RETAILING MANAGEMENT
A Planning Approach

Larry D. Redinbaugh
Graduate School of Business
University of Montana

57213

McGraw-Hill Book Company

New York   St. Louis   San Francisco   Auckland
Düsseldorf   Johannesburg   Kuala Lumpur   London
Mexico   Montreal   New Delhi   Panama   Paris
São Paulo   Singapore   Sydney   Tokyo   Toronto

To Donna Faye

RETAILING MANAGEMENT
A Planning Approach

34567890KPKP7987

This book was set in Times Roman by University Graphics, Inc. The editors were William J. Kane and Claudia A. Hepburn; the cover was designed by Jo Jones; the production supervisor was Judi Allen.
Kingsport Press, Inc., was printer and binder.

Library of Congress Cataloging in Publication Data

Redinbaugh, Larry D
  Retailing management.

  Includes index.
  1. Retail trade—Management.   I. Title.
HF5429.R347   1976   658.8'7   75-12950
ISBN 0-07-051366-X

Contents

iii

Preface

A retailer is an independent merchant middleman who acts as a consumer's purchasing agent and makes the customer's buying job as easy and convenient as possible. The essence of a retailer's operation is the active and prominent role he or she plays as a supplier of the right kind of merchandise, at the opportune time, and at the right price. Many functions, such as buying, bulk breaking, warehousing, financing, and risk bearing are performed by the retailer, and the success of a store depends upon the efficiency with which these and other retailing functions are performed and how well management has planned. Operational planning is an important factor that retailers will find essential if they are to succeed. Thus, this text focuses on retail business planning as a means of facilitating decision-making efficiency.

A planning approach to retailing management visualizes a retailing institution as a total system of interacting and related activities, each of which influence and affect the profitability of that business enterprise. In other words, managerial decisions in any one area of a retail business will directly or indirectly affect and influence all other activities within that institution. Managers have known for years that when a decision is made, it ultimately affects the business in some manner, and much has been written about planning in general. However, very little specific information has been provided for the student or retailing manager on the development of a retail business plan, and few, if any, textbook authors have gone into detail and provided a complete retail business plan for a viable business. Naturally, students and business managers are interested in why certain decisions are made, but they are also interested in the market conditions which lead to these decisions.

Many texts offer advice on "why" the manager should plan for the next year, but then they limit their material on retail business planning to sales forecasting and the purchasing of merchandise for resale. The author believes that a retail business plan begins with a determination of goals and objectives based upon market potential and is not complete until a provision has been made for the control of that retail plan. Although many retailers utilize retail business plans, many do not have these plans written on paper for easy reference purposes. Some retailers simply go from day to day, or week to week, with a general plan, but this practice is not adequate in today's highly competitive environment.

A major advantage of the planning approach to retailing management lies in its ability to provide alternatives for decision making. Retail business planning is a process whereby a retailer decides, at the present, what to do in the future. This process not only encompasses a determination of business objectives but also provides the necessary procedures for accomplishing these goals.

The planning approach does not attempt to be a panacea, but it does provide a thorough and systematic procedure for integrating and coordinating the activities of a retailing institution as a total operating system. This approach also encompasses many of the procedures and features of the traditional management methods and provides the retailer with a comprehensive and systematic method which will offer opportunities for increased consumer satisfaction, cost reduction, and greater profitability.

Part One of the text introduces the students to some of the more traditional retail store classifications. In addition, discussion focuses upon self-service, self-selection, limited service, and full-service retailing. In this part, in store retailing is discussed with attention being devoted to warehouse retailing, one of the newer retailing concepts. Nonstore retailing focuses on mail-order, door-to-door, automatic vending, and telephone retailing.

To complete Part One, a complete chapter on franchise retailing (which is generally associated with the small, independent retailer) has been added. In terms of the number of establishments, small retail institutions constitute the largest segment of retailing, but many retailing texts tend to neglect these independent retailers and emphasize chain stores and department stores instead. The material in this text attempts to strike a more objective balance between the various types, sizes, and kinds of retailing institutions.

Since retailing deals directly with the final user of a product, it is only proper that the student of retailing learn as much about consumer purchasing habits and patterns as possible. Thus, Part Two consists of a chapter on the market for ultimate consumers, cultural and social influences, and determinants of consumer purchasing behavior. Some retailing texts omit consumer purchasing behavior, which is an important determinant in the blend of a retailing mix. A retailer's sales promotional mix must not only attract consumers to the store, it must also induce them to purchase once they enter. Knowledge of consumer behavioral habits will help a student of retailing choose which promotional strategies and tactics to use.

Part Three introduces the retail business plan to the student, and each step of the plan is briefly explained. The retail business plan begins by defining the goals and objectives based upon a determination of market potential—not by sales forecasting as found in some retailing texts. It is from these goals and objectives that the remainder of the retail business plan takes shape. If the market potential is not evident, one need not go any further. It would be sheer folly to enter a market as a retailer if the sales potential were too inadequate to support a store. To date, little consideration has been given in retailing texts to actual market potential determination. Many retailers simply enter business with the hope that the store will be able to generate sales volume that is profitable.

From Part Three's introduction of the business plan, the remaining chapters cover in detail each step of the plan. Part Four explores in depth the opportunities of a retailer's potential market. Trading areas are defined, and consideration is given to population, social and economic factors, and sources of information. Retail store location and store layout and design are covered in Part Five. The location of a retail store is strategic because the site is not static but either deteriorates or grows more beneficial. Merchandise management—the heart of retailing—is discussed in Part Six. Beginning with resource determination, the text takes the student step by step through merchandise buying, assortment, and selection; negotiations with suppliers; and the receiving, handling, and pricing of the goods. Once the merchandise is moved to the selling floor, it becomes necessary to promote the goods for sale. Part Seven discusses the objectives of retail sales promotion, the importance of store image, personal selling, and how and why credit should be utilized as a sales promotional device.

A retail institution is only as good as the personnel associated with the business. Thus, Part Eight considers the management of the work force in a retail operation, i.e., recruitment, selection, training and evaluation, and compensation.

Since many retail enterprises fail from the lack of managerial efficiency and control, Part Nine of the book deals with the facets of financial planning and control. Sources of funds are explored, various types of credit are discussed, leasing advantages and disadvantages are probed, and return on investment is investigated. Further, merchandise control systems are discussed with the emphasis on the importance of merchandise control procedures. Discussion focuses on inventory turnover rates, their effect on profits, and alternate methods for increasing the stockturn rate. Finally, control and analysis of stock losses are investigated; these items are usually omitted from most retailing texts. In addition, specific suggestions are given for reducing the various kinds of stock losses.

Although the primary purpose of this text is to introduce students of retailing to basic concepts and practical applications regarding the planning approach to retailing management, retail store managers may also find this book valuable in decision making. An attempt has been made to introduce basic retailing theories and concepts as well as to offer suggestions on how a retailing manager can make value judgments concerning everyday activities. The book is designed to be practical, yet includes many concepts and theories on retailing which are explained in terms of benefits to the student of retailing. This text blends the "why" with the "how-to-do-it" approach and strikes a balance between current books on the market. An emphasis is placed on perceptive, creative, and innovative management, with stress on differentiation rather than "me-too" retailing.

Since there is considerable evidence to suggest that schools of business are turning away from the purely academic approach and are returning to more pragmatic methodology, the timing of this text is propitious. In some cases, colleges and universities have eliminated retailing from their curriculums because it was not considered to be "academic." However, recent observation shows that in some schools retailing courses are being reintroduced. This stems, in part, from the fact that many students are discovering upon graduation that the only jobs open to them are in the business fields. Many large firms are hiring any college graduate who has potential regardless of the college major, and thus many nonbusiness students are seeking basic, practical courses that can be utilized in the business world. This is evidenced by the increasing enrollment of nonbusiness students in our classes in the schools of business. Thus, a retailing course that is pragmatic can provide that basic education for the student, whether the individual is a business or nonbusiness major.

The retail business plan, which is the nucleus of this text, was designed from my experiences as a consultant to retailers. It has proved itself in the business world, and many of my clients have told me that it is a most useful tool in providing them with an overall perspective of their businesses. The students in my retailing classes are required to draft a retail business plan for either a new business or an existing store, and their reactions and reports have been most favorable. These experiences have led the author to believe that the plan has merit and can contribute to the field of retailing by being published in a textbook which can be utilized by both students and practitioners. Since the retail business plan has been tested in the market, there is little doubt that it has practical applications; however, not all students of retailing will agree. Some objection is to be expected since it does depart from the traditional approach to retailing. In summation, the retail business plan provides a logical, sequential, step-by-step procedure toward perceptive and innovative retail management.

Larry D. Redinbaugh

Part One

Introduction to Retailing Management

Chapter 1

An Introduction to the Retailing System

Many of us probably consider ourselves rather well informed on the subject of retailing. We are exposed to retail businesses nearly every day, and all of us have at one time or another made purchases from a retail store. As consumers, we take for granted a wide variety of goods and services from which we can make our purchases. We also patronize many different kinds of retail establishments, such as variety stores, grocery stores, gas stations, department stores, and furniture stores. Somehow these experiences as a consumer make us feel quite knowledgeable about retailing. Actually, however, these experiences only serve to provide us with a surface view of the various aspects involved in the operation of a retail store.

From a consumer's point of view, the most important aspect of retailing appears to be promotion and selling. We are continually subjected to many forms of retail sales promotion through radio and television advertisements, newspapers, leaflets, and instore displays. In some retail stores, we may also be approached by an overly eager or even aggressive salesperson who seems to "promote" a particular product. From these experiences, we may get the impression that this is what retailing is all about. But from the retailer's point of view, many other interrelated functions or activities must take place before consumers can purchase goods and/or services.

The field of retailing is becoming increasingly complex due to changes in the business environment. Today, because of rising costs, as well as a number of other factors, it has become more difficult for retailers to serve their customers effectively while operating a store at a profit. Thus, the purpose of this book is to focus on these retailing functions and activities, keeping in mind the idea of improving the store's efficiency so that consumers may be served more effectively by the retailer. By using the planning approach to retailing management, this text explores the methods and procedures by which retail managers and students of retailing can become more efficient. But more importantly, the planning approach to retailing management provides the retailer or student of retailing with alternatives for use in the decision-making process. Being able to choose from a number of alternatives is extremely helpful—and important—to the retail manager as adjustments to the rapidly changing business environment must be made.

In order to learn which of the retail store's activities are involved in this decision making, as well as what influences those activities, let us look at some of the underlying factors.

RETAILING MIX

The words "retailing mix" will be used in this text when referring to a retail store's activities and functions. Just what do we mean by these words? Retailing mix can be defined as a combination or blend of the store's goods and services, promotion, prices, merchandising, location, sales personnel, reputation, and image. It is the blending, or mixing, of these various elements that creates the atmosphere in which the retailer conducts the business—hopefully in a manner which will attract the greatest number of customers at a profit to the store. Since the retailing mix (the goods, location, prices, image) will vary from store to store, it is up to the store manager or owner to be perceptive and to determine what the best mix is for that particular store. The alteration of the items in the retailing mix is the primary concern of the planning approach to retailing management.

Whatever affects the satisfaction of the consumer or the profits of the store will probably, in turn, force the retailer to make a change in the retailing mix. Certain social, economic, technological, and competitive factors which are present in the business and economic environment will tend to influence the everyday decisions of the retail manager. Generally, some of these forces are beyond the control of the retail store manager. However, the manager must understand these forces and how they affect the business. He or she must also be able to alter the store's retailing mix in order to cope successfully with these influences.

SOCIAL FORCES

The social forces that affect the retailer include such factors as the following: Increases or decreases in population, changes in the age groups within the population, the mobility of the population, the desire for suburban living, the desire for increased leisure-time activities, and the changing attitudes among various segments of consumers. In today's retailing environment, a retailer must alter the retailing mix to cope with these social forces or risk failure.

For example, one of the more recent changes in social forces—a change in consumer attitudes—occurred during the 1960s. The consumerism movement of the early 1960s along with its continuing effect, encouraged the passage of laws and regulations by federal, state, and local governments. These laws and regulations have had a strong impact on retail managers across the country. For instance, retail advertising and sales promotional plans have been affected by the passage of laws monitoring retail store commercials. In October 1970, a federal law became effective prohibiting retailers from issuing a credit card except in response to a request or an application. In 1971 the Fair Credit Reporting Act became law; this law affects all retailers granting credit. During 1972, the Consumer Product Safety Act was passed, which was aimed primarily at producers. However, retailers are also involved if their stores sell these products to ultimate consumers.

Many regulations and laws have been passed primarily as a result of the consumerism movement, and these forces have directly or indirectly affected the retail stores' management. Although these constraints on the retailer have been made for the consumers' welfare, they nevertheless are an example of certain social forces which must be dealt with in the day-to-day operation of a retail store. Most of these forces are beyond the direct control of the retailer. However, the retailer must comply with all laws and regulations and must try to continue the successful operation of the retail establishment even though certain adjustments must be made.

ECONOMIC FORCES

Economic forces include such factors as the general level of the economy, interest rates, income, purchasing power, and inflation. These items, too, affect the retailer but are not under the retailer's direct control.

For example, both disposable (take-home pay) and discretionary (amount of pay left after necessities have been purchased) incomes have risen rapidly in recent years. This has increased the purchasing power of consumers throughout the United States. Along with this rise in disposable and discretionary incomes has come the increased demand from the consumer for more goods and services. Consumers are using goods and services at a rate never before attained. There is little evidence to indicate any reduction in this trend over the long range, although some drastic changes may develop over shorter periods of time because of the nation's general economic level and the level of unemployment. Thus, these factors must be considered and may affect a retailer's decision on opening another store or expanding a store's offering of goods and services.

Further, the steady growth of credit buying has encouraged consumers to "purchase today and pay tomorrow." Credit buying will probably continue to influence the retailer's decisions concerning the control of this powerful promotional tool. If the retailer is too lenient in extending credit, the results may be personal bankruptcy for the customer. If the store has a policy which unduly restricts credit, then the retailer will lose sales. As you can see, somewhere in between these two extremes, the retailer must find a balance which best suits the particular store.

TECHNOLOGICAL FORCES

More and more retailers are making use of technological advances in attempting to improve the store's operation and efficiency. Such items as electronic computers, data processing systems, and modern cash registers are being used to improve the operating results of retail businesses. Many of the large retailers have been using electronic equipment for some time to streamline employee payroll, credit customer billings, accounts payable, and inventory control, but there still remains room for improvement in these areas. Many of the small retailers have not yet utilized technological advances to improve their store operations. Fortunately, for the purpose of assisting these small retailers, some cash registers have been developed which aid in inventory control procedures. Information, such as style number, color code, date of purchase, and the name of the manufacturer, is included on the cash register ticket or slip as the sale is processed for the customer. These mechanical or electronic devices are relatively inexpensive and thus can be used effectively by the small retailers who cannot benefit from the use of large computers.

COMPETITIVE FORCES

While retailers have always had some competition, it appears that competitive forces are becoming increasingly severe for many retail businesses. Competition for the retail store comes from many sources. For example, many different types and kinds of retail stores offer the same or similar merchandise. Naturally, each of these businesses is eagerly competing for a portion of the consumer's dollar. In response to this aggressive competition, some retailers have been forced to change store policies, practices, and procedures in order to remain competitive—or in order to remain in business. Later in this book, we will discuss competition in more detail, as well as retail store failures, and what factors lead to business failure.

To this end, throughout this text, we will examine how a retailer can best adapt to a changing retail environment by the use of managerial techniques and proper retail business planning.

RETAILING DEFINED

There are many definitions of "retailing," but there is little agreement as to the precise explanation of the term. For the purposes of this text, the following paragraphs will explain some of the terms to be used.

"Retailing" includes all those business activities associated with selling goods and services to an ultimate consumer or final user for personal consumption.

A "retailer" is an independent merchant middleman (one who takes title to or owns the merchandise). This "merchant middleman" stands between a producer and a consumer and is the one who serves as the consumer's purchasing agent. Thus, the retailer makes the consumer's job of buying goods and services much easier by offering a convenient location and a wide assortment of merchandise. For this purchasing function, the retailer hopefully receives a reward (profit) from the operation of the business.

A "retail store" is the physical structure which serves as a warehouse from which consumers may select goods and services. These goods and services must be made available to the consumer at the right time, price, and place, and in the right styles, sizes, and colors if the retailer is to be successful. Failure to provide the right merchandise and service will result in consumers shopping elsewhere.

The term "warehouse" as used in this definition does not denote a warehouse such as that used by the wholesaler. Rather, the physical structure or retail store may be referred to as a "warehouse" in the sense that it is the place where consumers go to shop and compare merchandise, prices, and service. Unlike the wholesaler, the retailer provides a service to the consumer by breaking large units of merchandise down into single items so that the customer need not purchase in case lots.

THE RETAILING STRUCTURE

In the marketing of consumer products, retailing institutions are the final link in the distribution system. As goods are produced by manufacturers, they are moved along the channels of distribution from the manufacturer to the wholesalers and then to the retailers. Thus, the retailer often serves as the producer's representative in the marketplace.

Retailing is one of the easiest fields of business to enter because there are virtually no prerequisites. Once an individual has a business license and a location, operation may start with the aid of consigned merchandise (the retailer acts as an agent and does not pay for the goods) or the individual may offer some type of service. In the field of retailing, this relative ease of entry has created two phenomena which are somewhat related: (1) the stable total number of retailing institutions, and (2) the increasing rate of business failures.

Number of Retail Stores

A 1974 survey estimated that there were approximately 1.7 million retailing establishments in the United States. In 1967, combined total retail sales for these 1.7 million retail institutions was approximately $310 billion; but during 1974, the estimated total retail sales volume reached $529 billion. Table 1-1 provides more details about the relationship between the number of retail institutions and the total volume of retail sales. It is interesting to note from the figures provided in Table 1-1 that the number of retailing institutions has varied little since 1939. That

**Table 1-1   Retail Establishments and
Sales Volume for Selected Years**

Year	Number of stores (000 omitted)	Total sales (000,000 omitted)
1929	1,476	$ 48,330
1933	1,526	25,037
1935	1,588	32,791
1939	1,770	42,042
1948	1,770	130,521
1954	1,722	169,968
1958	1,788	199,646
1963	1,708	244,202
1967	1,763	310,214
1973	NA	488,000*
1974	NA	529,000*

*Estimated by Bureau of Competitive Assessment and Busi-
ness Policy.
  Sources: U.S. Bureau of the Census, *Census of Business:
Retail Trade,* for the years indicated.

is why the estimated number of retail institutions for 1974 has been estimated at
the same level of 1.7 million. For the past 35 years the number of retail stores has
remained fairly constant despite an increase in the total sales volume, as well as
an increase in population. Apparently, as some retail businesses fail, they are
replaced by an almost equal number of new retail stores.

However, there is one major shortcoming of the figures in Table 1-1. The
rise in the price level is not reflected in the total sales volume figures. Nevertheless, there has been an increase not only in retail sales per capita as measured in
today's dollars, but also an increase in the physical volume of goods sold at
retail.

Retail Store Failures

Each year, Dun and Bradstreet (a business reporting service) reports on the
number of retail store failures and the basic reasons for these failures. Dun and
Bradstreet reports that in 1972, 4,398 retail businesses had failed.[1] Table 1-2 lists
the basic reasons for these failures.

As you can see from Table 1-2, most retail store failures are due to two
controllable factors: (1) inexperience, and (2) incompetence. Inexperience and
incompetence often lead to a retailer's inability to generate a profitable sales
volume which is sufficient for maintaining a viable business. Managerial inefficiency is a result of a lack of experience in retailing management and proper retail
store planning. Often, individuals enter retailing because they have the desire to
"be their own boss." But many of these individuals have little knowledge of
retailing functions or business activities, so it is not surprising that many of them
fail within the first few years.

[1]*The Business Failure Record 1972,* Dun and Bradstreet, 1973, p. 8.

Usually, retail business failures are the result of a combination of causes. It is interesting to note from Table 1-2 that incompetence and inexperience in competing effectively will surely end in retail business failures. Most of the factors listed in Table 1-2 can be offset by acquiring managerial skills and drafting a retail business plan *before* entering the retailing field. Hopefully, this text will aid the student of retailing and the store owner-manager in acquiring the managerial expertise for the successful operation of a retail store. Certainly, retail business failures are to be avoided. But as long as inexperienced individuals are attracted to retailing and as long as the retailing field remains relatively easy to enter, the failure rate will continue.

Types of Store Failures   Some types of retail businesses appear to have a greater chance of failing than do other kinds of stores. Whether this failure rate is due to the kind of retail establishment, to a lack of managerial skill, or to a combination of both, is open to speculation (see Table 1-3). Certain types of retail businesses appear to have greater risks because of the nature of the merchandise being sold. For example, men's and women's ready-to-wear stores lead all other retail firms in the number of failures (97 and 88 per 10,000 operating retailers, respectively). In part, this is due to the risks associated with fashion merchandising. These risks include merchandise with a relatively short life span which is highly seasonal in nature and hence which requires frequent markdowns in price. Thus, slight errors in judgment on a buyer's or manager's part can be very costly—resulting in a store's financial failure. If an individual is considering opening a particular kind of retail business, it might be a good idea for that person to study Table 1-3 carefully.

Table 1-2   Reasons for Retail Business Failures

Apparent cause of failure	Percentage of retail firms
Incompetence	37.4
Unbalanced experience*	23.5
Lack of experience in the line	16.9
Lack of managerial experience	14.9
Reason unknown	2.5
Neglect	2.3
Disaster	1.3
Fraud	1.2
Total	100.0
Number of failures	4,398
Average liabilities per failure	$126,937

*Experience not well rounded in sales, finance, purchasing, and production on the part of the individual in case of a proprietorship, or of two or more partners or officers constituting a management unit.

Source: *The Business Failure Record 1972*, Dun and Bradstreet, New York, 1973, pp. 11–12.

Table 1-3   Retail Business Failures by Type of Business, 1972

Line of business	Failure rate per 10,000 operating concerns
Men's wear	97
Women's ready-to-wear	88
Cameras and photographic supplies	85
Infants' and children's wear	76
Furniture and furnishings	63
Gifts	60
Books and stationery	54
Sporting goods	49
Appliances, radio and television	42
Dry goods and general merchandise	34
Shoes	33
Toys and hobby crafts	30
Women's accessories	27
Auto parts and accessories	23
Jewelry	22
Drugs	22
Eating and drinking places	22
Bakeries	20
Lumber and building materials	17
Automobiles	17
Hardware	14
Grocery, meats and produce	13
Farm implements	10

Source: The Business Failure Record 1972, Dun and Bradstreet, New York, 1973, p. 5.

RETAIL STORE CLASSIFICATION

Retail stores differ from one another in many respects. Like human beings, they have personalities and characteristics which distinguish one from another. Some of these distinctions are: what they sell, whether they sell more than one product line, whether they are part of a chain (two or more stores), whether they are just a single store, and the extent of their services.

For example, one classification scheme segregates retail stores by the kind of business. In Table 1-4, a breakdown of retail sales by kind of business is given for the most recent years. Another method for classifying retail stores is according to the number of units or number of stores. Table 1-5 notes that during 1967 (unfortunately the most recent data for this classification) single-unit retail stores accounted for over 60 percent of all retail firms.

Another classification scheme is according to the number of services that a retailer provides to the customers. Some retailers provide their customers with a vast array of services; others allow the customers to serve themselves. In order to gain some insight into the internal operations of a retail store with respect to

Table 1-4   Retail Sales by Kind of Business—United States: 1972–1974
(Sales in billions)

	1972	1973*	1974*
Department stores	46,302	50,900	55,500
Variety stores	7,756	8,300	8,900
Grocery stores	88,340	95,400	102,000
Men's and boys' apparel stores	5,198	5,400	5,700
Women's apparel, accessory stores	8,386	8,800	9,300
Furniture stores	9,321	10,400	11,200
Household appliances	4,634	5,100	5,500
Restaurants and bars	33,891	36,600	39,500
Drugstores	14,523	15,400	16,300
Total retail trade	$448,379	$488,000	$529,000

*Estimated by Bureau of Competitive Assessment and Business Policy.
Source: U.S. Industrial Outlook 1974, U.S. Department of Commerce, p. 149.

the amount of customer services offered, let us devote our attention to a different method of classifying retail stores—one based on the amount of customer service.

Services Performed for the Consumer

A different way in which retail stores could be classified is by the extent of the services performed for the consumer by the retailer.

Retailers offer a wide spectrum of customer services—from practically no services (the self-service store) to a large variety of services (the full-service store). For a comparison of the number of customer services offered by different types of retail stores, let us look at Figure 1-1. We can determine from Figure 1-1 that self-service retailing offers the customer few, if any, services. With self-service retailing, the customer must perform the services, and for this reason, there is generally a price concession to the customer. One will also notice from Figure 1-1 that certain types of retail stores—grocery stores, discount retailers, warehouse retailers, mail-order retailers, and vending machines—force the customers to perform many of the services themselves. Generally, the only service

Table 1-5   Number of Single and Multiunit Stores and
Percentage of Sales

Size of store	Number of units		Total sales, %	
	1963	1967	1963	1967
Single store	1,488,166	1,543,182	63.4	60.2
2–10 stores	41,716	32,119	11.1	10.5
11–100 stores	1,675	1,797	9.7	10.7
101 stores or more	191	204	15.8	18.6

Source: U.S. Bureau of the Census, Census of Business: 1967, fig. 9, p. 28.

Decreasing Services .... Increasing Services			
Self-service	**Self-selection**	**Limited-service**	**Full-service**
Very few services	Restricted services		Wide variety of services
Price appeal	Price appeal		Fashion merchandise
Staple goods	Staple goods		Specialty merchandise
Convenience goods	Convenience goods		
Warehouse retailing	Discount retailing	Door-to-door sales	Specialty stores
Grocery stores	Variety stores	Department stores	Department stores
Discount stores	Mail-order retailing	Telephone sales	
Mail-order retailing		Variety stores	
Automatic vending			

Figure 1-1 Retail methods of service operation.

that may be offered to customers in a self-service store is the "checking out" of the merchandise.

This classification in no way indicates that this method of retailing is undesirable. As a matter of fact, it often is the most desirable from the consumers' point of view. As we will determine later, the extent and amount of customer service directly affects the operating expenses of the retail store.

On the other hand, the full-service retail store caters to the consumer by offering a vast array of services. For these services, the customer usually pays a higher price for the merchandise than would be paid for the same goods in a self-service store. As would be expected, the self-service retail store usually has lower operating costs than the full-service store. Retailing can be called a "labor intensive" type of business (i.e., labor costs may exceed 50 to 60 percent of a store's total expenses). Those retailers operating on a self-service or self-selection basis are able to maintain low labor costs.

Traditionally, retailing as opposed to wholesaling is a rather expensive type of business activity. This is due, in part, to the large number of customers who shop at retail stores where each individual is capable of generating only a small portion of the total sales volume. Thus, the amount of services extended to the customer readily affects the overall operating costs of a retail business.

Self-Service Retailing Self-service retailing was introduced to the public around 1915 by a grocery store, Piggly Wiggly of California. Originally, grocery stores were like other retail institutions of the time where a clerk assisted the customer in selecting from a limited line of merchandise. However, in the early 1900s, depressed economic conditions created a favorable environment for the establishment of a revolutionary type of retailing institution where the customers could save money. They did this by shopping in a less ornate building, by serving themselves from displays of merchandise, and by taking the goods to a checkout counter. The emphasis on price, or on saving money, had generated a new concept; but self-service retailing did not develop to any great degree until the 1930s. During the depression years self-service retailing evolved and expanded, becoming especially popular in the food field where entrepreneurs were seeking ways to combat rising operating costs and competition from chain stores.

From the rather austere conditions of the depression years, grocery stores have evolved into large-scale, self-service grocery supermarkets. For the large food retailer, self-service retailing has resulted in a number of economic advantages: division of labor, volume buying, price concessions (which come from volume purchases), ability to spread risks, large promotion budgets, and great assortments of merchandise for the consumer.

However, there are also some disadvantages associated with self-service retailing. In retailing institutions where self-service retailing is predominant (such as the grocery field), customers often complain that these marketing institutions are impersonal, sales clerks are unfriendly, chain stores push their own brands rather than name brands, and too much merchandise is prepackaged, especially meat and produce. Even though consumers voice criticisms against grocery supermarkets and the self-service method of operation, these retailing institutions will probably continue to expand because many customers do enjoy the privilege of shopping and comparing merchandise without being bothered by a salesperson. In fact, grocery supermarkets account for over 90 percent of total grocery sales according to a study conducted in 1970 by *Progressive Grocer*.[2]

Self-service retailing has become an accepted way for the customer to shop. In the 1970s with a trend of "individualism," many customers are demanding the right to examine merchandise leisurely and make a selection based on their own judgment without the help of a salesperson.

Self-Selection Retailing Self-selection retailing is closely related to self-service retailing, but the major difference is that with self-selection, a salesperson is available and can be called upon for assistance. In a self-selection retailing store, particular attention is devoted to the display of merchandise, as it is with self-service retailing. Merchandise is arranged on open tables, shelves, racks, and stands where the customer can make a complete inspection of the goods without the aid of the salesperson. Once a selection is made, however, the customer will hand the merchandise to a salesperson (not a checker) who completes the sales transaction. Or if the customer needs assistance during the selection of merchandise, a salesperson is usually close by and ready to assist. Variety stores are a prime example of self-selection retailing.

This type of retailing activity requires not only good "merchandising" techniques but also requires the judicious use of fixtures and lighting with a proper plan for merchandise layout and the smooth flow of customer traffic. The operating expenses for a self-selection institution are slightly higher than for a

[2]"Grocery Business Annual Report," *Progressive Grocer,* April 1970.

self-service type of business since additional salespersons and possibly more expensive merchandising techniques tend to increase a store's overhead.

Limited-Service Retailing   In a limited-service retail institution, services are usually limited to occasional sales assistance (especially in some departments), credit clearance, and merchandise returns. Customers will be offered sales assistance only if requested; otherwise, they are free to browse throughout the store. The major types of limited-service retailers are department stores, drugstores, and hardware stores.

In general, operating costs are higher for limited-service retailers than for self-service and self-selection retailers, but this is to be expected because of the difference in services performed. Thus, the gradual increase in the variety of services performed for customers is evident as an institution goes from self-service to full-service retailing.

Full-Service Retailing   Full-service retailing is a form of in-store retailing activity where a customer is met, given full consideration, and is assisted by a salesperson. Implicit in this type of retailing activity is the assurance to the customer that the salesperson is knowledgeable about the product or service and will be courteous and helpful. For several reasons this type of retailing activity has declined over the years. One major reason for the decline is that full-service retailing is a labor-intensive function which cannot take advantage of cost-saving, labor-saving, manufacturing-oriented automated devices. Labor costs associated with full-service retailing may be as high as 35 percent of sales volume, although these costs do vary considerably from store to store (i.e., expense variables include the nature and type of retail store, managerial expertise, location, and sales volume).

The proportionately higher operating expenses of a full-service retailer are economically justified in that the store is dealing directly with the ultimate consumer. Customers of a full-service store tend to purchase in small units and/ or dollar amounts; and they expect, and are offered, a greater variety of services which require considerable time and effort on the part of the store's staff. Also, many full-service retailers are small, and their inventory turnover rate is lower than for self-service retailers. Buying is often done in small lots, and full-service retailer rents may be higher than for self-service retailers. This is particularly true for a small, full-service specialty retailer located in a shopping center. But many customers are price conscious and patronize self-service retailers, and this has led to a decline in full-service retailing.

Even though full-service retailing is waning, this type of retailing activity will always be in demand by some customers. This is particularly true with certain types of goods (i.e., durables—where a salesperson must demonstrate features of a product and turn these product features into customer benefits, high-fashion merchandise—where the customer is seeking reassurance and assistance from the salesperson, or merchandise that must be fitted, special-ordered, or otherwise explained to a customer by a salesperson).

Classification Scheme

Although retail stores can be classified in numerous ways no attempt is made in this text to segment or classify them by all the various methods available since cross-classification could be quite confusing. For example, a furniture store (such as Wickes or Levitz) could be classified as a chain store (two or more stores centrally owned and operated), a specialty store (one which specializes in a single product line offering a considerable merchandise assortment), a single-product-line store, or a self-selection store.

RETAIL STORE CHARACTERISTICS

Although it appears to the casual observer that our retailing economy consists of large stores, this impression is a false one. Primarily, the retailing industry is made up of small, single units (see Table 1-5) which are operated by individual merchants. These single entrepreneurs tend to own and operate service stores such as restaurants, beauty shops, shoe repair shops, barber shops, small specialty stores, and gasoline service stations. According to the *1967 Census of Business,* approximately 68 percent of the retail stores in the country had an annual sales volume of $100,000 or less, which is considered by most standards to be a small retail business.

Advantages of Being a Small Retailer

There are several reasons why the number of small retail merchants has remained fairly high over the years. Many people have a desire to operate a small business and be independent. There is also a sense of pride that comes from owning and operating a small retail store. Further, some persons feel that the restraints imposed on them as employees of larger corporations are too repressive and ignore their creativity and individuality.

Although these entrepreneurs may appear small when compared to the giants in retailing (Penney's, Ward's, or Sears), nevertheless they often can compete effectively with the larger stores. The small retailer has an element of *flexibility* that is unmatched by any larger retail institution. Small independent retailers are able to offer merchandise which meets the needs of the local market. The personalized service that a small retailer is able to give the consumer is probably the greatest asset the store has. Decisions can be made more rapidly and efficiently since there is no need for the small retailer to check first with a central office. Whether it is a decision on what merchandise to order, what products should be deleted or added, or any other day-to-day problem, the retailer can handle these things directly and quickly. This flexibility is the major advantage of the small retailer and cannot be matched by the larger chain stores.

Disadvantages of Small Retailers

Naturally, small independent retailers in competing with larger retail institutions suffer from certain limitations. For instance, the small retailer generally does not have the financial resources of the larger stores. This factor may force the small retailer to pay higher prices than those paid by the large store for the same merchandise—due to the quantity discounts granted by the suppliers to buyers for large-volume purchases. This might force the small retailer into charging the final consumer a higher price than does the large store. (However, there may be exceptions to this situation as we will discover later in the book.)

Because of their greater financial resources, large retail stores are able to advertise and promote on a wider scale than the small retailer. Large retailers generally make heavy use of newspaper and television advertising whereas the small merchant may have to be satisfied with circulars and point-of-purchase displays. Thus, a small retailer may not be able to attract as many customers.

One may well ask the question, "How and why can small retailers continue to compete effectively with the retailing giants?" For the most part, small retailers do successfully compete by fulfilling a need in the marketplace. They are able to compete and accomplish this feat by differentiation—that is, by making the store "different" in some way which will attract customers. This can be done in various ways. A small retailer may locate his store near a larger store—which seems unwise—but he will remain open *later* than the larger store. Thus, he can take advantage of the higher traffic concentration. A small retailer may also compete by offering a larger variety of customer services. Perhaps differentiation can be accomplished by creating a special image for the smaller retail store. Or it may be possible for the smaller retailer to offer a goods and services mix which is especially appealing to a certain consumer group.

There are innumerable other ways in which a small retailer can effectively compete with larger stores. In part, this is what makes retailing so interesting. There is a place for nearly every type of retail store, and a place for both small and large retailers. It is not the store size which determines whether a store will be a success or failure. Rather it is: (1) the caliber of store management, and (2) the extent of experience combined with proper planning, which will determine the success or failure of a retail store. Each year there are many retail store failures. Unfortunately, the rate of failure for retail stores predominantly involves the smaller retailers. However, in the last two years, there has been an increasing number of large discount retailing chains that have filed bankruptcy. Although many factors may contribute to retail store failures, we saw earlier in this chapter that the underlying reasons could be condensed into just a few.

SUMMARY

From a consumer's point of view, retailing appears to emphasize promotion and selling. However, from a retailer's point of view, many other interrelated functions or activities must take place before consumers can purchase goods and/or services.

By using the planning approach to retailing management, we are able to explore the methods and procedures by which retailers can become more efficient. The planning approach to retailing management provides the retailer and the student of retailing with alternatives for use in decision making. Being able to choose from a number of alternatives is extremely helpful to the retail manager as adjustments to the rapidly changing business environment must be made.

A *retailing mix* is a combination or blend of the store's goods and services, promotion, prices, merchandising, location, sales personnel, reputation, and image which when blended create an atmosphere in which the retailer conducts the business. Retail store managers must be perceptive in determining what the best retailing mix is for that particular store.

Certain social, economic, technological, and competitive factors which are present in the business and economic environment will tend to influence the everyday decisions of a retail manager.

The *social forces* that affect the retailer include such factors as (1) increases or decreases in population numbers, (2) changes in the age groups within the population, (3) the mobility of the population, (4) the desire for suburban living, (5) the desire for increased leisure time activities, and (6) the changing attitudes among various segments of consumers.

Economic forces include such factors as (1) the general level of the economy, (2) interest rates, (3) income, (4) purchasing power, and (5) inflation.

More retailers are making use of *technological advances* in attempting to improve the store's operation and efficiency. Such technological advances include: (1) electronic computers, (2) data processing systems, and (3) modern cash registers. Some cash registers aid in inventory control by recording such information as style number, color code, date of purchase, and the resource.

Although retailers have always had some *competition,* competitive forces are becoming increasingly severe for many retail businesses. In response to this aggressive competition, some retailers have been forced to change store policies, practices, and procedures in order to remain competitive.

Retailing includes all those business activities associated with selling goods and services to an ultimate or final user for personal consumption. A *retailer* is an independent merchant middleman who stands between a producer and the consumer, and in effect, is the one who serves as the consumer's purchasing agent.

A *retail store* is the physical structure which serves as a warehouse from which consumers may select goods and services. These goods and services must be made available to the consumer at the right time, price, and place, and in a proper assortment if the retailer is to be successful.

In the marketing of consumer products, retailing institutions are the final link in the distribution system. There are approximately 1.7 million retailing stores in the United States. Each year many retail stores fail due to inexperience and incompetence. Inexperience and incompetence often lead to a retailer's inability to generate a profitable sales volume which is sufficient for maintaining a profitable business. Managerial inefficiency is a result of a lack of experience in retailing management and in proper retail store planning.

Like human beings, retail stores have personalities and characteristics which tend to distinguish them from other stores. Stores can be distinguished from one another in many ways—by what they sell, whether they sell more than one product line, whether they are part of a chain (two or more stores), whether they are just a single store, or by the extent of their services.

Retailers offer a wide spectrum of customer services—from practically no services (the self-service store) to a large variety of services (the full-service store). With self-service retailing, the customer must perform the services, and for this reason, a price concession is generally made to the consumer. A full-service retail store caters to the consumer by offering a vast array of services. For these services, the customer usually pays a higher price for the merchandise than would be paid for the same goods in a self-service store. The self-service retail store usually has lower operating costs than the full-service store.

Primarily, the retailing industry is made up of small, single units which are operated by individual merchants. Approximately 68 percent of the retail stores in the country had annual sales volumes of $100,000 or less, according to the *1967 Census of Business*.

The small retailer has an element of *flexibility* that is unmatched by any larger retail institution. Small independent retailers are able to provide more personalized service and offer merchandise which meets the needs of the local market.

The small retailer may have to pay higher prices for the same merchandise than those paid by the larger store because of the quantity discounts granted by the suppliers to buyers of large-volume purchases.

Because of their greater financial resources, large retail stores are able to advertise and promote on a wider scale than the small retailer.

It is not the size of the store which determines whether a retailer will be successful. It is the caliber of management and the extent of retail experience combined with proper planning.

REVIEW QUESTIONS

1 Explain the retailer's role in the marketplace and the reason for a store's existence.
2 What marketing functions does a retailer perform for the consumer?
3 How does one measure a retailer's efficiency in operating a retail store?
4 Discuss the environmental factors which influence a retailer's method of operation.
5 Define the following terms: *(a)* retailer; *(b)* retailing; *(c)* a retail store.
6 Why has the number of retail stores remained fairly stable throughout the past thirty years?
7 What are the reasons for retail store failures? How best can retail managers cope with this continuing problem?
8 Why do small independent retailers dominate the industry by sheer numbers?
9 Discuss why retail stores are classified in many different ways.
10 Why is retailing considered a service type of business?
11 How do you account for the fact that certain types of retail stores have a greater rate of failure than other types of stores?
12 Discuss some of the attributes and principles of self-service retailing. Why has self-service retailing become so popular?

13 Name some stores which operate on the self-service principle.
14 Why do full-service stores exist when the selling price of merchandise usually is greater than in self-service stores?
15 How do you explain that some consumers are price conscious, and others prefer to pay for many and varied services?
16 What factors have contributed to the increasing number of specialty stores in the past few years?

Chapter 2

Retail Methods of Operation

A retailer is an independent merchant middleman who stands between the producer and the ultimate consumer. Retailing includes all functions associated with the sale of goods and services to consumers for personal use. Most retailing is done through traditional retail stores and is referred to as "in store" retailing— as opposed to "nonstore" retailing (e.g., mail-order, door-to-door, and vending machines). It is in store retailing and the retail store as a business enterprise to which we now devote our attention.

IN STORE RETAILING

In store retailing refers to a business location—a retail store. It is from this location that a retailer makes the consumer's buying function as easy and convenient as possible. In essence, the retailer chooses a location where consumers will have easy access to the store, and he also tries to anticipate consumer wants and desires. Thus, the retailer acts as the consumer's purchasing agent by selecting merchandise available from a number of resources. Hence, a retailer's responsibility to the store's customers will include the provision of the right assortment of merchandise at a reasonable price in various sizes, colors, and styles which are appropriate for consumer use. In in store retailing, the merchandise is also stored at the retailer's place of business until the consumer purchases the merchandise.

As is true of all types of businesses, certain inherent risks are associated with operating a retail store. A retailer's justification for existence in the marketplace is based upon how well the store performs these purchasing functions for the consumer, and a retailer exists only because of the ability to perform these functions better than his competitors. Retailers have sought many ways to improve in store retailing functions and methodologies in order to compete more effectively in serving the consumer.

Warehouse Retailing

During the last few years, a relatively new concept of retailing has emerged and gained momentum; it is referred to as "warehouse retailing." Warehouse retailing usually involves the use of a warehouse or barnlike structure where merchandise samples are displayed in a showroom, but where the retailer's entire inventory is located in a storage room adjacent to the showroom. Usually the displayed merchandise is limited to a single line of goods, such as furniture, appliances, or carpeting. From the samples of merchandise, a customer makes a selection, and the item is brought to the customer from the warehouse or storage room. In some warehouses the customer must drive from the showroom to the warehouse to pick up the merchandise. The warehouse retailer offers the con-

Figure 2-1 Photograph of warehouse retail outlet. *(Courtesy of Wickes, San Diego)*

sumer very few services—no credit, no delivery, no installation—unless the consumer pays an additional fee.

The warehouse concept of retailing is based on selling only national brands of merchandise, such as furniture or appliances, right from the carton without providing the consumer any services. Warehouse retailing prices usually represent savings of 20 to 25 percent to the customer over what would be paid to the so-called traditional retailer offering the same brand of merchandise.

This concept of retailing is filling a void left by the discount retailer who has traded up merchandise lines. The discount retailer, in many instances, has upgraded all merchandise lines, and in this process, has had to increase the retail price of the merchandise to cover the costs associated with increased service to the consumer. Thus, the warehouse retailer has created a market for the consumer who wishes to save money by performing his own services, such as delivery and uncrating the goods. The consumer is expected to pick up and haul the merchandise. If installation is required, either the consumer can perform the work, hire an outside firm, or hire the retailer to perform these activities. In the case of carpet installation, mechanics may be hired by either the retailer or the customer to perform the work. If hired by the retailer, the consumer simply pays the retailer an additional fee for this service at the time of purchasing the carpet. The same basic principle applies in the event an appliance must be serviced and installed.

The warehouse retailing concept has also challenged and/or changed some established methods of pricing, gross margins, and servicing in single-product-line stores. Traditional markups on carpeting, furniture, and appliances, (single product lines) have been high when compared to the warehouse retailing concept. Operators of warehouse retailing institutions often buy merchandise directly from the manufacturer in large volume, or take the customer's order from samples, and then ask the customer to pick up the merchandise at the warehouse—enabling the retailer to offer lower prices and accept lower gross margins. At any rate, this concept is forcing traditional high-gross-margin retailers to reevaluate their retailing methods. Retailing experts believe that this concept of retailing will develop and grow as long as an inflationary economy forces prices upward, and the consumer believes that money can be saved by patronizing a warehouse retailer.

Usually the warehouse retailer is open seven days a week. The store hours are long—perhaps from 9 A.M. to 9 P.M. each day. The store location is usually near a railroad or highway interchange. These locations keep delivery costs low and also keep the land and rental expenses low in comparison with other locations. (These locations will be much less expensive than planned regional shopping-center locations.)

Generally the warehouse retailer sells for cash, although many offer some form of credit in a limited way. In some warehouses, credit transactions may make up about 20 to 30 percent of the store's sales, although this feature may well defeat the warehouse concept of limited services. The warehouse retailer sells furniture and carpeting much like the discount retailer used to sell appliances—name-brand merchandise with a price appeal. Generally only name-brand goods which move rapidly are offered by the warehouse retailer. The average stock turn may be six times each year or approximately twice that of the traditional retailer selling the same merchandise.

The warehouse concept has taken hold in the retailing environment and numerous small retailers have opened warehouse retail stores specializing in carpeting, appliances, and furniture. Perhaps the best known of the furniture retailers using the warehouse concept includes both Wickes and Levitz. Both of these retailers operate on a national level, whereas many of the independents operate only locally. Both Wickes and Levitz sell only fast-moving, brand-name furniture. The gross margins generally are less than those which traditional retailers (except on fair-trade items) maintain, and the store is usually located on less expensive land than could be obtained in a shopping center. With these two warehouse retailers, the merchandise is stocked on the premises, and the customer receives the goods at the store's loading-unloading dock. In some instances, the customer gets free delivery, although in most instances, this is an additional cost.

Discount Retailing

The in store method of discount retailing emphasizes the sale of name-brand merchandise (manufacturers' brands) with low price as the main appeal. Discount retailers carry a reasonably complete line of hard and soft goods with well-known, presold brand names, but this merchandise is consistently sold somewhat below the advertised or manufacturer's suggested retail price. Although the practice of selling merchandise at, near, or below a manufacturer's suggested retail price is nothing new in the retailing industry, this type of retailing institution did not gain wide acceptance until after World War II. Its growth is due to the expansion of mass merchandising techniques, mass sales promotion, and one-stop shopping. The discount retailing concept is simplicity itself—a one-stop shopping center selling only fast-moving, branded merchandise and selling these goods at cut-rate prices. The discount retailer usually is located in a free-standing store (which is less expensive and quicker to construct than more elaborate buildings). The rate of inventory turnover (RITO) is much faster than traditional retailers selling the same merchandise, and these savings are passed on to the consumer who patronizes these stores in order to obtain bargains. Prior to World War II, discount retailers consisted mainly of catalog stores where the consumer would order name-brand merchandise from a catalog at a discount. Delivery of the merchandise often took weeks and then, in many instances, the goods had to be returned because of customer dissatisfaction. Today, at a discount store, customers are able to inspect name-brand merchandise on the premises and usually are able to take the goods home with them after the purchase. This personal inspection of the goods is often the key to a customer's purchasing decision. Many consumers have a desire to examine the goods before making a purchase rather than waiting until after merchandise has been shipped from a catalog warehouse.

Figure 2-2 Photograph of discount store. *(Courtesy of FedMart, San Diego)*

By offering primarily name brands and a variety of staple goods, discount retailers have a more rapid turnover of merchandise, which results in the retailer's ability to accept a lower gross margin per item than many of the traditional retailers. Hence, this concept has also come to be known as "low-margin–high-turnover" retailing. Few services are offered by the discount retailer, leaving the consumer to perform many of the perfunctory duties of shopping. This also results in reducing the discount retailer's overhead.

Discount retailers typically operate somewhere on the shopping periphery where rents are low. They use plain, no-frill buildings with tile floors and no window displays, plain racks for the display of goods, and central checkout registers. Usually, but not always, the building consists of one story. Those discounters operating from multistory buildings are usually located in older areas of cities. Usually discount stores cost up to 50 percent less to build than conventional stores because they are one-story structures located outside a city's expensive downtown center. Today's discount retailers, such as K-mart or Woolco, may be 120,000 square feet in size compared to the 250,000 square feet in a conventional department store constructed in a planned regional shopping center. Some of these present-day discount retailers locate the building next to a food supermarket in a community shopping center or in a shopping-center strip.

Present-day discount retailers usually open their doors to the general public. There are a few "membership" stores where the consumer pays a small fee (usually a dollar or two) to become a member and receives a membership card. The store then allows only those card-carrying "members" to shop on the premises. But the number of membership stores appears to be declining as large-scale public promotion is becoming more evident. Many discount retailers appear to have promotional budgets as large as those of the large department store chains with whom they are directly competing.

Several factors have contributed to the success of the discount retailer. One is the overall improvement of retailing methods during the past twenty years. The discount retailer has become an aggressive merchandiser. Many of the discount stores are managed by perceptive managers who implement a strategy of creative merchandising. The second, though not as explicit, can be called fortuitous circumstances. Although some retailing ingenuity may be responsible, the success of the discount retailer is probably due more to circumstances as they have developed over the years.

During the 1930s, durable goods and household appliances were introduced to the consumer market when economic conditions were not favorable for a profitable sales volume on the part of either the retailer or the manufacturer. The quality of workmanship also left much to be desired, and during the 1930s, the frequency of appliance repair was high. As appliances were new to the public at that time and were classified as luxuries for many families, strong and persuasive salesmanship had to be used in order to sell these items.[1]

With the beginning of World War II, appliance manufacturing came to a halt as production facilities were channeled into war efforts. During the war years, people received high wages, full employment was achieved, and many women for the first time in history entered the labor force in great numbers. Since consumer goods and services were limited, most of these wages were invested in war bonds and other savings programs. At the conclusion of World War II, manufacturing efforts reverted to peacetime activities, namely, the production of consumer goods. Because of the unavailability of consumer goods during the war, many consumers had developed what economists refer to as a "pent-up demand." With the war over and money to spend, consumers were soon seeking ways to buy goods and services, especially household appliances and other durable goods. Yet having lived through the worldwide Depression years of the 1930s, these consumers were price conscious. This attitude of economy was quickly recognized by a small group of retailers who later referred to themselves

[1]William J. Stanton, *Fundamentals of Marketing,* 4th ed., McGraw-Hill, New York, 1975, p. 362.

as discount retailers, discounters, or low-margin–high-turnover retailers. This basic concept of name-brand merchandise sold with a price appeal is prevalent yet today with the discount retailer.

There is still another reason why this type of retailing establishment developed and grew after World War II. Manufacturers of appliances began to presell (advertise) their merchandise extensively to the consuming public via radio and magazines. Then during the late 1940s and early 1950s, the television medium also began to be commonly used by manufacturers to accomplish this preselling. Thus, many manufacturers' brands became well known and needed little selling effort on the part of the retailer. Quality control measures also became better at the manufacturing level and people began to trust manufacturers' guarantees and warranties on products. Since the consumer came to trust the manufacturer, it was easy for the discount retailer to gain a foothold in the marketplace. The customer no longer needed to turn to the retailer for the product's guarantee; the consumer simply turned to the producer for this service. Even today we find manufacturer-sponsored service centers which aid the consumer in case of product dissatisfaction or in the event of product repair and warranty.

Department Store Retailing

Department stores are large retail institutions handling many items of merchandise: men's, women's, and children's apparel; furniture; floor coverings; china and glassware; hardware; jewelry; and notions. The distinguishing characteristic associated with these retail stores is the "departmentalizing" or segmenting of product lines. Each line of goods has a space allocated to it, and each department is provided with a cash register to record sales and salespersons to assist the customers. In some instances, these spaces are leased to persons not affiliated with the department store.

Department heads, or buyers, are usually employed as the managers of each product line, and they are responsible for buying, pricing, and promoting the merchandise and for earning a profit within that department. Also, the department head supervises the salespeople working in that department.

Department stores are highly organized retail institutions. Although variations exist, one can normally expect to find most large department stores segmented into four divisions: (1) operations (general store manager), (2) sales promotion which includes public relations and advertising, (3) merchandising which deals with buying and selling, and (4) control which focuses on accounting and finance. In some instances, large department stores have added a fifth division: organization development and personnel relations.

Aside from the advantages of a specialized organizational structure and the division of labor associated with departmentalization, there are other important features of department stores. By departmentalizing, managers are better able to maintain closer contact with each line of merchandise. This enables store managers more quickly to detect any weaknesses in the product lines, and at the same time, to determine which merchandise is profitable. Also, gross margins are more easily adjusted on each product line when a store is departmentalized.

Figure 2-3 Photograph of department store. *(Courtesy of Bullock's, Los Angeles)*

Salespeople are more inclined to be better informed when allowed to concentrate on selling one product line. Inventories are more easily controlled and stock losses are readily determined when a store is organized along department lines. Finally, the customer also is better able to find what he or she is seeking if the merchandise is segmented and arranged according to a logical and systematic scheme.

Department stores suffer from some limitations as well as all other types of retail institutions. The departmentalization of merchandise may be a hinderance to the customer who wishes to purchase several items of a different nature. This customer is forced to go from department to department in search of the merchandise he or she wants. Customer buying habits and patterns differ with various customers purchasing similar items for different purposes. Although department stores attempt to arrange related goods together for consumer shopping convenience, as yet, no perfectly satisfactory system for department store layout has been worked out. There are just too many customer variables to consider in departmentalizing merchandise layout and display.

Generally, operating expenses are considerably higher for department stores than for retailers offering fewer services. Merchandise inventory turnover rates may be low in some departments, such as apparel that becomes rapidly out of date. Another limitation of some department stores is the lack of personalized service. Due to rising costs of operation, many department stores are functioning with fewer sales personnel. Customer complaints often focus on this lack of sales assistance, and some consumers will migrate toward specialty stores where personalized service may be more accessible. This customer complaint is justified in some instances, but many department store managers are trying to improve customer relations in an effort to meet competition and improve services.

Chain Store Retailing

Chain stores are retail institutions which consist of two or more units centrally owned and managed. The *Census of Business* uses classification categories beginning with 2, 4, 6, 11, 26, 51, and 101 units; but many independent retailers with two or three stores do not consider themselves chain stores. Normally, one thinks of a large number of units when reference is made to a chain store. Technically, however, two or more units constitute a chain.

Several distinguishing characteristics separate chain stores from independent retail units. First, the ownership of chain stores rests in one location. Chain stores usually have a main office from which a management team will direct many of the retailing activities. Individual stores in the chain have little autonomy and purchasing is centralized, as is pricing and promotion. Centralized management in chain stores leads to standardized operating policies among the many stores and, in turn, this often leads to greater efficiency of the organization.

A marketing strategy that is utilized by many retail chain stores for greater efficiency is called "vertical integration." Many retail firms are either partially or fully integrated; that is, they control two or more stages of the marketing process. For example, Standard Oil Company of California may control the drilling operations, distilling plants, pipelines, bulk tanks, and the retail outlets. Thus, this firm is fully integrated. Other retailers (such as Safeway Stores) maintain large distribution centers where they purchase from producers, place the goods in a warehouse, and distribute to the chain's own stores in their own trucks. This firm is only partially integrated. But these strategies may give larger retail institutions certain efficiencies and lower operating costs not available to smaller companies.

Chain stores are large-scale retailers and often enjoy competitive advantages associated with their relative size. Retailing chains are able to purchase in larger quantities than smaller stores and as a result, they receive greater price discounts on merchandise. In many instances, chain stores purchase directly from the manufacturer or producer, achieving additional economies. Often large-scale purchasing will lead to other benefits, such as advertising allowances, preferred treatment on goods that are in short supply, and even exclusive distribution rights to certain branded goods. These are benefits that normally do not accrue to the smaller retailer.

Chain stores also have the financial strength and resources needed to develop, promote, and guarantee their own brands of merchandise. Their adequate financial resources allow them to make more effective use of promotion media in blanketing a market with advertising.

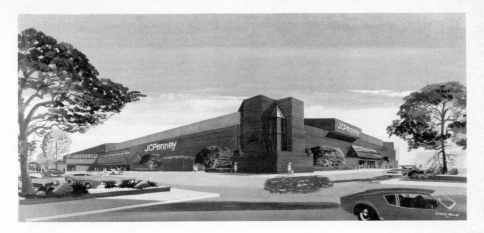

Figure 2-4 Photograph of chain store. *(Courtesy of J. C. Penney Company, Inc.)*

Also, many chain stores have the ability to spread risks. Any multiunit organization automatically spreads the marketing risks among its member stores. Often chains will open a store in a newly developing suburb before that store can support a profitable sales volume. This makes little difference since the store's losses can be absorbed by the others in the chain until the new store can support itself. However, even chain stores with their vast financial resources cannot afford sustained or consistent losses in many stores at the same time.

Many consumers credit chain stores with selling at lower retail prices than independent retailers, and chain stores promote this image with moderate success. In reality, however, one needs to scrutinize this claim closely because it may be misleading. Today, because of improved methods of operation, reduction of costs, and increased competitiveness, many independent retailers are matching the prices offered by chain stores. Many of the independent retailers are using innovative and creative merchandising techniques which rival those used by chain store managers.

Another reason why it may be misleading to compare prices of chains with those of independents is that the merchandise may not be the same brand or of the same quality. Comparing a house brand (the retailer's own brand) with a manufacturer's brand is not fair even though the products may be similar. The grades and qualities of merchandise vary, and comparison should be made only on *like* grades of different brands or on products of the *same* quality. Generally, producer's brands tend to be more consistent in quality than do middlemen's brands.

If chains do sell products at lower prices than independent retailers, it is often traceable to perceptive management and skill. Chain stores may be able to keep operating costs lower than those of independent retailers because of (1) more astute buying, (2) a better division and utilization of labor, and (3) a more efficient inventory control system. An effective inventory control system leads to wiser buying which, in turn, often leads to a faster rate of inventory turnover.

Careful managerial control which maximizes the inventory turnover rate and minimizes the number of slower moving items in stock will lead to lower operating costs and, hopefully, greater profit maximization.

Chain stores, as other retail institutions, suffer certain disadvantages. Standardization in operating policies among the individual stores of a chain which often leads to greater efficiency of the organization also leads to store inflexibility. Firms which are inflexible often suffer sales losses which stem from changes in local market opportunities. Chain store managers are not able to act without first getting approval from the central office, and this takes valuable time. Because of local conditions, what may be appropriate for the central office may not necessarily be good retailing strategy for an individual store manager. A chain store manager usually has very limited autonomy with respect to the product lines that are carried in inventory. Although it is often possible for store managers to reject certain standardized items, it is virtually impossible for that manager to offer goods which are not approved by the chain's central office. In this respect, independent retailers are much more flexible than chain stores. It is well to keep in mind that in chain stores any deviation from the standardization will most likely increase operating costs. Thus, the store manager must carefully weigh the results of any departure from the norm so that any additional costs incurred by the deviation will be offset by increased profits.

It also has been stated that chain stores suffer from a poor public image. In some instances, that is true. Certainly, small locally owned independent retail stores view chains with suspicion. The independents claim chain stores are guilty of absentee ownership, low employee morale, low wages, and long hours of operation, and chains do not pay their fair share of taxes. However, upon closer scrutiny, it would appear that much of this criticism is unwarranted. Chain stores have wide customer acceptance and changing social conditions have prompted them to become increasingly responsive to public sentiment. Today, chain stores have improved their social and business image and enjoy greater public support than at any time during their existence.

Specialty Retailing

Many in store retailing institutions are referred to as "specialty" stores since the operators of these stores *specialize* in a given kind of merchandise—such as furniture, shoes, jewelry, candy, bakery goods, men's and women's apparel, or linens. Specialty store retailers may carry only one line of merchandise, but the customer can choose from a large selection or assortment within that line. For example, a specialty store selling candles will offer to the customer a vast assortment of candles in many sizes, colors, shapes, and scents—a much larger variety of candles than one would find in a variety or department store. The assortment of merchandise within a product line in a specialty store is comparatively greater than in a general store that typically carries only a limited collection of many different kinds of goods.

Specialty stores not only give customers the advantage of a wide choice of one line of merchandise but also offer certain benefits to the operator or owner.

Figure 2-5   Photograph of specialty store. *(Courtesy of Bullock's, Wilshire, Los Angeles)*

First, a retailer specializing in one line of merchandise is better able to buy a larger assortment of goods than when the same amount of capital is invested in several lines of merchandise. For many retailers with limited capital, this is a distinct advantage.

Second, a specialty store retailer may be able to become more familiar with the sources of supply and with consumer demand when dealing with only one product line. While many retailers are knowledgeable about several lines of goods, they are less likely to react as quickly to market or economic changes as the specialty retailers. Since the specialty retailer's attention is devoted to one line of goods, he or she may have greater knowledge of consumer brand preferences, prices, styles, or fashion responsiveness and may be better able to keep abreast of market trends and basic market influences.

The major limitation or disadvantage of a specialty store is that a successful operation depends solely upon one line of merchandise. If consumer habits or market conditions change, the success of the store may be imperiled. Some critics of specialty stores point out that opportunities are missed to make sales of additional kinds of goods. Customers patronizing a specialty store usually do so in order to select from a wider variety or assortment of merchandise, but it is possible that the customer would purchase additional items if available.

NONSTORE RETAILING

Nonstore retailing was originally initiated as a method for serving the needs of customers unable to patronize retail stores. The inability to patronize existing retail stores stemmed from either the lack of time to shop in person or the customer's distance from these retail stores. Because of the needs of these individuals, three methods of nonstore retailing have evolved: mail-order retailing, door-to-door retailing, and automatic-vending retailing. Currently, another form of nonstore retailing which is gaining momentum is telephone retailing whereby a customer can order merchandise from a store by placing an order by telephone. Although this practice is not new, telephone retailing is becoming more popular, and many retailers are establishing telephone order desks.

Mail-Order Retailing

After its inception in the late 1800s, mail-order retailing received little attention or use. However, around the turn of the century, Sears, Roebuck and Company and Montgomery Ward and Company printed extensive catalogs which were sent to prospective customers. Mail-order retailing received its impetus by catering to markets which were not highly concentrated and were located primarily in rural areas. Since overall economic conditions were not as prosperous as today, many people did not have much discretionary income and so their purchases of consumer goods were quite limited. Since these markets would not support a regular retail store, mail-order retailing was one method by which market areas could be enlarged while also providing a service to the people in these remote areas. Today, even though economic conditions and population densities have changed, mail-order retailing is one type of nonstore retailing which continues to be popular with many customers.

Usually, mail-order retailing takes one of three possible forms: (1) the customer may purchase from a catalog, (2) the customer may order from an order blank appearing in a magazine advertisement, or (3) the customer may order from a form sent through the mails by the seller. Some mail-order houses are large; e.g., Sears, Montgomery Ward, J. C. Penney; and offer an exceptionally wide variety of product lines with considerable depth of assortment in each line. Other mail-order houses include the smaller, specialty stores such as Walter Drake and Sons, Eddie Bauer, Sunset House, and Miles Kimball. These specialty mail-order houses may limit the number of lines they offer—sometimes to only one or two lines—to such items as books, records, fancy foods, novelties, or sporting goods.

Over the years, retailing strategies and tactics for mail-order houses have been modified to meet changing competitive conditions. Many large mail-order houses, such as Sears and Montgomery Ward, maintain catalog order desks in

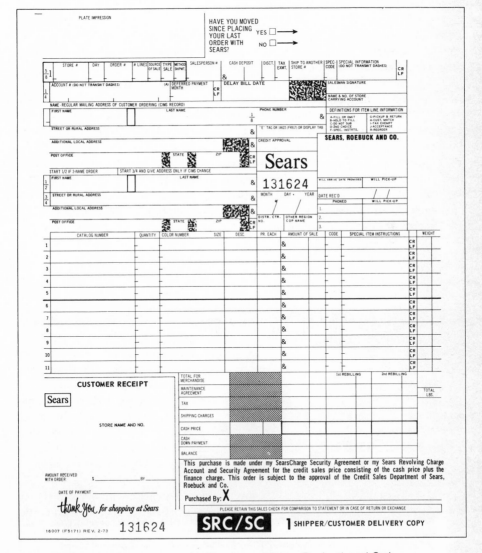

Figure 2-6 Mail-order form: sample. *(Courtesy of Sears, Roebuck and Co.)*

their retail stores, or the customer can request a catalog from the store. In the past, these mail-order retailers supplied free catalogs to potential customers, however, today the customer may be asked to pay for the privilege of obtaining a catalog. One reason for asking the consumer to pay is the high cost of printing and mailing the catalog to prospective customers, since there is little assurance that customers randomly selected will order from the catalog.

Some mail-order houses, like Sears and Montgomery Ward, have set up catalog offices in small communities where a customer personally can go to the store, browse through the catalog, and then place an order. When the merchandise arrives, a telephone call is made to the customer who is asked to pick up the goods as soon as convenient.

According to the *Census of Business,* mail-order retailing constitutes approximately 3.7 percent of the total retail sales whereas the total sales of nonstore retailers is 6.6 percent.[2] However, these figures are distorted because they do not include the mail-order business of department stores and producers, and they do not correctly reflect the fact that the mail-order business is highly concentrated in the giants of the department store industry (i.e., Sears, Montgomery Ward, J. C. Penney, and Spiegel).

Advantages and Disadvantages of Mail-Order Retailing   Mail-order retailing enjoys some definite advantages over instore retailing. One major benefit that emerges is that operating costs are usually lower for mail-order houses because they are usually located in low-rent districts, have lower labor costs per sales dollar, and maintain less expensive buildings and fixtures. Other advantages are not quite so obvious.

[2]U.S. Bureau of the Census, *1967 Census of Business: Retail Trade,* vol. 1, table S, January 1971, p. 30.

Figure 2-6a   Catalog distribution center. *(Courtesy of J. C. Penney Company, Inc.)*

It is believed by some students of retailing that with mail-order retailing there is a psychological advantage to the customer. It works this way. Almost all catalog prices for large mail-order retailers are quoted f.o.b. warehouse. This means that the customer is asked to pay freight or postage charges on the merchandise ordered. However, it is believed that the customer associates only the catalog price with the cost of the goods, while in reality, the freight or postage charges should be added to the cost of the merchandise. Some small specialty mail-order houses include the postage or freight charge in the catalog price of the merchandise, but with the increasing postal rates and freight charges, fewer and fewer mail-order retailers are doing this.

Specialty mail-order retailers have strong consumer appeal since many of their catalog items are not readily available from local stores. Another benefit of mail-order retailing is that the customer may leisurely look through the catalog without being hurried by a salesperson. Also, there is the distinct advantage of not having to drive to a retail store to shop.

On the other hand, mail-order retailing also has some definite disadvantages, both for the retailer and the consumer. For example, customers must place their orders from a catalog without being able to view or inspect the merchandise. In order to combat this disadvantage, mail-order houses offer liberal guarantees, return goods privileges, and detailed catalog descriptions of the products.

Another disadvantage for a customer is that delivery time for ordered merchandise may be long. Mail-order retailers have attempted to offset the slow delivery services of freight and mail carriers by establishing warehouses in many parts of the country. Teletypes and computerized facilities have reduced the order-delivery time in many instances, but the problem is still a major one.

A major disadvantage for the mail-order retailer is that this system is rather inflexible since once the catalog is printed, the price for an article is fixed. Price changes can be implemented by the printing of a catalog supplement. However, catalog changes and printing are expensive and are usually kept to a minimum since the publishing of a catalog is the largest expense for a mail-order house.

Future of Mail-Order Retailing   With the prevailing use of automobiles, good roads, self-service retailing, and shopping centers, mail-order retailing should be declining. However, this is not the case—even before the energy crisis appeared. There is something about the convenience of shopping by catalog and the elimination of the hassles with sales clerks, traffic problems, and parking that has led to the stabilization and slight growth of this method of nonstore retailing. Also, it is possible that mail-order retailing will continue to receive some additional stimulation from consumer revolts against the depersonalized methods of many in store retailing institutions.

Door-to-Door Retailing

Perhaps one of the oldest methods of retailing is where the buyer and seller meet in the buyer's home. This type of retailing is referred to as either "door to door" or "house to house." In some cases, door-to-door retailing is done through "cold canvassing" (i.e., the salesperson literally goes from house to house without advance selection of potential customers). In other instances, door-to-door retailing is the result of established routes or territories.

Door-to-door retailing is usually associated with producers; however, some retailers also sell merchandise door to door. For example, dairy producers and egg producers frequently market their products house to house via an established route, although these producers will also sell their products wholesale to in store retailers. Other producers who utilize only door-to-door retailing include:

Avon	Cosmetics
Fuller Brush Company	Brushes and household goods
Stanley Home Products	Housewares and cleaning supplies
Sarah Coventry	Jewelry
World Book Encyclopedia	Reference books
Tupperware	Plastic household/kitchen items
Amway Products	Detergents and cleaning supplies
Wearever Aluminum	Cooking utensils

From time to time, some retailers sell merchandise on a door-to-door basis, such as insurance salespersons and automobile dealers who visit prospects at home (especially in rural areas). Still others include salespeople of mutual funds, feed, rugs, draperies, vacuum cleaners, cleaning products, and magazines.

While many salespersons will prospect for customers by physically going from door to door, others have resorted to "party plans." Party plans occur where one customer acts as a host or hostess of a social gathering and invites many friends to the house. The basic purpose of having an individual sponsor a party is to gather together as many prospective customers as possible. Then, as part of the party-plan arrangement, the host or hostess allows the salesperson to "demonstrate" or make a sales presentation to the group. Orders for merchandise are taken and delivery usually follows in a few weeks. The host or hostess is rewarded for the hospitality shown to the salesperson by being given one or more gifts—although the value of the gifts usually depends upon the dollar amount of orders that were placed during the party. Underlying this strategy is the parent company's belief that the host or hostess will invite only those friends who are willing to make a purchase. Naturally, this arrangement benefits the salesperson since he or she has a number of prospective customers in one place rather than having to call on a number of individual customers. However, it should be noted that often the salesperson will visit the prospective customer after the party if there appears to be additional sales potential. This party plan has been quite successful for such companies as Tupperware and Wearever Aluminum Products since this is the *only* way to purchase these products. Housewives who wish to buy these particular brands have no choice but to resort to the party plan of retailing.

Advantages and Disadvantages of Door-to-Door Retailing   Although door-to-door retailing does not account for a very substantial portion of retail sales, it does provide an attractive service for many customers. House-to-house retailing offers the consumer personalized, at-home service without the burden of going to a store, locating the merchandise, and standing in line at the checkout counter. At the same time, it offers many retailing companies the opportunity of controlling their distribution structure, pricing mix, and promotional program.

For producers and retailers utilizing this method of retailing, there are some drawbacks. One important feature is that a salesperson must be well prepared in selling and closing techniques—although it is likely that a sales demonstration given to housewives is more easily and warmly received than one given to either wholesalers or in store retailers.

Door-to-door retailing is not inexpensive. One might assume that since the middleman is bypassed and there are no buildings to maintain there would be some cost savings to the customer. Instead products sold door to door tend to be more expensive than those available in retail stores. In some instances, however, it becomes extremely difficult to compare merchandise lines as many of these items are not similar.

Companies utilizing house-to-house retailing often maintain higher profit margins since retail prices are easier to control than if the product were sold through in store retailers. The largest single expense for door-to-door retailers is the commission paid to the salesperson. However, this is a variable expense and is incurred only *after* a sale has been made. This is a result of a traditional practice of compensating door-to-door salespersons on a straight-commission basis. Since most salespeople selling house to house pay their own expenses, the company is responsible only for a commission on the sale. It is interesting to note that the companies who utilize the door-to-door retailing strategy say the main advantage is the lower cost of doing business. However, lower costs of door-to-door retailing can be accomplished only if the company is more efficient in the performance of the wholesaling and retailing functions. Often this is not the case, and the higher net profit concept is an illusion. Many of the firms who utilize door-to-door retailing seem to have one major objective: they wish to maintain close control of the retailing activities even if the costs associated with this type of retailing are more expensive than other means of retailing.

Although this method of nonstore retailing generally runs counter to consumer buying habits, it is still accepted by many consumers. However, this acceptance of door-to-door retailing has led to the emergence of an unpleasant byproduct; the growth of fraudulent door-to-door selling schemes, which unfairly blot the reputation and trustworthiness of the legitimate house-to-house retailers. Some communities have retaliated by passing restrictive legislation which either limits or, in some cases, prohibits door-to-door selling. Salespersons involved in fraudulent operations are often thought to be drifters and floaters. Since it is rather difficult to supervise door-to-door salespeople, some town officials feel that they must prohibit *all* house-to-house retailing.

In summation, poorly selected sales personnel, the lack of supervision and high commission rates (approaching 50 percent in many cases) contribute to the problems associated with door-to-door retailing. But some companies appear to be extremely successful in using this method, so these problems are not insurmountable.

Future of Door-to-Door Retailing   Door-to-door retailing will undoubtedly continue to be used for products that lend themselves to home demonstrations, and some customers will always be attracted by the opportunity of purchasing directly from the source of supply. Similarly, the attraction of the high commissions associated with this type of retailing activity will always be of interest to some salespersons.

Automatic-vending Retailing

A third type of nonstore retailing is "automatic vending," whereby an amazingly wide variety of products are sold through coin-operated, mechanical vending machines. Usually, a company owns and operates the machines and rents or leases space in desirable locations.

According to the National Automatic Vending Association (a trade association for vending machine operators), this type of retailing accounts for approximately 2 percent of the total retail trade. Most of these sales dollars are generated by the sale of cigarettes, candy, soft drinks, hot beverages although other goods do lend themselves to automatic vending (such as hosiery, cosmetics, sandwiches, insurance policies, and food snacks). Other vending machines include amusement devices such as pinball machines, slot machines, and jukeboxes. However, the sales generated from these latter machines are not included in the 2 percent sales figure.

Advantages and Disadvantages of Automatic Vending   Automatic-vending retailing often reaches consumers where and when it is not feasible to do so by in store retailing. Usually, products sold through automatic vending machines are of low unit value, fairly standardized, small and uniform in size and weight, and well-known presold brands of a convenience nature. This type of nonstore retailing often complements in store retailing, allowing the customer to make purchases when the regular retail stores are closed.

However, automatic-vending retailing is expensive for the vendor. First, mechanical breakdowns are frequent; second, the pilferage rate is extremely high; third, items which are vended must be of low unit value, usually under one or two dollars; fourth, the machine must make change for the consumer if he does not have small coins available. Some of the newer, more modern vending machines allow a customer to exchange a dollar bill for coins, but unfortunately, these are not reliable and have become sources of irritation for both the vendor and the customer. Another source of irritation with the vending machine is that there is no opportunity to return unwanted merchandise.

Future of Automatic Vending   Even with the disadvantages listed above, the use of vending machines by customers who wish to purchase either impulse

Figure 2-7 Photographs of vending machines.

goods or other items of low unit value is increasing. Perhaps the greatest potential for this type of retailing lies in impulse items such as candy, soda pop, cigarettes, chewing gum, and snack items.

Telephone Retailing

Telephone retailing is not a new phenomenon but has received increased emphasis since the energy crisis. Currently, both large and small retailers are encouraging customers through their promotional material to order by telephone. Although telephone orders have always been solicited to some extent by large department stores, the practice has gained momentum because of shorter store hours, the shortage or high price of gasoline, and the cooperation of the public in an attempt to conserve energy and ease traffic congestion.

Advantages and Disadvantages of Telephone Retailing Telephone retailing offers a customer the advantage of shopping while at home without the inconveniences associated with inclement weather, parking and traffic problems, and babysitting arrangements. For the retailer, telephone selling is a means of obtaining additional business. The telephone can be used to revive inactive credit accounts, build customer goodwill, and contact existing customers when new merchandise arrives or when the store is having a special sale.

As with all other types of retailing, telephone retailing has certain limitations. Blind solicitation by telephone often annoys customers and should be used with discretion. High returns on telephone ordering can be expected because the goods often do not meet the customer's expectations. Delivery service or mail service must be provided by the retailer which may increase the store's operating expenses.

Future of Telephone Retailing   Those retailers who have maintained adequately trained staff for telephone retailing can expect to expand their business in the future. Telephone retailing appears to be on the increase, and retailers who plan for this type of retailing activity should be amply rewarded.

SUMMARY

A *retailer* is an independent merchant middleman who stands between the producer and the ultimate consumer. *Retailing* includes all functions associated with the sale of goods and services to consumers for personal use.

Warehouse retailing usually involves the use of a warehouse or barnlike structure where merchandise samples are displayed in a showroom, but where the retailer's entire inventory is located in a storage room adjacent to the showroom. Usually the warehouse retailer sells only a single line of merchandise. The warehouse concept of retailing is based on selling only national brands of merchandise right from the carton with price appeal.

Discount retailing emphasizes the sale of name-brand merchandise with price as the main appeal. Discount retailers, unlike warehouse retailers, carry a reasonably complete line of hard and soft goods with well-known, presold brand names, and this merchandise is consistently sold somewhat below the advertised or manufacturer's suggested retail price. The discount retailing concept is simplicity itself: a one-stop shopping center selling only fast-moving, branded merchandise at cut-rate prices. The discount retailer usually is located in a free-standing store. The rate of inventory turnover (RITO) is much faster than for traditional retailers selling the same merchandise.

Department stores are large retail institutions handling many different product lines. Generally department stores are divided into four divisions: (1) operations, (2) sales promotion, (3) merchandising, and (4) control.

Chain stores are retail institutions which consist of two or more units centrally owned and managed. A marketing strategy that is utilized by many retail chain stores for greater efficiency is called vertical integration; that is, they control two or more stages of the marketing process. Chain stores are large-scale retailers and often enjoy competitive advantages associated with their relative size. These advantages may include greater price discounts on merchandise, financial strength, great resources, the ability to spread risks, and in some instances, the ability to sell goods at lower retail prices than some independents. One reason for the latter may be that chains sell many house brands rather than national brands.

Many in store retailing institutions are referred to as *specialty stores* since the operators of these stores *specialize* in a given line of merchandise. Specialty stores provide consumers with a wide choice of one line of merchandise. The specialty store merchant is able to buy a larger assortment of goods than when the same amount of money is invested in several lines of merchandise. By specializing in one product line, the specialty retailer may have greater knowledge of consumer brand preferences, prices, styles, and fashion responsiveness than other types of retailers.

Nonstore retailing consists of mail-order, door-to-door, and automatic vending. *Mail-order retailing* allows the consumer to purchase merchandise from a catalog at his or her leisure. Generally, mail-order retailing benefits from lower operating costs than in store retailing. Delivery times, return goods, and the inability to inspect the goods are major disadvantages for the consumer.

Perhaps one of the oldest methods of retailing is where the buyer and the seller meet in a buyer's home. *Door-to-door retailing* is usually associated with producers although many retailers also sell merchandise door to door.

Automatic-vending retailing lends itself to an amazingly wide variety of products. Most of these products consist of the sale of cigarettes, candy, soft drinks, hosiery, cosmetics, and other low-unit-value items. Automatic-vending retailing is expensive for the retailer because of mechanical breakdowns, theft, and initial investment. Telephone retailing is used by some department stores to increase sales.

REVIEW QUESTIONS

1 Describe the role of the retailer in the distribution of goods and services to ultimate consumers.
2 What are the distinguishing features of warehouse retailing?
3 What factors contribute to the success of warehouse retailing?
4 What are the distinguishing features of discount retailing?
5 A number of discount retailers have failed in the past two years. What are some of the causes of retail store failure?
6 How and in what manner do department stores differ from other types of retail stores?
7 Discuss some of the reasons why department stores continue to enjoy success in a highly competitive retailing environment.
8 What distinguishes a department store organizational structure from the management structure of other types of retail stores?
9 What is chain store retailing?
10 Discuss the following statement: "Chain stores often have a competitive advantage over the small independent merchant."
11 What is vertical integration? Why do some chain stores use vertical integration?

12 How does specialty store retailing differ from department store retailing?

13 Discuss some of the advantages and disadvantages of specialty store retailing over department store retailing.

14 What factors contribute to the successful operation of a specialty store?

15 How did nonstore retailing begin?

16 Why does nonstore retailing continue to be successful when so many stores are serving the needs of the consumer?

17 Discuss some of the advantages and disadvantages of mail-order retailing.

18 What is the special appeal of a specialty mail-order retailer?

19 From the customer's viewpoint, what is the biggest disadvantage of mail-order retailing?

20 Door-to-door retailing continues to grow despite the rise and growth of planned regional shopping centers. What factors do you believe contribute to the success of door-to-door retailers?

21 Why do some producers continue to retail goods to the consumer by the door-to-door method of retailing?

22 What are the main disadvantages of door-to-door retailing?

23 Why do consumers continue to patronize door-to-door retailers?

24 What environmental factors contribute to the success of automatic vending as a means of retailing?

25 Discuss the advantages and disadvantages of automatic vending as a method of retailing.

26 What is one of the main limitations of automatic vending?

27 Discuss some ways in which telephone retailing can be used to a greater degree by retailers.

Chapter 3

Franchise Retailing

Independent retailers, as a group, have become increasingly effective in competing against corporate chain stores. Through the use and adaptation of the strategies and tactics used by the chain stores themselves, independent retailers have been able to compete successfully with the larger chains. The independent retailers have been able to compete more effectively by using some of the following tactics: (1) improving their merchandising practices by upgrading product lines, (2) eliminating slow-moving items after careful analysis, (3) adding new items which sell more readily, (4) improving store locations, layouts, and designs, and (5) maintaining better control over internal operations.

Another strategy which has worked extremely well and has grown quite popular with small retailers in competing against chains is the *contractual agreement* between a supplier and a number of independent retailers. This contractual arrangement between a supplier (either a manufacturer or wholesaler) and several small independent retailers is called a "franchise." In essence, a franchise is a contract which gives a retailer the right to do business under the name and image of that manufacturer or wholesaler. The reason franchises have become so popular is that many persons with a minimum amount of money can set up a retail business. Without the advice and help of the supplier or wholesaler, most of these persons would not be able to enter the retailing field. Thus, franchising has allowed the small retailer to compete effectively with many chain stores and has become an important segment in the retailing field. Hence, throughout this chapter, we will be taking a closer look at the elements involved in the contractual agreement called "franchising."

DEFINITION OF FRANCHISE

A franchise contract is a legal agreement between a company (franchisor) and an individual (franchisee). Through this contract, the individual is provided with an opportunity to conduct business within specific operating conditions, methods, and territorial limitations. But the franchise arrangement does allow individual ownership while reducing some of the risks associated with that individual independent ownership. For example, franchised retailers are often trained in retailing techniques at the parent company's training facilities. The prospective retailers may be provided with a standardized retailing plan to guide the operation of the business, and they may be given advice in areas such as expense control, tax matters, and merchandising practices.

For the privilege of obtaining a franchise from a company, the independent retailer (franchisee) must compensate the franchisor. Compensation to the franchisor may come from one of the following: (1) an initial fee charged each franchisee, (2) a royalty imposed on the gross sales of the franchisee, or (3) the profit from the sale of merchandise, supplies, and services to the franchisee. However, it should be noted that *any, all,* or *some* combination of these three fees may be imposed on the franchisee (independent retailer) by the franchisor (parent company).

Through a franchise agreement, an individual retailer is allowed to build an equity in his or her own business while receiving assistance from the parent company. A franchisee usually can sell the business at any time, although many franchise agreements have a stipulation that the parent company must be given the first opportunity to repurchase the franchise. The major reason that a parent company wants to have this opportunity is to protect its trademarks and good name. It is the franchisor's way of keeping control and preventing the sale of the franchise to an individual who does not meet the company's criteria as a franchise holder in terms of good reputation, reliability, capability, and good credit references.

TYPES OF FRANCHISING SYSTEMS

Usually, most people think of franchising as being particularly associated with the food industry, which is not incorrect; but franchising extends far beyond just the food industry. There are many types of franchising systems. Franchisors can be either wholesalers or manufacturers, and franchisees can be either wholesalers or retailers. But since the subject matter in this book deals with retailing, our discussion will be focused upon the retailer as a franchisee.

One type of franchising system that is quite common is the following. A number of small retailers may band together in an association in order to make volume purchases comparable to the chain stores. This arrangement or banding together may create a franchise relationship. For example, Associated Grocers and Certified Grocers (two of the largest retailer-sponsored franchises in the food industry) allow the independent retailer to purchase stock in the association (franchise arrangement). Thus, through this arrangement, the small retailer can buy merchandise at prices which compare favorably with the prices that chain stores obtain from producers.

Another example of a franchise system in the food industry is a wholesaler-sponsored association which consists of independent retailers, such as Independent Grocers Alliance (IGA) or Super Valu Stores. An association such as this grants a franchise to the wholesaler who, in turn, grants a license (or franchise) to member retailers (e.g., IGA Stores). This arrangement enables these members to purchase merchandise at favorable prices and likewise compete with larger retailers.

Another basic type of franchise exists whereby the manufacturer and the retailer join together to sell goods and/or services. This comes about when the manufacturer franchises the retail store. A manufacturer of automobiles, trucks, farm equipment, paint, petroleum products, and shoes may franchise (grant a license to) a retailer to sell these products. For example, one of the oldest franchise arrangements of this type is the automobile dealership. During more prosperous economic times, there is a large demand for automobile franchises, whereas during times of economic uncertainty, the demand lessens considerably. Currently, the large amount of capital needed to enter the franchised automobile business has probably limited the number of franchises available in this particular retailing field.

Farm equipment retailers are usually franchised, unless the store is owned by the manufacturer. Manufacturer-owned retail stores are becoming more common as the initial capital investment rises beyond the reach of many individuals. However, John Deere and International Harvestor do franchise retail stores when the conditions so warrant.

Paint manufacturers such as the Davis Paint Company and Mary Carter Industries, Inc., still franchise retail stores. Both require a modest investment from the franchisee. As of this writing, the Davis Paint Company required an investment of $18,000; while Mary Carter Industries required an investment of $12,200 by the franchisee.

In another form of franchising a manufacturer and a retailer join to franchise a single department in a large store. It is not unusual to find a shoe manufacturer franchising a shoe department in a large department store. These franchise arrangements are usually between the manufacturer and the department store operator. Also, it is fairly common practice to find a manufacturer of appliances (such as television sets, radios, and stereos) granting a franchise to a department within a department store. Most large department stores offer major, national brands of appliances, and the department will be franchised by the manufacturer. In some instances, however, the same manufacturer may also grant a franchise to a specialty retailer (one who deals in a single line of merchandise).

The franchising of services has become prominent in the last decade. For instance, accounting and tax services have been franchised for many years. H & R Block, Inc., is perhaps the best-known nationwide tax firm. Many of the automobile rental agencies are also franchised, such as Dollar-A-Day, Rent-A-Car, Thrifty Rent-A-Car, and Budget Rent-A-Car. Other franchised services include beauty salons, business services, carpet and upholstery cleaning services, and employment agencies.

Today, a variety of franchising systems exist and include manufacturers or companies selling franchises in fields such as:

Prepared foods	McDonald's, Dairy Queen
Accounting and tax services	H & R Block
Advertising services	Port-O-Sign
Art galleries	Heritage Galleries International
Automotive products and services	AAMCO Automotive Transmission
Automobile rentals	Hertz, Avis
Automotive agencies	Chevrolet, Ford
Beauty salons	Edie Adams Cut & Curl
Car washes	Robo-Wash
Doughnut shops	Mister Donut of America
Employment agencies	Western Girl, Manpower
Retail food stores	7-Eleven Stores, Hickory Farms of Ohio
Motels	Holiday Inn, Sheraton Inn
Paint stores	Mary Carter Industries
Rental services	A to Z Rentals

The list above is far from being comprehensive but should give you an idea as to the breadth and depth of the franchising arrangements in the retailing area. For a more complete listing of franchise offerings, consult the annual *Directory of Franchising Organizations* published by Pilot Industries, 347 Fifth Avenue, New York, New York 10016.

The field of franchising does offer a variety of opportunities to those individuals who wish to enter the field of retailing as entrepreneurs. In particular, for many persons with limited experience in retailing, franchising is one method by which a small businessperson can obtain guidance in management techniques while purchasing his or her own business.

THE FRANCHISE CONTRACT

Franchise contracts are binding legal documents which will vary somewhat to fit a particular market situation. Since a franchise contract is complicated and legally binding, a prospective buyer should inspect all aspects of the contract thoroughly before he signs the franchise. Every prospective franchisee should really hire an attorney to protect his or her interests *before* signing. This point cannot be stressed strongly enough. All too often, franchisees have failed to weigh all the ramifications of a franchise contract carefully. This failure, in turn, has led to financial disaster for far too many small independent retailers. Thus, some of the aspects which the prospective franchise buyer should investigate are as follows:

First, a prospective franchisee should find out how long the franchisor has been in business. Does the company have a good reputation and a good credit rating? (Perhaps a Dun and Bradstreet report would be in order.) For well-established reputable franchisors, the business failure rate among their franchisees is extremely low when compared to the failure rate of independent retailers. This is due, in part, to franchisors placing great value on their reputations and trademarks. In addition, franchisors will usually offer managerial assistance and, in some cases, financial assistance in order to prevent one of their franchisees from failing. A franchisor will provide or help the franchisee with the business planning, but this does not stop the franchisee from closely scrutinizing the agreement and investigating the prospects of success *before* signing a franchise contract.

Second, a franchisee should examine the selection and recruiting procedures used by the parent company. Generally, the more selective a franchisor is in selecting prospective franchisees, the better the chances of success for the franchise. In order to appraise the ability of the franchisor more accurately, a prospective buyer should talk with current franchise holders and visit the home office of the parent company. These discussions may lead to a more honest appraisal of the conditions surrounding a particular franchise.

Third, a prospective franchisee should investigate thoroughly the products and/or service he or she wishes to sell and determine the following: (1) saleability, (2) customer acceptance, (3) frequency of purchase, (4) seasonality, and (5) extent of availability. If the product or service is not universally used, accepted, or purchased frequently, a franchisee's prospects for success may be limited.

Fourth, will the franchisor grant a license for exclusive rights to a particular geographical territory? In some situations, franchisors pay little attention to competitive areas and are more interested in obtaining franchising fees. Thus, a franchisee could end up by having a similar store less than a block or two away.

Fifth, the franchisee should be aware of any practices, policies, or procedures required by the franchisor. It is possible that the franchise contract may become void if these methods or procedures are not followed by the franchisee.

Sixth, franchisees should determine market potential as would any independent retailer. All marketing factors, such as average income levels, age distributions, growing or declining market areas, and other demographics, must be carefully appraised before entering a market. A franchise holder will be in no better position than an independent retailer if the market will not support the business.

As an overall statement of caution, be wary of get-rich-quick business ventures because these opportunities do not exist in reputable franchising operations. Be sure to investigate thoroughly before investing.

ADVANTAGES OF FRANCHISING

Franchising has much to offer in an economic and social sense since it allows an individual the opportunity to be in business as an entrepreneur. For many persons, franchising may offer the only means by which they can enter retailing. Although franchising takes capital, as does any other business venture, often the amount required is minimal. It sometimes takes only a few hundred dollars (as for H & R Block, the accounting tax service franchise). However, it should be noted that other franchises may require thousands of dollars (e.g., Sheraton Inns: $250,000 and up).

Generally, one can open a franchised retail business with less cash than might otherwise be needed. For instance, a franchisee will not need to stock as much inventory as a comparable nonfranchised business. Usually, franchised retail businesses operate on a minimum, fast-moving inventory which reduces the amount and number of items which may be slow moving. This increases the rate of inventory turnover (RITO) for the franchisee, and in turn, reduces the amount of money invested in stock.

Usually, but not always, a franchisee can expect to receive some type of financial assistance from the franchisor. Some parent companies (the franchisor) will assist in lending money to franchisees; others will assist the franchisee by seeking credit sources through the parent company's connections. Because of the parent company's reputation and credit rating, it may be easier for a franchisee to obtain credit than if the individual were to seek funds as an independent entrepreneur.

Another benefit is that the parent company can offer the franchise holder a system whereby control is exercised over pricing, promotion, and merchandising. Since the franchisee may have limited retailing experience but have a strong desire to succeed, the availability of expert assistance is a strong selling point. Although the franchisee may be considered an independent small businessperson in reality, the franchisee has the backing of large-scale buying and promotional programs with the managerial know-how of a large concern. The preceding advantages are just several reasons why the rate of failure for franchise holders is much lower than it is for other independent retailers. The majority of small retail businesses fail for two principal reasons: a lack of retail business experience and incompetence.[1] The lack of retail business experience includes deficiencies in "sales, finance, purchasing, and production on the part of the individual" owning and operating the store.[2] Often, the franchise arrangement that offers managerial assistance to the individual helps to eliminate these problems.

In order to lessen the franchise failure rate, many franchisors offer training

---

[1]*The Business Failure Record 1972,* Dun and Bradstreet, New York, 1973, pp. 11–12.
[2]Ibid.

programs for prospective franchise holders. Training programs may run from several days to many weeks with the emphasis on managerial know-how. This permits a franchisee who has had no previous retailing business experience to enter the retailing business with at least *some* background.

Another benefit is that the parent company often has vast purchasing power, similar to a chain organization. Thus, all the advantages associated with large-scale purchasing accrue to the franchisees. Through the parent company, franchisees can achieve economies by purchasing directly from manufacturers or suppliers. Usually, franchisors can also secure favorable discounts and terms of sale which, in turn, are passed on to the franchisee. Of course, a "handling" fee is added to the cost of the merchandise to the franchise holder. This is just one method by which the franchisor obtains compensation for his role in the franchise arrangement.

Too, franchisors usually take advantage of large-scale promotional techniques. Many franchisors require franchisees to place a certain percentage of their gross sales in a promotional fund. Since each franchisee contributes to the promotional budget, the franchisor is able to advertise at both the local and national levels. Thus, in many instances, a franchisee benefits from national promotion even though he or she operates in a local area.

Another advantage for a franchisee is the benefit of the parent company's research. Most small independent retailers cannot, or do not, conduct research on expanding their market position through improved products and/or services. But most franchisors conduct marketing research on a continuing basis, are keenly aware of market conditions, and realize that research—like advertising— must be a continuous endeavor. Again, because the success of a franchisor depends upon the success of the franchisees, the parent company is constantly searching for new and improved retailing techniques.

Still another benefit that a franchisor provides is offering assistance to the franchisee in recordkeeping. This is extremely helpful to the franchisee, especially in areas which often cause problems for the small retailer—payroll, tax reporting, insurance, hospitalization coverage, and inventory control. Many franchisors offer assistance or actually require conformance to standard operating procedures in these areas. There is a fee associated with these services; however, by using these services, the franchisee is able to devote more time to operating the business by leaving the details to the franchisor. This one factor has contributed immensely to the success of franchise retailing.

DISADVANTAGES OF FRANCHISING

Even though there are many advantages to franchising a retail business, a franchisee must also consider any shortcomings. It is possible that the franchisor may become so dominant in the franchise arrangement that the individual may lose control of the business. For instance, some franchisors establish certain policies that may be detrimental to a local franchised business, even though other franchisees may benefit from such policies. Often, local market conditions are not the same as national marketing conditions. Since most franchisors tend to establish policies which reflect national marketing conditions, this one factor may prove disastrous for certain local franchisees.

Second, a franchisee may find that the franchisor's promotional policies and the fees for such promotion may be impractical. Again, the franchisor tends to select promotional programs which reflect national marketing trends rather than local market desires. Thus, when a franchisor decides that all franchisees must participate in a national promotional program, a local franchisee has little, if any, choice.

Third, some franchise contracts are written whereby the franchisor has much more protection than does a franchisee. This is another reason for having an attorney carefully review and explain the conditions of a franchise contract to a prospective buyer. In some instances, a franchisee cannot sell the business without prior approval from the parent company. In other cases, the parent company must be given the first opportunity to purchase the franchise from the franchisee. Although this practice serves to protect the franchisor, it may be detrimental to a franchisee. In some instances the purchase price is stated in the original contract. When the franchisee decides to sell the business, he or she has no choice but to sell it at the stated price to the franchisor; thereby resulting in a loss or no profit to the franchisee. In other cases, the parent company may have to approve the sale of the business to another individual, which could keep the franchisee from selling the business at all.

In summary, it would appear that the advantages of franchising a retailing business far outweigh the disadvantages. Basically, franchising was instituted to aid the individual or the small businessperson who wants to be in business. In most cases, defrauding or suppressing the franchisees is not one of the goals of the franchisor. Nearly all franchisors would like to have their franchisees express independence and individualism so long as the business is profitable and does not detract from the image of the parent company. The franchising of a retail business is founded upon the principle of proven business practices and policies, coupled with sound financial planning. When these ingredients are blended with proper training in management know-how, the franchised retail business has a good chance of being successful.

CHECKLIST OF PRECAUTIONS

As with any retail business venture, a number of precautions should be taken by an individual before investing in a business or a franchise. The checklist and the precautions that follow can be used by a prospective franchise buyer in determining whether or not to invest in a business. However, these precautions and the checklist should be used only as a guide or an outline and should not be used as a substitute for the advice of an attorney and a certified public accountant.

Precautions

As stated previously, any prospective franchisee should investigate the franchisor. For instance, some franchisors are selling franchises which do not have a proven method of business operation; that is, the franchises being sold are based on an idea, not on a proven retail plan. Only the most reputable franchisors will agree to sell a franchise if their business or businesses have been successful for a number of years.

If the franchisor has been in business for a number of years, the prospective buyer should ask to inspect the business. He or she should talk with the other franchisees or individuals who are knowledgeable about the franchisor's operations. This will help to reduce the number of frauds which have been increasingly evident over the past decade and will also give the franchisee a better idea of what he or she is buying.

A prospective franchisee should be extremely wary of any franchise which offers unbelievable profits on a small investment. Sound business practices and experiences tell us that this is virtually impossible with any retail business. If these types of investments could be made, the gravitation of individuals to the field would be unbelievably high, and the companies would not have to advertise.

A person seeking a franchise should also be cautious about the franchisor who insists on immediately signing a contract and receiving the down payment without first encouraging the prospective franchisee to investigate the parent firm. Many persons have been cheated out of their life savings by fast-talking salespersons selling franchises.

Finally, be wary of the franchisor who appears to be willing to make every concession that the franchisee wants. Franchise contracts serve to benefit and protect *both* the franchisee and the franchisor. Thus, any franchise contract must offer mutual concessions. Any franchise contract which is weighted toward either the franchisee or the franchisor is not likely to be a good contract. Basically, it is a business venture whereby two parties (the franchisee and the franchisor) enter into a retailing arrangement where both parties should be respected and protected against any adverse elements.

Checklist

Before entering into a franchise contract, the following checklist should be thoroughly reviewed by a prospective franchisee.

1 How long has the parent company (franchisor) been in business?
2 What is the financial strength and credit rating of the franchisor?
3 What does the franchisor offer in the way of bank references?
4 What does the parent company offer in the way of future plans for its own development?
5 How selective is the parent company in choosing franchisees?
6 Does the parent company insist that a prospective franchisee visit the home office?
7 Does the parent company provide a training period for new franchisees?
8 Insist on visiting the parent company's established franchises and ask questions about the parent company and how they treat their franchisees.

9 Determine exactly how much cash is needed immediately and how the remaining money is to be raised.

10 Establish how much equipment and supplies must be purchased, and make an inventory list.

11 Determine how the accounting procedures will be implemented and who is responsible for keeping records.

12 Determine who has the right to establish a location.

13 Review the contract for selling rights, promotional fees, and the like.

14 Determine what happens to the franchise should the business not meet the quotas set by the parent company.

15 Determine what type and kind of territorial protection the parent company offers against other franchises.

Certainly this list is not exhaustive in any sense of the word. However, it does provide an initial guide for the individual who desires to enter retailing through a franchise arrangement. Many well-established franchises do tend to reduce the chance of failure and ensure, to some degree, the opportunity for success. However, the person entering the retailing field (whether via a franchise or on their own) should still take all possible precautions. The franchise agreement or contract is *not* a substitute for allowing the prospective franchisee to neglect any of the fundamental details associated with entering business. Franchising may reduce the amount of risk for the franchisee in some technical areas, and the franchise checklist should be used as a guide in making any final decisions.

SOURCES OF CREDIT

When an individual makes the decision to enter retailing via the operation of a franchise, a capital investment will be required. This investment may be more—or less—than that required for opening a nonfranchised store. However, regardless of the amount of money, where does the individual obtain the necessary funds?

In some cases, funds will come from a person's savings account. There may be no need for the franchisee to borrow money. At other times, it may be necessary for the franchisee to obtain additional capital. If this happens, what sources are available? First, many franchisees will try to raise the additional capital from friends and relatives. Generally, raising funds in this manner is *not* the wisest choice since the result may be a family feud or loss of friendship.

It is more prudent to raise the necessary funds through the more traditional channels of financing. First, consult with a banker on the advisability of investing in a franchise. This consultation with a banker should take place *before* any commitments are made to the franchisor. A banker can often help by offering information on the local business environment; he can also serve as a consultant regarding the amount of money that can be loaned for a retail investment.

Although bankers have the reputation of being rather conservative, they usually will not turn down a sound investment. A good retail business plan will significantly assist the banker in determining whether funds will be loaned for the franchise; (the writing of a detailed business plan will be covered later in the text). If a banker cannot loan a person funds for a business venture, he or she may be able to help you find another source.

For some people, another source of possible funds for a franchise investment includes the Veterans Administration (VA). Since World War II, the VA has been engaged in the business of guaranteeing and insuring business loans. However, there is a restriction on the VA loans—one must be a veteran in order to qualify for a VA-guaranteed-and-insured business loan.

Another government agency, the Small Business Administration (SBA), was created by the Small Business Act of 1953. The SBA has field offices throughout the United States, and they are playing an increasingly important role in providing financial assistance for the franchised retailer. The SBA's basic purposes are to aid, counsel, assist, and protect the interests of small business concerns, including retailers. Small independent retailers seeking reliable and reputable franchises can receive loans from the SBA and also obtain advice on managerial techniques. Eligibility for financial assistance from the SBA is limited to small independent businesses (which include small franchisees) whose annual sales receipts do not exceed $5 million. If an individual is refused an SBA loan, it may be due to the agency's lack of funds, or in many instances, it may be due to the fact that the enterprise is not a sound investment or that the individual applying is not a good credit risk.

The sources above are just several sources from which funds can be obtained by the prospective franchisee. It is quite possible that by checking the local business scene, other sources may be found.

THE FUTURE OF FRANCHISING

The future of franchise retailing appears to be promising. Although no factual data are available, estimates are that franchise retailing is becoming a $100 billion industry. Over the past several decades, small independent retailers have been struggling to compete with chains, department stores, and grocery supermarkets. As a result, many independent businessmen have disappeared from the retailing scene to seek employment elsewhere. To a limited degree, franchise retailing has reversed this trend. It has helped to improve retailing managerial efficiency by establishing high operating standards for retailers. It also has allowed individuals to start small retailing establishments and to be in business for themselves. Even though the parent companies (franchisors) establish and control many of the operating policies in a franchise arrangement, nevertheless the franchisee is provided with an opportunity to develop and own a profitable retail business.

As with any retail business, there is an end to the number of markets which will support new retail businesses. Franchise retailing is no exception. There is evidence to suggest that in some fields of retail franchising—such as fast-food outlets—some businesses are being overdeveloped and oversold. On the heels of overdevelopment, an increasing rate of franchise failures will follow. This will result in a slowdown in some areas of retail franchising until territories can be found or developed which will support new franchises.

Another trend shows that parent companies (franchisors) are purchasing the more successful franchises, turning them into company-owned outlets. Thus, as in other retailing segments, franchised companies could develop into retailing giants.

Franchising, as a means of retailing, currently looks encouraging because of the economy in the retailing field. As profits become compressed, more and more retailing operations will become franchised. Franchising as a retailing methodology has adopted some of the standards and procedures used by manufacturers. These methods, in turn, will tend to ensure the success of the businesses by improving managerial efficiency, eliminating waste, and controlling expenses. This particular factor has added a measure of needed stability to the retailing environment. Franchising helps to broaden the economic base by making the entrance into retailing easier for the small businessperson. Thus, it undoubtedly will offer new opportunities in retailing to the small businessperson, and thereby, make an even greater contribution to the American economy.

SUMMARY

Franchise retailing has become an accepted and proven way of operating a retail business. A *franchise* is a contract which gives a retailer the right to do business under the name and the image of a manufacturer or wholesaler. The party granting the license is called the *franchisor;* the party purchasing the license is called a *franchisee.* A *franchise contract* is an agreement between a franchisor (parent company) and a franchisee (individual) whereby the purchaser is provided with the opportunity to conduct a business according to a definite plan. This plan includes the franchisor's name and method of operation, inventory requirements, recordkeeping, and the like.

Franchise retailing has encouraged the growth of small independent retailers by providing them with managerial techniques, skills, training, and know-how. Through a franchise arrangement, the small independent retailer is provided with a proven system of business with the franchisor overseeing the operation of the retail store. For this guidance, aid, and instruction, the franchisee must pay an initial fee, and in some instances, a percentage of the profits of the business. In essence, the franchisor and the franchisee become partners in business although the franchisee is supposedly an independent retailer.

Franchise retailing is not limited to the fast-food industry as the casual observer might think. Franchising extends to service businesses, automobiles, gasoline, household appliances, durable goods, building supplies, and the like. There are really no limits on what type of business can be "franchised."

One generally associates a franchise contract as an agreement between a manufacturer and a retailer. However, other types of franchises do exist although they are beyond the scope of this text.

Franchise agreements are legal and binding contracts which should be examined carefully by an attorney before an individual signs one. Many of the same common sense rules that apply to the entering of a business also apply to franchising. Investigating before investing is good advice anytime.

The main advantages of franchise retailing include: (1) the purchasing of a proven method of retail operation, (2) less capital is usually required (although there are times when this may not be true), (3) the benefits of marketing research by the parent company, (4) large-scale purchasing power through the franchisor (which may result in better merchandise at a reduced cost), (5) advice on financial planning and recordkeeping, and (6) training in management skills and techniques.

Franchise retailing suffers from some of the same limitations as other types of retailing. The franchisee may lose control over the business due to franchisor dominance. Franchisor fees may become excessive and reduce the profits for the franchisee. Some franchise agreements prohibit the franchisee from selling the business without prior approval from the franchisor.

It is wise for any individual contemplating the purchase of a retail franchise to first draft a checklist of considerations and thoroughly investigate the situation. The Small Business Administration may also be of assistance in making the decision on whether to purchase a franchise.

The capital investment in a franchise can be substantial. It is advisable for the franchisee to first obtain commitments of funds from some source, such as a bank or government agency, before signing or making any promise to a franchisor.

Franchise retailing will continue to develop and grow. Basically, it is filling a void in the marketplace and helping to reverse the trend of smaller retailers leaving the industry. For many persons, franchise retailing allows them the privilege of being "in business for themselves."

REVIEW QUESTIONS

1 How have small independent retailers become increasingly more effective competitors against chain stores?
2 What is a franchise?
3 Describe the elements of a franchise between a manufacturer and retailer or between a wholesaler and a retailer.
4 Write a letter to a franchisor of your choosing and request information concerning the requirements of becoming a franchisee and establishing your own retail business. Discuss these requirements before class members.
5 Discuss some of the areas that all prospective franchisees should investigate before signing any franchise contract with a franchisor.
6 Discuss some of the advantages of franchising as a means of entering retail business.
7 Discuss some of the disadvantages associated with franchising a retail business.
8 Why is the rate of failure somewhat lower for franchised retailers than for other small independent retailers?

9   Discuss future prospects for franchising in the retailing industry.
10 Explain why franchising has become so popular in some areas of retailing.
11 Visit a local franchised retail outlet. Discuss some of the aspects of franchising with the owner of the business. Write a short report discussing the pros and cons of franchising based on your interview with the local owner of a franchised retail business. Report your findings to the class for discussion.
12 Based on your findings from the above exercise, provide a checklist of precautions before investing in any retail franchise.

Chapter 4

The Market for
Ultimate Consumers

Many of us consider ourselves well informed on the subject of retailing. After all, we are surrounded by a world of retailing activity. Everywhere we turn retail stores and shopping centers confront us. We are constantly subjected to television, radio, and newspaper commercials which try to persuade us to shop at a certain store, purchase a certain product, or try a specific brand.

Some of us purchase items from retail stores on a self-service basis, and some of us prefer to have a salesperson assist us. At one time or another, most of us have observed the price and/or quality of the merchandise as we visit a variety of retail stores. Many of us have even worked in retail stores and therefore are of the opinion that we know quite a bit about retailing. We are treading on thin ice, however, since in retailing—as in many other fields—a little knowledge may prejudice our decision making in the wrong way.

Many retailers and students of retailing claim they have the consumers all figured out. They say they know and can predict what the customers will do and what they will buy. But in actuality, many of us in retailing do not know why consumers buy or why they do not buy certain merchandise. Many of us are still attempting to answer this complex problem. Since the interaction between the retail store and the consumer is so important to the success of a retailer, we will now devote several chapters to the study of consumer behavior. We will explore some of the theories surrounding consumer behavior, the managerial philosophy which directs the retailer's everyday decisions, and some of the environmental influences which affect consumers and their consumption patterns. Perhaps in this way we can learn more about why consumers purchase certain goods and why they do not purchase others.

THE RETAILING CONCEPT[1]

Retailing is "people business" in that all retailing activities tend to focus on the ultimate or final consumer. The retailing segment of the marketing process links the final consumer to the manufacturer by providing goods and services for the consumers' convenience. That is, retailers sell merchandise to household users for their personal consumption.

In retailing, there is a philosophy which emphasizes consumer satisfaction at a profit to the store. This philosophy of retailing is referred to as the "retailing concept." This retailing concept is based on the fact that all the retailer's plans, policies, and operations should be consumer-oriented. It also encourages the retailer to strive toward full customer satisfaction at a profit to the store. A retailer's only social and economic justification for existence is the store's ability to satisfy the customers' needs and desires. Thus, it is essential that all retailers be consumer-oriented. Those retailers who are not consumer-oriented and who will not adhere to the philosophy of the retailing concept will not be successful in our highly competitive retailing environment.

Under the retailing concept, the consumer becomes the nucleus of all retail planning, programming, and policy making. The retailer will develop a retail business plan with the consumer as the focal point. (Retail business planning will be discussed in considerable detail later in the text.) This text focuses on planning as a means for success in retailing. If the retailer wishes to be successful, he or she must implement the retailing concept into the retail store organization; retail planning should pervade the entire retail organization, whether large or small. All activities and functions should be coordinated and planned so that consumer satisfaction at a profit to the store takes place. In essence, this is the basis for retailing management.

IMPORTANCE OF THE CONSUMER

Perhaps an extension to the retailing concept should be the philosophy that the "consumer is queen or king." Inherent in this philosophy is the idea that the consumer is basically the one who determines what merchandise a retail store will carry. In other words, the goods carried in inventory by a retail store are strictly for the customers' convenience. The consumer also basically determines what services the store will offer, the hours of operation, what retail prices the

---

[1]Adopted from the marketing concept.

store will place on merchandise, and the caliber of sales personnel. With the wide variety of goods and services available today, the consumers are limited only by the amount of income they receive or the credit that is available to them.

Today's retailing environment can be characterized as one of *caveat vendor* (let the seller beware) rather than one of *caveat emptor* (let the buyer beware). In other words, today's retailer must be aware of the hazards of selling goods and services which are *unacceptable* to the consumer. There was a time when the buyer or the consumer had to be especially careful and all purchases were made at the consumer's own risk. Today's risk in retailing rests with the retailer. The consumer has such a wide variety of goods from which to choose that the retailer cannot be complacent and ignore the wishes of the consumer. In essence, the retailing market today has become a "buyer's market" rather than a "seller's market." With the growth and development of the consumerism movement, this point cannot be ignored.

THE MARKET

There are many markets: the stock market, the wholesale market, the grain market, the livestock market, and so on. But when we speak of *the market* in this book, we are talking about *the retail market*.

Someone may state that they are going to the market. What they really mean is that they are going to a grocery supermarket or to some other type of retail institution. Our definition of a market consists of three elements: (1) people, (2) people with money, and (3) people willing to spend their money.[2] Hence, a market consists of people with money who are willing to spend their money for goods and services. This is of special interest to retailers because it is the consumers' willingness to spend that makes a retailer successful. Consumers have needs and desires which can be fulfilled in some manner only with some good or service. To satisfy the consumers' demands, the retailer attempts to fulfill these needs and desires by providing the right goods, at the right price, at the right time. This is customer convenience and is the essence of retailing.

MARKET SEGMENTATION

In the preceding section, we discussed what constituted a market. By any sense of the imagination, the market is large. There is the world market, the European market, the United States market, and so on. Retailers cannot possibly cater to all these markets. Thus, there must be some segmentation or division of the larger market which the retailer can handle by offering the right merchandise, at the right price, at the right time.

Market segmentation consists of dividing a market which has different characteristics into one which has similar characteristics. For example, the

---

[2]William J. Stanton, *Fundamentals of Marketing,* 4th ed., McGraw-Hill, 1975, p. 49.

United States market varies from one section of the country to another because of differences in traditions, mores, customs, and habits. Educational levels, ages, sex, occupations, marital status, income levels, religion, and personal interests also vary. Thus, the retailer must find a segment or portion of that market that he or she can serve.

To divide a market into similar characteristics or features means that the retailer "carves out a niche" in the market and concentrates on that "niche." For example, by promoting price appeal, a discount retailer caters to the price-conscious-market segment. I. Magnin, an expensive women's specialty store, caters to the higher income market by offering prestige merchandise. Thus, each of the retailers above has a market segment which offers them greater opportunities than another segment of the total market.

Sex	Age	Income	Occupation
Female	0–5	$0–$4,999	Unskilled
Male	6–12	$5000–$9,999	Semiskilled
	13–19	$10,000–$14,999	Skilled
	20–34	$15,000–$19,999	Professional
	35–49	$20,000–$24,999	
	50–64	$25,000–$29,999	
	65 & older	$30,000 & over	

Education	Marital status	Social class
Grade school	Single	Upper-upper
High school	Married	Lower-upper
College	Separated	Upper-middle
Graduate school	Widowed	Lower-middle
Postgraduate		Upper-lower
		Lower-lower

Residence	Residential status	Personal interests
Urban	Tenant, apartment	Sports
Rural	Tenant, house	Travel
Suburban	Tenant, condominium	Theater
	Condominium, owner	Arts
	Homeowner	

Region	Climate	Religion
New England	Rain, snow, cold	Catholic
Middle Atlantic	Rain, hot, humid	Protestant
East North Central	Hot, dry, desert	Jewish
West North Central	Rain, cool	Other
South Atlantic	Cool, dry	
East South Central	Coastal	
West South Central		
Mountain		
Pacific		

Figure 4-1 Example of segmenting consumer markets by characteristics.

There is a market segment for men, for women, for teenagers, for children, for college men and women, for those over sixty-five, and so on. Each of these segments tends to have more similar characteristics than the overall total market. As you can imagine, it is much smarter for a retailer to concentrate on one market segment than to try to appeal to all segments of the total market. Trying to serve the total market is too great a task for one retailer and will only lead to ineffective retailing management. This should become even more clear to you by taking a look at Figure 4-1 which shows just a few ways in which a market can be segmented.

PRODUCT CLASSIFICATION

As it is necessary to isolate or segment a market for improved retailing efficiency, it is just as important to classify or categorize products according to their similar characteristics. In retailing, we classify consumer products according to three broad categories: (1) convenience goods, (2) shopping goods, and (3) specialty goods. This classification of consumer goods is based upon the way in which consumers purchase these items.

Because consumer satisfaction is the basic goal of retailing, this classification of goods and services focuses on the consumer, not on the products themselves. This classification of consumer goods has been criticized as confusing because there are no clear lines of demarcation between the three categories. Nevertheless, this grouping is useful in determining the type or kind of retail store. Generally, retailers readily and fully understand this classification of products. Why, you may ask? This scheme is based on the amount of time and effort spent by the average consumer in seeking each of these types of products (as we will soon discover). Since the consumer is our focal point or nucleus for the entire retailing program, retailers should keep this classification of products in mind. Later, this classification will aid you in making decisions on pricing, advertising, and sales promotion, and other elements of the retailing mix.

Convenience Goods

Convenience goods are those products which are usually low in cost and are purchased with a minimum of effort. Products in this classification include such items as milk, bread, meat, gasoline, toothpaste, and all other staple items. Generally, the consumer has a thorough knowledge of this type of product (or its substitutes) before going to the store. This product classification contains the items which are purchased on a routine and continuous basis. Usually, the consumer does not shop around for these products, although there may be some exceptions if the consumer is especially price conscious. For example, it is not uncommon for a housewife to patronize several grocery supermarkets in an attempt to save a few pennies on specially advertised items of the staple nature. However, the consumer will accept substitute products in this classification rather than spend time going from store to store. When the need for a convenience good arises, the consumer will purchase the item from the first store that offers the product. Convenience goods are products which are purchased frequently, and normally there is little brand preference. With some items in this convenience classification, there may be some limited brand preference. But substitutes are readily acceptable if the need is urgent. For instance, some manufacturers have attempted to instill brand preference for some of the company's products, such as toothpaste, but most consumers will accept a substitute toothpaste if one particular kind is not available in the store.

Because these products are found in many retail outlets, retailers of convenience goods have a lot of competition. Manufacturers of convenience goods have wide distribution systems which means that the consumer is able to purchase these products in many different types of retail stores. For example, toothpaste can be found in grocery supermarkets, drugstores, discount stores, service stations, and vending machines. The product is sold in many retail outlets for the consumers' convenience, hence the name, "convenience goods."

The retailer generally does not promote convenience goods unless the producer offers advertising assistance. At times, the retailer will advertise convenience goods at a special price which will attract a large number of consumers. If the retailer advertised the item at the regular price, this would only aid the other retailers (the competition) who are selling it also.

Convenience goods readily lend themselves to self-service retailing. Usually a retailer will offer several brands of a convenience product, and the consumer can select from the displays in the store. The burden of promotion generally falls on the producer, although the retailer may from time to time have special displays of convenience items so as to build store traffic.

Shopping Goods

Shopping goods are those products for which the consumer will shop and compare the different product features, prices, warranties, colors, styles, and other characteristics. Shopping goods are products about which the consumer does not have a thorough knowledge. Thus, the customer must shop for this information. Several trips to various stores may be made by the customer to seek this information and to compare one product with another.

Such items as automobiles, furniture, appliances, gifts, jewelry, furs, men's and women's apparel, and all durable goods fall into the shopping goods scheme of product classification. The unit value or price of shopping goods usually exceeds that of convenience goods. Also, the number of retailers offering shopping goods will be fewer than the number of stores offering convenience goods. The purchasing of shopping goods is much less frequent than that for convenience goods.

Retailers of shopping goods usually try to locate near one another for consumer convenience. Consumers wishing to shop and compare the different products will usually go from one store to another seeking advice and information on an item about which they lack knowledge. At times, the consumer may have decided on what *brand* to buy but not from which *retailer* to buy. Thus, the consumer is seeking the "best possible deal" on price, delivery, and customer service. Customer service is an important facet for the shopping goods retailer. Essentially, with shopping goods, the two factors of product and service are inseparable; but discount retailers have attempted to shift the service responsibility to the consumer. Most discount retailers who offer shopping goods have found it necessary either to provide services (such as delivery or repair) or to make arrangements with an outside firm to perform these functions. This is one reason for the success of the independent shopping goods retailer. The product and the service are provided to the consumer in a package. This combination tends to be successful since many consumers prefer their products be serviced by the retailer from whom they bought the item.

Shopping goods lend themselves to franchising. If a franchise contract is not used by the producer of shopping goods, there will be, nevertheless, a close working arrangement between the retailer and the manufacturer. It is common practice for retailers to purchase shopping goods directly from the producer. Shopping goods retailers also purchase in larger quantities from the producer in order to obtain maximum discounts and allowances. From the consumers' point of view—even though brands are quite important for shopping goods—the retailer's reputation may be more important than the manufacturer's name.

Shopping goods are promoted by the retailer to a greater extent than they are promoted by the producer. For instance, men's and women's apparel will be advertised, displayed, and priced by the retailer rather than by the manufacturer, except in the case of "fair-trade merchandise." (With fair-trade merchandise, the manufacturer sets the retail price or selling price of the goods, and usually the retailer must comply.) Again, this illustrates the point that in many instances the retailer is better known to the consumer than is the manufacturer. This is particularly true in the case of fashion merchandise. Here the consumer may not care who the manufacturer is but instead is more interested in the style and cut of the merchandise.

Specialty Goods

Specialty goods are those products which a consumer will make a considerable effort to find. Usually, there is a strong *brand preference* for specialty goods, and the consumer has full knowledge of the product. The consumer will accept no substitute and will continue to shop for the specific brand. Often, when a retail store is found which offers a favorite brand, the consumer will continue to patronize that store because the item can be purchased easily without expending extra effort to find the product elsewhere.

Specialty goods have a characteristic of brand preference, which makes both high-priced and low-priced products fall into this classification. For instance, a pipe smoker will usually insist on a specific brand of tobacco for his pipe. This makes it a specialty product. Other products such as automobiles, appliances, stereos, expensive men's suits, and some furniture, are also included in the specialty product category. Note that it is not the *price* as much as the *brand* which determines the specialty-product classification scheme.

Retailers featuring specialty goods are fewer in number than those offering convenience or shopping goods. Generally, there is only one retailer offering specialty goods in an area; this gives the retailer a competitive edge on the market as the store does not have to compete with other stores on this particular brand. There may be substitutes or other brands of the basic specialty product, but no other retailer in the area will offer the same brand.

Sometimes the manufacturer of specialty products will also utilize a franchise arrangement. When a franchise contract is used, the selection of a retailer is carefully and deliberately undertaken. This arrangement protects not only the retailer but also serves to protect the manufacturer. If a retailer knows that his or her store is the only one in a certain geographic area handling that certain brand, that retailer may make a greater effort to promote the product. However, the producer and the retailer will usually join in on any promotional efforts for specialty goods. It is usually a cooperative advertisement with the producer and the retailer each paying a portion of the promotional expenses.

JUSTIFICATION OF PRODUCT CLASSIFICATION

The previous classification of consumer products is based on the purchasing habits of consumers. Critics of this scheme state that the classification is one of buying habits only and that the products themselves should not be classified in this way. This criticism may be justified. However, the previous product classification (convenience, shopping, and specialty goods) does serve as a useful tool for both a retailer and a producer. By using this scheme, retailers, in particular, are better able to alter their retailing mix to improve customer service.

At the beginning of this chapter, we discussed the need for a retailer to be consumer-oriented. Since the consumer is the focal point of all retailing activities, we should use every available aid or device in order to strive for continued improvement in consumer service.

The previous classification of consumer products has given rise to retail store names. For instance in the business world, we talk of convenience stores, shopping stores, and specialty stores. There is nothing wrong with using this classification for retail stores. After all, the consumer (our focal point) has also come to refer to various retailers in this manner. If the consumer prefers this scheme, why should the classification be criticized and why should we question the consumers' reasons for placing stores in a category? What really is important is the following: the consumer has come to accept this classification method and for convenience sake has extended the scheme to retail stores. For the retailer and the student of retailing, it is important that we realize that stores often may carry more than one product classification. For instance, a retailer may offer the consumer mostly convenience goods (such as in a grocery supermarket), but a retailer may also offer a limited selection of specialty products, such as fancy foods or imported beers. If we study Figure 4-2, we can see that there are no clear-cut product categories. The products (and their classifications) tend to overlap one another. In other words, there are areas of grey because consumers

Impulse goods	Convenience goods	Shopping goods	Specialty goods
Soft drinks	Flour	Small appliances	High-fashion goods
Magazines	Sugar	Television sets	Pipe tobacco
Cigarettes	Coffee	Radios	Cigars
Candy bars	Bread	Automobiles	Cosmetics
Potato chips	Butter	Furniture	Watches
Popcorn	Eggs	Clothing	Motor oil
Chewing gum	Meat	Shoes	Wines
Beer	Paper products	Gift items	Liquors

Minimum shopping effort $\rightarrow$	Increased shopping effort $\rightarrow$ Some forethought and	Maximum shopping effort Considerable forethought
No forethought or prepurchase planning (no brand preference)	prepurchase planning (brand comparison)	and prepurchase planning (brand insistence)

Figure 4-2 Classification of consumer goods (based on consumer buying habits).

do not all shop in the same manner. Figure 4-2 can best be described as a "spectrum" or a continuum of product classification which has considerable overlap within each product category. Although this scheme tends to produce shaded areas, the classification does serve the retailer in determining the best mix of products and services. As for the critics of the classification, it can only be stated that until a better scheme is devised, this product category will continue to be used by retailers in an attempt to better serve the consumer.

OTHER PRODUCT CLASSIFICATIONS

In addition to the three main product categories just discussed, consumer products are classified or identified in other ways. The following definitions or categories are used in retailing and will be used throughout this text. The following brief explanations may assist you in understanding and clarifying the various retailing product categories.

Impulse Goods

"Impulse goods" are those products of low unit value which the consumer purchases with little or no forethought. Many products fall into this classification. They include soft drinks, peanuts, chewing gum, popcorn, magazines, razor blades, candy, snack items, and ballpoint pens. In short, any product which is purchased without any preplanning can be labelled an impulse good. Often, a retailer will place items of low-unit value near the checkout stands. While consumers are waiting in line to pay for their purchases, they often will select items from these merchandise displays. Consumers see the items and purchase *on impulse,* hence the name. As you might imagine, impulse items usually do not appear on shopping lists.

Soft Goods

The name "soft goods" is applied to such items as clothing, bedding, towels, and linens—items which tend to be produced from cloth. These are goods which are offered by department stores and specialty stores as their major product lines. Department stores and specialty retailers often offer extensive lines of linens, bedding, bathroom towels, and clothing for all age groups.

Durable Goods

Durable goods, sometimes referred to as "hard goods," include items such as home appliances, automobiles, and some furniture. Durable goods usually have a high unit value and are purchased infrequently. Some durables may have some trade-in value, and their purchase is deliberately planned (shopping goods).

Brown Goods

This classification of products is really a subcategory of durable goods. In particular, it refers to radios, stereos, and television sets.

White Goods

White goods can be either soft goods (linens or towels) or white goods can also indicate durable goods of the appliance line. When retailers use "brown and white goods," they probably mean durables. But to department store retailers who have "white sales," this would indicate bedding or linens.

Seasonal Goods

Many products are seasonal in nature. Fashion merchandise is seasonal according to style and color. Other products such as lawn mowers, antifreeze, overshoes, bathing suits, Christmas cards, winter coats, and garden tools have peak demands during certain periods of the year. Thus, they are considered to be "seasonal goods."

SERVICES

Service retailing deserves mention because approximately fifty cents out of every dollar we spend goes for some type of service. Many of us tend to think in terms of service only when it is connected with a product. However, there are many retailers who sell only services. Retailers of services include banks, insurance companies, doctors, dentists, beauty salons, barber shops, car washes, shoe repair shops, restaurants, motels, hotels, lawyers, and accounting services. The list is almost endless.

As we continue to become more dependent on the other people in our society, the trend toward spending more money for services increases. We Americans are highly interdependent upon one another. Today, most of us rely on others to provide the products and/or services which at one time we produced by ourselves. Also, many of the items that we once considered luxuries have become necessities in our daily lives. This service-luxury market of retailing has added a measure of stability to our nation's economy because of our interdependence upon one another for these products and services. Services and items that have become a part of our everyday consumption pattern have encouraged the growth of retailing since most consumers feel that they cannot postpone their purchases and therefore want the goods immediately.

DEMOGRAPHIC CHARACTERISTICS

"Demographics," or demographic characteristics, is the study of the statistics on births, deaths, marriages, the density of population, the size of the populace, and the distribution of the population.

Retailers should be interested in demographics because of their need to know the characteristics of the customers they serve. For instance, demographics can aid retailers in determining the type and kind of product assortment they should offer the consumer and where to locate a store. Demographics also give the retailer a profile of the type of customers that the store is dealing with. In addition, retailers can learn the population size and its projected growth, the distribution of these people within the trade area, the birth and death rates in the area, and the makeup of the population by age, sex, race, and nationality. All these facts will be helpful to the retailer in more successfully serving the customer.

Changes in Age Mix

There were 203 million persons in the United States in 1970;[3] by early 1974, this figure had risen to 212 million; and by 1984, the population in the United States is projected to reach 233 million.[4]

Within the total population of the United States, numerous and constant shifts are taking place. These shifts and changes in the age mix are quite significant for the retailer. For instance, persons between the ages of twenty and thirty-four are increasing in number more rapidly than any other age group. According to *U.S. News and World Report,* this age group will grow by 25 percent (or approximately 12 million people) during the ten-year period 1974–1984. Too, by 1984, this age group will account for approximately 57 percent of the nation's expected growth of 21 million people. The persons in this age group will be setting the trends in consumption patterns for our society. During this period of their lives, these people will get married, establish households, begin raising families, earn good incomes, and possess considerable disposable and discretionary income. In addition to setting trends for consumption patterns, this group of people will probably buy on credit, thereby obligating themselves for future payments. Just what does all this mean for the retailer? It may be wise for retailers to observe rather closely the changes in consumption patterns of this particular age group, especially in relation to his or her type of retail business.

[3]*Statistical Abstract of the United States,* 1973, pp. 12–13.
[4]*U.S. News and World Report,* February 25, 1974, p. 44.

For example, if a retailer is selling furniture or durable goods, the growth that is expected within this age group, together with their spending habits, would make this change in demographics rather significant.

It is also estimated that the number of households (one or more family members living together) will increase from 70 million in 1974 to more than 86 million by 1984.[5] This increase in households may expand the market for such items as home accessories, furniture, appliances, automobiles, clothing, garden supplies, plants, lawn mowers, and do-it-yourself building materials.

As we can see in Table 4-1, other major shifts in the population are taking place. The younger middle-aged group from thirty-five to forty-nine will continue to grow, but not as rapidly as the rate for the previous age group of twenty to thirty-four. A significant factor for retailers to consider in regard to the people in the thirty-five to forty-nine age bracket is that the income of most of these persons is rising rather rapidly. With this rise in income, the people in this age bracket will tend to move into larger and more expensive homes. This, in turn, will increase their need for furniture, appliances, home furnishings, carpeting, drapes, and other household items. Since many of these people tend to move to the suburbs, they may also need a second automobile. It is also possible that these people will upgrade their standard of living because of the rise in their incomes. The retailer may then assume that these persons will consume food which is higher in price and quality and that they will do more entertaining, thereby purchasing and consuming more liquor and soft drinks.

The number of persons making up the older middle-aged group from fifty to sixty-four will grow rather slowly during the decade of 1974–1984. However, it is important for retailers to take note that these people will have the *highest* average incomes of all the age groups. If a retailer wishes to attract this segment of the market, he or she should pay particular attention to promoting luxury goods, expensive services, and leisure-time-related activities.

The number of persons in the older age group, sixty-five and up, will continue to increase. This group of people will have considerable discretionary income which can be spent for travel and luxury items, as well as a variety of retailing and recreational services. Along with the recreational services, these persons will purchase clothing and equipment which will complement their leisure-time activities. Because of advancing age, this age group also tends to spend a larger amount of money on health aids and drugs than do the other age groups.

We have left the youngest age group, children and teenagers, until last because it is this group which will actually *decline* in numbers. This age group by 1984 will decrease by 2.1 million, or by 3 percent of the total population.[6] The significance of these figures lie in their makeup. The baby crop is expected to expand from 3.1 million in 1973 to an estimated 4.2 million by 1984.[7] However,

5Ibid.
6Ibid.
7Ibid.

Table 4-1 Population by Age Groups

AMERICANS:THE CHANGING AGE MIX

U.S. Population is in a slow rise—from 212 million today to an estimated 233 million in 1984.

But major shifts are ahead among various age groups, with broad significance for business and government.

Children and Teen-Agers

Now	75.7 million
1979	73.4 million
1984	73.6 million

Change, 1974–84:
Down 2.1 million, or 3%

Baby crop is expanding again, promising growth ahead in numbers of elementary-school children. But youths of secondary-school and college age will decrease all through the decade.

Young Adults, 20-34

Now	48.9 million
1979	56.5 million
1984	61.0 million

Change, 1974–84:
Up 12.1 million, or 25%

More than half of the growth in U.S. population will come in the young-adult group—the age bracket in which people start earning good incomes, get married, set up households, start families and spend in a big way.

Younger Middle-Age Group, 35–49

Now	34.5 million
1979	35.9 million
1984	41.1 million

Change, 1974–84:
Up 6.6 million, or 19%

Growth in this age group will come faster and faster in years ahead. These are the people that, climbing up the income ladder, move into bigger houses, become multicar families, and in general, upgrade living standards.

Older Middle-Age Group, 50–64

Now	31.4 million
1979	32.4 million
1984	32.2 million

Change, 1974–84:
Up 0.8 million, or 3%

This group, with highest average incomes, will grow slowly, then diminish in number. Result: Less lift for spending on services, leisure activities, expensive homes and luxury goods.

People 65 and Older

Now	21.7 million
1979	23.7 million
1984	25.5 million

Change, 1974–84:
Up 3.8 million, or 17%

Rapid rise in number of older people promises greater demand for apartments, medical care—and broader Social Security benefits. Older people also offer an expanding market for luxuries—such as fashionable clothing, books, recreation.

Source: Reprinted from U.S. News & World Report, Feb. 25, 1974, pp. 44–45. Copyright 1974 U.S. News & World Report, Inc.

the young people of secondary school age and college age will decrease in numbers over the next ten years. This is due, in part, to the nation's fertility rate hitting a record low of 1.91 children per woman during 1973.[8] The "replacement level" of 2.1 (the theoretical point at which births equal deaths), is expected to be attained by the early 1980s. This should stabilize the population of the United States. Of course, any population shifts or changes in the next few years could invalidate these estimates.

Any changes and alterations in the nation's age mix will undoubtedly bring about changes for the retailer. During the next decade, the retailer must be prepared to meet the challenge. The changing age mix will alter our nation's attitudes, way of life, and consumption habits and patterns, as well as affect our value judgments. For instance, the period of the sixties was a bountiful time for Americans. During this decade, we experienced previously unequalled abundance and what appeared to be unlimited resources, and our society became rather affluent. During the early seventies, however, it became apparent to us that there was a limit to our abundance and affluence. Many shortages developed. Such items as fuel, raw materials, manufactured products, and the like were in short supply. The consumer experienced some inconvenience and shortages in areas where previously there had always been an abundance. Consumers became frustrated, and anxieties never before encountered developed and affected consumers and their consumption patterns. Out of these frustrations and anxieties a simpler way of life is evolving. There appears to be an accelerated trend toward small town living and a movement to the suburbs. The retailer must also move and change to meet the demands of these consumers. Employment outside the metropolitan areas has also been increasing. All these social changes represent challenges to retailers.

Retailers will have to go where there is a market. This may indicate a change in store location or a more careful measurement of market potential in certain trade areas. It may represent a change in the retailing mix—the blend of products, services, price, promotion, and planning activities. It may alter the hours of operation for some retailers. This next decade (1976–1986) will require constant vigilance on the part of the retailers if they are to meet these challenges of social change successfully.

SUMMARY

In retailing, there is a philosophy which emphasizes consumer satisfaction at a profit to the store. This philosophy of retailing is referred to as the *retailing concept*. This retailing concept is based on the fact that all the retailer's plans, policies, and operations should be consumer-oriented. Under the retailing concept, the consumer becomes the nucleus of all retail planning, programming, and policymaking.

It can be stated that the "consumer is queen or king." It is the consumer

---

[8]Ibid.

who basically determines what merchandise the store will offer, since the goods carried by the store are strictly for the customers' *convenience*.

When we discuss the attributes of a market, we are referring to the three *basic elements of a market:* (1) people, (2) people with money, and (3) people willing to spend their money. It is the consumers' willingness to spend money that makes a retailer successful, assuming efficiency of operation.

Retailers cannot possibly cater to all markets; thus there must be some division or segmentation of markets. *Market segmentation* consists of dividing a market which has different characteristics into one which has similar characteristics.

In retailing, we classify consumer products according to three broad categories: (1) convenience goods, (2) shopping goods, and (3) specialty goods. This scheme is based on consumer purchase habits and patterns. *Convenience goods* are those products which are usually low in cost and are purchased with a minimum of effort. Convenience goods readily lend themselves to self-service retailing.

Shopping goods are those products for which the consumer will shop and compare the different product features, prices, warranties, colors, styles, and other characteristics. Shopping goods lend themselves to franchising or exclusive representation by a retailer.

Specialty goods are those products which a consumer will make a considerable effort to find. Usually, there is a strong brand preference for specialty goods, and the consumer has full knowledge of the product. Retailers featuring specialty goods are fewer in number than retailers offering convenience or shopping goods. There may be only one retailer offering specialty goods in an area.

In addition to the three main product categories, consumer products can be identified in other ways. For instance, *impulse goods* are those products of low unit value which the consumer purchases with little or no forethought. The name *soft goods* is applied to such items as clothing, bedding, towels, and linens. *Durable goods,* or *hard goods,* include items such as home appliances, automobiles, and some furniture. *Brown goods* are those durable goods such as radios, stereos, and television sets. *White goods* can be soft goods or can also refer to durable goods of the appliance line, such as refrigerators and stoves. *Seasonal goods* include fashion merchandise, lawn mowers, bathing suits, and the like.

In addition to retailing that emphasizes the sale of goods, *service retailing* is very significant since most of us as consumers spend approximately fifty cents of every dollar for some type of service. Retailers of services include banks, insurance companies, doctors, dentists, and beauty salons. Many of us rely on others to provide the products and services to make our life style more convenient.

Demographics is the study of the statistics on births, deaths, marriages, the density of population, the size of the populace, and the distribution of the population. Retailers are interested in demographics because of their need to know the characteristics of the customers they serve.

In 1974, there were 212 million people in the United States; by 1984, the population in the United States is projected to reach a total of 233 million. Persons between the ages of twenty and thirty-four are increasing in number more rapidly than any other age group. By 1984, it is estimated that this age group will account for approximately 57 percent of the nation's expected growth of 21 million people (1974–1984). Between 1974 and 1984, the number of households will increase from 70 million to more than 86 million. This increase in households will expand the market for such items as home accessories, furniture, appliances, automobiles, clothing, garden supplies, house plants, and so on.

The younger middle-age group from thirty-five to forty-nine will continue to grow, but not as rapidly as the rate for the twenty to thirty-four age group. A significant factor for retailers to consider in regard to the people in the thirty-five to forty-nine age bracket is that the income of most of these persons is rising rather rapidly.

The number of persons in the older middle-aged group from fifty to sixty-four will grow rather slowly during the decade 1974–1984. It is important for retailers to note that these people will have the highest average incomes of all the age groups. The number of persons in the older age group, sixty-five and up, will continue to increase. This group of people will have considerable discretionary income which can be spent for travel and luxury items, as well as for a variety of retailing and recreational services.

Children and teenagers will actually decline in numbers during the ten-year period 1974–1984. While the baby crop is expected to expand during this period, the young people of secondary school age and college age will decrease in numbers.

Any changes and alterations in the nation's age mix will undoubtedly bring about changes for the retailer. The changing age mix will alter our nation's attitudes, way of life, value judgments, and consumption habits and patterns. Retailers must be prepared to meet the challenges of the next ten years.

REVIEW QUESTIONS

1 What is the retailing concept?
2 Discuss the concept of the "consumer is queen or king."
3 Discuss why today's retailing environment is characterized as one of *caveat vendor*.
4 How does the text define a market?
5 Explain market segmentation and its basic purpose(s).
6 Discuss the classification of consumer goods.
7 Define the following terms: impulse goods, soft goods, durable goods, brown goods, white goods, and seasonal goods.
8 Explain the purpose of studying demographics.
9 Discuss the significance of the age groups in Table 4-1.
10 What do population shifts and trends indicate for retailers in the next decade?

Part Two

Consumers and Buying Behavioral Attributes

Chapter 5

Determinants of Consumer Purchasing Behavior

As we discussed in the last chapter, every retailer and every student of retailing needs to know why consumers purchase certain goods and services or why they do not purchase others. An understanding of consumer purchasing behavior is the retailer's foundation for developing a proper retailing mix. (As you will remember, a retailing mix is a combination of goods and services, price, promotion, image, prestige, location, and other characteristics which blended together will result in optimum sales and profits for the retailer.)

But how does the retailer find out what the consumer is thinking? We know very little about what actually goes on in the mind of a consumer making a purchase. In fact, many consumers, if asked, do not know why they purchase one item in preference to another. A consumer's purchasing decision is a complex aggregate of factors which may include such things as: peer group influence, learning experiences, motivation, attitudes, beliefs, personality traits, perception, and cognition. Consumer purchases are rarely the result of a single factor. Instead, purchasing decisions are usually based on a number of factors which may change over a period of time. Fluctuations and changes in income level, life style, acquired learning experiences, and group influences are just a few of the things which may alter a consumer's purchasing decision.

A retailer may be able to obtain certain market information on potential customers such as their level of income, but less will be known about how and why these individuals spend their incomes. In order to gain more insight into the purchasing behavior of consumers, one needs to study consumer motivations, attitudes, and buying habits. A retailer must understand the reasons *why* consumers purchase a given brand or product, or *why* consumers shop at one store rather than another. A retailer must appeal to the consumers' conscious and unconscious motives or lose their patronage. As you will remember, the basic purpose of every retailer is to satisfy the customer at a profit to the store. An understanding of the principles of consumer purchasing behavior will allow a retailer to develop a retailing mix which will satisfy most of the store's customers.

THEORIES OF CONSUMER PURCHASING BEHAVIOR

It may appear to the casual observer that when a customer makes a purchase, it is a simple and routine procedure. In the case of an impulse purchase, this may be the case. However, many consumer purchasing decisions are a result of a set of complex factors which even the consumer does not understand. For instance, why does a customer pick up and look at an item but later return that same item to the shelf? Why do consumers have brand choices, product preferences, and favorite retail stores? Being able to answer these questions with some authority is possible only if we study in considerable detail consumer behavior and its role in the purchasing decision.

Several disciplines aid retailers and students of retailing in determining the behavior of consumers when they shop. These disciplines help to answer such questions as: Why do customers purchase or not purchase certain merchandise? Why do consumers respond to certain types of advertising and sales promotions? Why are consumers attracted or repelled by certain retail stores? The disciplines or areas of study that can help the retailer answer these questions are: (1) psychology, (2) sociology, and (3) social psychology.

Psychology is the study of individual behavior. Retailers and students of retailing are interested in individual behavior, but in some instances, the discipline of psychology may focus too narrowly on specific behavioral characteristics. Retailers generally are more interested in *groups* of people, therefore, the following discipline may be of greater assistance to the retailer.

Sociology is the study of group behavior. The study of sociology provides us with explanations of how various groups may react to certain stimuli. Thus, it may help the retailer in deciding how consumers will react to such things as advertising, point-of-purchase display materials, the outward appearance of a store, the interior design, and the like. Along with sociology, the following discipline can be quite helpful to a retailer.

Social psychology is concerned with the behavior of individuals as they are influenced by the various groups of people around them. We know that peer groups and social groups often play a significant role in affecting an individual's purchasing habits and patterns.

Any one of these disciplines alone does not provide us with a theory which explains *all* consumer purchasing behavior. But each of these disciplines contributes some insight and gives us a possible explanation for certain types of consumer buying behavior.

Even among themselves, psychologists do not agree on which factors provide the best explanation of a consumer's purchasing behavior. Different schools of thought provide different answers. However, most psychologists do agree on one thing: that a consumer's learning process is the real key to a better understanding of any purchasing behavior. Although no single learning theory has evolved to explain purchasing behavior, several existing theories offer some insight as to why consumers behave as they do.

Over the years, several theoretical models have been developed which attempt to explain consumer purchasing habits.[1] Each of these studies has contributed a small portion to the complex field of consumer purchasing behavior. Too, these studies have partially provided answers to why consumers purchase, and why they do not purchase. With this thought in mind we now turn our attention to these specific theories of consumer behavior.

Stimulus-Response Theory

The stimulus-response theory of consumer behavior was introduced by psychologists such as Pavlov, Skinner, and Hull.[2] Although the original experiments were conducted in the laboratory on animals, these men believed that all human beings learn a pattern of behavior in a similar way—by responding satisfactorily to an applied stimulus. A *correct* response to a stimulus provides the individual with need satisfaction *(reward)*, and an *incorrect* response results in a *penalty*. Thus, established behavioral patterns are the result of continued repetitions of the same stimulus. This basic concept is used today by many retailers in their advertising and sales promotion.

A slight variation of this stimulus-response theory was advocated by Watson.[3] Watson stated that if one repeated the same stimuli over and over, there would be a consolidation of response patterns. In other words, from this basic fact has come the idea that advertising themes and ideas must be repeated over and over again, so as to ensure a given purchasing response. Thus, if a retailer selects an advertising theme which creates a certain image for the store and the retailer continually repeats this theme, it should reinforce the store's image in the consumers' minds. According to the stimulus-response theory, this theme (stimuli) must be repetitive and continuous. The consumer must be constantly reminded of the basic image or idea the retailer is attempting to communicate.

[1]Philip Kotler, "Behavioral Models for Analyzing Buyers," *Journal of Marketing,* October 1965, pp. 37–45.
[2]Several books are available on this theory: see Ivan P. Pavlov, *Conditioned Reflexes,* Oxford, London, 1927; B. F. Skinner, *Science and Human Behavior,* Macmillan, New York, 1953; Clark L. Hull, *Essentials of Behavior,* Yale, New Haven, Conn., 1951; Clark L. Hull, *A Behavior System,* Yale, New Haven, Conn., 1952.
[3]John B. Watson, *Behaviorism,* The People's Institute, New York, 1925.

Although a retailer wants a certain consumer response, the consumer *may* give an entirely different reaction.[4] For instance, a retailer will want the consumers to respond to an advertisement by purchasing a certain product or brand. If the consumers do not respond to the retailer's advertisement, or if they respond to the advertisement by purchasing a different brand or product than the ones advertised, we can assume that this was an incorrect response. As you probably have observed, there are many inappropriate or incorrect responses in the marketplace. Retailers spend considerable sums of money in attempting to obtain the correct consumer response; some retailers advertise every week in the hope of obtaining a correct consumer response. It is a challenge for the retailer to create an appeal (stimulus) which will obtain a correct response from the consumer.

At times retailers fail to understand that an advertisement does not always produce a correct response from the consumer. It is difficult for a retailer to present an advertisement which will be acceptable to all persons. Similarly it is hard to convince consumers to react according to the retailer's wishes. For example, an advertisement which emphasizes youth may "turn off" older consumers; an advertisement which appeals to older persons may repel younger consumers. This brief illustration emphasizes the importance of a retailer knowing the profile of the consumers in the store's target market. (A target market consists of a group of consumers with similar characteristics which the retailer wishes to attract to the store; i.e., women between the ages of eighteen and thirty or men between the ages of twenty-eight and thirty-five.) The theme of the store's advertising must be acceptable to the customer grouping if the correct responses are to be obtained. If the store does not receive correct responses from the consumers, the retailer has wasted the funds spent on advertising and sales promotion.

Cognitive Theory of Consumer Behavior

Some psychologists reject the stimulus-response theory as being too mechanical.[5] These people adhere to another theory of consumer behavior which is called the "cognitive theory." Advocates of the cognitive theory believe that the learning process is much more complex than a simple stimulus-response reaction. They think learning is influenced by such factors as past experiences, acquired beliefs, personal philosophies, and personal attitudes. They think consumers react only after *perceptive thinking* which is goal-oriented, not by a stimulus-response action.

However, this cognitive theory does not explain why so many consumers buy impulse items for need satisfaction. (Impulse purchases are those to which the consumer has given little or no thought, are unplanned, and are made on the

---

[4]Arno K. Kleimenhagen, Donald G. Leeseberg, and Bernard A. Eilers, "Consumer Response to Special Promotions of Regional Shopping Centers," *Journal of Retailing,* vol. 48, Spring, 1972, pp. 22–29.

[5]Ernest R. Hilgard and George H. Bower, *Theories of Learning,* Appleton Century Crofts, New York, 1966.

spur of the moment.) Since many retailers rely upon impulse purchases for additional sales volume, it would be helpful if this consumer behavior could be understood.

Supporters of the cognitive theory of consumer behavior believe that people are problem solvers. In other words, they believe that consumers receive a stimulus, but they respond only after they have solved the problem. This thought process is called logic and is why we say consumers are reacting in a "logical manner."

It is true consumers solve problems almost every day. For instance, a consumer solves a problem when deciding in which store to shop. Problem solving is involved when a consumer decides to try a new product for the first time or chooses a different brand of the same product. Also, a consumer is problem solving when he or she ponders whether to purchase an item on the installment plan or whether to withdraw the money from a savings account.

A consumer's problem solving is aided by a variety of learning experiences. Consumers have favorable experiences with some products and brands and unfavorable experiences with others. This is true also for experiences with various retailers and retail stores. Consumers who have a favorable experience with a product, brand, or store, will most likely use these learning experiences to evaluate new products, brands, or stores. Anything new to the consumer will be evaluated in light of previous experiences, whether favorable or unfavorable. For these reasons, it is important for retailers to understand why consumers respond or fail to respond to certain stimuli.

Generally, it is much easier for a retailer to adapt to the consumers' responses than it is to attempt to change the consumers' behavior patterns, especially if these behavior patterns have been established for a long time. If patterns of purchasing behavior have developed over a long period of time, it becomes difficult—if not impossible—to alter these consumer patterns. This is particularly true if the person obtains satisfaction from the purchasing of *certain* goods and services.

Psychoanalytical Theory

Still another theory which can be used to partially explain why consumers purchase or do not purchase goods and services is known as the "psychoanalytical" school of thought and was founded by Sigmund Freud.[6] According to Freud's theory, each individual has three parts in his or her mind: (1) the "id," (2) the "ego," and (3) the "superego."

The "id" contains our basic instinctive drives or needs which cannot be fulfilled because of social customs. The "ego" is the conscious planning center in our mind which finds releases for urges and drives. The "superego" then channels these drives and urges into socially acceptable behavioral patterns which tend to reduce feelings of guilt and remorse.

---

[6]For a more detailed analysis of the Freudian psychoanalytic model see Philip Kotler, *Marketing Management, Analysis, Planning, and Control,* 2d ed., Prentice-Hall, 1972, pp. 106–108.

Since individual drives and urges may be antisocial, they are controlled to some degree by the ego. The ego maintains a balance between the id (needs and drives) and the superego (which is our conscience). In order to determine the consumers' hidden drives and needs which result in purchasing behavior, advertisers and retailers have resorted to methods of "motivational research." Motivational research is composed of psychological tests and resultant statistical data which can be used to define specific consumer behavioral patterns. Motivational research methods are quite complex and detailed and are beyond the scope of this text.[7]

Freud's studies also pointed out that he believed that sex or sexually related biological feelings were the basic determinants of one's personality. We do know an individual's personality and behavioral patterns are closely related. They are highly interdependent characteristics which cause a person to react favorably or unfavorably toward certain stimuli. For example, a consumer may have a favorable attitude toward one retailer yet be repelled by another store. Or a consumer may be attracted to or repelled by one product or another and "turned on" or "turned off" by certain advertisements.

Although the Freudian theory has been modified or discarded by some scholars, his theories have not been completely abandoned and should not be underestimated. For example, the Freudian influence is often revealed in the branding of products, in advertising, and in personal salesmanship. Retailers often try to make certain products "sex symbols," or they will ascribe sex appeal to certain goods. Often this process begins with the manufacturer and extends through the retail store into the store's promotional appeals. For instance, Freudian appeals are used by retailers in advertising such products as perfumes, cosmetics, and shaving lotion.

Freud's theories have contributed to the understanding of consumer purchasing behavior because they provide a basic explanation of the functioning of the conscious and unconscious mind. And it often is the consumers' unconscious level to which retailers can make subtle appeals.

MOTIVES AND MOTIVATION

A lot of time and money is spent on advertising and sales promotion in an attempt to get consumers to buy products and services at a particular store.[8] Retailers, therefore, should be interested in the *why* and *how* of consumer motivation. In a retailer's market segment, there are a number of people with money, desires, and needs; the retailer must attempt to match the store's offerings with those desires and needs. Every element in the retailing mix is focused toward the goal of

---

[7]For a more complete analysis of motivational research see Joseph W. Newman, *Motivation Research and Marketing Management,* Harvard, Cambridge; L. Edward Scriven, "Rationality and Irrationality in Motivation Research," in Robert Ferber and Hugh G. Wales (ed.), *Motivation and Market Behavior,* Irwin, Homewood, Ill., 1958, pp. 64–72.

[8]For a detailed discussion of consumer motives see C. Glenn Walters, *Consumer Behavior, Theory and Practice,* rev. ed., Irwin, Homewood, Ill., 1974, chap. 7.

motivating consumers to buy. Because of the complexity of the human mind, however, motivation is one segment of consumer behavior about which we know little. Consumers cannot really explain why they are motivated to purchase one item instead of another or why they will patronize one store over another. When asked these questions directly, consumers will state one or more reasons for such behavior patterns. However, in reality, they may react in a completely different way. Thus, the full understanding of this subject is yet to be grasped.

We know that a motive is an urge or a drive which stimulates an individual to seek satisfaction for a particular need. This need that must be satisfied may be either hunger, thirst, security, or prestige. Further, sometimes consumers' motives are latent or dormant and must be stimulated in some manner in order to activate their latent motives since the consumers are not consciously aware of them. Stimulation may be accomplished through powerful promotion and communication; thus by using certain stimuli, we can *sometimes* get people to act.

Ego Motives

The ego is that part of our personality which focuses on the "self." We often hear the phrase, "He has a big ego," which really means that the person is self-centered. Or we may hear "She needs her ego boosted," which means that this person needs to be reassured or that this person's self-image needs support.

But we all have egos and associated with our egos are certain motives or needs which must be satisfied. Thus, many consumers purchase products or services to enhance their egos. After all, what is in a label or a brand name? Through advertising and promotion, consumers have been given the idea that a certain brand or label will enhance their egos. Hence consumers, through the use of certain products, hope the people around them will view them more favorably.

Assume for a moment that a person earning $6,000 a year shops at Neiman-Marcus (an expensive department store that caters to a relatively high income group). That person in an economic sense probably cannot afford to shop at such a prestige store. However, it may be important to that person to be seen in the store by his or her peers, or it is important for that person to be able to tell others that the item came from Neiman-Marcus. This person is shopping at Neiman-Marcus because of an ego motive.

Because of the ego, retailers and salespersons in retail stores also make use of the "you approach" in selling merchandise. Have you ever noticed how many mirrors there are in a women's fashion merchandise store, or how the salesperson will turn the customer around to view a suit of clothing before the mirror?

The desire to enhance the ego is why consumers purchase certain brands of products. For example, automobile dealers make good use of the "you" or "ego" approach to trade customers up to higher priced models. Seldom do any of us purchase basic transportation; instead we purchase *status* and *prestige*. The products we purchase enhance our egos and help us to rank ourselves in a higher position among our peers. Because of our diverse ego motives, status symbols come in all forms and with a variety of products and/or services which help to enhance our various egos.

Emotional Motives

Another type of motive that is evident among consumers is one that is called an "emotional motive." Many consumers will purchase goods and services that to the observer seem to involve little if any logic. We have heard the phrase, "It was an emotional response," and it is true that the human emotions of love, fear, pleasure, and achievement, may often dictate the type of purchase made.

For example, most of us have a desire to be attractive to the opposite sex. Retailers have been able to capitalize on this emotional aspect of consumer behavior by selling large quantities of perfume, shaving lotion, cosmetics, clothing, and the like. Not too long ago, a man would not be caught using a hair spray or a deodorant. Today, many men use both. Men are using these products because they think it will make them more attractive to the opposite sex. Women (and some men) purchase large quantities of cosmetics and hair colorings. Again, consumers, through the use of these products, hope to become more acceptable to the opposite sex or their peer groups; and this emotional motive probably explains this particular behavior.

Many emotional motives play an important role in consumer behavior. For instance, most of us have a strong desire to be accepted by our peers. None of us likes to be scorned by social groups so we conform to the norms or standards of these groups. Retailers make use of these emotional motives by advertising that a certain product will make you acceptable to those around you.

In the case of fashion merchandise, women will spend considerable sums of money to purchase an "original" dress or gown. This shows the person's desire to be accepted and admired by the group. Yet it also shows the person's desire to stand out from the group and possibly even to be envied by those within the group. This is an emotional motive which makes us wish to be liked, envied, and admired. Thus, many of us will resort to individual hair styles, custom-made suits, special cars, and other types of goods which we hope will make us "liked" by our peers.

Rational Motives

In contrast to emotional motives, some consumers are quite rational or logical about their purchasing decisions. Usually, rational motives are based on economics, that is, money considerations. Retailers will stress value, good buys, economy, and the like, in order to appeal to the more rational consumer. Most of us like to consider ourselves rational. But perhaps it would be better to state that we purchase rationally in a very emotional manner.

Several rational motives stimulate consumers to purchase goods and services. The first of these rational motives is *economy*. Many of us like to make a "real buy," meaning that we think the price is right. That is why a retailer's special sales event will stress economy. Many of us patronize sales events whether we need the merchandise or not. If the item is really needed at the time of the sales event, a purchase would be rational (because it was on sale). But if the item was not needed at the time of the sales event, a purchase would be emotional (because we thought money was saved just because the item was on sale). Basically, discount retailers and warehouse retailers are appealing to the consumers' rational motives of economy. These retail stores have become popular because the consumer believes that the merchandise is being purchased for a lower price than in another retail store. In some instances, this may be true. In other cases, it is possible the same item could be purchased in a "regular" retail store for the same price or for less. However, these retailers have successfully appealed to a consumer motive and have obtained huge customer followings.

Efficiency is another rational motive which stimulates consumers to purchase such items as power saws, electric mixers, and toasters. In other words, any item which may reduce the amount of time spent performing a certain chore will appeal to our efficiency motive. In short, one can state that the efficiency motive is a matter of convenience; and in our highly mechanized and technological society, this motive is an important one.

The third rational motive is *dependability*. Most of us try to purchase dependable, durable, and reliable goods—that is, ones which will last for a long time without maintenance or repair. This is the reason why many durable-goods retailers stress dependability in their advertising. Some retailers also offer their customers "service contracts." Under a service contract, a retailer will take care of all maintenance within a stated time period. In some instances, a three-year service contract may be sold to the consumer desiring dependability. Some retailers (such as Sears, Roebuck and Company) have had considerable success in selling service contracts with appliances. By emphasizing "trouble-free" use of a product, the retailer is appealing to the dependability-motivated consumer.

Patronage Motives

Patronage motives are those which encourage consumers to shop at one store rather than another. Of course, patronage motives are a primary concern of every retailer. Retailers are constantly seeking ways in which they can increase the store's number of customers (patronage). All the elements of the retailing mix are focused upon inducing consumers to come to the store and browse, thereby increasing the opportunities for the consumers to purchase goods or services. Since consumers are attracted or repelled by certain retail stores because of their personality or image, it is important that the retailer develop a store image which will appeal to the customers. In this way, the retailer can possibly encourage the consumers to "patronize" the store. (How to build a store image will be covered in a later chapter.)

Consumers are often motivated to patronize a retail store because of its location. It is not unusual for a store's location to attract or repel a customer. The rise and growth of planned regional shopping centers has done much to attract consumers to certain retail stores. But upon closer investigation, one will discover that planned regional shopping centers attract only certain types and kinds of retail stores. For instance, a discount retailer will not normally be located in a regional shopping center. The discount retailers prefer to be located somewhere on the outskirts of an area where rents are lower. Since the outskirts of a trade area usually suffer from a "lower" consumer image, a discount retailer doesn't care because the consumer expects this type of store image. In fact, if a discount retailer were located in an expensive or exclusive shopping area, it is possible that many economy-minded customers would not patronize that store because the image would be wrong.

Other patronage motives include the merchandise and service mix that the store makes available to the customers. Some consumers will patronize a certain retail store because of a vast assortment of goods. Other consumers will patronize a certain retail store because they offer a full line of customer services (such as delivery, gift wrapping, credit, installation, and liberal return privileges). This is why some retailers stress "service and selection" rather than price. These retailers are hoping to attract customers who are interested in service and selection.

Finally, one patronage motive which often ranks high in the consumers' mind is the reputation of the retailer. A retailer develops a reputation from the manner in which the business is conducted with the customer. Once customers find a retailer they trust, they are very likely to return again and again to that same retailer. Generally, it takes a long time for a retailer to develop a reputation of respect and trust. But if all business transactions are geared toward developing a reputation for fair business practices, a store's patronage will increase. Word-of-mouth advertising is inexpensive promotion, and it can be invaluable in enhancing the store's image. Of course, it can also work the other way.

PERCEPTION

Consumers are exposed to a large number of environmental influences which, in some manner, affect or alter their purchasing behavior. Since each of us perceives or senses these environmental influences in a different manner, we place different interpretations on these factors. Each of us has our own "frame of reference," that is, each of us views the same environmental influences in a somewhat different way. Thus, "perception" is another important aspect in understanding consumer behavior. One author has defined perception "as the particular interpretation one gives to objects or ideas observed or otherwise brought to the consumer's attention through the senses."[9] Through their perception, then, consumers place different emphasis on these factors because of their learning experiences, their personality traits, their attitudes and beliefs, and the manner in which they see themselves.

Because of the factors noted above, consumers tend to be selective regarding the environmental influences that surround them. They are constantly exposed to various stimuli—some of which they screen out. Actually, only a small portion of the stimuli in the environment is perceived by them as individuals. The other environmental influences and stimuli are blotted out or ignored because they are not relevant.

[9]*Ibid.,* p. 13.

For these reasons, a retailer must strive to attract the consumers' attention (perception) in some special manner. This is why a retailer tries to develop something unique for the store's advertising and sales promotional programs. The store's advertising and sales promotion must be different from competing stores' efforts if the consumers are to be attracted to that store.

In a consumer's selective process of perceiving certain influences or stimuli, a product, brand, or retail store does not really exist until it is consciously recognized by the consumer. When the consumer sees that a product, brand, or retail store exists because it fulfills a need, then it can be stated that perception has taken place. Until this recognition has occurred, there is no perception on the part of the consumer.

To make this situation even more complex, consider the following illustration. A retailer perceives a stereo as being a necessary item for rounding out the store's product line. A consumer may see this same stereo as being a source of entertainment. Another customer may view the stereo as being a luxury item which is unaffordable. Still another consumer who lives alone sees the stereo as a companion (i.e., the stereo is psychologically fulfilling since there is sound in the room when the set is turned on just as though a human being was present). And there may be other consumers who do not even know that the stereo set exists because it has never entered their field of perception.

What does all this mean to the retailer? In essence, it means that every retailer is limited to the extent to which the consumers can be reached through advertising and sales promotion. Thus, it is wise for the retailer to develop some image, advertising, or promotion which differentiates the store from its competition. This differentiation must fall into the realm of perception for both customers and potential customers. In reality, the sales promotional message must be applicable to the consumer if it is to be perceived and if the consumer is to act by purchasing the merchandise.

ATTITUDES

An attitude is a position or belief that an individual holds concerning any number of things. It may be a point of view about certain events, happenings, products, brands, services, or stores. An attitude may be either favorable or unfavorable. Stated another way, we can say that an attitude is an evaluation of worth or merit. For example, an attitude held by a consumer about a certain brand is an evaluation of that particular brand's potential in need satisfaction. The same may also hold true for a certain retail store. Thus, a consumer's attitude is formed through an evaluation of all the characteristics and experiences that the brand or store holds for the consumer. Again, these may be either favorable or unfavorable.

An attitude may be largely emotional or it may be very rational. Attitudes usually vary in intensity. A consumer may have strong feelings (attitudes) about certain brands, products, or stores; or a consumer may be apathetic (indifferent toward a certain brand, product, or store). Consumer attitudes reflect a judgment on the part of the individual. For these reasons, it is important for us to explore how consumer attitudes are formed, changed, and measured.

Over the years, The Survey Research Center at the University of Michigan has conducted studies which concentrated on consumer buying intentions regarding products, brands, and product types. Rather consistently, these studies have indicated that consumer buying intentions and actual purchasing decisions are closely related. That is, consumers' purchasing behavior is influenced by their attitudes. Of course, consumer attitudes may change which, in turn, may alter their buying behavior.[10]

Formation of Attitudes

Just how are attitudes formed? Generally, an individual's attitudes are acquired or formed from past experiences. Thus, the attitudes of consumers will come from personal experiences with a product, a brand, a store, the service of a store, or by doing business with an individual retailer. These personal experiences may be either favorable or unfavorable which will affect the way the consumer reacts. From these personal experiences, there develops a "frame of mind" which we call an attitude. For this reason, it is very important that the retailer conduct all business dealings in the most equitable manner. For example, too many retailers act as though they know what is best for the customers, rather than determining what the customers' wishes really are. Instead, retailers should focus directly on the consumers' wishes since it is what the consumers think (attitudes that may be formed) about a store, a brand, or a product that will determine their purchasing behavior. Also, it is the consumer satisfaction which will determine to a large degree whether a retailer will be successful or unsuccessful.

Secondly, consumer attitudes may be formed by a person's association with various groups of people. For instance, the family, the school, the church, the work groups, the peer group (those with the same social standing), and other social groups help to shape, to some extent, a person's attitude toward certain things. For example, if someone in a peer group finds a certain product or store unacceptable, it is quite likely that the other persons in that peer group will also find that product or store unacceptable.

The measurement of consumer attitudes is beyond the scope of this book. However, it is important for a retailer to understand that attitudes strongly affect a consumer's purchasing behavior.[11] Once the consumer has formed an attitude, it may be extremely difficult to alter or change this opinion.

How can a retailer get the consumer to perceive that the store, its merchan-

---

[10]See George Katona, *The Powerful Consumer,* McGraw-Hill, New York, 1960, pp. 52–53; James H. Myers and Mark I. Alpert, "Determinant Buying Attitudes: Meaning and Measurement," *Journal of Marketing,* October 1968, pp. 13–20; Seymour Banks, "The Relationship of Brand Preference to Brand Purchase," *Journal of Marketing,* October 1950, pp. 145–157.

[11]For a discussion on attitude measurement scales, see James F. Engel, David T. Kollat, and Roger D. Blackwell, *Consumer Behavior,* Holt, New York, 1968, pp. 170–173; James H. Myers and William H. Reynolds, *Consumer Behavior and Marketing Management,* Houghton Mifflin, Boston, 1967, pp. 150–157.

dise offerings, its services, and the like, offer the most satisfaction? In essence, a retailer has only two choices: (1) a retailer can attempt to change the consumers' attitudes so they are in agreement with the store's retailing mix, or (2) a retailer can change the store's retailing mix to fit the consumers' attitudes. Once the consumers' attitudes have been determined, the retailer probably will find it easier to alter the retailing mix. It is best not to change the retailing mix through trial and error, though. But the retailer can make sure that the mix correlates with the consumers' attitudes. Without this correlation, a retailer may find that the store will suffer a loss of profitable sales volume.

The attitudes of the consumers are not under the control of a store owner-manager and are somewhat difficult to alter or to change. But since the elements of the retailing mix are under the direct control of the store's management, they are easier to alter. Thus, it is probably wise for the retailer to take the route of least resistance with a greater chance for success.

For example, even though a consumer has had an unpleasant experience with a retail store, product, brand, or service, that consumer may be receptive to a change in attitude. Depending on the experience, the consumer's negative attitude may be weak, or the person may be receptive to learning something different. If a consumer's attitude is completely rigid, the retailer may have no chance of altering it; but the retailer will not know this unless he or she tries. This altering of a consumer's attitude is usually done through powerful and persuasive promotion or personal selling. The success of this attempt to change the consumer's attitude will depend upon the believability of the message, whether spoken or in print, and the receptiveness of the consumer.

At times it may be feasible for a retailer to use special incentives in an attempt to alter or change consumer attitudes. For example, such special incentives as coupons, large trade-in allowances, or special terms may sway a consumer enough to try a brand or product that currently runs counter to that consumer's attitudes.

PERSONALITY

An individual's personality is made up of the characteristics or acquired attributes which make each person different from another person.[12] For our purposes, it is good to know that a consumer's personality traits will affect and influence his or her purchasing behavior, and numerous studies have been conducted on personality traits and their relationship to consumer buying behavior.[13]

Although we are certain that personality traits do influence the consumer's behavioral purchasing patterns, we are not sure to what extent or just how these purchasing decisions are influenced by personality. One explanation is that both

[12]Adapted from C. Glenn Walters, *loc. cit.*

[13]See James F. Engel, David T. Kollat, and Roger D. Blackwell, *Consumer Behavior,* Holt, New York, 1968; David Riesman, et al., *The Lonely Crowd,* Yale, New Haven, Conn., 1950.

personality and environmental influences shape the consumer's behavioral patterns. We do know that certain products are purchased by consumers with certain types of personality. Personality traits also play some role in the behavioral patterns of consumers. But as yet, this evidence is rather inconclusive.

LEARNING

Learning is the change in a consumer's behavioral patterns, thought, or actions due to past experiences.[14] Learning is the acquiring of knowledge and the understanding of something that was previously unknown to a person. Consumers tend to learn from their experiences. If the experiences are favorable and pleasant, a reinforcement and strengthening of the attitudes takes place. The more firm the reinforcement, the stronger the belief. The greater the belief, the more likely certain behavior will become a habit or an established pattern of behavior. For instance, if a consumer forms a habit of purchasing a certain brand or product or of patronizing a certain store, it may be quite difficult to alter this habit or behavioral pattern. Why is this so? Essentially, the consumer's mind is *closed* to learning because these past experiences have been rewarding and reinforcing. By the same token, if these past experiences have not been rewarding and have not reinforced learning, the consumer's mind may be *open* to trying new brands, products, or to patronizing a different store.

In addition, other factors also influence the consumer in purchasing behavior and consumption patterns. All consumers are influenced to some degree by their own backgrounds and by cultural and social group influences. In order to gain greater insight into these factors, we will now devote our attention to cultural influences and social standing.

SUMMARY

Every retailer and every student of retailing needs to know why consumers purchase and why they do not purchase goods and services. An understanding of consumer purchasing behavior is a retailer's foundation for developing a proper retailing mix.

Three major disciplines will aid a retailer in better understanding why consumers purchase certain merchandise. These three areas of study include psychology, sociology, and social psychology. *Psychology* is the study of individual behavior. *Sociology* is the study of group behavior, and *social psychology* is concerned with the behavior of individuals as they are influenced by the various groups of people around them.

The *stimulus-response theory* of consumer behavior indicates that people learn a pattern of behavior in a similar way—by responding satisfactorily to an

---

[14]Adapted from C. Glenn Walters, *op. cit.,* chap. 10, "The Effect of Learning on Consumer Behavior."

applied stimulus. A correct response to a stimulus provides the person with need satisfaction, a reward; and an incorrect response results in a penalty.

The *cognitive theory* of consumer behavior rejects the stimulus response theory as being too mechanical. Consumers learn and react only after perceptive thinking which in most instances is goal-oriented. Thus, supporters of the cognitive theory believe that people are problem solvers.

The *Freudian psychoanalytic theory* of consumer behavior indicates that much of a consumer's actions are related to biological feelings which are the basic determinants of one's personality. An individual's personality and behavioral patterns are closely related. Freudian appeals (sex objects) are used by retailers in advertising such products as perfumes, cosmetics, and shaving lotion.

A *motive* is an urge or a drive which stimulates an individual to seek satisfaction for a particular need. The ego motive is that part of our personality which focuses on the "self." The desire to enhance the ego is why consumers purchase certain brands of goods.

Emotional motives are those which involve little if any logic. Many emotional motives play an important role in consumer behavior. In contrast to emotional motives, some consumers are quite rational or logical about their purchasing decisions. Usually, rational motives are based on economic considerations, such as price, value, or durability.

Patronage motives are those which encourage consumers to shop at one store rather than another. Retailers are constantly seeking ways in which they can increase the number of the store's customers. Consumers may patronize a store because of location, the merchandise and service mix, or the reputation of the retailer.

Perception is the particular interpretation one gives to objects or ideas observed or otherwise brought to one's attention through the senses. An understanding of consumer perception is necessary to a retailer in developing the proper store image. A retailer needs to develop a store image through advertising that is different from competing stores.

An *attitude* is a position or belief that an individual holds concerning any number of things. An attitude may be either favorable or unfavorable, emotional or rational; but attitudes are acquired or formed from past experiences. It may be a personal experience with a particular store, brand, or product. Once a consumer has formed an attitude about a store, product, or brand, it is easier for the retailer to alter the retailing mix than attempt to change the consumers' attitudes.

An individual's *personality* is made up of the characteristics or acquired attributes which make each person different from another person. Personality traits do influence the consumer's behavioral purchasing patterns.

Learning is the change in a consumer's behavioral patterns, thoughts, or actions due to past experiences. Consumers tend to learn from their experiences, and if these experiences are favorable, there is a reinforcement and strengthening of attitudes. The more firm the reinforcement, the stronger the belief. The greater the belief, the more likely certain behavior will become a habit or an established pattern. The patronizing of a certain store can become an established pattern of behavior.

REVIEW QUESTIONS

1   Why should a retailer know something about consumer purchasing behavior?
2   Define psychology; sociology; social psychology.
3   Discuss the stimulus-response theory of consumer behavior.
4   What is the basis of the cognitive theory of consumer behavior?
5   Explain the psychoanalytical theory of consumer behavior.
6   What is a motive?
7   Define ego motives. Emotional motives.
8   How can a retailer cater to a consumer's rational motives?
9   Discuss ways in which a retailer can encourage patronage motives.
10   What is perception?
11   How do attitudes differ from consumer perceptions?
12   How are consumer attitudes formed?

Chapter 6

Cultural and Social Group Influence on Consumer Purchase Behavior

It can be said that we are a product of our environment since our behavioral patterns are heavily influenced by the world around us—our society and its culture. But just what is culture? Culture can be defined as the sum total of ways of living which is handed down from generation to generation. Our attitudes, philosophies, biases, are shaped by the culture and its forces. It establishes patterns of behavior and enforces group standards. Our culture or society rewards and punishes individuals for acceptable or unacceptable behavior and is a significant factor in determining the behavioral patterns of all persons.

Similarly, the manner in which an individual behaves is also influenced to some degree by the various social groups to which that individual belongs—such as the family, social groups, and reference groups. Our behavioral styles, values, mores, and traditions are passed on through the family and social groups and affect the manner in which we behave. We tend to conform and behave within the framework that culture (society) has provided for us through the norms which are imposed on us to act in a certain way. Thus, consumer behavior is also affected by the cultural and societal environment in which we live.

These cultural standards and norms affect consumer behavior in the marketplace. The retailer also complies with these cultural norms by remaining open for business during certain hours, by dealing honestly with the customer, by closing at a certain time, and by complying with the various laws and regulations imposed by society. Ethical standards, business practices, and laws affect both the consumer and the retailer and have resulted in the consumer market as we know it today. Within the total consumer market, there are many smaller markets which differ from one another in some way. Retailers must be aware of the differences in these various markets. The people who reside in one market will have a different and varied cultural background from those persons who reside in another market. Why is this so important to the retailer? The differences in cultural influences will affect the way in which consumers react to certain stimuli. Every section of the country has regional and local differences due to cultural variations. Retailers will have to make use of acceptable cultural appeals if they are to be successful.[1] Certain appeals may attract some consumers, other appeals or stimuli may repel some consumers. Thus, it is important that retailers know which appeals to use.

CULTURAL INFLUENCES

Even though we are a product of our environment and our cultural ways are handed down from one generation to another, certain cultural changes do take place slowly over a period of time. For instance, younger people tend to be more receptive to cultural changes than do older persons. Thus, most of the advertising and sales promotion appeals that are used today would have been unacceptable to consumers twenty years go.

To some degree, cultural changes make some of us more tolerant of new ideas and of changes in traditions, habits, customs, and mores. As might be expected, some of these cultural changes have taken place more readily than others. These cultural changes have affected retailers and their response has altered the manner in which many goods and services are marketed today. The discussion which follows focuses on some of the market responses to cultural changes.

Impulse Purchases

Consumers today make frequent trips to the store to purchase goods and services which is a change from the consumers of twenty to forty years ago. Also, many of the consumers' purchases are impulsive in nature; that is, purchases are made with little or no preplanning or forethought and no shopping list.

Many products fall into the category of impulse purchases—items such as cigarettes, candy, chewing gum, soda pop, or beer. Most consumers purchase these items and many others in a sudden and seemingly unconscious manner. Thus, any item purchased on the spur of the moment with no preplanning may be considered to be bought on "impulse." Because of this change in consumer behavior, self-selection and self-service retailers have encouraged consumers to

---

[1]Philip Kotler and Gerald Zaltman, "Social Marketing: An Approach to Planned Social Change," *Journal of Marketing,* vol. 35, July 1971, pp. 3–12.

purchase on impulse. They have increased the use of open displays, attention-getting devices, and prepricing of items. The manufacturer, too, has aided the retailer by packaging items in attention-getting, vividly colored, attractive wrappers which also encourages consumers to purchase on impulse. Impulse items are considered by retailers to be "silent salespersons" in that they induce the consumers to purchase on the spot. And today's consumers have responded by increasing their number of impulse purchases.

Convenience Orientation

Over the years, the American consumer has become convenience-oriented. We have become accustomed to an affluent society, and with this affluence, consumers are spending greater sums of money on items which are easy and ready to use. For example, the consumer can purchase many food items which are preprepared. Many food items need only to be put into the oven to heat or can be fixed with a minimum of preparation. The aerosol can is another example of consumer convenience, and it has been adapted to many products, including cheese, whipping cream, deodorants, hair sprays, and room deodorizers—to name just a few.

The popularity of one-stop shopping (where the consumer can purchase many items at one or several adjoining retail stores) again demonstrates the consumers' desire for convenience. Along with one-stop shopping convenience, there has been a general increase in the number of hours retailers remain open, again for consumer convenience.

Today, the extended and increasing use of buying on credit is certainly a change from the attitudes held by consumers forty years ago. A cultural change is certainly evident in this one area. The growth of credit purchases has been a response by business people to the consumers' desire to have something today but pay for the item over an extended period of time. This, too, is a convenience for the consumer. Most consumers do not wish to postpone their purchases for any length of time, and this has resulted in our nation's extensive credit network. Certainly retailers, as business people, have encouraged this use of credit.

Another convenience-oriented change in our technological society has been our clamor for push-button, labor-saving devices. For example, most kitchen appliances are operated by push buttons—for convenience, as well as ease of operation. The labor-saving mixer, ice crusher, blender, automatic toaster, self-defrosting refrigerator, self-cleaning oven, electric range—all are convenience-oriented items which have been accepted and demanded by consumers. The acceptance of this cultural change to convenience items is due to the convenience and labor-saving advantages that these items offer the consumer.

Leisure-Time Activities

Another cultural change in recent years has been the increase in leisure-time activities. These activities have encouraged the sale of such items as pickups and campers, pleasure boats, tents and camping equipment, fishing gear, recreational vehicles and motor homes, travel trips and package tours, snowmobiles, skis, motorcycles, and sports clothing. As long as the consumer has discretionary income (income which is left after paying the necessities of rent, groceries, and utilities), the market for leisure-time items will continue to grow. However, the leisure-time market is subject to the ups and downs of the economy, and any unemployment will curtail this market. Luxuries, which basically make up the leisure-time market, are usually the first items to be eliminated from a consumer's budget when economic activities take a downturn. But retailers have capitalized on and expanded their leisure-time offerings, and many consumers have responded by purchasing a wide variety of these goods.

With the increase in the number of working wives, this change in our culture has also brought about the development of the leisure-time market. Since both husband and wife work, the weekends are devoted to "togetherness" and leisure-time activities in which the whole family can participate. This family "togetherness" has come to replace the family dinners and gatherings of a generation ago. Thus, although cultural influences do change, in some instances cultural patterns are simply altered to conform to previous behavioral traditions.

Trading Up

Another cultural influence which has affected consumers' behavior has been the desire to improve our life style. This life style improvement, of getting or buying something bigger and better, is referred to as "trading up." Most of us want to improve the quality of our lives and enjoy some luxuries. Thus, retailers have been quick to capitalize on this basic human characteristic of desiring something "new and improved." For instance, retailers of durable goods almost always try to get the consumer to purchase the "top-of-the-line" item because it offers many features that are lacking in the less expensive models. Also, there is more profit for the retailer on the sale of the more expensive goods. And once the consumer has used the more expensive model, he or she is unlikely to return to a less expensive model with fewer product features.

For example, most automobiles are sold with optional items, such as air conditioning, vinyl tops, power steering, automatic transmissions, and the like. The optional item list is nearly endless. For many consumers, buying a car with many optional features represents an improvement over the basic or previous model. By buying optional items, the consumer is trading up. Through the use of optional items in today's market, compact automobiles offer some of the features that the luxury car offers. Consumers want these luxuries because of their desire to improve or trade up to a more expensive model.

Other ways in which consumers have traded up their standard of living include the following. Eating fancy foods and frequently eating at restaurants are indications of improving one's standard of living. Other examples include extensive travel, the purchase of higher priced dresses and suits, and the increased demand for Scotch, wines, gourmet foods, art, and entertainment. Once consumers have experienced these luxuries and this higher standard of living, it is very difficult for them to return to a more austere way of living.

It is a basic human characteristic to want an improved and higher standard of living. Therefore, these cultural changes will probably be long lasting. Retailers, too, will probably continue to cater to the market and to the consumer who desires to trade up to something better.

SOCIAL INFLUENCES

A consumer's purchasing decisions are influenced to some degree by the cultural surroundings and social groups with whom the individual interacts. This process is referred to as "social interaction," and it affects an individual's values, attitudes, and philosophies. Social interaction is the personal involvement of an individual with a group of persons. In turn, this involvement or interaction influences a consumer's decision on what is purchased or not purchased, which store to patronize or which store to avoid, or which brands to buy and which brands not to buy. This social interaction provides the consumer with a certain amount of self-satisfaction and self-fulfillment. As long as this satisfaction continues, the individual will continue to be a member of that social group. However, if the group reacts negatively, that consumer probably will seek other social groups in order to gain satisfaction.

Social and Reference Groups

Our behavioral patterns are also influenced to a considerable degree by the numerous small groups to which we relate. These groups include social groups (such as churches, lodges, fraternities, sororities, and clubs), reference groups to which an individual does not belong but wishes to belong, and the family. What is important to the student of retailing is that each of these groups has a set of values, attitudes, and beliefs which serve as standards or norms for expected behavior. Each member of the group tends to share the same values, attitudes, and beliefs, and thus will conform to the group's behavioral patterns.

For example, if an individual belongs to a group that plays bridge and then dines out afterward, each person will assume a role that is expected. He or she will arrive at the prescribed hour, dress in an appropriate manner, behave in an acceptable manner, and order foods and drinks which conform to the group's established and expected patterns of behavior. Too, students who visit the ski slopes will conform to group influences and pressures by purchasing similar equipment, by dressing in the popular styles of clothing, and by socializing in the lounge after a long day on the slopes. Failure to comply with the social group's norms of expected behavior usually results in a penalty—rejection of the individual by the group.

Knowingly, or perhaps unknowingly, a consumer's buying decisions and purchases are also influenced to a considerable degree by the reference groups of which he or she is a member. A reference group is one to which an individual belongs or wishes to belong. If an individual is not a member of a certain social group but desires to be a member of it, the group will still exert some influence over that person's behavior. This bonding together of individuals from various social groups has certain ramifications for retailers. For instance, consumers may wish to be identified with celebrities, movie stars, or other prominent persons. Even though most people who play golf do not socialize with Jack Nicklaus, Arnold Palmer, or Lee Trevino, consumers do tend to purchase golf equipment which has been endorsed by these professionals. The use of testimonial advertising by manufacturers often carries over to the retail level of business activity.

It has been demonstrated through studies of purchasing behavior that reference groups are extremely influential. They change buyer attitudes, affect perceptions, and motivate and direct the purchase of goods and services by consumers.[2] In part, this behavioral pattern stems from the word-of-mouth advertising from satisfied members of the group. This is especially true if the advertisement comes from a member of the group who is considered by others to be the "opinion leader." Thus, it becomes important for retailers to aim their advertising and promotion to these small reference groups.[3] Reference-group opinion leaders, through their influence, will determine to a great degree what brands or products the group's members will purchase, what styles and fashions of clothing they will wear, to what clubs the members will belong, and even what types of vacations these members will take.

One author has suggested three principal reasons for the impact of word-of-mouth advertising on purchasing behavior:[4]

1   It is more reliable and dependable.
2   It offers reinforcement which is lacking in the mass media.
3   It provides information which is often reinforced by social pressure.

Often, new products are purchased by a consumer upon the recommendation of a friend.

Family Influences   Of the small reference groups to which an individual belongs, the family unit is probably the one which has the strongest effect on a person's behavioral pattern. This is particularly true in regard to the family's purchasing decisions. Many families—but not all—act as a buying unit as well as an earning unit. That is, many working wives "pool" their incomes with the family unit in order to improve the standard of living for the entire group. With more and more working wives in the labor force (currently in excess of 40 percent), family units have become powerful decision makers in the acceptance or rejection of goods and services. This is an important point for the retailer to remember in planning promotional programs as well as in deciding what goods and services to offer.

[2]M. D. Beckman, "Are Your Messages Getting Through?" *Journal of Marketing,* 1967, pp. 34–38; James E. Stafford, "Group Influences on Consumer Brand Preferences," *Journal of Marketing Research,* February 1966, pp. 68–75.

[3]Ernest Dichter, "How Word-of-Mouth Advertising Works," *Harvard Business Review,* November–December 1966, pp. 147–166.

[4]Johan Arndt, *Word of Mouth Advertising: A Review of the Literature,* Advertising Research Foundation, New York, 1967, p. 25.

According to one author,[5] there are four questions which a retailer should ask:

1 Who influences the buying decision?
2 Who makes the buying decision?
3 Who makes the physical purchase?
4 Who uses the product?

It is evident from the questions above that four different people could be involved in the buying process. Or one individual might perform all four functions. Or these decisions might be the result of some husband/wife/child combination.

Although purchasing decisions may be made independently by either the husband or the wife, there is evidence which suggests that a family member's influence varies widely from product to product.[6] For example, a wife may select the roses for her garden; the husband may purchase the fertilizer for those roses; but together, they may decide to hire a landscape gardener to design a formal garden.

Approximately one-half of the total number of American families have children living at home. These family units are especially important to retailers. Expenditure patterns for family units with children indicate that proportionately higher amounts of a family's income are spent on food, clothing, shelter, and recreation. You can see why this fact would be important to a local retailer who had a store in an area with a large number of families with children.

This is why some retailers and/or producers advertise on national television during the early evening hours or during children's programs. They believe the children will influence their mother's purchasing decisions; especially for some products.[7] Although this may be true at one time and with certain products, most mothers tend to purchase what they believe their children should have rather than what the child may want. However, some observations indicate that the child does directly influence the purchase decision, especially on impulse items.

In some respects, young teenagers or children in the preteen years have also become influential in family buying decisions. In addition, these children have become purchasers of goods and services in their own right. Many teenagers have part-time employment or liberal allowances, and they have a tendency to spend almost all this money for goods and services. Thus, many retailers have catered to these groups by selling popular records, clothing of a fad nature, food, and tickets to popular entertainment which appeal to the youth market. The

[5]William J. Stanton, *Fundamentals of Marketing*, 4th ed., McGraw-Hill, New York, 1975, p. 112.

[6]David M. Heer, "The Measurement and Basis of Family Power: An Overview," *Marriage and Family Living*, vol. 25, 1963, pp. 133–139.

[7]Louis A. Berey and Richard W. Pollay, "The Influencing Role of the Child in Family Decision Making," *Journal of Marketing Research*, February 1968, pp. 70–72.

young adults and teenagers who live in the family unit also continue to exert an influence on purchasing decisions made by the family unit. For instance, both young adults and teenagers who work or have allowances have rather substantial incomes to spend on goods and services. These young people are, in turn, influenced by their peer groups. This peer group influence may alter the family unit's effect and change their spending habits. As time goes on, and these young adults leave the basic family unit, their consumption patterns and buying behavior will gradually change to reflect their own attitudes and ideas.

Overall, the woman in the family unit does the family purchasing and exerts a considerable influence on family consumption patterns.[8] However, if the male member of the family unit is present, he also will have a considerable influence on the purchase of certain goods. Males influence the purchasing decisions of products that tend to be more expensive. For instance, when major purchases are made (such as automobiles, appliances, furniture, and the like) wives will probably ask the husband to join in the decision to purchase.

Although most women continue to do the majority of the shopping, men have become increasingly less inhibited about appearing in stores to buy a variety of items. Self-service and self-selection retail stores have encouraged more men to shop for goods. In addition, the longer hours of operation, with stores open in the evening and on Sunday, have made it more convenient—and even possible—for men to shop, since normally they would have been working during store hours.

OTHER SOCIAL INFLUENCES

When Consumers Purchase

It is quite significant for retailers to know *when* consumers purchase goods and services. For instance, at what time during the year do customers make their purchases? Are there some days of the week that are better shopping days than others? During what hours do the majority of consumers purchase goods and services? If a retailer discovers that the majority of the store's customers purchase on a seasonal basis, then the retailer must adapt the store's buying and inventory to this habit. Or the retailer may try to extend the season in order to smooth out the sales volume. For example, many retailers attempt to extend the Christmas season by having pre-Christmas sales events. It is fairly common in some parts of the country to find Christmas merchandise on sale in the stores by late October or early November. Other retailers have attempted to extend the spring season by offering spring clothes in late February and selling these items until late May or early June. Other retailers have had moderate success with extending the vacation season or the sale of seasonal items through preservation facilities and special sales.

---

[8]See Harry L. Davis, "Measurement of Husband-Wife Influence in Consumer Purchase Decisions," *Journal of Marketing Research,* vol. 8, August 1971, pp. 305–312.

Grocery supermarket operators have definitely adapted their promotional programs to the time of the week when people buy groceries. Most of the grocery stores advertise every Wednesday or Thursday, with the advertised prices being good through Sunday. Thus, most of the grocery shopping and buying is done on Thursday, Friday, and Saturday in order to take advantage of the special prices.

Over the last few years, many retailers have elected to stay open during the evening hours for the convenience of the consumer. Because of their work schedules, many consumers have formed the habit of shopping only during the evening hours. Thus, it is significant for a retailer to know when consumers make their purchases since the store must be flexible to meet the consumers' demands.

Where Consumers Purchase

A retailer should also consider two aspects of *where* consumers purchase their goods and services: (1) Where was the decision made to purchase the item? (2) Where was the actual purchase made? It is possible that the decision to purchase an item was made in the home, stimulated by a retailer's advertisement. Or it could be that the preliminary decision was made at the family home, but the final decision was made in the store because of the sales presentation. Or perhaps one member of the family decides to purchase a birthday gift of clothing or jewelry, but a specific decision is not made on an actual item until he or she can look at the store's offerings. Then a final decision is made on a gift.

As you would expect, a retailer's sales promotional program should try to be directed to the place where the decision to purchase is made. If the decision is made in the home, then the retailer must gear the sales promotion so that the advertising will enter the house. Usually, this is done through the use of the daily newspaper or a circular that is mailed to the residence. If the consumer's decision is made in the store, then point-of-purchase display materials and merchandising techniques should receive special emphasis. Also, the sales personnel of the store should be properly trained to assist the customer and close the sale if the decision is made in the store. This is particularly true with the sale of durable goods. If a retailer is selling mostly impulse items, the emphasis will be on the display and arrangement of merchandise.

How Consumers Purchase

How consumers purchase will directly affect how a retailer responds with product and service offerings, price appeals, and promotional programs. If consumers prefer self-service or self-selection, the retailer must merchandise the items in a manner which will facilitate the consumers' purchasing decisions. If family units are large with a number of children, the retailer may find that the customers prefer to buy in larger quantities. Thus, large economy packages would sell much more readily than small individual packages. Conversely, if the store's customers are primarily elderly people living alone, the individual serving packages would be the items to stock.

Another aspect of how consumers purchase is represented by the one-stop shopping that has become so popular. The demand of consumers for one-stop shopping has contributed to the retailers' use of scrambled merchandising techniques (i.e., the adding of unrelated lines of merchandise to the basic offerings). Good examples of this are a grocery supermarket offering childrens' clothing and a drugstore selling food products. It is very possible that a retailer will be forced to alter the store's offering in order to keep the customers satisfied.

One other aspect of *how* consumers purchase goods and services is their demand for buying on credit. Credit will be covered in more detail in a later chapter. However, it is well at this point to emphasize consumers' demand for purchasing on credit rather than paying for items in cash. In order to remain competitive, many retailers have had to offer credit terms. About the only type of retail business which does not offer credit is the grocery store; and this is due, in part, to the low gross margins on food items.

Other services, such as free delivery, gift wrapping, installation, and alterations, may also be demanded by the consumer. These are important considerations for the retailer because these services attract consumers to the store. If the competition provides such services, the retailer may have to provide them or be faced with a loss of customer traffic. Consumers generally are convenience-oriented. During prosperous economic times, customers will pay the retailer for providing such additional services. But it also becomes apparent that these services are the first to be eliminated by the consumer should economic conditions worsen.

From the above, it becomes readily apparent that the retailer must consider and survey when, where, and how the store's customers purchase their goods and services.

FAMILY INCOME

The overall amount of family income and the age groups within the family are significant social factors which influence purchasing and consumption patterns. Some families have a large amount of income; others may be at or near the poverty level.

The youth market (ages four to twelve) is important to certain retailers because some retailers specialize in catering to the needs of this age group. This youth group can influence parental purchases; and toward the upper age limits, these youngsters spend considerable sums of money on themselves.

Increasingly, the teenage market (ages thirteen to seventeen) accounts for large amounts of funds spent for such items as records, clothes, snack foods, and entertainment. Some retailers cater to this age bracket by promoting "juniors," "misses," and "young adults," products. Fad clothing is of particular interest to this age group, and a number of specialty retailers are marketing directly to these young people. For instance, such specialty retailers as "Jeans and Things" and "The Gap" are examples of retailers specializing in clothing that currently is popular with this age group. (It should be noted that this clothing market is in no way limited to the teenage group as young adults also purchase items from these stores.)

The young adult market (ages eighteen to thirty-four) is quite important to certain retailers because many of these people purchase bigger, more expensive items. Automobiles, furniture, and household appliances are often purchased by this age group. Many people in this group may be getting married, starting a family, or entering professions; thus, they are buying appropriately related items. This age group, too, makes extensive use of credit.

The mature years (ages thirty-five to fifty-five) are the years in which consumers become more stable and settle down in homes. With the purchase of a home comes the inevitable buying of new furniture, lawn and garden supplies, patio equipment, and household repair tools. When people reach the upper part of this age group, they will spend more money on travel, entertainment, a second home, or move to a condominium. Again, the consumption pattern may be repeated. Usually the income level of this age group also rises substantially as many persons in this age bracket are in their peak earning years.

The senior group (ages fifty-five and up) becomes significant for retailers because this group of consumers differs from the former groups. Incomes may peak and soon decline as age rises. Also, the consumption of food usually decreases during this period of life. The living style is well established, and durable goods are usually purchased for cash. A routine has taken over, and the group looks forward to retirement years. Medical expenditures may rise, travel may increase, food expenditures may drop—although eating out may increase, and other patterns may develop.

What is the significance of these various age groups and their incomes? Retailers should be aware of the differences in income distribution among these groups and carefully watch for any changes that develop. Sales promotion and merchandise selection must be carefully tailored to meet the changing patterns of purchasing and consumption between these age groups.

SOCIAL CLASSES

A consumer's perception and buying behavior is the result of the social class to which he or she belongs. Social classes do exist in the United States, although some people may disagree. But these social classes arise from the differences among human beings in educational level, income level, family background, intelligence, and other sociological factors. Hence, a person's buying behavior is greatly influenced by the social class to which he or she belongs or aspires to belong. There is considerable mobility between the social classes, especially in the movement of people upward from a lower to a higher class. An understanding of this upward social mobility is necessary if the retailer is to assist customers in selecting the right merchandise, in trading up to higher priced goods. (Trading up is the term given to the process whereby customers will purchase more expensive items than the lower priced ones for which they originally asked.)

Over thirty years ago, a well-known sociologist, W. Lloyd Warner, developed a stratification or classification for the groups in the American society.[9] It is Warner's sixfold classification of American society which is used to study social behavior and movement. This social class structure is important to all retailing institutions because no retailer can attempt to serve customers in all segments of society.

W. Lloyd Warner defines the six classes of American society as follows:

1 *Upper-upper class* (Less than 1 percent of the total population). The upper-upper class includes the aristocracy of birth and wealth. These people are wealthy and professionally prominent, and they uphold family traditions and values and are instrumental in influencing community and governmental affiars. Probably few cues are taken by the other classes from this elite group since entry into this social class is by birth or marriage, and there is little upward social mobility into this social class.

2 *Lower-upper class* (About 2 percent of the total population). The lower-upper class consists of the "new" rich. These people are self-made millionaires who have moved into this social strata either because of hard work, lucky circumstances, or both. This social class includes wealthy executives, owners of large businesses, and other successful professional people.

3 *Upper-middle class* (About 10 percent of the total population). The upper-middle class consists of mostly successful professional and business people, many of whom are college educated. Many business executives, owners of smaller businesses, and professionals (doctors and lawyers) belong to this social class. It is this group of people that is very status conscious. Most of the individuals in this social class are "strivers." They also tend to buy goods and services which will reflect favorably upon their image. Their interests are broad and diversified, and they tend to influence, to some degree, the people who are ranked below them in social status.

4 *Lower-middle class* (About 35 percent of the total population). The lower-middle class includes the "white collar" workers, clerical workers, and some highly paid "blue collar" workers. To the people in this social class, there is a real sense of responsibility—doing a good job, maintaining a well-cared-for home, and giving a college education to the children. Members of this group exert considerable effort to move upward although in reality, there may be little opportunity to do so. Nevertheless, the social pressures of "keeping up with the Joneses" tends to force this group to try to live well.

5 *Upper-lower class* (About 40 percent of the total population). The upper-lower class includes the so-called "average" people—i.e., semi-skilled workers and employees of small establishments, many of whom earn average to good incomes. These people also enjoy the good life, but do not appear to be striving for upward social mobility as the class above them.

[9]For further discussion of social class structure, see W. Lloyd Warner and Paul Lunt, *The Social Life in a Modern Community,* Yale, New Haven, Conn., 1941; W. Lloyd Warner, Marchia Meeker, and Kenneth Eells, *Social Class in America,* Science Research, Chicago, 1949; W. Lloyd Warner, "Classes Are Real," in Gerald W. Thielbar and Saul Feldman (eds.), *Issues in Social Inequality,* Little, Brown, Boston, 1972, pp. 8–9.

6 *Lower-lower class* (About 12 percent of the total population). The lower-lower class is made up of all the unskilled workers and many of the unemployed people. Because of the low income level of this group, these people are often apathetic or unconcerned with self-betterment or improvement since they are primarily concerned with survival.

In locating a person's position on the social-class ladder, Warner considered an individual's source of income, occupation, and place of residence. Occupation was considered a prime determinant of one's social standing since many lower-middle class people may earn as much, or more, than a family in the upper-middle class. But the expenditure and consumption patterns of the social groups will vary widely. For example, let us take three individuals all earning approximately the same income, $15,000. One is a small businessman, one is an independent plumber, and the other is a college professor. Just by knowing their occupations, we can realize that each of these individuals will spend their incomes on different products in different stores. They will entertain in different social circles and will spend their leisure time in different manners. Thus, it is important for retailers to know that an individual's socioeconomic class will affect his or her buying habits, as well as the reception of a store's promotional appeals.

Traditionally, retailers have relied upon people's income as a measurement of buying power. However, income alone is not the only determinant of social class or buying habits and patterns. Although most of the population falls into the middle-income groups, there are wide patterns of buying behavior because of differences in educational levels, philosophies, prejudices, and preferences. A wise retailer should take a close look at the social classes in the "target market."

CONSUMERISM

Today's consumers are well-educated and informed people who basically reject the doctrine of *caveat emptor* (let the buyer beware) and assert themselves in many ways so as to exhibit a doctrine of *caveat vendor* (let the seller beware).

Consumerism, or the consumer movement, is evidenced by the various groups of people who have become more active, aggressive, and vocal in their support of consumer interests and protective legislation. Such groups include Consumers' Union, the Sierra Clubs, Common Cause, and Public Interest Research Groups (PIRG). Since the marketplace has become increasingly complex, the relationship between the buyer and the seller has become rather impersonal. Thus, the consumer movement has focused attention on many aspects of all business activities, but notably advertising and sales promotion. In addition, the retailing industry has also received increased attention from the consumer advocates in that the public is evaluating the role of the retailer and the functions or services performed for the consumer. Some of the other areas of consumer concern have been credit and installment sales transactions, guarantees and warranties on products, and price gouging. In short, any retail business function which appears to be *de*consumer-oriented has come under scrutiny. Increasingly, public concern has focused on the role of the retailer and other business people and whether their proper function should be to aid the consumer or confuse the consumer. Also, the consumer is interested in whether the retailer's functions or services add to the retail price of a product rather than assist the consumer in the purchasing decision.

Consumerism in the 1960s

In the early 1960s, the consumer movement began to be felt in the retailing trade. The consuming public began to reject the old adage, "Let the buyer beware." Today, this adage has been turned around to where it now means, "Let the seller beware."

In his first message to the Congress in 1962, President John F. Kennedy spoke of four basic consumer rights:[10]

    1   *The right to safety*—to be protected against the marketing of goods which are hazardous to health or life

    2   *The right to be informed*—to be protected against fraudulent, deceitful, or grossly misleading information, advertising, labeling or other practices, and to be given the facts needed to make an informed choice

    3   *The right to choose*—to be assured, wherever possible, access to a variety of products and services at competitive prices; and in those industries in which government regulations are substituted, an assurance of satisfactory quality and service at fair prices

    4   *The right to be heard*—to be assured that consumer interests will receive full and sympathetic consideration in the formulation of government policy and fair expeditious treatment in its administrative tribunals.

Consumerism and the consumer movement has become a popular issue of the times with academicians, better business bureaus, consumer advisory groups (such as Action Line and Call for Action), and Public Interest Research Groups (PIRG), organizing to demonstrate their concerns for the protection of the buying public. The more traditional public interest groups, such as Consumers' Union and the Sierra Clubs, are both active and aggressive in protecting the basic rights of consumers. Too, some individuals are well known for being the spokesmen for consumers. These persons include Ralph Nader, who wrote the book *Unsafe at Any Speed,* and is given credit for the failure of General Motors' Corvair car; Vance Packard, who authored *The Hidden Persuaders* which deals with advertising and sales promotional appeals; Jessica Mitford, who wrote *The American Way of Death;* and David Caplovitz, who wrote *The Poor Pay More.* These books have been widely read by the public and have helped to make the consumer aware of the protection from business interests that is available.

---

[10]Warren G. Magnuson, "Consumerism and the Emerging Goals of a New Society," in Ralph M. Gaedeke and Warren W. Etcheson (eds.), *Consumerism,* Canfield, San Francisco, 1972, pp. 3–4.

Although these books make sound reading material, it is wise to be somewhat objective in digesting the contents.

Basic Issues of Consumerism

Consumerism and the consumer movement are fundamentally based on three separate, but interrelated, issues. These issues are: (1) inflation, (2) protection of individual consumers, and (3) business practices.

Inflation   One of the greatest continuing concerns Americans have is the issue of inflation and its effect on the consumer. Inflation in the United States has been climbing at a rate which far exceeds the tolerance of many consumers. Inflation hits the "pocketbook" of all consumers, but it affects the poor to an even greater degree than it does the upper-middle income groups. Inflation is an income-eroding device; that is, inflation slowly eats away our real incomes and leads to consumer discontent. In other words, our wages and income do not purchase what they once did, and it costs us additional money just to maintain our current standard of living.

Even though inflation is one of the major issues of American consumerism, the rate of inflation in the United States is not as high as it is in other parts of the world. Thus, while prices are soaring in this country, they are not rising as rapidly as in the other parts of the world. It may take Americans some time to adjust to the current rate of inflation, but there does not appear to be any abatement of this major issue at this time. Therefore, inflation will continue to be a target for the consumer movement throughout this decade.

Protection of Individual Consumers   Currently, the consumer movement is focused on a second issue which is getting considerable attention. This issue is the protection of the consumer, and in particular, the protection of minorities.

The consumer movement has been actively seeking the protection of individuals by having both the producer and the retailer guarantee the safety of products, especially for children. Dangerous toys have had a considerable amount of valid criticism from consumer movement advocates. Plastics, flammable materials in bedding, and the like have also received considerable attention. Lack of pollution control equipment on automobiles and in manufacturing plants has also been under attack. The consumerism movement has helped to force the passage of labeling laws, and now all retailers are required to inform consumers about their rights before signing any documents.

For the past fifteen years or more, the protection of minorities has been the subject of heated debates. Equal housing opportunities, right-to-work laws, more jobs for minorities—these issues are the concern of the consumer movement as well as all Americans.

Business Practices   Business activities, including retailing, have been under attack by the consumer movement for some time. One must allow that some of the criticism of business and its practices has been justified. However, since the movement first began during the early 1960s, business people have become quite conscious of practices, policies, and procedures which may reflect unfavorably upon them. Many business people have been the most staunch supporters of ethical business practices. For every unethical business firm, there are many other firms who have never resorted to unethical business practices.

Advertising and Promotion   Two elements of business practice appear to be more visible to the consumer and the consumer movement than any other function of business activity. These visible elements include advertising and promotion.[11] Through advertising and promotion, the retailer represents the producer, and in most instances the consumer looks to the retailer for fair play in advertising and promotion.

It is clear that a retailer may take several measures in order to assure the consumers that the store is not trying to mislead them but is trying to do everything possible to guarantee the product and/or service. First, the basic function of any retail advertising and promotion program is to inform the consumer about the product or service and its merits. In informing the consumer about a product's attributes, honesty should prevail throughout the promotion. Also, the advertising should be in good taste and comply with the traditions, mores, and customs of the community.

Second, a retailer should not make claims about the product or the store which cannot be supported with proof. Puffery and exaggeration should be avoided if the retailer wishes to obtain the trust and confidence of the consumer.

Third, if the retailer offers a product warranty and installation, the consumer expects fulfillment of these guarantees. If there is a charge for such items, this must be explained fully to the consumer.

Fourth, if the retailer is selling on credit, which includes the majority of retailers, then the consumer should receive a full explanation of all credit and service charges. Payment-due dates, repossession, and the like, should be explained to a credit customer before that person obligates himself or herself to the store.

Finally, it is only common sense that a retailer conduct business in an ethical and honest manner in order to gain the confidence of the consumer; for without the consumers, the retailer will be out of business. In essence, the consumer movement or consumerism is a result of mistrust; but if the retailer backs up all claims and deals fairly with consumers, there will be no reason for mistrust on the part of the consuming public.

---

[11]For a more detailed description of advertising and promotion and its effect on the consumer, see *Action Guidelines,* National Business Council for Consumer Affairs, published as a consumer service by Montgomery Ward, 1972, pp. 1–64. Although this particular study deals mainly with producers, the retailer is directly involved because the retailer is the final link in the distribution system.

SUMMARY

Culture is defined as the sum total of ways of living which is handed down from generation to generation. Our attitudes, philosophies, and biases are shaped by the culture and its forces.

Cultural standards and norms affect consumer behavior in the marketplace. Generally, a retailer complies with these cultural norms by remaining open for business only during certain hours, by dealing honestly with the customer, and by complying with the laws and regulations imposed by society.

Because of cultural influences, consumers make frequent trips to the store to purchase goods—often merchandise of an *impulse* nature. Many products fall into the category of impulse purchases—items such as cigarettes, candy, chewing gum, soda pop, and beer.

The American consumer is *convenience-oriented*. Many foods are prepared and ready to bake in the oven. One-stop shopping caters to the customer as a matter of convenience. The extensive and increasing use of credit buying is also a matter of consumer convenience.

A significant cultural change over the years has been the increase in *leisure-time* activities. These activities have encouraged the purchase of such items as campers, pleasure boats, tents, fishing gear, recreational vehicles, and motor homes.

Another cultural influence which has affected consumers' behavior has been the desire to improve our life style. The improvement of our life style is referred to as *trading up*. Many of us desire to improve the quality of our lives and enjoy luxuries. Once we have enjoyed these luxuries and the improved life style they bring, it is difficult to revert to the more austere life.

Our behavior patterns are also influenced to a considerable degree by the numerous small groups to which we belong or desire to belong. These small groups are called *reference groups,* and the bond which develops between persons in these small groups affects the manner in which we consume goods and services. Of the small reference groups to which an individual belongs, the family unit is probably the one which has the strongest effect on a person's behavioral pattern.

Because of varying social influences, a retailer should know *when, where,* and *how* consumers purchase. By knowing something about these characteristics of consumers, a retailer is better able to develop an optimal retailing mix.

The overall amount of *family income* and the *age groups* within the family are significant social factors which influence purchasing and consumption patterns.

A consumer's perception and buying behavior is the result of the *social class* to which he or she belongs, or aspires to belong. W. Lloyd Warner determined that there are six social classes of people in the United States: the upper-upper, lower-upper, upper-middle, lower-middle, upper-lower, and lower-lower.

Today's consumers are well-educated and informed people who basically reject the doctrine of *Let the buyer beware,* and assert themselves in many ways, which then exhibits the doctrine of *Let the seller beware.*

Consumers have *four basic rights* as stated by the late President John F. Kennedy in his first message to Congress in 1962. These basic rights include the right to safety, the right to be informed, the right to choose, and the right to be heard.

The *basic issues of consumerism* include inflation, protection, and ethical business practices. Retail businesses have come under scrutiny because of deceptive advertising and promotion, and in some instances, because of a failure to inform consumers about credit transactions.

REVIEW QUESTIONS

1 What is culture?
2 What influence does our culture have on the manner in which we consume goods and services?
3 How and in what manner has culture contributed to consumers making so many impulse purchases?
4 Why are consumers so desirous of convenience and the purchase of convenience goods?
5 What factors contribute to the growth of leisure-time activities?
6 What does trading up mean?
7 How can a retailer capitalize on the trading-up process?
8 Define reference groups. How do reference groups influence our behavior?
9 Why does the family have a great influence on an individual's behavioral patterns?
10 Why is it important for a retailer to determine when, where, and how consumers purchase goods and services?
11 What is the significance of family income?
12 Discuss the various social classes in the United States.
13 What is the significance of social class structure?
14 Define consumerism.
15 What are the four basic consumer rights as stated by John F. Kennedy?
16 What are the basic issues of consumerism?

Part Three

The Retail
Business Plan

Chapter 7

The Retail Business Plan

Retail business planning is a process whereby a retailer decides at present what to do in the future. It encompasses a determination of objectives and includes the necessary procedures for accomplishing those objectives. These procedures for attaining established goals are referred to as "retailing strategies and tactics." Usually, retail business planning will provide a number of strategies and tactics from which the retailer can select the best alternative for a certain set of market conditions.

A retail business plan is a written document which specifies systematic, orderly, and integrated procedures for achieving certain predetermined objectives within a specified period of time. Briefly, a retail business plan should state what is to be done, how it is to be done, by whom the work will be performed, and when the work is to be completed.

Nearly all large and small retailers, consciously or unconsciously, enter into some form of business planning. Many retailers will often have just a mental view of their business plan. On the other hand, more sophisticated retailers will develop very elaborate written business plans. However, every retailer, regardless of the size of operation, will benefit from proper business planning and the development of a retail business plan.

BENEFITS OF RETAIL BUSINESS PLANNING

Retail business planning may be a conscious or an unconscious effort, it may be formal or informal, or it may be scientific or unsophisticated. Nevertheless, retail business planning is worthwhile, necessary, and inevitable.

Sophisticated and scientifically conceived retail business planning will lead to a number of benefits. First, the proper use of retail business planning forces a retailer, whether an independent owner or a hired manager, to sit down and put in writing the objectives for that retail business. Objectives are usually for the ensuing year, although goals may be established for a longer period of time—say three to five years. This often is the most difficult step in the retail-business-planning process because it requires a manager or owner to outline very specifically the goals of the store. A retail firm's objectives should not be stated in vague language, but should be realistic and stated in a clear and precise manner. All too often a retailer's goals will be stated in a general way such as, "to increase sales and profits and to provide customer satisfaction." But this type of goal will not be effective. Objectives for the store should state answers to *specific* questions such as: "By what percentage is the store going to increase the sales and profits? By what means are sales and profits going to be increased?" In this way the manager or owner is forced to appraise the total business environment accurately from many angles—the retailer's market position, competitors' positions, product lines and merchandise assortment, financial resources, store location, market potential, and consumer demand. As stated above, this part of retail business planning is extremely difficult. But once the goals of a retail store are definitively outlined, they help to guide the store toward success.

Second, retail business planning leads a manager or owner to develop and improve coordination of the store's retailing activities. Managerial decisions made in any area—such as finance, purchasing, and promotion—will directly or indirectly affect and influence other aspects of the retail business establishment. Each retailer has to visualize the business as a total system of interacting and related activities, each of which influence and affect the profitability of that business enterprise. Thus, much thought must be given to the consequences of any managerial action.

Third, retail business planning causes a retailer to become more efficient by improving performance standards for control of the store. An effective retailing control system has two facets: internal and external. Internal controls can and may be altered from time to time by the management (i.e., purchasing, pricing, and promotion), but external controls may be beyond the scope of the management's capability (i.e., government regulations, general economic conditions, and aggressiveness of competition). Thus, at all times, a retailer must analyze internal and external controls and time schedules to determine if they are commensurate with the store's stated objectives.

Fourth, retail business planning results in a more effective utilization of resources (i.e., personnel, finances, physical facilities, and equipment). Formal planning assists retailers in optimizing a blend of people, money, and facilities by establishing goals and providing the necessary strategies and tactics for achieving store objectives.

ELEMENTS OF A RETAIL BUSINESS PLAN

Each retail business plan is different and must reflect the special needs and interests of a specific retail business; however, most retail business plans contain certain elements in common. These principal points include:

1   A written statement of a retailer's goals and objectives
2   A determination of a retailer's potential market and a sales forecast for the ensuing year(s)
3   An evaluation of the retail store's location (new or existing)
4   A determination of the store's interior layout and exterior design
5   A resolution of the number of resources from which a retailer will purchase merchandise for resale to the consumer
6   The negotiations with resources (suppliers) for the terms of sale
7   A provision for handling incoming merchandise (receiving, checking, marking, and the movement of goods)
8   A general pricing policy and pricing strategies and tactics to be used by the store to stimulate profitable sales volume
9   The promotional policies and strategies to be used by the store
10   The management's policies and practices for handling the store's personnel
11   A complete financial analysis of the business (including an analysis of sales, expenses, and profits)
12   A merchandise control system (inventory control procedures)
13   An expense control system (accounting procedures)
14   A system for the control of stock losses

Each of the points listed above will be discussed briefly; then in order to understand the various elements of a retail business plan more clearly, a separate chapter will be devoted to each point of the retail business plan.

1   Statement of Goals and Objectives

Since a retail business plan is designed to accomplish certain goals and objectives, it is necessary for either the owner or manager to state clearly in writing the goals of the retail store or firm. Written goals and objectives are much more useful and explicit than those which are not spelled out in writing. A retailer's objectives must be succinct and specific; e.g., the store will have $1 million in sales next year, the store or firm will increase last year's sales by 11 percent, the store will sell 750 units, or the business will obtain a 10 percent rate of return on investment. These goals and figures are much more precise than vague terminology, such as "the firm or the store will increase sales and profits over last year," and precise goals are much easier to work with because they provide a better guide for the store's management.

The basic purpose of having written goals and objectives is to provide a specific target for the management of a retail institution. Of course, the sales and/ or profit target that is established as a goal must be realistic and based upon the potential market which exists for the retail store.

2 Retailer's Potential Market

A contributing factor toward the failure of new retail stores is management's error in determining the market potential of a trade area. In recent years, a considerable amount of marketing research has been done in the field of market-demand measurement; but despite efforts to encourage retailers to research and measure market potential, retailers still tend to enter business without any analysis of retailing opportunities in a trade area. A proper analysis of market potential leads to improved managerial decisions in appraising potential sales volume, developing the retail business plan, and implementing and controlling a retail business plan. For example, let us assume that a large department store chain is attempting to decide in which of several suburbs it should locate a branch store. An analysis of market potential and expected sales volume in terms of gross sales in each suburb will be a helpful and guiding factor.

There are three basic trade areas: (1) primary, (2) secondary, and (3) a fringe area. Although retailers may utilize several techniques to estimate market potential in a trade area, one of the most widely used devices is the "index-of-buying-power" method. Probably no factor in itself is more important to the success of a retail store than the *number* of people living in a trade area and the *amount of purchasing power* held by these people. The trade area for a particular kind of retail store should be researched and analyzed from several points of view: (1) social considerations, (2) economic conditions, (3) extent and aggressiveness of competition, (4) location and ease of access, and (5) potential sales volume.

3 Retail Store Location

The location of a retail business is of paramount importance as it does not remain static but either improves or deteriorates. Many retail businesses fail because of poor location. The actual store site should be selected carefully since location greatly influences the future success of a retail store. The primary social and economic justification for the existence of a retail business is its ability to serve a consumer group. Thus, a retail store should be conveniently located and, in effect, should go to the customer. More attention is currently being devoted to retail store location because of the rising costs of land and the increasing rate of retail store failures. But retail store failures are not limited to small independent retailers; increasingly, there are instances of chain store failures which are due, in part, to poor retail store location. Many retailers will simply open a business in an area where a vacant building exists and will give little or no thought to the location of the store or to the potential of the trade area surrounding the store.

4 Store's Interior Layout and Exterior Design

Every retail institution has a personality or image which either attracts or repels consumers. Although the basic purpose of interior store layout and design is to promote profitable sales volume, many retailers give little thought to the value of merchandise arrangement, fixtures, space allocation, or decoration. Sufficient attention should be devoted to a store's interior so that the proper atmosphere is created for the type of customers being served. A store's exterior should offer an invitation to the consumer to enter and browse.

Other factors such as lighting, use of color and music, and the attitude of sales personnel will also create impressions which often are long lasting. In order to be successful, a store image that is created should be consistent with the overall managerial philosophy concerning merchandising and promotion. If the store's appeal is to be one of economy and is based on low-priced merchandise, then an elegant and richly decorated interior is not expected by the consumer.

Each retail store should be physically arranged in accordance with a definite floor plan. Consideration should be devoted to selling areas, nonselling areas, traffic flows, and patterns. Customers should not be able to enter and leave via a straight path through the store as traffic flows and patterns should be designed to encourage consumer browsing and purchasing. Lighting should not detract from the merchandise but rather highlight the items on display. Creativity in interior store layout and design is not expensive and each store interior should have an identity all its own. The exterior, or store front, should offer some differentiation from other competing store fronts. A storefront serves to identify a store, and this impression of the store on the part of the consumer may be a lasting impression. Therefore, it is important that attention be directed to an inviting and pleasing store appearance.

5 Retail Resource Determination

There is an old adage, "One cannot do business from an empty wagon." In other words, a retailer must have the correct merchandise, at the proper time, and at the right price for the customer if the business is going to be successful. Upon starting a new business, retailers are faced with the immediate problem of determining lines of merchandise, as well as the extent of those product lines. Generally, there are two main sources of supply: producers and middlemen. A retailer may purchase from both supply sources, but care should be exercised that purchases not be spread out between several resources offering the same type of merchandise. By limiting the number of resources, a retailer will be better able to take advantage of both quantity and cash discounts, establish a rapport with suppliers, and still be able to stock the latest styles and fashions for the store's customers.

6 Negotiations with Resources (Suppliers)

Before the actual purchases are made, a retailer will find it necessary to negotiate with suppliers on a number of factors. One major point is price, which will vary depending upon the quality, quantity, and various discounts allowed by the vendor. Also, a retailer is concerned with the period of time allowed before payment must be made to the resource. This time period is often referred to as "dating," and together with the price of the merchandise, is called the "terms of sale." Other factors which are often negotiated between a retailer and a vendor include guarantees against a price decline, return of merchandise, and transportation charges.

7 Handling Incoming Merchandise

Once merchandise has been purchased and the method of shipment agreed upon, the goods must be received, checked, marked, and placed on the selling floor. A shipment of merchandise should be inspected as it is received from the carrier (truck, airplane, etc.) and a record should be made. Merchandise also should be checked against the invoice for any discrepancies in price, quantity, or quality of goods. In large stores, these functions are usually delegated to specialized personnel, or at times, a buyer may wish to perform these activities. In a small retail operation, the proprietor or a salesperson will carry out all of these functions. But careful planning and organization in handling incoming merchandise will yield important reductions in costs associated with receiving operations.

8 Pricing Policies, Strategies, and Tactics

Before a retailer makes store purchases, a general pricing policy should be established although specific retail prices will be marked on the merchandise as it is received at the store. A general pricing policy may follow one of three possible routes: (1) pricing above the competition, (2) pricing below competitive levels, or (3) meeting competition with pricing strategies and tactics. Although general price levels of merchandise are determined by many factors, specific retail prices are under the control of the retailer.

Proper pricing of merchandise may maximize store profits, although pricing strategies and tactics alone will not ensure a successful retail operation. The price of a product or service may determine the demand for an item and may have a psychological effect upon the customer. Customers often rely upon the price of an item as an indicator of the quality of that product, but a retailer may temporarily reduce prices on an item in order to attract customers. This pricing tactic is called "leader pricing" and may be used as a "loss leader." Loss-leader pricing really is a misnomer because the underlying pricing strategy is to build greater store traffic and to increase total sales and profits even though selling one item at or below the retailer's cost. A pricing policy has three basic purposes: (1) to cover the original cost of the merchandise, (2) to cover a retailer's operating expenses, and (3) to provide a profit to the retailer. But a retail pricing policy, together with the store's pricing strategies and tactics, must have consumer appeal in order for it to be profitable for the store.

9 Promotional Policies, Strategies, and Tactics

A retailer should establish a general promotional policy for the store which may be determined in part by the image that the retailer wishes to project to the consumer.

Sales promotion in retailing includes advertising, personal selling, displaying of merchandise, and any other strategy and tactic which will induce a profitable sales volume for the retailer. Essentially, a retailer will combine advertising, personal selling, and displaying of merchandise to obtain a sales promotional mix which will attract customers to the store and entice them to make purchases.

Generally, there are two major classifications of retail sales promotion. The first form is advertising to attract consumers to the store—via newspapers, radio, television, and direct mail. The second form is concentration on instore sales promotion. This includes window displays, floor displays, point-of-purchase display materials, personal selling, and incentives for the store's personnel (such as "spiffs" or "pm's" [prize money] which stimulate profitable sales volume for the store).

All too often a retailer determines a retail sales promotional budget based on intuition or past sales. This technique advocates that sales promotion is a result of sales, when in actuality, sales should be the end result of retail sales promotion. Thus, a retail sales promotional budget should be based on the goals and objectives that the retailer has established for retail sales promotion.

10 Management's Policies for Store Personnel

Retailing has been referred to as a "people business," meaning that retailers work with customers and employees every day. The importance of the humanization of a retail business cannot be overemphasized.

Staffing may be one of the most important managerial functions of retail store management. Employees must be organized for the successful operation of the store, and retailing activities must be performed satisfactorily from the viewpoint of both the customer and the retailer. The management of retail personnel includes the recruitment, selection, training, and compensation of employees. These activities may vary considerably with the size of the store. For the independent retailer, personnel may be limited to one or two part-time employees. At the opposite extreme, large chain stores will have thousands of employees throughout the organization with a formal personnel department to handle all recruitment, selection, hiring, training, and compensating of employees. Whether large or small, centralized or decentralized, the activities associated with the management of retail personnel must be handled efficiently.

11 Financial Planning and Analysis

There is no substitute for adequate and proper financial planning for either a new or an existing retail business. Small independent retailers often begin business without adequate funds or proper financial planning, and this has led directly, or indirectly, to a high rate of retail store failures. Inadequate financial planning is not limited to small retailers. In some instances large chains miscalculate their revenues and expenses—although these errors in judgment may be offset by the overall profits of the chain organization. That is, one store in the chain may lose money, but the entire chain system may be profitable.

Financial planning is usually, but not always, limited to budgeting for the operation of the retail business. Financial analysis is concerned with controlling sales, expenses, and profits. Sales analysis may determine that some products or product lines should be eliminated since they are not profitable for the store.

Retail sales transactions are often vital indicators of a store's current performance and can be checked against past or anticipated sales for more effective financial planning. Typical retailing costs include the purchase price of the merchandise, delivery charges, wages, rent, promotional expenditures, equipment costs, and depreciation. These operating costs must be controlled since, in the final analysis, a retailer is primarily interested in the amount of profit. A retailer's profits should be analyzed and compared with similar retail operations, with the expected return on investment, and by product line(s). Profit analysis can provide a basis for taking corrective action for attaining greater control and efficiency in the store.

12   Merchandise Control Systems

Merchandise control systems vary from store to store because of factors such as the size of store, type of merchandise, and philosophy of the management. Like all other elements of a retail business plan, a merchandise control system must be tailored to each store; but as with other systems, there are common elements. All merchandise control systems are designed to aid management by providing precise information on the movement of merchandise. This, in turn, aids the buyer in the performance of the purchasing functions. Merchandise control systems help reduce out-of-stock items and keep investments in slow-moving merchandise at a minimum. In essence, the basic purpose of any retail merchandise control system is to provide a balanced relationship between investment in inventory and the fulfillment of the customers' wants.

13   Expense Control Systems and Analysis

In order to determine what progress has been made toward the goals and objectives set forth in the retail business plan, an analysis of operating expenses incurred must be made by the store's management. It is important to determine not only the dollar amount of retail expenses, but also their classification. Dollar amounts are necessary for operating purposes, but the classification of retail expenses is essential for determining which expenditures should be modified. Whether retail expenses should be reduced or increased depends on the results expected as outlined in the retail business plan. Retail expense control and analysis is necessary for reasonable profits. Since expenses vary considerably by the type of business (e.g., self-service to full-service stores) and are affected by other factors (e.g., size, location, and assortment of merchandise), expense control and analysis should concentrate on methods by which certain types of expenses can be controlled and/or reduced.

14   System for Control of Stock Losses

Stock or merchandise losses vary by the type of retail store and the efficiency of retailing management. Stock losses may range from about 0.5 percent of sales for a well-managed department store to approximately 6 percent for those retail stores which are not well controlled. Although these figures are only estimates, it is believed that they accurately reflect the increasing problem of stock losses.

Basically, there are two main classifications of merchandise losses: (1)

shoplifting and (2) employee theft. Other reasons for stock shortages include breakage, cash register mistakes, and the failure to correctly weigh or measure certain types of goods. Although a retailer cannot completely eliminate merchandise losses, positive steps can be taken to keep these stock losses at a minimum, and the key to low stock losses is proper managerial control.

In order to introduce you to a retail business plan, we are introducing the following material for your consideration. This is an actual retail business plan that was developed by the author for a retailer in the Midwest. The names have been changed, but all the data are factual.

The retail business plan was for a new specialty store that sold only one line of merchandise—carpeting. Some of the elements in this retail business plan may not apply to your situation, but you will be able to use this plan as a guide in tailoring a plan for your own store.

RETAIL BUSINESS PLAN: WAREHOUSE CARPETS, STATEVIEW, MINNESOTA

Objective

The objective of Warehouse Carpets is to obtain $500,000 in gross sales during the first year of operation which will yield a 30 percent return on the owner's investment.

The elements in the retail business plan for Warehouse Carpets will include the following:

1   Determine the potential market for carpet in the Stateview, St. Maria, and Elkhorn trade areas.

2   If an appraisal determines that there is an adequate market demand for carpet in these trade areas, a specific store location will be selected complete with costs of land and building.

3   Suggest ways in which the building can be designed and arranged—both exterior and interior.

4   Select and determine the approximate number of resources from which Warehouse Carpets can purchase carpet for resale.

5   Suggest methods for handling incoming merchandise, receiving, checking, and marking; and make further recommendations for any special handling equipment.

6   Recommend a general pricing policy and pricing strategies and tactics.

7   Recommend a general promotional policy and promotional strategies and tactics; determine an advertising and sales promotional budget for the first year of operation.

8   Make suggestions for staffing together with training and compensation of retail store personnel.

9   Calculate a break-even point for the proposed retail store, together with a contribution margin analysis.

10   Calculate a return on investment (ROI) given the estimated first-year expenses for the proposed business.

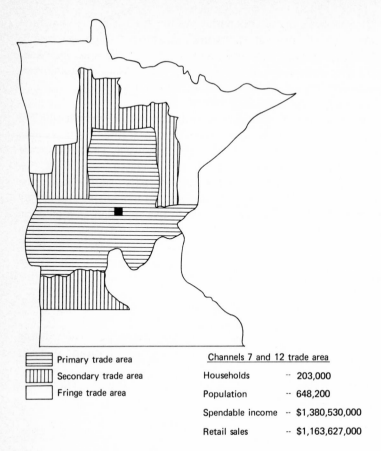

Primary trade area
Secondary trade area
Fringe trade area

Channels 7 and 12 trade area

Households	--	203,000
Population	--	648,200
Spendable income	--	$1,380,530,000
Retail sales	--	$1,163,627,000

Figure 7-1 Trade-area coverage.

    11 Suggest methods for control of expenses and for the reduction of stock losses.

POTENTIAL MARKET

The trade area of Stateview, St. Maria, and Elkhorn consists of 33 counties in two states. The western portion of the trade area extends into another state, South Dakota. This is a rural, farming and livestock area with one major city of 50,000 population which is St. Maria. This is the proposed city for the location of the new store.

    The total trade area consists of 203,000 households of which 190,100 are equipped with television sets. The total population of this trade area is approximately 648,200 with a spendable income of $1,380,503,000. Retail sales for the previous year reached $1,163,627,000.

    New construction is expected to total 333.4 million square yards of floor area during 1975—which is at a low level due to rising interest costs associated with home purchases.

Assumptions In analyzing the potential market for carpet in this trade area, it is necessary to first make some assumptions. First, it is being assumed that each household in the trade area consists of 900 square feet as a minimum. This allows a total potential of 100 square yards of carpet for each household. Second, if carpet retails for an average price of $5 per square yard, the total potential sales volume for this trade area is equal to $101.5 million. However, not every household in this trade area will be completely carpeted. Some provision or adjustment must be made for this fact.

It can be assumed that each household in this trade area can absorb one-third of this estimate due to the fact that some rooms in these houses are not yet carpeted, and some rooms which are carpeted will soon need replacement carpet. These assumptions reduce the total potential market for carpet in this trade area to $33.8 million. For a comparison of dollar value and market potential for carpet in this trade area, see Table 7-1.

Competition In appraising the potential market for carpet sales in this trade area, one must consider the number of competitors and the aggressiveness of these competitors.

This trade area consists of thirty-one retailers who offer carpet to the consumer at retail prices. Many of these retailers operate from their homes and install the carpet they sell. They are called mechanics, and they sell many yards of carpet in this manner.

Four large, national department stores in the trade area sell carpet in various fabrics and colors. In addition, there are two specialty carpet retailers. The department store chains are not "pushing" carpet and are considered to be nonaggressive. The two specialty carpet retailers are perceptive merchandisers and constitute very aggressive competition. These retailers should be considered direct competitors, whereas the department stores may be referred to as indirect competitors as carpeting is not the department store's main line of merchandise.

Other Considerations This trade area has about 70,000 summer homes. For the most part, these homes are not carpeted. However, these homes do constitute additional potential business in that each can make use of high-

Table 7-1   Potential Market in Yards Based on Number of Yards per Household*
(In Millions)

Carpet, $/yd	100 yd/ household	50yd/ household	30yd/ household
$9	$182,700	$91,350	$60,900
8	162,400	81,200	54,130
7	142,100	71,050	47,366
6	121,800	60,900	40,600
5	101,500	50,750	33,800

*Base: 203,000 households in the trade area.

density, rubber-backed nylon carpet. These homes can be considered "plus business."

RETAIL STORE LOCATION

In selecting a site for the proposed retail store, consideration must be given to traffic count and accessibility to the location. In addition, adequate parking for customers is an absolute necessity.

One possible site is the former Joe's Supermarket on West Main Street near the Westroads Shopping Center. This building is vacant and contains approximately 17,500 square feet. The rental fee based on an annual lease arrangement is $2.50 per square foot net. The store can be remodeled at the tenant's expense. This site is not being recommended because: (1) the rental fee is too high in relation to potential sales, and (2) the image of the grocery store may be retained by the new tenant. The store should be able to develop an image in keeping with the theme of "Warehouse Carpets."

A second possible location for the proposed store is on the corner of East St. Maria and Lincoln Avenue. This site is a vacant lot which can be purchased for $50,000. The lot measures 120 feet on East St. Maria and 110 feet on Lincoln Avenue. The construction of a building suitable for Warehouse Carpets would cost $60,000 (approximately 14,000 square feet at $4.28 per square foot).

The third possible site, and the one that is being recommended for Warehouse Carpets, is a five-acre parcel of land located near the Westroads Shopping Center. This property is located on a highly traveled four-lane street and has ample room for expansion. The parcel of land is valued at $160,000. A building can be constructed for $64,000 (15,000 square feet at $4.28 per square foot). By using a formula for rent determination (12 percent for building rent and 10 percent for land use), the annual rental fee would be $23,700 ($16,000 for the land and $7,700 for the building). This rental fee is clearly within the limitations set forth for this type of retail business in this trade area. In addition, there is the possibility of the owner selling off a portion of the five-acre parcel and still being able to provide customers with adequate parking. Another alternative includes the possibility of constructing complementary stores on the land and renting these facilities to other retailers. The land, in addition to the store, appears to be a sound investment for future appreciation.

EXTERIOR STORE DESIGN AND INTERIOR ARRANGEMENT

A concrete block structure of 15,000 square feet is to be constructed on the specific site just recommended. The building is to have one large window facing the street, which will allow the consumer to observe carpet displays in the showroom. Approximately 3,000 square feet of the building is to be apportioned for the showroom; approximately 300 square feet should be allocated to office space; and the remainder is to be used for storage of carpet rolls and equipment.

The building is to have a loading dock at the rear with a door 12 feet high and

24 feet wide to facilitate the loading and unloading of carpet rolls with the aid of an electric forklift.

To facilitate the carpet displays in the showroom, use will be made of roll drums. These roll drums will allow the consumer to turn samples over for observation and inspection and also allow the salesperson an opportunity to compare different grades of carpet.

RESOURCES

Most carpet manufacturers produce basic carpet lines, fibers, qualities, styles, patterns, and colors. Branding in carpet is not as important to the consumer as the color, fabric, or pattern. Since carpet manufacturers produce almost identical carpeting, there is little incentive for the retailer to purchase from a large number of resources. It is more prudent for the retailer to concentrate purchases in as few resources as possible and still allow adequate coverage of the carpet lines. This policy on purchasing carpet will allow the retailer to take all discounts as they are granted by the resource.

It is recommended that Warehouse Carpets maintain an average inventory of approximately 200 rolls of carpet. This inventory can be purchased from six resources. Additional resources will result in a waste to the retailer; a fewer number of resources could result in shortages during times of labor problems or strikes at the production level.

EQUIPMENT AND HANDLING

Carpet retailing with the "warehouse theme" takes special equipment because of the bulk of the merchandise and having to move the heavy rolls of carpet from one location to another. In order to maintain an inventory of approximately 200 rolls of carpet, it is necessary to have fourteen bays of carpet storage racks. Since the store is new, it will be necessary to invest in "racking equipment" to facilitate the storage of these carpet rolls. The items needed include:

	Equipment needed	Unit price	Total price
32	U2P-48144R Uprights 16,800-lb capacity	$23.73	$ 759.36
112	pair 35A0-120 shelf beams, 34-lb capacity/pair	16.45	1,842.40
32	BBT-48-in back-to-back ties	2.97	95.04
	Total, f.o.b. Michigan City, Indiana		$2,696.80

A forklift suitable for this retail operation is the Clark Electric Model EC500-40E. This forklift has a capacity of 4,000 pounds and a lift height of 156 inches. A 4,000-pound forklift meets the federal government requirements under the Williams-Steiger Occupational Safety and Health Act of 1970. The price of the forklift is $13,250 including an eight-foot rod which is used to insert and raise the carpet rolls.

All incoming merchandise is to be inspected for damage upon arrival from the common carrier. Invoices are to be compared with the purchase order to detect any discrepancies, then forwarded to the accountant for payment. After the merchandise has been inspected and marked, it is to be placed on the storage rack provided according to the scheme established by the retailer for color, style, and fabric.

PRICING POLICIES, STRATEGIES, AND TACTICS

The general pricing policy for Warehouse Carpets is to promote quality carpet at list prices which are substantially below those of traditional retailers. The store will stock and promote as the main price line a carpet which retails for $5.99 per square yard. This price line is to become the main central theme for Warehouse Carpets. Normally, this quality and grade of carpet would retail for $8.99 in a department store. In addition, Warehouse Carpets will offer the consumer other price lines of carpet. One line of goods will have a retail price of $4.99 per square yard, and the other line will be priced to sell at $2.99 per square yard.

In order to trade the customer up to more expensive merchandise, Warehouse Carpets will offer carpeting at $7.95, $9.95, and $11.95 per square yard.

After a customer has been shown the main price line of carpet which will sell for $5.99 per square yard, the salesperson will attempt to trade the customer up to a more expensive line of merchandise. This should be accomplished with some ease, since the same brand and quality of carpet will sell for $2 to $3 more per square yard at other stores.

In order to maintain a complete line of carpet, it is necessary for the store to stock less expensive carpet in limited amounts. For instance, a limited amount of nylon carpet which would sell for $1.88 to $2.29 per square yard could be offered from time to time to build and increase store traffic.

In order to maintain the "warehouse concept" for retailing carpet, the store must maintain an inventory of approximately 200 rolls of carpet. This inventory is to include the following:

Number of rolls of carpet	Retail price
50	$ 1.88–2.29
60	5.99
40	7.95
30	9.95
20	11.95

It is not necessary to stock all these rolls of carpet at all times. It is suggested that these figures be used as a guide to buying and stocking carpet for Warehouse Carpets. Reorder points must be established after the store has been in operation for a few months.

PROMOTIONAL POLICIES, STRATEGIES, AND TACTICS

Warehouse Carpets will stress the "warehouse concept" and the main theme will be one of "quality merchandise at low prices." In order to reach potential customers in the trade area, use will be made of Channels 7 and 12 television stations. The cost of commercial television spots on these two stations is $28 for class AA advertisements. This rate is based on 260 exposures per year, 6:30 P.M. to 10:00 P.M. daily.

The promotional rate for 30/20-second spots on both channels is $39 based on 260 exposures from 6:30 P.M. to 10:00 P.M. daily. These promotional strategies will cost $7,280 and $10,140, respectively.

Warehouse Carpets will make use of television spots in ten-second lengths until the consumer has become familiar with the warehouse concept in retailing carpet. During the first year of operation, the store will double ten-second exposures on both television stations. This will bring the total television budget to $14,560 for the first year. This figure does not provide for a "grand opening event."

Eight local newspapers are published in the trade area. Warehouse Carpets will use these mediums for the grand opening and also make use of these newspapers for special events. Advertising in each of the eight local newspapers once a month in addition to the grand opening will cost a total of $21,294 of which $9,646 will be used for the St. Maria Times. These totals bring the promotional budget to approximately $40,000 for the first year of operation.

STAFF AND TRAINING

Warehouse Carpets will begin business with one well-experienced salesperson, who also will act as the sales manager and general manager. This individual is responsible for the movement and turnover of carpet inventory, maintenance of store profits, and the training of any junior salesperson that may be hired in the future. To commence business, one junior salesperson will be hired and trained by the sales manager.

The gross profit plan of compensation (30 percent) will be used for all sales personnel. This method of compensation will encourage salespersons to maintain the retail price of carpet without resorting to price cutting in order to obtain the sale. This plan for compensation also encourages salespersons to stress quality and customer benefits, even though the main theme is price appeal.

An accountant will be hired to work one-half day each week to maintain the accounting records for Warehouse Carpets. Daily posting will be done by the sales manager.

BREAK-EVEN AND CONTRIBUTION MARGIN ANALYSIS

A break-even point will indicate to a retailer at what point a certain volume of sales will meet or cover a store's total expenses, both fixed and variable. Given these total expenses, a break-even analysis is useful as a managerial tool in determining the needed sales volume for a store. A sales break-even point for a retail store can be determined by using the following formula:

$$BEP = \frac{total\ fixed\ and\ variable\ costs}{average\ gross\ profit\ margin}$$

It was determined by management that an average gross profit margin of 30 percent would be maintained on all retail sales. The store's total fixed and variable expenses totalled $88,710. The expenses for the year were broken down into the following categories:

1. Rent	$23,700
2. Advertising and sales promotion..	40,000
3. Depreciation on store equipment..	2,410
4. Utilities	3,000 (estimated)
5. Supplies	600 (estimated)
6. Telephone	1,200 (estimated)
7. Insurance	1,200 (estimated)
8. Miscellaneous	1,000 (estimated)
9. Interest on $130,000 at 12 percent..	15,600
Total fixed and variable costs	$88,710

$$BEP = \frac{\$88,710}{30\%} = \$295,700\ in\ gross\ sales$$

Contribution Margin

Definition: That percent of $1 in sales available to pay fixed expenses and contribute to profit.

$1		Sales dollar
	−0.70	Cost of goods sold
	+0.035	Discount income (actual cost of goods = 0.665 of each sales dollar)
	−0.09	Commission (0.3 × 0.3)
	−0.01	Employer's payroll taxes (10% × 0.09¢ = 0.01¢)
	−0.765	
−0.765		
$0.235		Contribution margin

RETURN ON INVESTMENT

Assume: All net cash inflow invested in similarly profitable ventures. Otherwise, net profit would sit idly by earning a lower or zero return which would drag down the overall return.

Assume: Operations of at least eight to ten years with at least $500,000 sales volume each year.

Assume: Contribution margin as per break-even cost analysis at 23.5 percent (0.235¢) of each $1 sales available to pay off fixed costs and contribute toward profits.

Assume: "Investment" = total average assets which in this case is the total investment by the lenders.

Assume: Return on this "investment" equals net cash inflow generated (cash inflows less cash outflows) plus interest.

$$\text{ROI (lenders)} = \frac{\text{net income} + \text{depreciation} + \text{interest}}{\text{average assets}}$$

$$\text{ROI} = \frac{23.5 \,(500,000 - 375,000) + 2400 + 11,600}{145,000}$$

$$\text{ROI} = 30 \text{ percent (approximates true interest rate of return using present value tables)}$$

EXPENSE CONTROL

Since this is a relatively small retail store, the supervision of expenses will be under the direct control of the manager. The manager will maintain the suggested gross profit margin of 30 percent on sales; the salespersons' salaries will come from the 30 percent commission based on gross profit; and, further, measures will be taken to ensure compliance with federal employer's payroll taxes.

The rent, equipment depreciation, and advertising and sales promotional budget are accurate for the first year of business. Variable expenses, such as utilities, supplies, discounts to contractors and employees, and sample expenses, will have to be monitored.

STOCK CONTROL

Carpet is merchandise which lends itself to considerable waste and expense to the store if the mechanics become careless in making room cuttings. In order to keep stock shortages to a minimum, the sales manager will supervise all instore cuttings to take advantage of all short pieces of carpet. These short pieces of carpet can be sewed together by matching the texture and color with a minimum of waste. If this practice is not carried out as a matter of store policy, considerable shortages of merchandise will result. Waste carpet pieces not used by the store personnel can be sold as remnants at special sales events.

SUMMARY

A *retail business plan* is a written document which specifies a systematic and integrated procedure for achieving certain predetermined objectives within a specified period of time. The retail business plan should state what is to be done, how it is to be done, by whom the work will be performed, and when the work is to be completed.

Retail business planning leads to a number of benefits. First, objectives for the business are put in writing. Second, retail business planning leads to improved coordination of retailing activities. Third, retail business planning leads to an effective retailing control system. Fourth, retail business planning results in a more effective utilization of resources: personnel, money, and physical facilities.

Although each retail business plan is tailored to the store, most retail business plans contain common elements. Each retail store should have a *target* which is referred to as goals or objectives. The basic purpose of having written goals is to provide management with a specific target toward which to guide the business.

Management should make a determination of the *market potential* of a trade area before entering business. Probably no other single factor is more important to the success of a retail store than the number of people living in a trade area and the amount of purchasing power held by these people.

The *location* of a retail business is a significant factor because the value of the store site does not remain static but either improves or deteriorates. Many retail businesses fail because of poor location. Some retailers will simply open a business in an area where a vacant building exists and will give little or no thought to the location of a store or to the potential of a trade area surrounding the store.

A retail store's *design and interior layout* is important because every retail business has a personality or image which either attracts or repels consumers. Creativity and innovation in exterior design and interior store arrangement is not any more expensive than the "me-too" phenomenon. Each retailer should strive to make the store have an identity all its own, which then differentiates the store from competing stores.

Every retailer should strive to have the *correct merchandise* at the right time and price if the store is going to be successful. Generally, there are two main sources of supply—producers and middlemen. Usually a retailer will find it necessary to purchase merchandise from both types of resources.

Negotiations with resources include the price of the merchandise which is a major point. Other factors such as discounts, allowances, and the period of time allowed before payment must be made to a resource usually are negotiated. Together, these items of negotiation are referred to as *terms of sale*.

After the merchandise has been purchased by the retailer or the store's buyer, some provision must be made for receiving, checking, marking, and placing the goods on the selling floor. Careful planning and organization in *handling* incoming merchandise will yield important economies and reductions in costs associated with receiving operations.

Before a retailer makes store purchases, a *general pricing policy* should be established although specific retail prices will be marked on the merchandise as it is received at the store. A general pricing policy may follow one of three possible routes: (1) Pricing above the competition, (2) pricing below competitive levels, or (3) meeting competition with pricing strategies and tactics. The proper pricing of merchandise may maximize profits for the store, although this alone will not ensure the successful operation of the business.

Sales promotion in retailing includes advertising, personal selling, displaying of merchandise, and any other tactic which will induce a profitable sales volume for the retailer. Essentially, a retailer will combine advertising, personal selling, and the displaying of goods to obtain a sales promotional mix which will attract customers to the store and entice them to make purchases.

Staffing may be one of the most important managerial functions of retailing. Employees must be organized for the successful operation of a store, and retailing activities must be performed satisfactorily from the viewpoint of both the consumer and the retailer.

There is no substitute for adequate and proper *financial planning* for either a new or an existing retailing business. Small independent retailers often begin business without adequate funds or proper financial planning which has led directly, or indirectly, to a high rate of retail store failure.

Merchandise control systems vary from store to store because of factors such as size of store, type of merchandise, and the philosophy of the management. All merchandise control systems are designed to aid management by providing precise information on the movement of merchandise. This, in turn, aids the buyer in the performance of the purchasing functions.

In order to determine what progress has been made toward the goals and objectives set forth in the retail business plan, an *analysis of operating expenses* incurred must be made by the store's management. Whether expenses should be reduced or increased depends on the results expected as outlined in the retail business plan.

Stock losses vary by type of retail store and the efficiency of management. They may range from about 0.5 percent to a high of 6 percent of sales, which greatly reduces the profits of a store.

REVIEW QUESTIONS

1 What is retail business planning?
2 What is a retail business plan?
3 What are the benefits of retail business planning?
4 Discuss the most common elements found in retail business plans.
5 What is the basic purpose of having a set of goals in writing?
6 What step of the retail business plan is the most difficult to accomplish?

PROJECT

You are to develop a retail business plan for either a new store or an existing retail business. If you select to develop a retail business plan for a new store, you are to begin by stating your goals and objectives. You are to follow each step in the retail business plan as provided for you in the text.

If you select an existing retail business, you are to seek the consent and cooperation of the owner/manager of the store. Some of the elements in the book's retail business plan may not apply in your situation. Nevertheless, tailor the plan to the store you have selected.

This retail business plan will consist of approximately ten to twelve pages of constructive material. The report and plan should be typed, double-spaced, and well documented. Upon completion of the retail business plan, give a ten-minute presentation to the class members in order that they can share in your experiences.

Part Four

Market Opportunities

Chapter 8

A Retailer's Potential Market

One of the most common causes of failure of new retail stores is management's error in determining the market potential (possible total sales) of a trade area. In recent years, there has been a considerable amount of marketing research done in the field of market-demand measurement. But despite efforts to encourage all retailers to research market potential, many simply enter business without making any analysis of the retailing opportunities in a particular trade area. A proper analysis of market potential leads to improved managerial decisions in appraising a retailer's potential sales volume, in developing a retail business plan, and in implementing and controlling the retail business plan. For example, a large department store chain is attempting to decide in which of several suburbs it should locate a branch store. An analysis of market potential and expected sales volume in terms of gross sales in each suburb will be a helpful and guiding factor.

Retailers may utilize several techniques to estimate market potential in a trade area, but one of the most widely used devices is the "index-of-buying-power" method.[1] Probably no factor in itself is more important to the success of a retail store than the number of people living in a trade area and the amount of purchasing power held by those people. In order to determine the "market" for a

[1] See "Survey of Buying Power," *Sales Management,* published annually.

particular kind of retail store, the trade area should be researched and analyzed from several points of view: (1) population characteristics, (2) social conditions, (3) economic conditions, (4) extent and aggressiveness of competition, (5) location and ease of access, and (6) potential sales volume.

POPULATION CHARACTERISTICS

A market potential for goods and services must be in evidence before a retailer enters business. In other words, there must be adequate market demand for the type of goods and services a retailer is going to offer, or there is little, if any, need for a retailer to enter a specific market. If market demand is not present, a retailer will not be able to develop the demand, no matter how persuasive the retail sales promotion and advertising.

Although many factors affect the success of a retail business, probably no single item determines a retailer's success to any greater extent than the number of people residing in a potential market area. The population of a potential market determines the number of potential customers a retail store might hope to attract. However, the total number of people residing in a potential market area will not alone guarantee a retailer's success. Although population in a specific trade area creates a potential market for food, clothing, and shelter, the retailer's volume of sales will depend not only on the number of people but on their level of disposable and discretionary incomes. Basically, it takes three ingredients to make a market: (1) people, (2) people with money, and (3) people with money *who are willing to spend it.* [2]

Before entering a market, a retailer should gain some knowledge about the population rate in the trade area. Is the rate growing or declining, and how will it affect the particular retail business? For an overall view of population characteristics, a retailer can review *Current Population Reports* which are population estimates published by the Bureau of the Census of the United States Department of Commerce. This publication, which is distributed frequently but somewhat irregularly, contains details on population characteristics such as growth, shifts in population, and age groupings by both regions and states. Another valuable source for pertinent data regarding population characteristics and buying potential is the annual volume published by *Sales Management,* "Survey of Buying Power." These publications provide detailed, up-to-date information and also give some insights into growth patterns, birth rates, population shifts, and trends in various markets among regions, states, cities, and environs.

It is important for a retailer to know whether or not the population of a potential market area is increasing, decreasing, or remaining stable. If the number of people is increasing (other factors remaining constant), the sales volume potential of a retail store can be expected to increase in the future. The reverse is also true when a trend indicates a decrease in the population. However, a stable population could be a more favorable environment in which to

[2]William J. Stanton, *Fundamentals of Marketing,* 4th ed., McGraw-Hill, 1975, p. 49.

analyze potential. A trading area which is stable is also one of maturity, and it probably has a more even and constant expenditure pattern than the more volatile, cyclical, and rapidly developing markets. A stable market often has a great potential and deserves investigation as to its population characteristics and buying power.

Another aspect of a market's population that should be analyzed when determining sales potential is the average age of the people. Younger people tend to be more active, consume greater quantities of food, purchase more clothing, and may be more mobile than more mature groups. However, the older segment of our society should not be ruled out as not having potential for certain types of goods and services. The number of people over sixty-five is increasing both absolutely and as a percentage of the total population. These people are logical prospects for health food, prescription and proprietary drugs, certain cosmetics, cruises, and foreign travel tours. Thus, there is market potential for every age group; an analysis should be made of each trade area a retailer plans to enter or is currently operating in.

The marital status of potential market consumers bears investigation as the purchasing and consumption habits of married people differ from single persons. This is particularly true for durable goods, such as household appliances, furniture, carpeting, and even nondurables, such as maintenance supplies for the home. Single people often live in apartments whereas married persons may reside in a home. Since homeowners generally spend more time in their homes and more money on the home than do apartment dwellers, consumption patterns may vary considerably between the two groups.

SOCIAL CONSIDERATIONS

Social considerations are important to retailers because every market differs in its composition. Some markets are homogeneous; others are heterogeneous. In other words, markets are either alike in characteristics (homogeneous) or they are totally different in characteristics (heterogeneous). Similarities or differences reflect cultural influences which, in turn, influence buying behavior. Culture can be defined as a totally "learned way of life," and the life style of the persons in a trade area differs considerably from market to market. These differences are due, in part, to family influences, religion, and education, which affect a person's beliefs, attitudes, and behavior. Also, a person's behavior is determined to some degree by the people with whom this person interacts. Although these phenomena are quite complex, some social characteristics can be isolated and may aid a retailer in determining the proper retailing mix.

Borrowing money and the use of credit has become an accepted pattern of behavior for most Americans. A retailer who does not offer credit terms in some form will probably find that his or her market share will be fairly restricted.

For most people, there is an overriding desire for conformity. This trend has received impetus from suburban living and the rise of young executives and blue-collar workers from the lower social classes. Other social characteristics include the desire for one-stop shopping, self-service, and impulse buying. Customers often go shopping without a specific list of items and go home with several bags of goods of unplanned purchases. Increases in both disposable and discretionary incomes have fostered this type of social phenomenon, and retailers should recognize that people have accepted this pattern as a way of life. Of course, this pattern could change if economic conditions force the consumers to alter their purchasing behavior. But in order to be successful, retailers will have to accommodate the customers regardless of their wishes.

ECONOMIC FACTORS

The economic factors of a potential market can be determined from several sources. For example, many business periodicals and newspapers provide information on general economic conditions. *Sales Management's* "Survey of Buying Power" provides information on income and its distribution by cities, counties, and states. Other economic factors to be examined by a retailer are the extent and aggressiveness of competition, the type and nature of industries in the area, the stability and reliability of income from these industries, and existing and proposed transportation facilities. These factors should be analyzed for support of or the detraction from the proposed or existing retail business.

Consumer buying power, as measured by the amount of income in a trade area, is an important determinant as to the potential of a market. Part of the income received by the working people in a trading area often makes up a retailer's sales dollars. Generally, a trade area of low income leads to a lower sales volume for all retailers. Conversely, when income levels are relatively high in a trade area, a retailer can expect to share in higher sales volume, assuming that other factors are equal. In other words, it is assumed that the retailer will put forth a reasonable effort to gain those available sales dollars.

It is not only important to determine the amount of income in a trade area, but it is also significant to determine how this wealth is distributed. Income distribution is important because it will influence sales of luxury items and other high-quality merchandise.

A retailer should analyze the source of income for a trade area. If income is derived from factories or cyclical industries, a trade area may experience some fluctuations of income. If people's income is derived from governmental service agencies, one can expect a somewhat greater stability of income in that area. But whatever the source of income for a trade area, the sales volume for retail stores will reflect the nature of this income.

COMPETITION

All retailers have competition, either directly or indirectly. It is important for a retailer to know everything that is capable of being known about the store's competition. Both the number of competitors and the aggressiveness of these retailers should be analyzed. This can be done in a number of ways; for example, a simple survey of the trade area will determine the number of retailers. Some of these retailers will be direct competitors; i.e., they sell basically the same type and kind of goods that the proposed business will offer. Other retailers are competing for the same customer dollars but on an indirect basis; i.e., just so many dollars will be divided among the various retailers in a trade area or community.

To further illustrate direct and indirect competition, let us look at a men's clothing store. This store will directly compete against other men's clothing stores. However, somewhat more indirectly, this men's clothing store will compete with department stores, discount stores offering men's clothing, shoe stores, large chain stores, and even to some degree, variety stores which sell men's clothing.

Competition may be aggressive or it may be rather apathetic and nonaggressive. Aggressive competition in a trade area usually results from the well-established stores which have perceptive management. These competitors usually keep abreast of retailing trends and offer the customer many services, quality merchandise at reasonable prices, and other conveniences (such as adequate parking and long hours of operation).

On the other hand, it is entirely possible to find a trade area in which there are several older stores where management is apathetic and nonaggressive; that is, the management is not sensitive to the demands and wishes of the customers. These types of retail outlets offer an advantage to the aggressive retailer. Apathy can stem from unusually large sales volume and profits, a declining interest in the business, old age, or simply management complacency. In determining the store's goals and retailing strategies, the retailer should appraise the caliber of competition in a proposed trade area. This appraisal can be done by observation, by comparison shopping, by talking with competitors' customers, and by talking with the local chamber of commerce.

TRANSPORTATION FACILITIES

Since the mobility of our society affects retailing institutions, the means of transportation by which people travel from place to place should be examined. The density and distribution of traffic (including pedestrian) will influence a market's potential retail sales volume. If people move about by automobile, the roads, streets, and parking facilities of a trade area should be examined for accessibility. These factors are not the sole determinants of selecting an area or location in which to locate a retail store; nevertheless they do have a direct bearing on market potential. If customers cannot easily go to a place of business, they probably are not potential customers, and their purchases will be made elsewhere. Customers residing near the boundaries of two trade areas may favor one shopping area over another because of easier access by automobile or public transportation. Natural boundaries, such as rivers, lakes, and hills, may direct traffic into irregular configurations which are not favorable to one trade area, thus lessening the potential of that market. Traffic analysis is a must in the determination of a market's potential; and even if that area's customers are pedestrians, they must arrive via some means of transportation.

Customers will travel various distances to shop at a store, but usually one can expect people to travel only relatively short distances. For many customers, a drive of 2 to 3 miles is the farthest they will travel to go shopping for basic necessities. For others, especially in rural or suburban areas, it is not uncommon for people to travel distances up to 40 miles.

PRIMARY TRADE AREA

Trade areas are geographical locations from which retailers "pull," "draw," or "attract" customers, and these areas vary considerably in size, location, and density of population.

One method of defining a trade area is to determine the geographical boundaries of the advertising media. For example, a television station or a daily newspaper is limited in its viewing audience or readership. This area may be defined as a general trade area. However, this general area may not be satisfactorily delineated to a retailer in a large city because the television stations and newspapers may cover a much larger area than the retailer serves. Thus, we need to clarify further the boundaries of a trade area.

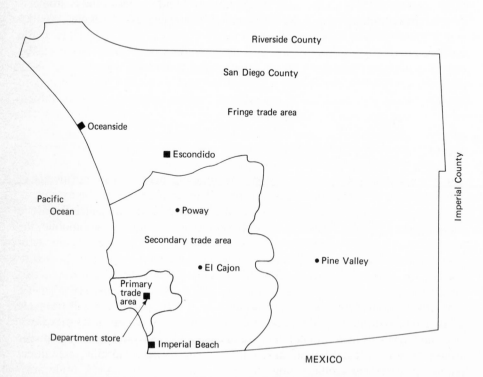

Figure 8-1 Primary, secondary, and fringe trade areas.

A primary trade area is one from which a majority of a retailer's customers are attracted to the store. For example, Sears defines their primary trade area as the area in which 75 percent of the store's credit customers reside. This definition is workable for Sears because of the large number of credit customers, but it may not be applicable for a smaller retailer selling goods for cash or for a smaller retailer using some universal credit card (such as Master Charge or BankAmericard).

In a metropolitan area, a retailer is likely to find that the store's primary trade area is within a few miles of the business. Primary trade areas can be expanded or contracted by the "pulling" power of the store, competing retailers, or some other attraction, such as entertainment.

Primary trade areas for shopping centers are usually much larger than primary trade areas for neighborhood stores. The attraction and reputation of anchor stores reaches far and wide, especially in the absence of other large chain stores. Anchor stores are those major chains, such as J. C. Penney, Sears, Bullock's, or The May Company which are a center's major retail stores.

SECONDARY TRADE AREA

Secondary trade areas become more difficult to delineate. However, it is reasonable to expect that occasional customers may reside outside the primary area and in a secondary trade area. Naturally, customers residing in a secondary trade area are not frequent patrons as are those customers who reside within a few miles of the store. For example, Sears defines a secondary trade area as one in which the next 15 percent of the store's credit customers reside. Another illustration might be the residents of Del Mar, California, who sometimes drive to San Diego to shop. Since Del Mar is approximately 25 miles from San Diego, these customers would be classified as living in a secondary trade area. Patronization of the specialty stores and shopping centers in San Diego by persons living in Del Mar cannot be expected to be as frequent as those residing nearby, however, it is not unreasonable to assume that Del Mar residents will drive the distance to shop perhaps ten or twelve times each year. Consequently, these purchases can be considered as "plus sales" for retailers in San Diego.

FRINGE TRADE AREA

There is a third trade area which extends far beyond the primary and secondary trade areas. This trade area is referred to as "a fringe trade area." The fringe area makes up the remaining total potential customers that may patronize a retail store. By using the previous example of Sears, it can be stated that the store's fringe-area customers make up the remaining 10 percent of the total customers. (The primary trade area accounted for 75 percent; the secondary trade area accounted for an additional 15 percent; thus, the fringe area accounts for the remaining 10 percent.)

The percentage figures that store management assigns to the various trade areas will depend on each manager's philosophy, the goods and service mix, the store location, and reputation of the store. Many variables determine the amount of "pulling power" that a store may have. It is entirely possible that a store's primary trade area may include 90 percent of the total potential customers with the secondary trade area accounting for the remaining 10 percent. In summation, it is well for a retailer to consider primary, secondary, and fringe trade areas for potential customers.

STARTING A NEW RETAIL BUSINESS

There are two methods by which one can begin a retail business: One is to open a new store, and the other is to purchase an existing business. As you would expect, there are advantages and disadvantages to both methods.

A new retail store may be opened either in a new location or on a previously occupied site whether it is a similar type of store or a different type. The advantages in opening a new store include the following:

1 Being able to develop a store's own image
2 Having the discretion to purchase and offer to the public the type of merchandise that the retailer prefers
3 Having the choice of pricing merchandise to meet the demands of the customers
4 Being able to start with a new structure or a newly remodeled building with appropriate equipment and fixtures
5 Not having to pay an existing businessman for "goodwill" or "blue sky"

When a retailer begins a new business, that person can either open the business in a new building or remodel an existing building. If a retail business is started in a new location, with either a new or remodeled building, a retailer is better able to develop the proper image for the store. A store's image is conveyed to the customers from the outward as well as the inward appearance of the structure. A new building looks inviting and does not suffer from deleterious or harmful images left behind by the previous retailer since it is often difficult to change the image of a store. Customers often retain prior store images even though a new owner may take over a business with an entirely different product line. For some reason, an existing structure which has not been remodeled carries with it the image of the former tenant. For example, a structure in a shopping center in San Diego has had three tenants in the past seven years. Each of these tenants has offered a similar type of goods, each not bothering to remodel or change the image of the structure. The first two failed to gain enough sales volume to pay the expenses associated with the lease arrangement. It remains to be seen if the third tenant can become successful in the same location, although it is doubtful at this time as to the ability of the store to remain viable.

However, a retailer may be successful where others have failed if the image can be changed. One major contributing factor is a complete remodeling of the structure. If a storefront is changed, the interior design and layout altered and rearranged, and new lighting fixtures added, then the basic image of a store has changed. Another factor that is often overlooked by retailers is the installation of carpeting, a relatively minor expense in the opening of a new business in an existing structure; but what a difference it can make. New floor coverings, paint, paneling, and/or wallpaper will disguise an existing structure and create a new, personal image for the beginning business.

When a retailer develops and opens a new retail store, that person is free to purchase the type, kind, and style of goods he or she wishes to offer for resale. It can be said that "the retailer starts business with a fresh offering" since he or she does not have to dispose of merchandise acquired from the previous owner.

It is of paramount importance for the retailer before opening a store to determine the price lines of merchandise that the store is going to offer the public; and assuming that the retailer has done the research well, he or she will have determined the proper price lines that should be stocked for resale. To reiterate, the first impressions obtained by the buying public are often lasting. The retailer should carefully evaluate merchandise prices and offerings for the store's opening event.

Still another advantage of opening a new business lies in not having to pay a previous owner "goodwill." When a retailer purchases an existing business, normally that person will have to pay the owner for the established customer following. There is nothing tangible in purchasing goodwill as we will determine shortly even though it may be a definite advantage to the new store owner.

PURCHASING AN EXISTING RETAIL BUSINESS

Sale offerings of retail businesses can be found in newspaper advertisements, real estate listings, or can be carried by word of mouth. Since many reasons for selling a business may be given by an owner, the prospective buyer should determine the real cause *why* the owner is selling. Some common reasons for selling include: retirement, poor health (which may be an overworked excuse), desire to make a profit (in addition to regular owners, there are individuals who purchase *failing* retail enterprises and then by remodeling, cost cutting, or developing a clientele, show a profit on the books and sell the business within several years), or inability to operate a profitable enterprise.

If the latter reason is given, the prospective buyer should make every effort to determine the exact cause of the business failure. Businesses often fail because of the lack of managerial know-how and inadequate financing; and it may be that the prospective purchaser can overcome these obstacles. If a prospective buyer can determine *why* the existing business is for sale, that person will be better able to determine a fair market price for that business and will lessen the chances of paying too much.

Purchasing an existing business can mitigate the problems associated with assembling resources and equipment, choosing the location of the store, and hiring personnel. However, a prospective buyer should carefully evaluate just what is being purchased to determine a fair market value of the assets. This takes considerable time and talent. If the prospective buyer does not take adequate time to evaluate the assets of a retail business, he or she may be chagrined to discover that it was a mistake to purchase the business. The prospective buyer should consult with an accountant and an attorney before agreeing to a price on an existing business. A good, reliable information source on existing businesses is the Dun & Bradstreet Report. Although this information will cost the prospective purchaser a fee (unless he or she is a member in good standing with the association), the price of this information is minimal in comparison to the purchase price of a retail business and the accompanying risks involved in the purchase.

Just how does one evaluate or place a value on an existing business? Price may be determined by establishing values for all the assets. It does not follow, though, that this will be the selling price because the owner may ask a considerable amount for goodwill or blue sky. However, by establishing a value for the assets of a business, one does have a point from which to begin bargaining. In some transactions, not all of the assets are purchased from the previous owner. For example, the new buyer may lease or rent the building, lease the existing equipment, and purchase only *certain* existing stock. If such an arrangement is made, the new buyer does not need as much working capital. Under another arrangement, the previous owner may retain the accounts receivable, or the new owner may wish to continue selling on credit, which will result in a determination of the worth of the accounts receivable. Caution should be exercised in determining the value of existing accounts receivable. This may well be the real reason for the sale of the business; that is, the previous owner was unable to keep the accounts receivable under proper control. This phenomenon often happens with small retail businesses because most owners try to maintain the goodwill of the customers and never refuse them credit. Of course, it is likely that the retailer would be better off *not* doing business with a customer who refuses to pay the account on a regular basis.

Usually, the greatest amount of money for an existing business is invested in the inventory of that business. Therefore, the prospective purchaser should carefully analyze the stock in order to determine its fair market value accurately. Often one will find stock which is basically unsaleable or could be sold only if it were marked down drastically. (Markdowns will be covered later in the chapter on pricing.) The value of stock items can be adequately determined from invoices or from price lists of resources. Since it is possible that some of the merchandise is seasonal in nature, one must give consideration to the current demand for that merchandise. A new owner may find that he or she is in the position of warehousing or storing the seasonal merchandise for six months or more before final sales can be consummated, and stored or warehoused merchandise does not make any money for a retailer. Since merchandise may actually deteriorate in value, be stolen, become soiled, or be damaged by fire or vermin while in the warehouse over a period of several months, lengthy storage should be avoided if at all possible.

Evaluation of the building and equipment is not too difficult for a prospective purchaser. The fair market value of the real estate can be determined from a real estate appraiser for a fee, and equipment values can be determined by pricing similar new equipment and deducting a fair and reasonable value for the depreciation. Nearly all manufacturers of store equipment are eager to supply prospective new owners with price lists of comparable equipment. It then becomes just a matter of judgment as to the rate of depreciation of the used fixtures.

That intangible asset, the valuation of goodwill, is somewhat more difficult to estimate than placing a price on a tangible asset. Goodwill can be defined as the difference between the fair market value of tangible assets and the asking price. Some consider this difference as being "blue sky." Blue sky originally was used to allude to fraudulent securities; however, the term is now applied to the intangible assets of the business and the value which should be placed upon the right to conduct business. With franchises, the franchisee (purchaser) pays a predetermined amount for the privilege of using a sign, logo, or other symbol which has been promoted over a period of time and has an established clientele. With a nonfranchised business, goodwill probably will be subject to negotiation between the buyer and the seller.

After a retailer has appraised the potential market, either to open a new store or to purchase an existing business, store location then becomes an evaluation problem. In the case of a new store, site location studies will always be undertaken. In the case of an outright purchase of an existing store, the new owner must decide whether to stay at the same site or relocate the business. This is especially true today where the changes in population and buying habits are subject to wide fluctuations and may readily affect the viability of a retailing business.

In the next chapter, we will deal directly with specific site location and also consider population mobility as it applies to store location.

SOURCES OF INFORMATION

In an attempt to determine a potential market, a retailer has at his or her disposal several reliable sources of secondary information. Mention has already been made of *Sales Management's* "Survey of Buying Power," which annually gives reliable estimates of population, income, and its distribution. This source can be used to update some of the *United States Census of Population* data.

The *United States Census of Population,* published by the Department of Commerce, is probably the single most important compilation of descriptive consumer data. Such data are presented by states, counties, cities, and sections of cities. Age, income, occupation, and family status are only a few of the many factors presented in this reliable source. This source has one serious limitation, however. Data are only taken every ten years, and the report is not available until two years later. Estimates may be made by the various business journals, and it is well to obtain these estimates if possible.

Another source of statistical data which is valuable in determining a retailer's potential market includes the *County and City Data Book: A Statistical Abstract Supplement* published by the United States Department of Commerce. This source provides population estimates by county, region, division, and state. Other sources include the *Statistical Abstract of the United States, The Editor and Publisher Market Guide,* and the *County Fact Book.* This latter source is published each year and provides data on county governments, population characteristics, revenue and taxation, transportation, employment, and selected statistics on retail trade by metropolitan areas and by county. Most states also publish a *Statistical Abstract* which provides similar data.

In addition, the Bank of America publishes a *Small Business Reporter* which is valuable as an aid for selected retail businesses. The *Small Business Reporter* is available from any branch of Bank of America, or from the corporate offices in San Francisco. These publications cover many types and kinds of businesses and are available for $1 per copy.

The Small Business Administration, SCORE (Service Corps of Retired Executives), radio, television, and newspaper offices, often are of assistance in determining the consumer profile of a trade area.

When a retailer cannot find data on potential markets, primary data must be gathered through the use of a marketing survey. At times, it may be prudent to make use of test markets, although this technique usually is restricted to producers of consumer goods. After a marketing survey has been taken, a retailer must exercise good judgment in making an estimate of the market potential of a geographic area.

SUMMARY

One of the most common causes of failure of new retail stores is management's error in determining the market potential (possible total sales) of a trade area. While retailers may utilize several techniques to estimate market potential in a trade area, one of the most widely used devices is the *index-of-buying-power* method. Probably no factor in itself is more important to the success of a retail store than the number of people living in a trade area and the amount of purchasing power held by these people.

A *market potential* for goods and services must be in evidence before a retailer enters business. Before entering a market, a retailer should gain some knowledge about the population rate in the trade area. Is the rate growing or declining, and how will it affect the retailer's particular store? If the number of persons is increasing and other factors remain constant, the sales volume potential of a retail store can be expected to increase in the future. The reverse is also true when a trend indicates a decrease in the population. Younger persons tend to be more active, consume greater quantities of food, purchase more clothing, and may be more mobile than more mature groups.

Social considerations are important to retailers because every market differs in its composition. Some markets are homogeneous; others are heterogeneous. Similarities or differences reflect cultural influences which, in turn, influence buying behavior.

Consumer buying power, as measured by the amount of income in a trade area, is an important determinant as to the potential of a market. It is not only important to determine the amount of income in a trade area, but it is also significant to determine how this wealth is distributed.

All retailers have *competition,* either directly or indirectly. Both the number of competitors and the aggressiveness of these retailers should be analyzed.

Since the mobility of our society affects retailing institutions, the means of transportation by which people travel from place to place should be examined. *Traffic analysis* is a must in the determination of a market's potential, and even if that area's customers are pedestrians, they must arrive via some means of transportation.

A *primary trade area* is one from which a majority of a retailer's customers are attracted to the store. *Secondary trade areas* are those beyond the primary trade area. Customers residing in a secondary trade area are not frequent patrons of a store. *Fringe trade areas* include consumers who would only occasionally visit a store, perhaps once or twice each year.

There are two methods by which one can begin a retail business. First, a person may open a new store, and second, one may purchase an existing retail business.

The advantages of *opening a new retail store* include: (1) being able to develop a store's own image, (2) having an opportunity to purchase fresh merchandise, (3) being able to price the goods to meet the demands of the consumer, (4) having the opportunity to start business with a new or remodeled building and fixtures, and (5) not having to pay an existing businessperson a price for blue sky or goodwill.

Sale offerings of retail businesses can be found in newspapers, real estate listings, or through word-of-mouth advertising. It is well for a prospective buyer of a retail store to first determine the real reason *why* the present owner is selling the business. A prospective buyer must take time to *evaluate the assets* of a retail business in order to determine a fair and just price. Usually, the greatest amount of money for an existing business is invested in the inventory of that business. Therefore, the prospective purchaser should carefully *analyze the stock* in order to determine its fair market value accurately.

The *fair market value* of the real estate can be determined from a real estate appraiser for a fee, and equipment values can be determined by pricing similar new equipment and then deducting a fair and reasonable value for the depreciation.

Sales Management's "Survey of Buying Power," the *United States Census of Population,* business journals, and marketing surveys can be important sources of information for retailers appraising a potential market for profitable sales volume.

REVIEW QUESTIONS

1   Why do many small retailers fail to make estimates of market potential?
2   What factors should be evaluated in determining a trade area potential?
3   Which market factor is most important in determining the potential of a trade area?
4   Where would you begin looking for secondary data concerning a specific trade area?
5   What is the significance of determining the age of persons residing in a trade area?
6   Discuss the importance of social considerations of a trade area and the possible impact on a new retail store's business.
7   Explain how economic factors determine the merit of a trade area.
8   How does one measure the possible impact of competition on a retailer's business volume?
9   How do you evaluate the transportation facilities in a potential market area?
10 Define the various trade areas.
11 How do you determine whether an area is a primary, secondary, or fringe trade area?
12 What are the advantages of opening a new retail business?
13 What are some of the advantages of purchasing an existing store?
14 How do you go about evaluating an existing retail business?
15 Name some sources where you may find information concerning market potential.

Part Five

Establishing a Retail Store

Chapter 9

Retail Store Location

The location of a retail business is of paramount importance since a store's environment does not remain static but either improves or deteriorates. The actual store site should be selected carefully because the future success of a retail business may depend on the store's location.

The primary social and economic justification for the existence of a retail business is its ability to serve a customer group. Thus, a retail store should be conveniently located and, in effect, should *go* to the customer. Because of population shifts and movements, the increasing number of planned regional shopping centers, continually rising land costs, and changing urban social conditions, greater attention is being devoted to retail site location.

Another reason retail store location is a critical element is the rising rate of retail store failures. Retail store failures have not been limited to small independent retailers, but increasingly chain store failures also have occurred which are due, in part, to poor store location. Many retailers will simply open a business in an area where a vacant building exists and will give little or no thought to the location of the store or to the potential of the trade area surrounding the store. If one retail store has failed at a specific location, it may be because of the lack of customer traffic and poor location. However, we periodically witness the failure of one retail enterprise, and almost immediately another retail business will move

into the same building. It probably can be assumed that little in the way of
marketing research or location research was done before the new owner moved
into the same building. Simply stated, the building was vacant and the rental fee
inexpensive. However, under close scrutiny, one probably could determine that
this may be the most expensive venture for the new retail store. Why, one may
ask? Because in a dynamic retailing environment such as ours, the life span of
most retail locations and facilities is relatively short-lived. Even the largest
planned shopping centers with all the marketing resources and expertise, are
faced with the problem of retail store mortality due to: obsolescence, changes
and shifts in population, construction of newer shopping centers with the latest
features, and the ever-present changing consumer desires. A retail store is much
like a human being. It has a birth, growth, maturation, and a decline. These
stages of life may be very short, or they may be of longer duration. In today's
economic marketplace, one cannot expect the same retailer to be at the same
location forty or fifty years. Retail locations should constantly be reevaluated to
determine whether they are meeting current expectations and future goals. Retail
store location is a continuous problem, not one that is finished when the store
opens for business. It may vary in importance through the life cycle of a retail
store, but nevertheless it is a pivotal or critical portion of the retail business plan
and will be approached in a logical and systematic manner in this chapter.

THE IMPORTANCE OF RETAIL SITE LOCATION

In the evaluation of market potential and the determination of anticipated sales
volume for a retail store, several areas of trade may be analyzed. Any one trade
area, or perhaps all analyzed trade areas, may yield a sufficient dollar volume of
sales to support a retail store. However, specific site location of a store is a
prerequisite to a profitable sales volume.

The value of specific site locations tends to change over time. Some values
change rather quickly, and others slowly become less valuable over a longer
period of time. Retailers often will continue to occupy a specific location long
after the site has lost its customer appeal. It is often difficult for a retailer to
decide to move a place of business to a new location because of a fear of the loss
of patronage. However, the store may be losing enough customers and enough
sales each year to more than offset any costs associated with moving to a new
location.

No single factor by itself determines the value of a specific site, but three
elements when combined will aid in the determination of the worth of a location.
These three elements are: (1) the general trade area, (2) traffic flow and its
analysis, (3) the population and its mobility.

THE GENERAL TRADE AREA

Generally, a retailer has some idea or preference as to the general area where the
store will be located. The choice probably has been narrowed down to a state or

to a specific town or city. If the town is rural and Midwestern, the trade area may extend for many miles in all directions. Some Midwestern towns have considerable "pulling power" and attract customers from miles away. But within larger cities, the trade area may be limited to a geographical area or radius of a few miles or perhaps even less if the store serves only a neighborhood. In this instance, the neighborhood store's trade area will consist of only a few blocks.

When we speak of a trade area, our discussion is focused on the geographical area where most of a retailer's customers reside. It may be that the store's customers reside within a short radius of the store, or it may be that the majority of the store's customers live many miles from the store. It is an area which is limited in scope either by natural or artificial boundaries (rivers, lakes, streets) or simply by that store's ability to attract customers for whatever reasons. The size and shape of a trade area are not clearly defined and there are no neat, concentric zones whereby one can categorically say that so many customers come from this area and so many come from another area. It is possible that 80 percent of a store's customers live within a very short radius of the store; 10 percent live many miles from the store; and the remaining 10 percent live far beyond what normally would be expected to be within the store's trade area. Some people will drive varying distances to patronize a specific store. Others may have to depend on public transportation. Depending on the type of retail store, this either enhances or restricts the trade area of certain stores. Too, trade areas tend to overlap. Trade areas will vary in size depending on the nature of the goods sold (durable goods will expand a trade area). Also, the size of the trade area will be affected by the attitudes and social characteristics of the people residing within the trade area (when they shop, frequency of shopping, how far they will travel). There is no simple formula for determining the boundaries of a trade area. However, several tools can aid the retailer in making the decision whether or not to locate a store in a certain trade area.

Social Characteristics

The social considerations of the local population should weigh heavily on the decision to locate a store in a particular community. For instance, several specific areas should be analyzed and evaluated in terms of a retail store location in a community: (1) the population characteristics of a community, (2) the attitudes and progressiveness of the people residing in that community, (3) consumer buying habits, and (4) any special features which would attract customers from some distance.

1   Population Characteristics   Probably no one single factor is more important than the population of a community. A retailer needs people, people with money; and these people must have a willingness to spend their money. The sheer *number* of persons residing in a trade area will in itself *not* determine whether a trade area has potential. A retailer must determine whether the population is increasing, decreasing, or remaining static. In the past few years, the population of many communities (especially the suburban areas) has risen sharply because of new housing developments. Others have slowly waned over the years (including many downtown areas). The specific causes of changes in population must be analyzed in order to provide the retailer with an accurate picture of the status of a trade area.

In determining the trade area's sales potential, the population of a trade area should first be analyzed for age distribution. It is possible that smaller, rural communities may have a higher proportion of older people, while the newer, suburban communities of the metropolitan areas consist primarily of younger families. Older people tend to be less active, consume less food, buy less clothing, entertain less frequently than younger persons, and in all probability will not increase their overall consumption of various consumer goods. The purchasing habits of senior citizens tend to be relatively fixed due to financial circumstances or long-standing habits. Thus, their consumption patterns are not easily changed or altered. Social security benefits do increase occasionally since the federal government periodically grants a cost-of-living increase to social security recipients. However, there is in effect little increase in the purchasing power of these individuals. Of course, senior citizens do purchase some types of goods in a consistent manner, and a retailer may wish to cater to these people. For example, a drugstore may find that senior citizens will increase sales and profits. Food stores offering smaller sizes or individually packaged units can cater to older persons' wants and needs. Travel agencies and other leisure-time or recreational stores can make money by concentrating on the older and more wealthy age group. Thus even though the older persons' buying habits may be semifixed, there is a definite market for these people.

A trade area which has a large proportion of younger married people is often preferred by retailers over the community which consists of mostly older people. Young married couples generally have rising incomes, whereas older people may be living on fixed incomes from pensions and social security benefits. Younger couples or families tend to be the major purchasers of furniture, new cars, household items, and lawn and garden supplies. They also tend to socialize with other young people, which places them in the market for many items in the food and drink category. All in all, the younger people probably provide a better overall market potential for a retailer, although this does not suggest in any way that the older retired persons should be neglected. They, too, are potential consumers, only in a different way and exhibit different buying habits and patterns. This is one of the reasons we studied consumer behavior in the earlier chapters.

The average family size is also an important population characteristic because a retailer should adjust the merchandising mix to suit the needs of the family. If a family size tends to be large (with three or more children in a family), a retailer should offer merchandise which suits the economy of a larger family. Food should be available in large "family-size" packages, inexpensive clothing may be stocked for the children, washers and dryers may be in demand, and so on. If the family size is smaller, then it may be more prudent for the retailer to offer merchandise in smaller packages or units.

2 Attitudes and Progressiveness The attitudes and progressiveness of the people in a trade area should be evaluated and considered because a progressive community will promote and attract more persons to that area. The more people that a trading community attracts, the more likely the purchasing power of the area will be increased. One standard which has been used for many years and is still quite accurate in depicting the attitudes and progressiveness of the people residing in a community, is the status of the public school system. Some communities will support in every way their school system, or they will consistently veto any improvement bonds for schools. Since these actions depict the general philosophy of the local residents, the consequences may determine whether or not a community is attractive to new residents.

The existence of local, active service organizations (i.e., Rotary, Kiwanis, Chamber of Commerce, or Jaycees) may reflect a certain progressiveness on the part of the citizens of that community. It has been shown that the communities which promote such clubs are usually a more progressive place in which to reside, especially in smaller communities or the suburbs. Any new retailer should become an active member in one or more of these organizations.

3 Buying Habits An investigation and analysis of the buying habits of the residents of a trade area or community is absolutely necessary. Any given community may have buying habits and patterns which are different from what a retailer expects. People may not purchase from local retailers but may drive to a planned regional shopping center. Or residents residing near a local shopping center may for some reason shop elsewhere. Thus, a retailer needs to find out potential customers' shopping habits and patterns, or the retailer may discover too late that the trade area will not support a retail business.

A retailer should also become aware of the customers' preferred hours of shopping. In some communities, the bulk of the shopping may take place in the evenings or on the weekend since both husband and wife work. In other areas, the main shopping might take place during the afternoon or early morning hours. What does all this mean to a retailer? It means that a retailer must schedule the store's personnel, hours of operation, and promotional activities around the buying habits and patterns of the potential customers. This is particularly critical for a retailer entering an area with a new business.

4 Special Features Some trade areas have features which are considered to be assets in attracting customers to the community. Historical monuments, museums, parks, resorts, athletic arenas, zoos, theaters, and colleges are just a few of the special features of a community. These features attract people from long distances and are responsible for increasing the flow of people into a trade area. Most likely, increased numbers of people will result in greater sales volumes for many merchants; although there is no guarantee that the increased population will result in higher sales. It is up to the retailer to attract these potential customers into the store.

Economic Considerations

Several economic considerations will qualify or disqualify a community as a prospective trading area in which to locate a retail store. These economic considerations include the following: (1) income, (2) competition, (3) transportation facilities, and (4) services.

1 Income The total retail sales potential of a trade area is closely related to the income received by the people residing in that area. This income, or a certain portion thereof, can be considered to be a retailer's potential sales dollars. The number of persons employed in a family, the total average income for each family, and the regularity and frequency of their income are indicative of the ability of the residents to purchase goods and services. Since total retail sales within a trade area are closely related to the purchasing power of the residents of a community, a retailer must be aware of the amount of money that will be available for buying goods and services.

Similarly, the source of the income within a trade area is also significant. Most retailers would prefer that their customers have a consistent, steady income rather than an income which is subject to wide fluctuations. For example, local, state, and federal government payrolls in general are relatively secure and steady. However, payrolls derived from the production of durable goods (such as autos) or from mining are subject to wide variations in work schedules (i.e., strikes and other work interruptions). Thus, a retailer should consider the source of income before locating a store in a certain trade area.

Income distribution also influences the sales volume for most merchants. If a retail store wishes to offer luxury items, then a retailer had better be sure that enough residents of that community have relatively high incomes. Generally, over the past decade, incomes have been rising and are quite widely dispersed across the nation, but in some communities the total income is highly concentrated and held by a few families. As you may readily conclude, these trade areas may not be the best areas in which to locate a store. There are, of course, exceptions to this situation. Some communities have a high median income (such as Grosse Pointe, Michigan; Beverly Hills, California; and Evanston, Illinois) where the majority of families are wealthy. The wealth is not concentrated in any one family, but is held by nearly all the families residing in the community. These areas offer great opportunities for retailers of certain high-class goods, high-fashion clothing, and various other luxury items.

How does a retailer go about determining the distribution of income in a trade area? First, one can make a determination of the kind, type, and price of homes in the trade area. Since a certain level of income is required before a person may buy a specific-priced home, this will give a retailer some idea as to the monthly or annual income of the homeowners in that trade area. Second, the proportion of home ownership (as opposed to families that are renting) reflects the dispersion of income as homeowners are generally more stable and better off financially. Third, the median educational level of a community often reflects how income is distributed. For example, are there a lot of professional people in the area—or a large number of factory workers or junior executives? Fourth, the per capita retail sales for any trade area will reveal the income pattern in a trade area. Perhaps one of the best sources for obtaining estimates of the distribution of income by counties is the "Survey of Buying Power" which is published annually by *Sales Management* magazine. This survey provides an accurate portrayal of the income and its distribution for any county in the United States. Unfortunately, this source is limited to larger areas than might be preferred by some retailers, but it is an excellent reference for obtaining per capita income data.

2   **Competition**   Every retailer has competition, whether it is direct or indirect. Direct competition is that which comes from those retailers offering similar or comparable goods and services. For example, when one grocery supermarket competes directly with another grocery store, when one men's clothing store competes directly with another men's clothing store, or when one shoe store competes directly with another shoe store, this is *direct* competition.

Indirect competition comes from other retailers who offer unrelated goods and services but who are competing for the same consumer dollars. An example of indirect competition would be a grocery supermarket and a clothing store. Primarily, these two retail institutions sell unrelated goods. But since the consumer has only x number of dollars to spend, each retailer must compete against other retailers for a portion of those dollars. Thus, the grocer in attempting to entice the consumer to buy more food is competing indirectly against the clothing store that is hoping the consumer will purchase clothing instead.

A retailer's competition should be surveyed and analyzed for quantity, quality, and extent of aggressiveness. A large number of competitors may be in the area; they may or may not be aggressive, perceptive to trends in retailing, or a threat to a new retailer. Also a number of competitors may not be competing directly since the goods they offer may not be like those offered by the prospective retailer. In other words, a women's ready-to-wear store may not have to compete directly with a department store but may be competing directly with another women's ready-to-wear store.

Relative competitive strength can be determined by analyzing certain facts and figures: (1) the number of competitors, (2) the length of time each has been in business, (3) the annual sales volume of each competitor, and to a lesser extent, (4) the aggressiveness and perceptiveness of these retailers. Of these factors, the annual sales volume of a competitor is probably the most difficult to obtain. However, one can estimate these figures from census data, trade association figures, and by asking other competitors. Surprisingly, when competitors are approached and asked certain leading questions concerning another business firm's sales figures and financial facts, one can extract fairly reliable data. Ask the question, "Who sells more women's ready-to-wear apparel than anyone else in the area?" Most of the retail firms competing with the store in question will know, within a fairly reliable tolerance, the sales figures and financial conditions of their competitors. By observation, one can appraise the aggressiveness and perceptiveness of competing retail store managers.

3 Transportation Facilities Traffic analysis and how it affects retail store location will be dealt with in greater detail later in this chapter. But since many consumers move about by car, one should pay particular attention to the roads, streets, and parking facilities in a trade area. These factors themselves do not determine a store's location, but the status of transportation facilities available may favorably or unfavorably affect the sales potential of a community and ultimately the store. Streets should be wide, paved, and well lighted. If the area has a planned regional shopping center, all roads should lead to the center. Parking must be provided since so many customers shop by automobile. Depending on the area, public transportation may be important for the retailer. Also, one can view adequate parking and good roads as another means of appraising the progressiveness of a community.

4 Services When one refers to services within a trade area, it usually means the banking, newspaper, and public service institutions that are present.

The local banking facilities should be analyzed from the retailer's viewpoint regarding what the bank can do for the retailer and the store. Whether for basic financing or for future use, such as for additional working capital, a retailer should find a bank that best suits the store's needs. A retailer will need a checking account at a local bank so that daily and weekly deposits can be made easily and conveniently. Thus, a retailer should check the services available in the local banks and select one which fits the store's needs.

All retailers have to advertise in some manner. Not all retailers make use of a newspaper, but it is well to appraise the circulation of the newspapers in a community. If a community has more than one newspaper, the circulation of each should be determined. Most newspapers appeal to certain groups, and it is advisable for a retailer to determine which group of consumers subscribes to each newspaper. Then a retailer should make an evaluation of the current advertisers in the local newspapers. What type of advertisements does the newspaper carry? What type of appeals are used by competing retailers? Does the newspaper have favorable rates? Since newspapers are the largest, most effective, single source of retailer promotion, a retailer will most likely use this medium for advertising. Television and radio stations also should be investigated as possible sources for advertising and promotion, since these mediums have become effective for some types of advertising of certain products.

TRAFFIC FLOW AND ANALYSIS

The amount, kind, and type of traffic that passes any specific location is highly significant to retailers because—usually—the heavier the traffic count, the greater the potential sales volume. Procedures used in an analysis of traffic will vary with the type or kind of retail business that is to be located on a specific site.

First, for retailers who handle items of low unit value, an analysis of the number of people passing a particular location is of great importance. It is also important to those retailers offering impulse goods or those providing fast-food services. With these types of goods and services, a retailer needs a high traffic count in order to survive financially. For example, retail stores needing a large number of people passing by include: fast-food establishments, variety stores, dry-cleaning facilities, drugstores, food stores, and specialty shops (such as tobacco stores, magazine shops, and bakeries).

In analyzing the traffic flow by a specific site, one should take into consideration a number of factors. For instance, the volume of customer traffic passing a particular site will vary with the time of day, the day of the week, the weather, the sales events of other retailers, or any other variable that may be evident at the time. It is important, therefore, to count customer traffic at different times and to provide allowances for variances. Any unusual condition may distort a traffic analysis and will end in a pedestrian and/or car count which is inaccurate. It is not unusual to find auto traffic detoured or rerouted due to construction, especially during the summer months. When this type of situation is encountered, it is difficult to obtain an accurate traffic flow and count. However, this is an uncontrollable variable that a retailer must consider. The construction and erection of lane dividers may prevent auto traffic from turning into certain shopping areas. Thus, information on city streets or highway plans should be obtained if possible. Usually, these plans can be discussed with the city planning officials or obtained from city records.

Further, an attempt can be made to analyze traffic as to the number of potential customers for specific types of goods and services. To illustrate, say that a large number of men pass a women's ready-to-wear store, or a large number of women and children pass a men's clothing store. In other words, a large number of persons *per se* passing a particular site does not *alone* constitute a good location, especially if those passing the location are not potential customers for a specific good or service. For example, statistical data have shown that women influence many of the purchasing decisions of any household. So for retailers wishing to offer women's and children's apparel, home furnishings, and grocery items, an analysis of the female traffic would be quite important. For sporting goods, automobiles, and men's furnishings, it would be more significant to obtain a traffic analysis of the men passing by. Also, there is a greater tendency for men to shop in self-service and self-selection stores which is an important factor for a retailer to consider.

There is yet another factor concerning traffic which must be carefully evaluated. The age distribution of the people who pass a certain location should be carefully examined. Adults usually will not be interested in youth-oriented items (unless they have teenage children). Similarly, teenagers probably will not be interested in purchasing furniture and appliances. However, both groups may be interested in fast-food items and other impulse goods.

The number of couples passing a certain location can be particularly significant if a retailer is offering home furnishings or appliances, since purchasing these items is usually a family-shared decision. Even the age of these couples may be important. Younger couples may be comparison shopping for home furnishings and appliances, but older couples may just be window shopping or passing by. As one can see from these examples, it is extremely important for a retailer conducting a traffic analysis to know the profile of a consumer group that is being analyzed for potential customers.

When evaluating an existing store, it is significant for a retailer to determine the number of persons entering the store. The basic purpose is to appraise the potential sales volume that can be obtained from that existing store. Thus, allowances should be made for those consumers who do not actually make a purchase. If one is able to determine the number of consumers that actually made a purchase and determine the average purchase price, it would be possible to predict the anticipated sales volume for that store for a period of time. However, caution should be exercised in this area. Any changes in the retailing environment or mix could readily alter these figures.

POPULATION AND ITS MOBILITY

One of the more recent significant factors affecting retail store site location has been the mobility of people. Because of population mobility—whether from rural to urban, urban to suburban, or community to community—customers' shopping habits and desires change. This movement of population has brought about several new developments in the manner by which retailers locate their stores.

Retailers who are starting new businesses realize the need to locate in the more heavily populated areas. Also, many existing retailers are being forced to reevaluate old retail sites which may result in the closing of some older stores and the opening of new stores at another location closer to the urban and suburban populations.

As we will see from the following paragraphs, population mobility has contributed to the clustering of retail stores or shopping centers, which affects the selection of a retail store site.

Planned Regional Shopping Centers

Perhaps the greatest influence on retail site location has been the movement of retail stores (which followed the population) from the downtown areas to the suburbs. This phenomenon has given rise to modern, planned, regional shopping centers. Planned regional shopping centers are controlled and directed "units" which provide the consumer with complementary shopping. By complementary shopping, we mean one store tends to complement another in the shopping center. The owners or managers of the planned regional shopping center, usually a large insurance company or other financial institution, offer leases only to those retailers who are financially strong and who offer both goods and services in a variety of forms, and complement the other stores in the center.

Planned regional shopping centers usually start by having two or more anchor stores which probably are national or regional retailing chains. These

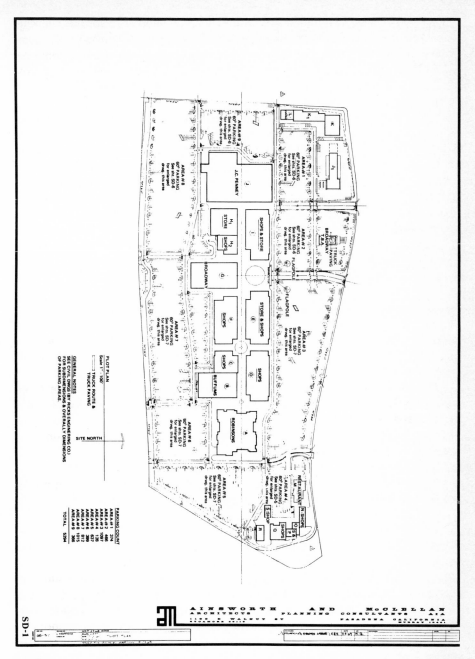

Figure 9-1 Planned regional shopping center. *(Courtesy of Fashion Valley Management Association, San Diego)*

retailing giants serve as a "nucleus" around which a number of specialty stores are clustered. Planned regional shopping centers have become autonomous units which are totally self-sufficient in all respects. These centers can be thought of as little cities within themselves since a consumer can purchase nearly any good or item of merchandise. These centers also provide adequate parking which is one of the major shortcomings of the downtown shopping districts.

Today's planned regional shopping centers are large complexes offering as much as, and sometimes more than, one million square feet of shopping area on 70 to 80 acres of land. Planned regional shopping centers of this magnitude often serve 200,000 to 250,000 people, with some people driving to the center from as far away as 30 miles. Many of the newly constructed regional shopping centers of this size offer fully enclosed, air-conditioned malls for the convenience and comfort of the consumer. One of the first planned regional shopping centers in the upper Midwest which offered these features was Southdale just south of Minneapolis, Minnesota. Dayton's, a regional chain store, serves as one of the anchor stores in this planned shopping center. In another planned regional shopping center in Costa Mesa, California, three anchor stores form the nucleus for the South Coast Plaza Center: Bullock's, The May Company, and Sears, Roebuck and Company. In a regional shopping center in San Diego, California, the anchor stores consist of Penney's, Robinson's, The Broadway, and Buffum's.

With rapidly rising land costs, many of the newly planned regional shopping centers are being constructed on two or three levels (whereas the first ones were usually on one level and spread out). Some centers even offer multiple levels of auto parking. Many are quite elaborate and offer such aesthetically pleasing features as water fountains, landscaping, pieces of sculpture, paintings, and recorded music. Many regional centers also have special events and entertainment for their patrons at various times during the year. Psychologically, customers are placed in a better purchasing mood when surrounded with such a pleasant environment. Although these items are planned to make shopping centers more pleasing and to attract consumers, caution should be exercised. The decor should not detract from the stores and from the merchandise these stores have to offer.

Several planned regional shopping centers have been constructed in downtown locations in connection with urban renewal projects. Generally, these centers serve the people who work downtown and usually do not make any special attempt to serve the suburban residents. It remains to be seen over a period of time what level of success these downtown centers will enjoy. It is always possible, however, in highly developed downtown areas with large numbers of working people and/or tourists passing through that this type of project could be quite successful.

Nearly all planned regional shopping centers have an association to which the retailers in the center must belong. The shopping center association acts as a guiding hand in the regulation of store hours, advertising, public relations, and the arrangement of store leases. Retailers, in turn, benefit from the association by having a common bond of belonging, which usually leads to improved customer

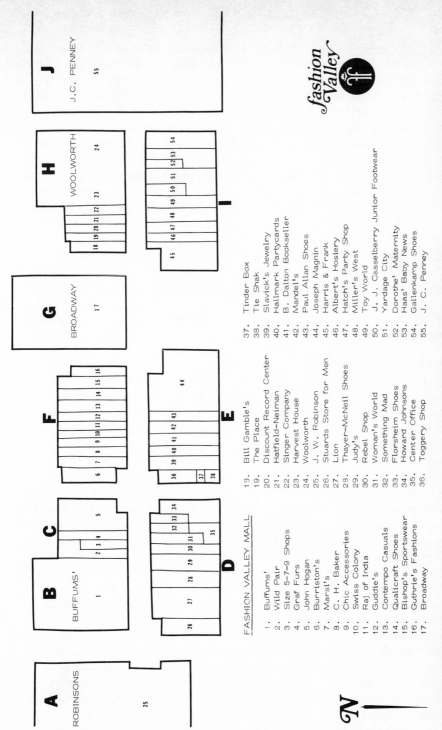

Figure 9-2 Store layout of planned regional shopping center. (*Courtesy of Fashion Valley Management Association, San Diego*)

FASHION VALLEY MALL

1. Buffums'
2. Wild Pair
3. Size 5-7-9 Shops
4. Graf Furs
5. John Hogan
6. Burriston's
7. Marsi's
8. C. H. Baker
9. Chic Accessories
10. Swiss Colony
11. Raj of India
12. Guddie's
13. Contempo Casuals
14. Qualicraft Shoes
15. Bishop's Sportswear
16. Guthrie's Fashions
17. Broadway
18.
19. The Place
20. Discount Record Center
21. Hatfield-Neiman
22. Singer Company
23. Harvest House
24. Woolworth
25. J. W. Robinson
26. Stuards Store for Men
27. Lion
28. Thayer-McNeil Shoes
29. Judy's
30. Rebel Shop
31. Woman's World
32. Something Mad
33. Florsheim Shoes
34. Howard Johnsons
35. Center Office
36. Toggery Shop
37. Tinder Box
38. Tie Shak
39. Slavick's Jewelry
40. Hallmark Partycards
41. B. Dalton Bookseller
42. Mandel's
43. Paul Allan Shoes
44. Joseph Magnin
45. Harris & Frank
46. Albert's Hosiery
47. Hatch's Party Shop
48. Miller's West
49. Toy World
50. J. J. Casselberry Junior Footwear
51. Yardage City
52. Dorothe' Maternity
53. Haas' Baby News
54. Gallenkamp Shoes
55. J. C. Penney

19. Bill Gamble's

service. For example, a customer who believes that one of the stores in the center did not properly satisfy a complaint may take the matter up with the shopping center association, which then acts as a mediator in the dispute. The association acts as an overall management system for the center, resolving retailer conflicts and problems as they arise.

The anchor stores may act as developers of planned regional shopping centers. For instance, some regional shopping centers have been developed by The May Company department stores. The Broadway department store in Southern California also plans and develops shopping centers as do several other major stores, such as the following: Allied Stores Corporation; Sears, Roebuck and Company through its Homart Development Company; Food Fair Properties, Inc., which develops for Food Fair Stores; and the Gamble Development Company which was formed by the Gamble-Skogmo, Inc., Stores. These retailing giants sponsor, plan, and develop regional shopping centers, and also serve as the anchor stores. These retailing stores then seek specialty retailers to complement the center or even find one or more additional anchor stores for a center. Thus, a center may be planned, sponsored, and developed by a retailer such as Broadway, but will also include other large retailers such as Sears, Penney's, Montgomery Ward's, or Robinson's.

Leases

The shopping center association usually negotiates a lease for space for the specialty retailers which will lend support to the anchor stores. At times, leases will be negotiated directly with the developer of the center. The retail members of the shopping center association are assessed fees which are used to support the association in its public relations and advertising work.

These leases usually are negotiated on a square footage basis, that is, a flat rental fee plus a stated percentage of either gross or net sales, or some combination of these arrangements. Lease arrangements vary considerably from center to center and different geographical locations, and may be from $10 to over $17 per square foot per year. For example, one West Coast planned regional shopping center offers two plans for specialty retailers: (1) if a specialty retailer desires a 900 square foot space in the center, the annual rental fee would be $17.50 per square foot per year; or (2) if a retailer needs more space in the center, a 3,000-square-foot store would cost the tenant $10 per square foot per year. Both of these are minimum rental fees which are then credited to a fixed percentage of gross sales, such as 8 percent in this instance. Also, in addition to this minimum rent a retailer is required to pay for common area maintenance, real estate taxes, and dues for the merchant's association. These assessments approximate $1.50 per square foot per year. Other leases may contain provisions for increased rent due to inflationary factors or a "step-up" provision which increases the rent as the merchant's sales volume rises. In many instances, the landlord or owner of the center provides only the building shell. The retailer (leasee) is required to install air conditioning, electrical wiring, plumbing, and the storefront. In essence, the retailer must improve the property from the basic "shell" structure. In addition, the retailer must bear all expenses for store fixtures and display cases.

Since leases vary considerably with respect to provisions and restrictions, it would be well for any retailer contemplating a move to a planned regional shopping center, before signing a lease, to have an attorney review the provisions of the lease. Since shopping center leases are expensive, considerable profitable sales volume must be generated. Several factors that affect the potential profitability of the retail store could also lead to reduced sales for retailers. Reduced net profits could create a hardship for many small retailers if their rent fee is tied to the sales volume since the rent fee continues, and the lease is a legal binding contract.

Usually, planned shopping centers are built only after considerable research indicates that the market in a particular trade area has potential. For the small specialty retailer, leasing space in a regional shopping center eliminates some of the steps in the retail business plan. However, in the more rapidly developing urban and suburban areas, certain developers of planned shopping centers are not exercising caution. Some centers are being constructed too close to already existing centers, which may lead to inadequate sales volume for both centers. You may find several planned shopping centers within a mile of each other, even though each offers basically the same type of goods and services. These risks should be carefully weighed by an individual retailer before signing a lease for space in a shopping center. Of course, refined marketing research techniques should be employed by the developers of a shopping center so as to prevent catastrophic consequences for the retailers involved as well as the owners of the center. In planning regional shopping centers, careful attention must be devoted to: market potential, competition, desirability of anchor tenants and supporting tenants, and provision of the proper retailing mix (both in terms of retailers and in terms of goods and service offerings).

During its first year in existence, planned regional shopping centers may average $100 a square foot in gross sales, rising to over $200 a square foot after the center has become established. The sales and sales-supporting area of the anchor stores, such as Penney's, Sears, Bullock's, Ward's, Dayton's, or others, will consist of approximately 200,000 square feet. The supporting stores of the center (such as men's and women's specialty apparel stores) may have around 7,200 square feet of space. Other specialty stores range from 1,850 to 23,000 square feet depending on the type of retail business. A variety store such as J. J. Newberry's may occupy 37,000 square feet in a planned regional shopping center. Since the center should make it easy for the customer to shop, the merchandising mix within the center should be highly selective. Paying close attention to these details and features will contribute to the profitability of the planned regional shopping center and the retailers leasing space in the center.

Neighborhood Shopping Center

A forerunner to the planned regional shopping center was the neighborhood shopping center in which there are from five to fifteen stores mostly offering convenience goods and services. The purpose of the neighborhood shopping center is to serve the immediate needs of approximately 2,500 to 7,500 people and be located within a few minutes drive of those families. For example, a neighborhood shopping center may consist of one grocery supermarket, a drug-store, possibly a variety store, and several small service stores. Service stores may include a shoe repair store, a dry-cleaning establishment, a barbershop, a beauty salon, possibly a bank, and other specialty shops. Whatever the combination of stores, the neighborhood shopping center serves the purpose of meeting the immediate needs of the people who live in that area.

Most of these neighborhood centers are constructed by an individual, or company, who owns the land or a small corporation who has purchased it. There is often little or no planning in the neighborhood development. Since many of these centers are not well planned, they may not be very accessible, and the immediate trade area may not have enough potential customers. As a result, the stores in the center will often suffer a loss of retail sales. It is not uncommon to find several neighborhood shopping centers within a few blocks of one another. Many recently constructed neighborhood shopping centers seem to be a result of not knowing what to do with idle commercial land. However, enough proof is available to conclude that the same type of planning should go into neighborhood shopping centers as goes into planned regional shopping centers. The same principles apply—it is only a matter of degree.

Isolated Store Sites

It is not uncommon to find isolated stores which are far removed from any neighborhood or planned regional shopping center. Many are convenience stores such as local grocery stores, gasoline service stations, office-supply specialty stores, or restaurants. Others may include discount stores, which tend to locate in a lower rent district of a city, or furniture and decorating establishments. Isolated stores generally are found along major roads or along crossroads where accessibility is easy, especially for customers who are attracted from considerable distances. Most of these isolated stores attract customers by using powerful and persuasive advertising and retail sales promotion; they do not rely solely on the traffic passing by. When such stores are located along main roads of travel on the way to a planned shopping center, a high volume of traffic will pass these places of business, and it is possible that many customers will stop and shop. However, to be effective, these retailers will have to employ "traffic stoppers," that is, ways and means of getting customers to stop, shop, and buy. As land costs continue to rise, it is possible that more retailers may gravitate to such locations in order to reduce costs and stay away from the higher priced neighborhood or planned regional shopping centers.

SPECIFIC RETAIL STORE LOCATION

The proper location of a retail store is probably one of the most important steps in developing a retail business plan. A good location will contribute significantly to the success of a retail store. Although the location will not offset management inefficiencies it will, nevertheless, play a vital role in the viability of a retail store. Before any sales can be made, customers must be able to find the store easily and be able to park while shopping. As with the appraisal of the market potential, the selection of a specific site must also follow certain market considerations.

As you discovered in the evaluation of a general trading area, a determination of the estimated sales volume generated by a specific location must be made as accurately as possible. Thus, it becomes a matter of "macro" versus "micro" in the estimation of sales volume for a particular location. In other words, how does a retailer go about determining sales volume for a specific location? One can make accurate estimates of a location's potential annual sales volume in several ways. First, it is well for a retailer to know how well the proposed store's competitors have done in previous years in selling comparable goods and services. Although these figures may not be obtainable directly from the retailers, they can be gotten from other sources, such as competitors, trade associations, and the like. Even the sales representatives from the suppliers and the wholesalers are good sources of such information. A survey of competitors, pitting one against the other, will often lead to well-informed estimates of the sales volume for a particular store. As stated previously, competitors often will reveal which retailer is the leader in a community.

Still another method of estimating the sales volume for certain goods is to take the total sales figures for an area and divide by the number of retailers selling these goods. You will remember that this total sales figure can be obtained from *Sales Management's* "Survey of Buying Power." Another source may be a city or country publication or the chamber of commerce may have materials with total sales figures for a city or a town. It is well that a retailer seek answers to the following questions before locating in a particular site:

1   Where do the proposed or existing stores' customers live?
2   How often do the customers visit the store?
3   How long have the customers or potential customers lived in the trade area?
4   How are the customers or potential customers segmented among women, men, couples, and children?
5   What is the major source of income, and what income groups are represented in the trade area?

After a retailer has made a determination of the possible sales volume for a specific location, a sales volume target or goal must then be set for that store. This figure should be realistic because existing retailers in the trade area are usually in a better position to counter any retailing mix which a new retailer may employ. For new retailers, this is an important and often overlooked consideration.

Among larger retailers, chains in particular, formulas are often used in determining the sales potential of a specific location. Often a comparison is made of a comparable store in a similar location, although this method has its drawbacks. First, comparable stores in so-called similar locations may differ in sales volume because of differences in: (1) the buying habits of the population, (2) the traditions of the population, (3) the mores of the people, (4) the customs of the area. Rarely does one find two cities or localities which are identical. But without relying too heavily upon sales figures, comparing one store to another may provide one with a very general estimate of sales volume.

Perhaps a more sophisticated technique of determining sales volume for a specific site is to use a formula, such as sales per counter foot, sales per square foot, or by using a traffic count. For example, one food store chain in California projects a proposed store's sales volume in the following manner. Management determines the number of adult residents in a specific trade area. This number is multiplied by $12, which has been determined as the average per capita weekly food expenditure. From this figure, a determination is made as to how much competing food stores will extract from the area. Then management adds to this figure a factor which accounts for any "plus" trade in food sales drawn from other areas. This methodology works fairly well for determining potential food store sales volume because food items are fairly standardized and the weekly consumption of food remains reasonably stable. People tend to eat about the same amount of food although dollar figures can fluctuate due to rising food prices.

For example, during the summer and fall of 1973, there was a meat shortage. Grocery supermarkets experienced a major drop in meat sales. This was a result of the consumers refusing to buy meat at the higher prices which had risen sharply during the summer because of a general meat shortage throughout the country. However, the total food dollars spent by the customers remained fairly constant. The consumers were boycotting meat, but they were buying some other food product in its place. Thus, the per capita food expenditure remained fairly constant.

The method given above works fairly well for food but is somewhat less reliable for determining the sales volume for other types of goods—especially items which fall into the discretionary classification. With impulse items and luxury items, it is much easier for the consumer to withhold his or her purchase than with food items. Also, there is less standardization with discretionary items than one finds with food items.

TRENDS IN RETAIL STORE LOCATION

As has been stated before, retail store location is perhaps one of the most critical elements of the retail business plan. Thus, in selecting a specific store location, the retailer continues to search for an improved way or means that will eliminate some of the risks. A method that is receiving increasingly greater attention is the use of written models and computer analysis. Written models represent factual situations. A model expresses the relationship between a set of marketing variables and serves as a guide for making decisions. When constructed, a model will include those variables necessary for site location evaluation: (1) population, (2) population density and concentration, (3) spendable and disposable income, (4) traffic flow and analysis, (5) buying power, and so on. Any variable deemed appropriate can be included in the construction of a model. The basic purpose of including variables in a model is to determine the interrelationships of these variables.

Since many business decisions concerning store location may be based on educated guesses, hunches, past experiences, or executive intuition, the retailer must have more reliable information for improved decisions. A model which includes the many variables deemed essential for store location serves as a frame of reference for the decision maker. Valid models will reveal the relationships of these variables under consideration and will serve to add clarity to the problem of retail store location. This process is called "explication" which means an explanation or interpretation of the relationships among the variables. Therein lies the value of models for use in retail store location selection. Since models aid in the prediction of probable sales results from various site locations, their use will continue to grow as retailers become aware of their value in the selection of store locations.

In the final analysis, a retailer should define the store's objectives, determine the type and size of the store, the goods and service mix the store will offer to its customers, the type of promotional appeals to be used, and establish policies on growth for the store. After these analyses have been done, the economic base of the trade area should be analyzed, a study should be made of the population and its characteristics, and a survey of the competition and its aggressiveness should be completed.

SUMMARY

The *location of a retail business* is very significant since a store's environment does not remain static but either improves or deteriorates. Because of population shifts and changes, the increasing number of planned regional shopping centers, continually rising land costs, and changing urban social conditions, greater attention is being devoted to retail site location.

Yet another reason retail store location is a critical element is the rising rate of *retail store failure*. Even the largest planned regional shopping centers with all the marketing resources and expertise, are faced with the problem of retail store mortality due to: obsolescence, changes and shifts in population, construction of newer shopping centers with the latest amenities, and the ever-present changing consumer desires.

The value of a specific retail site tends to change over time. Some values change rather quickly whereas others slowly become less valuable over a longer period of time. Retailers often will continue to occupy a specific location long after the site has lost its consumer appeal.

Although no single factor by itself determines the *value of a specific site,* there are three elements when combined that will aid in the determination of the worth of a location. These three elements are: (1) the general trade area, (2) traffic flow and its analysis, and (3) the population and its mobility.

Generally, a retailer has some idea or preference as to the general area where the store will be located. There are several factors to keep in mind in making a decision whether or not to locate a store in a certain trade area. For example, the *social considerations* of the local population should weigh heavily on the decision to locate a store in a particular community. These social considerations include: (1) the population characteristics of a community, (2) the attitudes and progressiveness of the people residing in that community, (3) consumer buying habits, and (4) any special features which would attract customers from some distance.

Probably no one single factor is more important to a retailer than the *population* of a community. However, a retailer must determine whether the population of a community is increasing, decreasing, or remaining static.

Often a trade area which has a large proportion of younger married couples is preferred by retailers over a community which consists mostly of older persons. Young married couples generally have rising incomes, whereas older persons may be living on fixed incomes.

Generally, a younger, more *progressive community* will promote and attract more people to the trade area. The more people that a trading area attracts, the more likely the purchasing power of the community will be increased.

A retailer should *analyze the buying habits* of the residents of a trade area because the people living in the community may have buying habits and patterns which are different from what a retailer expects.

Several *economic considerations* will qualify or disqualify a community as a prospective trade area in which to locate a retail store. These economic factors include: (1) income, (2) competition, (3) transportation facilities, and (4) services.

The amount, kind, and type of *traffic* that passes any specific location is highly significant to retailers. Usually, the heavier the traffic count, the greater the potential sales volume.

The *mobility of population* is important to retailers because population mobility—whether from rural to urban, urban to suburban, or community to community—causes customers' shopping habits and desires to change.

Planned regional shopping centers are controlled and directed units which offer the consumer complementary shopping convenience. Usually, planned regional shopping centers have two or more anchor stores which may be national chain stores. Planned regional shopping centers often gross $200 a square foot after the center has become established.

Neighborhood shopping centers serve the immediate needs of about 2,500 to 7,500 people located within a few minutes drive.

Isolated stores are removed from both planned regional shopping centers and neighborhood shopping centers. Many isolated stores are convenience establishments such as local grocery stores, gasoline service stations, office-supply specialty stores, service stores, and restaurants.

There are several methods by which a retailer can make accurate *estimates of a location's potential* annual sales volume. First, a retailer should know how well the proposed store's competitors have done in previous years in selling comparable goods and services. Second, sales figures from *Sales Management's* "Survey of Buying Power" will provide a retailer with total sales volume data for an area. Third, a city, county or chamber of commerce may have data concerning sales potential of a trade area.

Before settling on a specific site, a retailer should obtain answers to the following questions: (1) Where do the proposed, or existing, store's customers live? (2) How often do the customers visit the store? (3) How long have the customers or potential customers lived in the trade area? (4) How are the customers or potential customers segmented among women, men, couples, and children? (5) What is the major source of income, and what income groups are represented in the trade area? After these questions have been answered, the retailer is ready to establish a sales-volume target for the store.

REVIEW QUESTIONS

1 Why is retail store location so significant to the success of a retailer?
2 Discuss the three elements which when combined aid in the determination of the worth of a retail store location.
3 Discuss the importance of the social characteristics of a general trade area.
4 Explain the importance of the economic considerations of a general trade area for retail store location.
5 Discuss the importance of traffic flow and analysis in determining a retail store location.
6 Why is the analysis of consumer profiles valuable in determining a retail store location?
7 What is a planned regional shopping center?
8 What are anchor stores? What are complementary retail stores?
9 Discuss some of the merits of leasing space in a planned regional shopping center.
10 How does a neighborhood shopping center differ from a planned regional shopping center?
11 Discuss the conditions under which it may be more prudent for a retailer to locate a store in an isolated area.
12 List a number of factors which bear directly on a retailer's decision to locate a store on a specific site.
13 Discuss some of the trends in retail-store-site location.

Chapter 10

Retail Store Design
and Interior Layout

Although the basic purpose of exterior design and interior layout is to promote profitable sales volume, many retailers give little thought to merchandise arrangement, fixtures, space allocation, or decoration. Sufficient attention should be devoted to a store's exterior design and interior layout so that the proper atmosphere is created for the type of consumers being served. Every retail institution has a personality and image which either attracts or repels customers. Other factors—such as lighting, use of color and music, and the attitude of sales personnel—will also create impressions which often are long lasting.

In order to attain a proper impression, the store image that is created should be consistent with the overall managerial philosophy concerning merchandising, pricing, and promotion. For example, if a store's appeal is to be one of economy and is based on low-priced merchandise, then an elegant and richly decorated interior is not expected by the consumer and would be out of place in a discount retail store.

Creativity in interior store layout and design is not expensive, and each store interior should have and promote an identity all its own. A retail store should be physically arranged in accordance with a definite floor plan. Consideration should be devoted to selling areas, nonselling areas, traffic flows, and traffic patterns. For example, customers should not be able to enter and leave the store along a straight path. Instead, a traffic flow pattern should be designed which encourages customer browsing and purchasing. Lighting should not detract (by being too bright or by using very elaborate fixtures) from the merchandise but rather should highlight or spotlight the items on display. Colored lights and rock music may lure younger persons to a store. The combinations of design, lights, and music which can be used in exterior and interior design and layout are limited only by the retailer's creativity and, to some extent, finances.

After a retail site has been selected, the physical facility must be prepared for occupancy. This preparation will include either the design and construction of a new structure or the design and remodeling of an existing building. In either case, it is important to keep in mind that the basic retailing functions are the same. However, the efficiency and expediency with which these retailing activities are performed vary considerably. For instance, in a small retail store, these retailing activities may be performed differently from those performed in a large store. But whether a small store or a large store, the degree of efficiency is affected by the amount of planning and the type of arrangement in which these functions are organized for performance. In this respect, both a large and a small store could suffer from a degree of inefficiency because efficiency depends upon the internal organization and how well it was set up to carry out the processes within that retail store. Thus, the interior and exterior design and layout could readily affect those processes.

RETAIL STORE EXTERIORS

The newly constructed or remodeled retail stores of today are not reminiscent of retail stores of years ago. Today, much of the retail store construction reflects the use of natural materials, such as stone and wood. In some instances, use is being made of concrete, steel, copper, and brick. There has been and is a trend away from the rectangular buildings which give the appearance of many "boxes" in a row. Currently, the construction theme leans more toward some type of individualism rather than the identical "me-too" structures of a decade or two ago. Retailers are beginning to become aware that the front or outside appearance of a retail store often sells the consumer on that particular retail institution and the exterior of a store should reflect the image of a viable institution. Further, a store front should extend an invitation to the consumer to enter and spend some time browsing and inspecting merchandise. This often leads to retail purchases—which, after all, is the basic goal of every retailer.

Many consumers judge a retail store by its outward appearance. A well-designed store will feature an attractive front and entrance, at times pleasing window displays, and an entry which is particularly inviting to the consumer. The physical storefront, together with window displays and the entrance, often "sell" the consumer on that particular store. Since there is considerable latitude in designing a physical storefront, window display area, and entryway, each retail store should be designed to reflect a personality and image all its own. Too often, retail stores reflect the owner's concern for cost savings with a me-too

Figure 10-1 Photograph of storefront. *(Courtesy of Bullock's Wilshire, Woodland Hills)*

type of frontal design and structure since management can copy or buy ready-made plans, whereas for a few extra dollars or an extra bit of creative effort the store could have a much improved or even innovative outward design. Sometimes only a small additional amount of money is required to design the front of a retail store creatively, but the difference to the consumer may be well worth the expense.

Retail storefronts should be designed with the consumer in mind and should extend an invitation to the consumer to enter, browse, compare, and shop. Since a retail storefront is always in evidence before the consuming public, much like a television celebrity, it should "dress" for the occasion—the only difference being that the occasion never ends for the retail store. Even after closing hours, people often stroll along and window shop. Through the good use of window displays, the retailer has an excellent opportunity to arouse consumers' interest so that they will return to the store during shopping hours.

Store entrances should be wide, attractive and inviting, and should avoid the customer congestion that accompanied the use of revolving doors a few years ago. The more modern storefronts often are completely devoid of doors during hours of operation. Many doors have been replaced with flows of air (warm or cold depending on the location and climate) in an entryway which allows easy access to the store's interior. This type of store entrance is much more inviting to the consumer, providing an atmosphere of "openness." During closing hours, a large door then secures the store for the night.

Of course, one could well ask the question, "Why devote so much time and attention to the design and structure of a retail store?" Since land and construction costs continue to rise in all parts of the country, the retailer is caught in a profit squeeze and should reduce costs wherever possible. At the same time, a retailer should attempt to maximize the dollars spent to design a retail store by making prudent use of space allocation, materials, and other factors which will differentiate the store from competing retail institutions. This could well provide a retailer with the competitive edge needed in today's retailing environment. It is for these reasons that the retailer needs to obtain maximum efficiency from all aspects of the operation of the business. For example, a nationally franchised fast-food retailing chain recently purchased a 7,500-square-foot corner of land in downtown San Diego, California for $75,000. By the time a building is constructed, equipment and fixtures are installed, and lighting is provided, this franchised retailer will have made a total investment of nearly $250,000 *before* opening the doors. Thus, all physical operational aspects of the business had better be oriented toward bringing in the customers, or the retailer may find the store in financial trouble.

To provide another example, one West Coast fast-food chain breaks down construction costs in the following manner:

Land size	20,000 square feet minimum
Land cost	$5–$10 per square foot depending on location and traffic count
Building	2,000 square feet; total cost of building: $90,000
Site work	Paving, parking: $25,000
Equipment, signs, lighting	$50,000

Even leasing costs are expensive for a small retail store. For instance, a well-known, small convenience store recently leased 2,400 square feet of space in a neighborhood shopping center for 20 years at a price of $252,000. These figures indicate that the store rental is $1,050 each month, or $12,600 per year for the next twenty years. This is approximately 44 cents per square foot rental fee each month, which indicates that the store must generate considerable profitable sales volume in order to be able to meet expenses each month. In other instances, planned regional shopping centers charge a minimum of $17.50 per square foot plus 8 percent of gross sales for any retail store up to 3,000 square feet. Larger facilities in planned regional shopping centers may rent for $10 per square foot per year plus 8 percent of gross sales.

A newly located and constructed grocery supermarket will cost approximately $1.5 million before it is completed, exclusive of inventory. A large discount retailer may invest a total of $5 million, whereas a large department store may cost as much as $15 million. As a result of continuing rising costs of design, construction, and layout, retailers are becoming increasingly more conscious of the importance of cooperating with architects; land appraisers; lighting, heating, and air-conditioning engineers; marketing specialists in store equipment and layout; and designers for interior store color coordination.

RETAIL STORE DESIGN AND INTERIOR LAYOUT

Objectives

The basic objectives of retail store design and interior layout are twofold:

1   To attract consumers to the store for the maximization of profitable sales volume and to obtain the greatest gross margin per square foot of selling space
2   To design and arrange for the performance of retailing operations and activities, with overall objectives of keeping retailing expenses at a minimum

Gross margin, sometimes referred to as gross profit, is the difference between the cost of the merchandise and the selling price of those goods. Different kinds of merchandise carry different gross margins, or markup. Markup is expressed as a percentage of the retail price and is the difference between the cost of the merchandise and the selling price. This will be covered in greater depth later in the text.

In order to meet these objectives, a retailer should devote considerable thought and attention to the elements which compose the above-mentioned goals. These elements include the proper allocation of space to each section or department, the location and arrangement of sections or departments which are compatible with one another, and the apportionment of nonsales space, which lends support to the selling areas of a store.

Profit Maximization

Profits can be maximized if particular attention is devoted to the gross margin per square foot of selling area. Gross margin is usually expressed as a percentage of sales and may vary considerably for different types and kinds of merchandise. Different types of merchandise also occupy varying amounts of floor space. For example, furniture is large and bulky and requires a lot of floor space. The gross margins on furniture are relatively high when compared to other merchandise, due in part to the considerable space occupied and in part to the infrequency of purchase. Depending on the type of retail store (discount or the more traditional furniture store), gross margins range from 40 to 100 percent of the selling price. However, selling space is also expensive since furniture is bulky and occupies a lot of floor area. Thus, this fact may also justify the relatively high gross margins associated with furniture retailing. To place furniture in proper perspective, one must realize that the display of furniture often requires two to three times the amount of floor space as the display of glass and glass stemware or silver flatware. This basic retailing phenomenon of space allocation and space occupancy has given rise to the warehouse retailing concepts fostered by large national chains, which sell the same merchandise at much lower gross margins than the traditional furniture retailers.

When merchandise is sold in a store, the retailer has "marked up" each item; that is, the merchant has added to the cost of the merchandise an amount which will cover the store's expenses and provide the store with a profit. Merchandise which carries a markup in relation to the space occupied and the rate of inventory turnover (RITO), will produce the greatest dollar gross margin within a given period of time if the goods are located where the largest number of consumers will be able to purchase them. Some types of merchandise turn over very rapidly, but the markup percentage may be so small that the goods contribute only a small portion of the total gross margin of the store. Yet other merchandise may sell more slowly but may carry a large enough gross margin to make an important contribution to the total gross margin for the store.

In a retail store, different classifications of merchandise occupy varying amounts of floor space. The different areas of floor space, or the different departments, may produce varying rates of gross margin. For instance, in a grocery supermarket, the grocery department may produce the largest percentage of total sales for the store but may rank lowest as a producer of gross margin per square foot of selling area. The dairy department may rank below the grocery department as a producer of sales volume for the store, but may outrank the grocery department in gross margin per square foot of space occupied. For instance, the following illustration has been provided by one West Coast grocery chain (which prefers to remain anonymous):

Department	Percentage of store sales	Gross margin, cents/sq ft	Average mark up, %
Grocery	39	26	17
Meat	36	61	18.5
Produce	13	47	23
Dairy	13	64	21
Bakery	6	27	25
Frozen foods	3	25	24

From the above figures, it becomes apparent that a retailer should determine the amount of space to be allocated to certain departments or to certain classifications of merchandise. Basic considerations include the physical characteristics of the goods (whether the merchandise is small or bulky) and the amount of money returned to the store (the gross margin per square foot of space occupied). In order to attain a given sales volume for large bulky items, such as furniture, the retailer must allocate more space than for china and stemware. Or, as in the case of the grocery supermarket, it may be wise to allocate additional space for dairy items and meat products because of the relatively high gross margin per square foot of selling space occupied in the store.

It is rather obvious that the right merchandise should be located in the right place within a store. However, from a practical viewpoint, not all merchandise can be strategically located in a store. The placing of goods in a store requires considerable study and skill in merchandising techniques, but there are some basic fundamentals which will aid a retailer in the arrangement of the merchandise in the store and, in turn, may lead toward higher profits for the retailer.

Placement of Merchandise

Impulse items are goods which customers will buy "upon sight" even though they had no prior thought of purchasing these items. Goods that are purchased on impulse are small in size, of low unit value, have a rapid rate of inventory turnover (RITO), and carry a relatively high gross margin when compared to other goods. Since impulse goods must be seen to be purchased, they should be located where the items will be viewed by the greatest number of customers.

In department stores with multiple stories, merchandise of an impulse nature usually is found displayed on the main floor. In small, single retail stores, placement of impulse goods should be along the main aisles where there is high customer traffic or at the ends of the main aisles or gondolas. Merchandise placed in these locations will be seen by the greatest number of people. Since impulse items rely "upon sight" by the customer to be purchased, it is only good merchandising strategy to place such items in the areas of greatest sales potential. Merchandise which cannot be seen by the customer often is not purchased simply because the customers are hesitant to ask salespeople for assistance.

Some types of merchandise exert strong "pulling power"; that is, these goods seem to attract a lot of consumer attention. A retailer can build and direct customer traffic by the strategic placement of these items in the store. For instance, have you ever wondered why most grocery supermarkets locate the meat either on an outside aisle or near the rear of the store? This is done in order to direct customer traffic through the store or to the rear of the store. While the customer is on the way toward the meat counter, he or she will pass many other items and may select and purchase them. Since the evening meal is usually planned around some type of meat or fish dish, the grocery supermarket management is employing good sound merchandising strategy by directing the consumer through several areas or around other areas, before reaching the meat counter. It is possible and may be a good idea for a retailer to experiment with various locations for certain types of merchandise. It may lead to a better merchandise arrangement which will lead to increased gross profit margins per square foot of selling area for the store. In turn, this may lead to greater net profits from the sale of merchandise which has been located in areas of greater consumer exposure.

Merchandise which requires considerable deliberation on the part of the consumer, should be located away from impulse items. Failure to do so often causes congestion in the store during the busier hours of operation. People who are comparison shopping or thinking about a major purchase often ask the salesperson many questions and do not appreciate being interrupted by other shoppers. In the case of a durable good, the consumer may wish to examine the merchandise physically, or even ask for a demonstration. Thus, merchandise which may have to be demonstrated should be located near an area where space and facilities are available, and the demonstration can proceed without interruption. This is the best way for a salesperson to obtain the undivided attention of the prospective customer and, in turn, the best opportunity for a potential customer to ask questions and not be bothered in the deliberation of the purchase decision.

Since many customers frequently use and purchase related merchandise at the same time, goods which are used together should be located in adjacent areas. For example, men's neckties, tiepins, and cuff links should be placed near the men's shirts. Paint brushes, thinner, rollers, and paint should be placed together. Film should be located near the cameras, as should flashbulbs and other camera accessories. The placement of similar merchandise can also assist the sales personnel resulting in "plus selling" or plus sales, which in turn may indicate higher sales volume and profits for the retailer. Since so many customers shop without the benefit of a shopping list, the salesperson should always be alert to assist the customer in the purchase of related merchandise. Suggested or plus selling is where the salesperson suggests to the customer that the purchase of a related item could be used, such as a necktie to go with a shirt or paint thinner to clean paint brushes or to thin the paint. Suggested selling, or "plus selling" can save the customer money and time since it may eliminate a return trip to the store (or a competitor's store) for additional items, and the retailer benefits from additional sales volume. A failure to suggest the purchase of additional items to the customer is a very common failing of many merchandisers. This appears to be especially true in today's retailing environment where depersonalized service appears to be more prevalent than the personalized retailing. For those salespeople working on a commission basis, suggesting and selling additional merchandise to the customer can mean more money in their pockets. In many instances, the customer appreciates this type of personalized service and does not resent a salesperson's offering further suggestions for purchasing merchandise.

BASIC DETERMINANTS OF INTERIOR STORE DESIGN AND LAYOUT

The interior design and layout of any retail store depends on a number of factors: (1) the amount of floor space with which one has to work; (2) the nature of the store (self-service, self-selection, limited service, or full-service); (3) the type, kind, and amount of merchandise offered for sale; and (4) the personal preference of the owner/manager, since to some degree, the interior of the store reflects the personality of the owner-manager—creative and innovative, conservative and reserved, or somewhere in between.

In today's highly competitive retailing environment, retailers should strive to make the interior of the store as attractive and inviting as possible. It does not cost much more to design a store's interior so it reflects an individualized, agreeable atmosphere. Consumers like to browse and shop in an aesthetically attractive store; space allocation and apportionment aid in developing a pleasing store interior.

Interior Space Apportionment

One of the first steps in planning interior space allocation is to determine the number of square feet available. After this has been accomplished, space then must be apportioned to the selling and nonselling areas (receiving, marking, and storage of goods). Before finalizing a retail store's space allocation, the retailer should review a number of factors which influence and affect to considerable degree the interior space allocation of a retail store: for example, such factors as the type of retail store operation (self-service, etc.), type of goods handled, need for sales-supporting areas, width of aisles, receiving, storage room requirements—each of these must be placed in the proper perspective and relationship to each other. It is this "total overall plan" for the store's interior with which we are concerned. The store must function as a "total operating system" if it is to be successful and profitable.

Selling Areas   In any retail store, the selling areas are most important to the store's success. Nonsales or supporting areas assist the overall operation but are not as important as the revenue-generating selling areas.

Table 10-1   Space Allocation for a Mini-Department Store

Retail store size	In sq ft
Total selling area	32,000
Total non-selling area	7,000
Total	39,000

Total selling area	In sq ft
General merchandise	10,000
Prescriptions and social expression (includes cosmetics, health and beauty aids, greeting cards, gift wrapping, and paperback books)	6,000
Franchised cosmetics (Max Factor and Revlon, for example)	1,000
Fabrics	3,200
Fashion merchandise	8,300
Glassware, housewares, cleaning supplies	2,500
Seasonal items (Easter, back to school, Christmas, Thanksgiving, Valentine's Day, etc.)	1,000
Total	32,000

Figure 10-2 Location of goods in selling areas. *(Photograph courtesy of FedMart, San Diego)*

It is equally important for small stores to be well designed with respect to selling areas as it is for large department stores. Space in a small store is usually more limited than in a large store, and this lack of space may create an even greater need for good floor planning. Close attention must be devoted to the displaying of goods because improper layout reduces the amount of merchandise that can be attractively merchandised and displayed.

Each type of retail store should be viewed as having prime selling space, and the sales-supporting areas should be designed around the selling areas of the store. Although there are no set procedures by which one can arrange the interior of a retail store, certain fundamental standards of arranging a store's interior should be considered.

1 *Convenience Goods* Self-service and self-selection retail stores are good examples of retail institutions which offer convenience goods to the consumer. Convenience goods are those which require little purchasing effort on the part of the customer and virtually no selling effort on the part of the retailer. Some examples of convenience goods include food staples like flour, sugar, coffee, bread, eggs, meat, and some paper products. However, the arrangement of convenience goods within the store is significant if customers are to purchase these items.

Convenience goods should be located in high traffic areas. Aisles should be fairly wide to accommodate customer traffic flow and to allow ample space for browsing and inspection of merchandise. In addition, convenience goods must be arranged on the shelf in order to facilitiate the purchase of such items. For instance, nearly all modern grocery supermarkets are arranged with wide aisles, low shelving, and the merchandise is often at eye level for consumer convenience.

2 Impulse Goods   Impulse goods are those which are purchased with little or no forethought on the part of the consumer. Examples of impulse goods are soft drinks, magazines, candy, chewing gum, snack-food items, and cigarettes. These items should be placed in high traffic areas, preferably near the ends of the aisles and the gondolas. For instance, potato chips, candy bars, and other snack items in grocery supermarkets are usually placed near or on the end of shelving, or on the end of the aisles. Ladies' hosiery is another impulse item that is usually displayed in a prominent area at eye level where the

Figure 10-3 Location of goods in selling areas. *(Photograph courtesy of FedMart, San Diego)*

consumer will easily see such items. Often, items of this nature are arranged on a rotating rack near the end of a gondola. For instance, some grocery supermarkets offer sewing materials to the consumer on a spindle, which may be serviced by a rack jobber. (A rack jobber is a full-function wholesaler who sells nonfood items primarily to grocery supermarkets.)

3 *Shopping Goods*   Shopping goods are those goods for which a consumer spends considerable time and effort in comparing different brands or makes of the same product. Such factors as product features, styles, as well as price, are compared and evaluated by the consumer. Shopping goods are so named because a consumer "shops" and compares different brands and product features. Some examples of shopping goods include appliances, television sets, automobiles, radios, and furniture.

A retail store that sells shopping goods should give careful consideration to the in store "direction" of customer traffic. Traffic should be deliberately routed through the areas which will induce the most merchandise comparison and stimulate purchases. Usually, but not always, the higher priced merchandise is placed near the rear of the store so that the customer must walk past all the goods. In this way, the customer is exposed to more goods and thus may be encouraged to buy. Also, after inspection of the less expensive items, a salesperson may often more easily persuade the customer to purchase a higher priced item.

For example, it is not unusual for a retailer to display a low-priced, customer-traffic-building item in the window or near the door. This sales promotional tactic will "pull" traffic into the store. The rest of the merchandise is then displayed in price-ascending order toward the rear of the store. A salesperson (after greeting the customer at the front of the store) is able to direct the customer's attention to the desired item(s), pointing out product features and customer benefits as they walk along the aisle. The strategy behind such an arrangement of the interior of the store is to get the customer exposed to as much merchandise as possible, because the greater the exposure, the more likely the customer is to purchase merchandise. Since higher priced items usually have more features than less expensive items, it is easier for the salesperson to keep the consumer's interest as they go through the store. Generally, one will discover that this arrangement (lower priced to higher priced goods) occurs in the stores selling high-fashion apparel, household appliances, and furniture.

4 *Specialty Goods*   Specialty goods are those which a customer will seek out even though considerable effort is required on his or her part. This could include certain goods in the convenience or shopping goods classifications because this product scheme is based on the buying habits of a majority of consumers. Therefore, it is conceivable that there is considerable overlapping between the product classifications. Specialty goods can best be described as those for which a customer deliberately goes out of the way, spends a lot of time searching, and specifies a certain brand of merchandise.

Actually, the original classification of consumer goods according to this scheme was predicated upon consumer buying habits. However, in essence, the

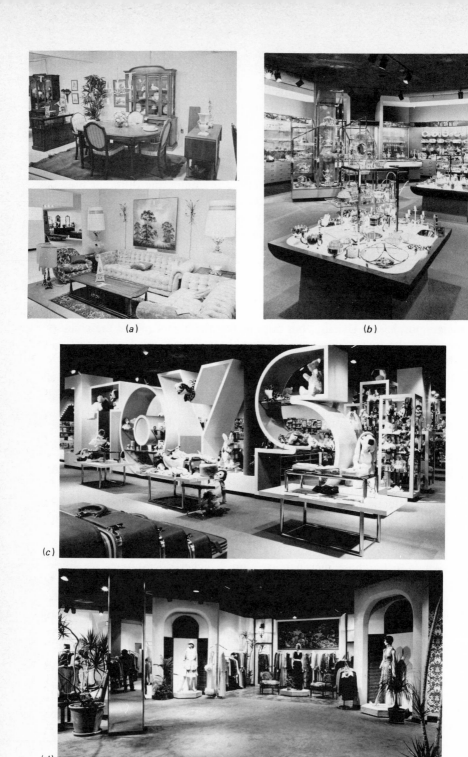

Figure 10-3a Location of goods in selling areas. (a) *(Photograph courtesy of Wickes, San Diego); (b) (Photograph courtesy of Bullock's, Los Angeles); (c) (Photograph courtesy of Bullock's, Los Angeles); (d) (Photograph courtesy of Bullock's, Los Angeles)*

amount of buying effort expended by the consumer is the determinant—that is, the consumer exerts very little effort on the purchase of impulse items and a great deal of effort on the purchase of specialty goods. Some examples of specialty goods include high-fashion merchandise, pipe tobacco, certain cosmetics, watches, some household appliances, and other items where brand preference by the consumer is a dominant purchase consideration. In other words, the consumer is unwilling to accept a substitute brand when purchasing specialty goods.

Usually specialty goods are associated with full-service retail stores. Since an inquiry usually must be made on the part of the customer, the salesperson may direct the customer to the correct area or department of the store or may assist the customer directly. In many instances, the salesperson must obtain the goods from behind the counter, from a locked rack, or from a special selling area. The basic strategy behind this approach is to have the salesperson persuade or sell the customer the merchandise. The approach is the opposite of self-service retailing where the customers serve themselves.

5 *Other Considerations*   If a retail store has more than one story, it is wise to display a portion of its offerings on the main level. This is referred to as "split departments" and is used by the retailer to promote a more complete offering to the customer. For example, high-fashion women's apparel may be on the third floor, however, the window display will offer one item from that department and one from the children's clothing department on the second floor. This tactic encourages the shopper to enter the store for further inspection, passing many items of merchandise on the way to the third floor and thereby encouraging the consumer to make an additional purchase. The more a retailer can expose a consumer to various goods, the greater the tendency for the consumer to buy.

Reserve merchandise or stock items should wisely be located near the selling area as customers do not like to be left alone for a very long period of time. A store's reserve merchandise or stock includes the items for which there is no room on the selling floor. If reserve goods are placed a long distance from the selling area, there is also wasted effort on the part of the salesperson if very many trips must be made. The more quickly items can be taken from the reserve stock, the more efficient customer service will be, and the customer will appreciate not having to wait long for the merchandise.

It is well to arrange the interior of a retail store so that complementary items are placed next to each other. Men's ties and shirts should not be far from the suit department in a specialty store. Shoes, socks, and accessories, too, should be placed in close proximity. This allows the customer to inspect the goods easily, and it also allows the salesperson to accomplish the plus selling mentioned above. For example, the current trend in clothing is toward the layered look or coordinates, both in women's and men's clothing. Since many accessory items carry relatively high gross margins, the additional selling of complementary items could add more sales volume and profits to the prudent retailer.

There is yet another purpose in carefully designing and arranging the exterior and interior layout of retail stores. From a managerial point of view, a retail store should be designed for a maximum of economic efficiency and ease of maintenance. The design should also provide adequate selling space, and have ample provisions for sales-supporting areas. A well-designed retail store facilitates the movement and flow of customer traffic and, at the same time, creates a pleasant environment for the customers' shopping convenience. Retail stores should be designed to help in the profitable operation of the type of business that is being conducted in that structure. For example, if a retail store is specializing in women's shoes, the exterior should be designed to attract women. Inside the store, merchandise should be arranged to allow ease of inspection and fitting. Mirrors and areas of carpeting should be available so that the shopper can view herself and, at the same time, not damage the goods while they are being fitted.

Prior retail store statistics indicate that a well-designed retail store—one that is effectively planned with respect to interior layout—will have an appreciably higher sales volume than a retail store which is poorly designed and arranged.

Nonselling Areas Nonselling areas or sales-supporting activities include receiving, marking and pricing, the storing of merchandise which is to be offered for sale, and customer service areas. These nonselling functions associated with retailing management also need to be arranged for operational efficiency of the store. Since these retailing functions in themselves will be covered in detail later in the text, coverage in this portion of the book will be devoted to the importance of locating these nonselling areas in an accessible position in relationship to the selling areas of the store.

1 *Receiving* Receiving merchandise in a small retail store is a simple operation which may amount to nothing more than signing a delivery receipt. Convenience and efficiency, in this case, dictate that the space allocated for receiving be near the rear of the store, with some provision for storing and marking the goods until they are moved to the selling areas of the store. In large retail stores, the receiving area may be the basement, the rear of the store, or some other area determined by ordinances regulating the flow of trucks. In either case, the space must be adequate to meet the needs of the store. The allocated space should have a relatively low value for purposes of selling and should be as close as possible to the stock room to reduce moving costs. A receiving area and the stock rooms should be close to the selling area in order to minimize the inconvenience and inefficiencies of moving the merchandise to the selling areas.

2 *Marking and Pricing* The marking of goods should take place immediately following receipt of the merchandise in order to minimize handling of the goods and to keep errors at a minimum. Goods that are unwrapped, inspected, and compared with the purchase order and the vendor's invoice should be marked and priced immediately and then moved to either the selling floor or to the storage area. Since the invoice is in hand as the goods are inspected, there will be less chance of mismarking and mispricing, or allowing the merchandise to reach the selling floor without a mark or a price.

3 *Storage* The storage area should be as near the selling area as feasible, as previously mentioned. In some instances, goods may be stored in remote

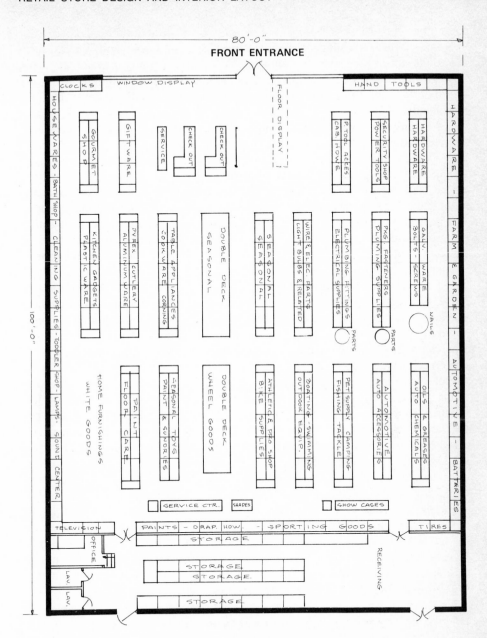

8,000 SQ. FT. PROTOTYPE STORE

Figure 10-4 Interior store arrangement. *(Courtesy of Coast-to-Coast Stores)*

areas, but this procedure leads to wasted effort and increased costs. For example, several warehouse furniture stores, such as Levitz and Wickes, have the goods stored very near the selling areas and the customer may actually walk through the storage area of these stores. This is a definite selling point as the consumer knows there will be no wait if the decision is made to buy the merchandise.

4 *Customer Service Areas*   Since a retail store is basically a customer service institution, the layout and design should have some provision for those areas which provide allied services to patrons. Such services include gift wrapping, return goods, customer complaints, decorating advice, checkrooms, postal facilities, utility payment counters, and restaurants. Usually only the large department stores or stores located in planned regional shopping centers will provide such a vast array of customer services. Small retailers may offer none of these services or perhaps just one or two customer services, but if a customer service is offered by the store, adequate space should be given for its proper functioning.

The allocation of interior space for customer services should be predicated on: (1) the frequency of usage, (2) the time during the shopping period when these services may be used, and (3) the customers' buying habits. Some customer services may be used by the individual at the beginning of the shopping tour, whereas others will be sought near the finish of the shopping trip. Still other customer services should be located near the merchandise which stimulates the use of such services—gift wrapping, mailing, credit, tailoring, and alterations. Since customers are more likely to shop for merchandise when they are less fatigued, they are more likely to take advantage of the customer services when they are tired. Thus, the customer service areas (like restrooms, wrapping desks, and postal services) should be located near each other. This will afford the consumer the most convenience.

Since some areas of a store are more valuable for selling areas than others, consideration should also be given to the value of such space. Generally, the less desirable the store space for selling, the more desirable the space will be for customer services. Often multistory department stores will provide space near the top floors for customer services, allowing the customer to take an elevator or an escalator to the customer service area. In many instances, these service areas also offer lounge and restroom facilities for the convenience of the customers in order to provide relaxation from the rigors of shopping.

CUSTOMER TRAFFIC FLOWS AND PATTERNS

Directly or indirectly, the flow and direction of customer traffic in a retail store may stimulate profitable sales volume for the owner. Thus, a retail store's entire layout and interior design should be considered from the viewpoint of how it affects or alters the direction and flow of customer traffic.

In general, customer traffic should be directed toward the areas where the emphasis is on the merchandising of goods. Special sale events or regular displays of goods should enjoy the fullest exposure to customer traffic. This particular merchandising strategy can be accomplished by carefully placing shelving, tables, or other display fixtures, or by offering narrow or wide aisles which attract or repel customers. If a retailer wishes to direct customer traffic toward a certain display of goods, this feat may be accomplished by offering the customer the easiest route to these goods. The wise use of point-of-purchase display materials (signs, lighting, tables) may be used to divert or direct customer flow and traffic patterns. It is necessary to keep in mind at all times the advantages of having customer traffic directed around and through all major displays and toward special promotional merchandise displays. The basic purpose of customer traffic control is to direct as many customers as possible past as many displays as feasible thereby increasing the purchasing opportunities for the customer. Since a retailer's goal is to stimulate customer satisfaction through the purchases he or she makes at a profit to the store, customers will appreciate being directed to the special values in the store. In turn, the retailer benefits by increasing the sales volume of the store.

Some areas or departments within the store are natural generators of customer traffic. The areas or departments which tend to attract more customer traffic should be placed in a relatively inaccessible part of the store. Areas which may be weak in attracting customers should be located near a readily accessible area of the store. This merchandising strategy will provide a retailer with a balanced arrangement within the store. Also, the arrangement of areas or departments will provide the best direction and flow of customer traffic.

To expand on this concept and to provide some illustration of this retailing strategy, think about the promotion of impulse items near the entrance or exit of a store. Impulse items, as you remember, are those which are purchased with little or no forethought on the part of the consumer. Thus, in order to sell impulse items, they must be located where customers will readily see and purchase these items, that is, at the entrance or exit of the store.

Another example would be the merchandising of special sale goods. Sale items usually are placed in the entryway or near the doorway of a retail store. Although this arrangement does result in a certain amount of customer traffic congestion, the strategy is to "pull" the customer into the store to inspect the merchandise. Once the customer has made a selection from the merchandise on sale, the traffic path should lead to the cash register which is beyond the display of the regular goods. Thus, the retailer is getting maximum customer exposure to the various displays of items as the customer walks through the store.

To provide other examples of strategic placement of goods which may alter or direct the flow of customer traffic, notice the traffic pattern in the next grocery supermarket you visit. Usually, customer traffic in a grocery supermarket is directed around the periphery or outside of the store. The customer enters the store and takes a basket or shopping cart near the entrance. The traffic path may then go past some impulse items—plants, magazines, or bakery goods. Next comes the display of fresh fruits and vegetables, followed by dairy products with meat, fish, and poultry products (the nucleus of most meals) in the *rear* of the store. Almost all the canned goods and packaged items and some paper products are displayed near the center of the store on shelves or gondolas which must be passed in their entirety. These shelves must be passed by the grocery shopper, and they provide the staple items. Impulse items are placed at the ends of the aisles where full exposure is offered to the consumer.

In a specialty retail store, customer traffic may be directed to a seating or viewing area; e.g. high-fashion merchandise stores for women's clothing. As the customer is being shown select merchandise by models, the person is comfortably seated on a chair and possibly given something to drink (coffee, tea, or a soft drink). If a fitting is desired by the customer, the fitting rooms are close by, and the area is surrounded by mirrors for a personal inspection of the fitting. If a purchase is made, the salesperson may take care of the entire transaction without the customer having to leave the area; the customer may not have to walk through the store except to pay for the purchase. In such specialty stores, a through-the-store traffic pattern without a salesperson in attendance is discouraged.

Large department stores will usually direct customer traffic indirectly toward the less rapidly moving merchandise. For example, furniture and household appliances are usually found on or near the top floors of the store and bargains are displayed in the basement or on the first floor of the department store. The first or main floor of a department store usually displays merchandise that is small in size, has a rapid rate of inventory turnover (RITO), and requires little purchasing thought and effort on the part of the customer. The department store's "customer directory" or information booth serves to divert traffic flow to the less used departments or areas.

Tables are often used to display either regular or sale goods in department stores and are placed in the wide aisles—hence, the name "aisle tables." These tables serve to interrupt the flow of traffic and cause the customer to slow down and inspect the merchandise on display. Many retail stores are designed with wide aisles for rapid customer flow, but this practice is really self-defeating for the retailer. Wide aisles encourage the customer to walk rapidly through the store, whereas the merchandising strategy should be to slow down the customer, providing an invitation to purchase goods and services. The more perceptive retail managers will not allow the consumer an opportunity to walk hurriedly through the store without having the chance to inspect goods for possible purchase. Customer traffic flows and patterns are under the direct control of the retailer. Every retailer should carefully study the store, the space allocation, and the possible direction and flow of customer traffic for maximum exposure to the goods on display.

CREATIVE LIGHTING AND DISPLAY

Creative lighting and the innovative display of merchandise is important in stimulating profitable sales volume for a retail store. Creative lighting is both a technical and an artistic problem that should be handled by a lighting engineer with the assistance of an interior decorator. Few retailers have the background and knowledge to judge lighting and its effect on merchandise displays. Although manuals and materials are available to inform a retailer about lighting, initially it probably would be best to have an expert give the retailer some guidance. Theater people often can provide valuable advice on just how to "highlight" certain merchandise through the correct use of lighting.

The basic purpose of creative lighting in a retail store is to attract and focus attention to the displays of merchandise, which in turn will encourage the consumer to make purchases. Since creative lighting has some psychological effect on the customer, good lighting should highlight the merchandise rather than call attention to the fixtures. For instance, some department stores have very elaborate chandeliers, which are objects of beauty in themselves and may enhance the physical appearance of the store; but they do nothing to highlight the goods on display. Currently there is a trend among the more modern department and specialty stores to make use of "focal lighting" or spotlights to highlight and call attention to certain areas or to certain merchandise displays. By utilizing these types of lighting fixtures, the customer sees only the goods on display, not the lighting fixture itself; the lighting fixture is somewhat hidden or camouflaged as it should be.

Lighting an area with special emphasis will encourage a customer to browse and shop more slowly. Proper lighting in a store suggests an environment which is clean and inviting. Creative lighting may be thought of as an effective competitive strategy since past experiences have shown that customers are attracted to those retail establishments which are well lighted. Too, the use of creative and proper lighting reveals the true color of materials which may be an inducement toward a consumer purchase. Creative lighting will pay for itself and should be carefully planned and coordinated with the arrangement of merchandise. With the current energy shortage, it is even more important that a retailer give consideration to effective and creative lighting.

FIXTURES AND EQUIPMENT

Retail store fixtures include such items as display cases, gondolas, shelves, counters, tables, cases, and cabinets. Retail store equipment generally refers to elevators, air conditioners, sales registers, escalators, and delivery trucks. Terminology differs somewhat between what constitutes fixtures and equipment; in this text, however, the fixtures will be those items associated with the display, service, and sale of merchandise. Retail store equipment will be those items concerned with both selling and nonselling activities.

It is important to consider carefully the amount of funds available for the purchase of fixtures and equipment. The purchase of these items must be in keeping with the image of the store. If a retail store is offering self-service, racks and counters must be used which facilitate self-service and self-selection by consumers. If a retail store is offering high-priced jewelry, proper display cases must be utilized for the protection of the merchandise; usually jewelry cases have locks which can only be opened by a salesperson. If only a limited amount of funds is available for the purchase of fixtures and equipment, the money should be carefully allotted among these items, in harmony with the goals and objectives of the store. Some retail stores make use of cabinets and wardrobes as occasional pieces throughout the store. Since many of these cabinets and wardrobes fall into the "antique" classification, they often add to the decor of the store's interior while successfully displaying certain types of goods. However, these fixtures should not detract from the merchandise that is for sale.

Display tables and shelving should be low enough for a retailer to be able to see the other aisles and shelving. This will often lead to better observation and visability (creating an atmosphere of openness) and could also lessen the chance of goods being stolen. Low shelving, gondolas, and tables tend to create an open atmosphere and make a small store appear larger than it actually is. Tables and shelving tend to direct traffic as do other types of fixtures. Fixtures need not be expensive but should be both attractive and functional. Some retailers make good use of handmade carts, tables, and other types of fixtures for the display of merchandise; the creative and innovative use of any type of fixture is boundless.

For multilevel department stores, it is necessary to install both elevators and escalators if the retailer wishes to provide full access to the merchandise. This equipment will offer rapid movement of customers from one floor to another and eliminate aisle congestion.

Practically all department stores today are offering air-conditioned facilities. This customer convenience has come about regardless of location since the advantages of air conditioning offset the initial costs of installing this equipment. The customers are more relaxed and comfortable in an air-conditioned environment, and they are encouraged to shop even on warm days, which probably will contribute to higher sales volumes for many retail stores. Also, a retail store that is air-conditioned provides a better working environment for the store's employees, thereby improving employee morale. Finally, if one's competitors air condition their stores, a retailer has little choice but to follow suit.

SUMMARY

The basic purpose of exterior design and interior layout is to promote *profitable sales volume* for the store. Every retail institution has an image which either attracts or repels customers. The *store image* should be created which is consistent with the overall managerial philosphy of the owner-manager.

Creativity and *innovativeness* in interior store layout and design is little more expensive than less creative layout and design.

Every retail store should be designed and arranged according to some definite *floor plan*. Special attention should be devoted to space allocation. The sales and nonsales areas must be in harmony with each other.

A *well-designed store* will feature an attractive front and entrance and make use of creative window displays. Storefronts should be designed with the consumer in mind. The front of a store should offer the consumer an invitation to enter and browse.

Both *construction and land costs* are rising rapidly and a retailer should obtain the maximum for the funds spent on design and arrangement. Customers prefer to shop in those retail stores where there is an atmosphere of openness and pleasantness.

The *correct utilization of space* will maximize a store's profits and minimize the retailer's expenses. These objectives may be accomplished by devoting attention to the various gross margins obtained from different types of merchandise per square foot of occupied selling space. The gross margin is the difference between the cost of the merchandise and the selling price of those goods. Markup is expressed as a percentage of the retail or selling price and is the difference between the cost of the goods and the retail price.

Since all merchandise cannot be strategically located in a store, consideration should be given to the *placement of goods* within the store. Some types of merchandise exert greater pulling power than other types of goods. Goods with great pulling power should be placed in strategic areas where customers will walk past other merchandise which does not attract customer attention.

The *basic determinants* of interior store design and layout include the actual number of square feet available for both selling and nonselling areas, the nature of the retail business itself, the type, kind, and amount of merchandise the store will offer to the consumer, and the personal preferences of the manager-owner.

It is important to give full consideration to both *selling* and *nonselling* space allocation and location. These are complementary in nature and should be arranged for optimal efficiency.

The *flow and direction of customer traffic* in a retail store may stimulate profitable sales volume for the owner-manager. Since the direction of customer traffic is under the control of the retailer, careful study of directing consumers past certain strategic points of a store's interior should be made for operating efficiency and the maximization of profitable sales volume. Some areas of a store are natural traffic generators; others have less customer attraction. Management should plan the direction and flow of traffic carefully in order that the less attractive areas in the store receive sufficient customer exposure. Customer traffic can be discreetly directed throughout the store by the careful and prudent placement of tables, fixtures, and shelving.

Creative use of lighting can enhance a store's environment and stimulate purchases by highlighting certain displays and types of merchandise. Lighting is to be utilized as a sales stimulator, not as works of art which detract from the merchandise itself. The creative and innovative use of lighting by the perceptive retailer will stimulate profitable sales volume for the store by providing an atmosphere conducive to consumer buying.

Planning should focus on the best utilization of equipment, and the *fixtures and equipment* should be in keeping with the store's image and management's goals. Professional advice from the experts in the field of lighting and equipment can well be worth the price of such assistance; few retailers are experienced in these fields and should seek advice and assistance before undertaking any expenditures.

REVIEW QUESTIONS

1   Explain precisely the basic purposes of exterior store design and interior layout and space apportionment.
2   What are the two major objectives of retail store design and interior layout?
3   Explain how store profits can be increased or maximized by devoting special attention to the gross margin per square foot of selling area.
4   Assume that you have just purchased an existing store. How would you go about determining space requirements for layout purposes?
5   Why do some types of merchandise seem to have greater "pulling power" than other types of goods?
6   Where in a store's interior would you locate merchandise which has a rapid rate of turnover? Why?
7   Why should merchandise which is related be located in adjacent areas?
8   What are the basic determinants of interior store design and layout?
9   What factors determine the ratio of selling to nonselling space in a retail store?
10 Distinguish between convenience goods, impulse goods, shopping goods, and specialty goods.
11 What is the purpose and relationship of the nonselling areas to the selling areas of a store?
12 Discuss the merits of directing customer traffic flows and patterns within a store.
13 Why should special attention be devoted to creative and innovative lighting in a retail store?
14 What are the benefits of creative and innovative lighting in a store?
15 What value lies in the careful selection of display fixtures? Which should a retailer use: open or closed displays? Why and under what circumstances would each be used?

PROJECTS

1   Prepare a written report on the interior design and layout of one of the following kinds of retail stores: (1) a men's specialty clothing store, (2) a women's ready-to-wear store, (3) a large grocery supermarket, (4) an independent furniture retailer, (5) a national chain variety store, or (6) a family type of restaurant. Make a sketch of the interior space apportionment; make an accurate estimate of the total square footage available for both selling and nonselling areas; and offer constructive suggestions for the improvement of the design and interior layout which would involve a minimum of capital expenditures. Make a five-minute presentation to the class on your project.
2   Prepare a written report on the exterior design and construction of any retail store of your choice. Pay particular attention to the image or personality that the store projects to the consumer. Make a sketch of the storefront and the entrance. How are the window displays arranged? Make some suggestions for improving the storefront and entrance, together with constructive criticism for improving the window displays.

Make use of photographs or sketches to illustrate your points. Make an estimate of the costs of changing the storefront and entrance. Present your findings to the class members.

3 Go to a large department store, grocery supermarket, or discount retailer, and seek permission from the manager-owner to observe customer traffic flows and patterns. You are to *observe* only, since this is "observational research." Write a short report on your findings and observations. Special attention should be devoted to the following: (1) How did the customers enter the store? (2) Where did the customers first go after entering the store? (3) What is the merchandising strategy of the store with respect to directing the customer toward certain displays? (4) Can you suggest any improvements in the direction of customer traffic in the store that you visited? (5) Discuss the results with the store manager or owner; then make a short presentation to the class on your findings.

CASE PROBLEM

Alexander's is a men's specialty store located in a planned regional shopping center in a Western city of 1.5 million people. The shopping center requires that all stores remain open the same hours each day—from 10:00 A.M. to 5:30 P.M. Monday through Thursday, from 10:00 A.M. to 9:30 P.M. on Fridays, and from 10:00 A.M. to 4:30 P.M. on Saturdays. The center is closed all day on Sunday, except from November 10 through December 24. The shopping center appears to have sufficient customer traffic although a new planned regional shopping center three miles distant may have some impact on the center's overall sales. The center's management believes that this is a temporary situation and that customers will return to the center once the novelty of the new center has worn off.

The center was well researched and planned. Alexander's storefront boasts a modern decor of stone and wood, which Alex Alexander (the owner) had installed. The storefront has two display windows approximately the entire width of the store (50 feet) except for the entrance, which has two doors, each 48 inches in width. The doors swing either way (that is, inward or outward) and are kept closed because of the controlled environment within the store. The storefront does not carry any identification except for a small painted sign on the door.

Alex Alexander, the proprietor, changes the window displays about every ten days, depending on when he is able to find someone to perform this duty. A firm which specializes in window decorating and displays is located near the center in a neighborhood shopping area. This firm is operated by Shela Johnson, a graduate of the local university, who majored in art and design. After taking the advice of a friend, Shela enrolled in a retailing course at the university and became interested in window displays and store arrangements. Shela abandoned her previous plans to enter a large advertising agency and opened her own business which specializes in rearranging retailers' window displays.

Shela charges $18 per hour for changing window displays and generally she spends two to three hours on each window display. In addition, Shela charges extra for background materials, signs, and lettering. After Shela has finished a window display, the customers often make compliments on her work. Alex has used Shela from time to time to work on the store's window displays, but because of the expense, he is considering performing the window-display work himself.

The interior of the store measures 50 feet wide by 125 feet long. Approximately 25 feet of the store's length has been allocated to storage and a small tailoring shop. This leaves Alex with about 50 by 100 feet of selling area.

Alex has always prided himself on handling some of the best men's clothing available. Suit brands include Hart-Schaffner & Marx, H. Freeman and Sons, and a house brand called Cal-Clothes. The store has six showcases where men's shirts are displayed, and several other cases where underwear, sweaters, socks, and accessories are stored.

Men's suits are displayed near the rear of the store, and most of the front of the store is uncluttered, which creates an atmosphere of openness. The floor is covered with tile, and the walls are painted a light green. Lighting includes fluorescent lights in the ceiling. Two full-length mirrors are near the middle of the store.

Alex has been in business eighteen years, six at the present location. The store caters to the upper-middle-class male market. Suit prices range from $135 for the Cal-Clothes brand to $240 for the H. Freeman and Sons brand. Alterations are free and the store operates on a cash-only basis. Last year's gross sales were $750,000. Alex has a liberal return-goods policy, but generally the customers are well satisfied. The store makes no deliveries, but Alex's wife does some gift wrapping during the holiday season.

Customer traffic appears to become congested near the cash register which is near the front of the store. At times, salespeople bump into one another. Alex employs six salespersons, two of whom are women. It has been observed that some customers come to the storefront and after viewing the congestion near the cash register, leave the store and are not seen again. Some customers have had to wait as long as fifteen minutes before being served by a salesperson.

Alex has considered hiring more salespersons in order that the customers can be better served. There is no room for expansion of the store, and Alex has dismissed the idea of relocating the store. Besides, he has twelve years remaining on the lease with the shopping center.

Question: How can you alleviate some of the problems encountered by Alex in the operation of the store?

Part Six

Merchandising Management

Chapter 11

Product Line and Resource Determination

There is an old adage, "One cannot do business from an empty wagon." In other words, a retailer must have: The right goods, at the right time, at the right price, for the right customer. Failure to comply with any one of these fundamentals of retailing management will result in an unsuccessful business. When starting a new business, retailers are faced with the immediate problem of determining what product lines the store should offer and the extent of the products within those lines. A product line will consist of products which are intended to be used for the same purposes, such as housewares, cosmetics, men's clothing, hardware, and so on. As for the extent of the offering within a product line, a retailer may decide to offer only a few products representative of the product line. Or a retailer may make a decision to offer a wide variety of colors, styles, and sizes of a product line. For example, usually a specialty retailer carries a vast assortment of goods from a product line (such as clothing) since they "specialize" in offering a wide assortment of one type of merchandise.

When the retailer has decided what product line or lines to offer, he or she then must find a supplier from which to obtain the goods. Two broad classes of resources or suppliers are available to retailers: (1) producers or manufacturers and (2) middlemen or wholesalers. Resources may also be referred to as vendors or sources of supply (manufacturers or wholesalers). These terms may be used interchangeably and are often so used within the business world.

A retailer may purchase from many resources. However, the retailer should safeguard against buying from too many sources. There are some definite advantages in limiting the number of resources. A retailer will be better able to take advantage of both quantity and cash discounts, establish a rapport or better working relationship with the suppliers, and yet still be able to stock the latest styles and fashions for customers. At times it may be necessary to purchase from many resources in order to be able to stock the right goods; but if the sources of supply are carefully picked, a retailer will be able to improve the buying function. A reduction in the number of suppliers also reduces the amount of paperwork for a retailer. A retailer cannot buy goods from every available source. All purchases from suppliers should be carefully planned and coordinated with the retailer's goals and objectives.

DUTIES AND RESPONSIBILITIES OF A BUYER

Whether a buyer for a large department or the owner of one's own business, a retail store buyer is a key individual in the merchandising activities for that store. Purchasing merchandise for resale to final consumers is the primary role of any buyer, whether in a large chain or a neighborhood store. A buyer's function is pivotal or the key element in purchasing the products for a retail store. The same principles and duties apply regardless of the retail outlet involved.

Basically, a retail store buyer has four main duties and responsibilities: (1) the purchasing of goods and services for the store's customers; (2) working with and assisting the supporting personnel (salespeople, stock clerks, and assistants); (3) sustaining a profitable operation in a department, division, or store; and (4) maintaining a mutually beneficial relationship with the resources (suppliers) from whom purchases are made.

Purchasing Goods and Services

The major function of a buyer, whether a retail store is large or small, is to determine what to buy, how to price the merchandise, how to display the goods, and how to promote the merchandise. This is a tremendous responsibility for one individual, and no other single retailing function is more important. A buyer usually is guided by the general policies of a store as to what type of goods to buy, but the sources of supply, pricing, and promotion become the responsibility of the buyer. A buyer may delegate these duties to others in the store, but it is the buyer who is ultimately responsible for the success or failure of the performance of these retailing activities.

Without the proper merchandise aided by selective promotion at the right price, time, and place, a retail store is not going to be successful. The buying function requires that a buyer have a working knowledge of selling trends of various types of merchandise as well as the rate of movement of items by color,

size, fabric, and style and that he or she know by whom these goods are manufactured. Detailed information about these characteristics of merchandise will
lead a buyer to better buying decisions.

Duties to Supporting Personnel

The buyer also has a definite responsibility to amiably and efficiently work with
assistants and other personnel employed in that retail store. A buyer can be
considered to be the director of the sales team by the people supporting the
department, division, or store. The buyer is the person in charge of directing all
retailing activities in order to accomplish a smooth flow of coordinated work
efforts between a department and other departments or between the department
and top management. Such work efforts include the following: (1) coordinating
and integrating a department's promotion with the store's overall promotion, (2)
working with other personnel to create a total system for uniformity of decisions
and customer relations, and (3) working with all other departments or sections
of the retail organization. Without the total support of all salespeople, assistants,
and stock clerks, the buyer will not achieve success. The buying function is
basically one of total team effort, with each individual playing a key role in the
success of this vital activity.

Responsibility for Profits

A buyer must be thoroughly familiar with the principles of expense and profit.
Some large retailers, such as Sears, place the responsibility for departmental
profits directly on the buyer. Thus, a buyer must be able to interpret and analyze
statistics and records and analyze information on trends and rates of movement,
as a guide to wise purchasing decisions. Knowledge of competitors, their merchandising strategies, and their day-to-day promotional activities should also be
learned by the buyer. A buyer should be creative, that is, he or she should be
able to devise new ways in which goods can be effectively promoted and
displayed. The merchandise that is purchased must be sold to the customers at a
profit to the store if the buyer is going to remain in that role. Buyers who do not
show a profit for a department, division, or store, are soon seeking other types of
employment.

　　In essence, a retail store buyer acts as the consumer's purchasing agent by
assembling goods and services from the many sources of supply. It is the buyer's
role to successfully coordinate customers' wishes with those of the management.
If the buyer is able to satisfy the wants and desires of customers, then management probably will be satisfied if a profitable sales volume is generated by the
store. A successful retail store buyer exists only because of his or her ability to
serve and satisfy customer wants and desires at a profit to the store.

Responsibility to Resources

Many buyers in the field of retailing believe that their function has been fulfilled
as soon as the department, division, or store shows a profit. This is a rather short-

sighted view, however, because a buyer also has certain *ethical* responsibilities to the suppliers. It is the buyer's duty to see that honest ethical business practices are used in dealing with the resources or suppliers. For instance, it is unethical for a buyer to return goods to a manufacturer for credit which were not actually damaged in transit, defective because of a producer's carelessness, or otherwise the fault of the producer. Merchandise which has been damaged by the store should be marked down and sold by the store. Many questionable practices take place between buyers and resources, and there is no justification for such business practices. There is a mutual business relationship between a buyer and a resource, and this relationship should not be damaged by either party taking advantage of the other. It is the buyer's responsibility to see that the supplier gets paid on time and that no undue influence is placed on the resource to accept late payments which carry unwarranted cash discounts. Although the accounting department actually issues payment for the merchandise, the buyer should determine that all terms of the transaction be properly fulfilled.

MANUFACTURERS AS RESOURCES

When a retailer purchases goods and services from a manufacturer or producer, it is referred to as a "direct" purchase or transaction. The practice of buying merchandise from a manufacturer or producer is generally restricted to large retailers. Some manufacturers have a policy of not selling directly to large retailers and will sell goods only through various middlemen (such as wholesalers, brokers, and jobbers). This policy may also include several other merchant middlemen (wholesalers) or agent middlemen (brokers).

There is one major exception to the rule that only large retailers purchase directly from manufacturers. In the field of fashion merchandise, even small retailers buy directly from the producer. The inherent nature of fashion merchandising dictates that a retailer (large or small) purchase directly from the source of supply—the producer or manufacturer. Changes in consumer demand and seasonality of the merchandise make this condition necessary even for a small retailer. Expedience is the watchword in fashion merchandising. Generally, the shorter the channel of distribution, the more rapidly merchandise can be delivered. (A channel of distribution from the producer to a retailer is shorter than a channel from the producer to the wholesaler to the retailer.) Short channels of distribution eliminate as many middlemen as possible without losing their effectiveness.

It is also possible that a retailer is able to purchase fashion goods for less money from the manufacturer than from a wholesaler. A wholesaler, or other middleman, must have a markup on the merchandise to cover the costs of operation which, in turn, could reflect a higher price to the retailer. However, purchasing merchandise through a middleman, such as a wholesaler or agent, may not always result in a higher price for goods to a retailer. The price of merchandise to a retailer depends on the efficiency of the distribution process and the effectiveness of the middleman involved in the process.

Advantages of Buying Directly From Manufacturers

As might be expected, several advantages may accrue to a retailer when purchases are made directly from the manufacturer.

First, there is the possibility that items purchased directly from a producer are fresher than goods purchased from a wholesaling middleman. For some goods such as hardware, building supplies, and the like, this is of little consequence since these goods do not deteriorate with age. But with merchandise such as food, women's wear, or fashion goods, a more rapid movement is necessary in order to take advantage of the shifts in consumer demand.

Second, a retailer may be able to purchase the same goods for less money from a manufacturer than from a wholesale merchant. Wholesale merchants must charge for handling the goods and add a percentage of markup to these goods. If a retailer is able to purchase in sufficient quantities from a producer, there may be an added advantage of quantity discounts. However, it is not conclusive whether retailers save money by purchasing goods directly from manufacturers. Some manufacturers have a one-price policy; that is, all buyers, whether they are wholesalers or retailers, pay the same price. In this case, a retailer would save money by purchasing directly from the producer. However, some manufacturers have variable pricing policies for wholesalers and retailers; and in this case, whether a retailer could purchase goods for less by buying directly from the producer would depend upon the efficiency of the wholesaler. It is best for a retailer to price and compare goods and services offered by *both* the manufacturers and the wholesalers.

Third, if an item must be returned to the manufacturer for any reason (repairs, servicing, or replacement), it probably will be returned to the customer more quickly if it does not have to be sent to the producer via the route of the wholesaler. As you can imagine, considerable time is lost in returning goods through long channels of distribution. Such slow service should be avoided since it could impair the good will between the customer and the retailer.

Fourth, a retailer may receive faster deliveries when purchasing goods directly from a manufacturer. The producer knows immediately if the goods are in stock and whether delivery can be made promptly. If a retailer places an order for goods with a wholesaler, considerable time may elapse before the order is returned indicating that the merchandise is not in stock at this time. Also, it is possible that a wholesaler may not stock all items from a manufacturer because of slow movement, lack of funds, or for other reasons.

Fifth, generally, manufacturers' representatives are more helpful to retailers in providing specialized, detailed information about the merchandise and national market conditions. This information is usually reliable and may be more current than that possessed by merchant or agent middlemen.

Sixth, the elimination of wholesaling middlemen may allow a retailer the opportunity to coordinate advertising and retail sales promotion with purchases. For instance, by purchasing directly from the producer, the retailer can rely on a specific delivery date. Promotion and advertising for this incoming shipment of goods can begin ahead of the delivery date, and the sales event can commence as soon as the goods arrive. In essence, delivery dates may be more reliable when purchases are made directly from the producer, thus, the timing of retail sales promotions can also be more precise.

MIDDLEMEN AS RESOURCES

When a retailer purchases goods and services from a middleman (wholesaler, broker, or jobber), it is referred to as an "indirect" purchase or transaction. The practice of buying merchandise from middlemen is not limited according to retail store size since nearly all small retailers purchase from wholesaling middlemen. Large chain retailers generally purchase directly from manufacturers. However, they also purchase merchandise for fill-in purposes from wholesaling middlemen or will make use of a wholesaling middleman to purchase merchandise that is not available directly from the producer. Some producers may have a policy of distributing *only* through a wholesaler; thus even large retailers have no choice but to obtain this merchandise from a middleman even though the price of this merchandise may be higher than if the goods could have been purchased directly from the producer. Therefore, in order to be able to offer certain kinds of goods to the consumer, large retailing chains must also purchase from the wholesaling middleman who carries those goods.

Occasionally, a retailer may purchase from another retailer, but this practice is usually limited to one-time purchases or to the purchase of goods for replacement for out-of-stock items.

Some retailers, such as grocery supermarkets, drugstores, hardware stores, variety stores, and even department stores, utilize the services of a special wholesaling middleman, called a rack jobber.[1] A rack jobber performs many "merchandising" functions for these self-service retailers. A rack jobber is able to furnish many nonfood items for the retailer. This eliminates the buying function for the retailer, and generally it can be assumed that the rack jobber stocks only the more rapidly moving items. Usually the rack jobber sells merchandise to a retailer on a "guaranteed-sale" basis. That is, if after a certain period of time the merchandise does not sell, the rack jobber takes the merchandise and grants a credit to the retailer.

Rack jobbers are increasing in importance due in part to the scrambled merchandising techniques employed by these retailers. Since many grocery supermarkets are seeking nonfood items with higher gross margins than foods, it would appear that the rack jobber will continue to fulfill the role of supplying these retailers with fast-moving, nonfood items.

One of the major advantages of a retailer using a rack jobber is the limited investment in merchandise. For instance, a retailer's investment is limited to the "rack merchandise"; there is no stock in the storeroom. All the merchandise

[1]For a complete, detailed study of a rack jobber, see Larry D. Redinbaugh, *The Rack Jobber: A Marketing Institution,* unpublished master's thesis, The University of Nebraska, Lincoln, Neb., June 1966.

appears on the racks provided by the rack jobber. Thus, the rack jobber is a specialist in purchasing, merchandising, and stocking nonfood items for the retailer.

A truck jobber is a wholesaling middleman specializing in fast-moving, nationally advertised, food items, such as potato chips, candy, dairy products, tobacco, bread, and snack items. Like the rack jobber, the truck jobber performs certain merchandising functions for the retailer. The truck jobber is primarily limited to the food field, calling on grocery supermarkets. The main advantage to a food retailer is having the truck jobber furnish perishable items on a frequent basis, which reduces the retailer's risk of loss of goods due to perishability.

Advantages of Buying from Middlemen

A retailer benefits from several advantages when buying merchandise from a middleman.

First, wholesalers and other middlemen often represent several principals (manufacturers or producers) and thus will have a greater assortment of goods from which a retailer can choose. This wide variety and selection of merchandise helps a retailer to serve customers better. Since many manufacturers tend to specialize in certain limited lines of goods, a retailer is more likely to obtain a greater selection from wholesaling middlemen because most represent more than one producer. Thus, a retailer may have a wide choice of several manufacturers' goods even while limiting himself to just one middleman. By concentrating purchases in only a couple of wholesalers, the retailer will eliminate the disadvantages that arise from doing business with many resources. By purchasing from fewer resources, a retailer is better able to take advantage of any discounts (cash or quantity) and probably can receive better or preferred service from these wholesalers.

Second, many retailers are able to obtain merchandise in smaller quantities from wholesalers than could be purchased from manufacturers. Typically, manufacturers like to sell only in large quantities. This policy may give the buyer an attractive price, but it also may result in overstocking a small retailer. Overstocking usually results in a low "rate of inventory turnover" (RITO) which then reduces the profitability of the store.

Third, wholesale middlemen may have better local market information than do manufacturers. Manufacturers generally cover a large territory, whereas wholesalers limit their market coverage to smaller geographical areas. So wholesalers are usually better informed about local market conditions than are manufacturers. Information about local market conditions is usually of more benefit to retailers than information on national markets.

MANUFACTURERS AND MIDDLEMEN AS RESOURCES

Most retailers purchase goods and services from *both* manufacturers and middlemen. As one may conclude from the previous discussion, retailers who utilize both manufacturers and wholesaling middlemen as resources enjoy certain benefits. It is unlikely, in most cases, that a retailer could rely solely upon one or the other as the only source of merchandise.

Large retailers generally tend to favor purchasing most of their merchandise directly from manufacturers, and use wholesalers for fill-in purchases. Small retailers generally purchase most of their goods indirectly from wholesale merchants and obtain directly from manufacturers only items that are not available from a local wholesaler.

In summary, a retailer must select resources that will be able to supply the right merchandise and goods, at the right price, at the right time in order to satisfy the needs and desires of the customers.

RESIDENT BUYING OFFICES

The world's largest wholesale market for consumer goods is in New York City. It has become difficult for many retailers to contact resources because of the size of the market and their distance from New York. To overcome some of these limitations, the "resident buying office" has been developed.

A resident buying office is located (whether in New York or near some other large wholesale market such as Los Angeles, Chicago, or Dallas) for the purpose of facilitating the purchase of soft consumer goods. The buyer in a resident buying office (resident buyer) does not purchase merchandise in the name of the office for resale to retailers but instead buys in the name of the retailer, receiving compensation for performing the buying services.

The name "resident" was derived from the fact that the individual who does the buying permanently resides in that city. The title of "buying office" has thus evolved from the fact that the resident buyer maintains some sort of facilities which are referred to as the "office."

Types of Resident Offices

There are basically two types of resident buying offices: (1) an independent office and (2) a store-owned office.

Independent Office   The independent resident buying office often serves many different, noncompeting retail stores, and membership is usually made up of both large and small retailers. An independent resident buying office charges fees to retailers based either on a contract arrangement or on annual total sales volume. Contractual arrangements between the resident buying office and a retailer usually are based on an annual agreement. The amount of services provided by the resident buyer will vary according to the fee paid by the member retailer. (The types of services they offer will be covered later in this chapter.) The greater the membership fee, the more services the resident buyer provides for the retailer. Some companies represented by independent resident buying offices include the Certified Buying Service, the Independent Retailers Syndicate, and the Atlas Buying Corporation.

Store-Owned Buying Offices   Store-owned resident buying offices are controlled by either a single, large retailing chain or by a group of retail stores. If
the resident buying office is owned by a single retail store, it is referred to as a
"private" buying office. If the resident buying office is owned and operated by
several noncompeting retail stores, it may be called an "associated" or "syndicated" buying office. Syndicated buying offices include those owned by the
Associated Dry Goods Corporation and Allied Purchasing Corporation. Probably the best known resident buying office of this type includes the Associated
Merchandising Corporation (AMC). AMC serves some thirty major department stores, including Dayton's of Minneapolis and the Dayton-Hudson organization, which has stores in the Midwest and on the West Coast. The Allied
Purchasing Corporation services the Allied Stores Corporation by maintaining
buying offices in major cities of the United States, such as Dallas, Los Angeles,
Chicago, and Miami.

Services Offered

As previously mentioned, retailers may belong to an association which has a
buying office, or a retailer may have his or her own resident buying office. The
resident buyer offers a number of services which aid in the buying functions of a
retail store. These services are as follows:

First, resident buying offices provide a retailer with information on new
resources, new merchandise and products, changes in market conditions, trends
in merchandising, and other retail management aids.

Second, resident offices often offer a retailer what is known as "special
order" privileges. It may be too costly for a retailer to visit the manufacturers'
places of business to inspect merchandise. So the resident buyer located in a
resident buying office can perform this function for a retailer who is located in
another part of the country.

Third, resident buyers are often influential in settling disputes between a
retailer and a manufacturer and/or wholesaler. Returned goods are often routed
through a resident buying office rather than have the retailer attempt to get the
vendor to accept the merchandise directly. Because of the distance involved,
vendors know that resident buying offices can switch to other resources or
suppliers more quickly than retailers can. Further, the resident buyer in any
negotiation is anxious to please the retailer. So the manufacturer is more likely
to settle any disputes quickly and keep the goodwill of the resident buyer since
a considerable amount of business may be involved. Many manufacturers never
see the retailer with whom they conduct business. All business representations
and transactions are done from the resident buying office with the resident buyer
making all the arrangements for the retailer.

Fourth, a resident buying office can provide a retailer with information on
selected merchandise, offer training to the retailer's sales personnel, and in
some instances, attend fashion and trade shows for the retailer. These services
often vary considerably from one resident buying office to another. Before

joining a particular resident buying office, a retailer should give careful consideration to the type and amount of services offered. A retailer should pay only for those additional services which are needed to complement the retail store and the purchasing function.

In summary, a resident buying office serves as a helpful aid to the buyer of a large department store. The local buyer is provided with up-to-date information on the pulse of the market and is able to keep current on changes in national market conditions, trends in merchandising, styles, and fashions. Any information a local buyer can receive about national market conditions may help to improve his or her performance. In addition, a local buyer will usually make one or two trips each year to New York (or some other major wholesale market) where personal contacts are renewed and strengthened with the resident buyer.

DETERMINATION OF PRODUCT LINES

In advance of purchasing any merchandise, it is extremely important for a retail store buyer to determine the number of product lines a store will offer for sale. As previously defined, a product line is an assortment of goods or products intended basically for the same use.

With our modern market system, it is becoming increasingly difficult to isolate retail stores in terms of the types and kinds of merchandise they offer. Nevertheless, it is important for a buyer to predetermine the number of product lines to be offered and the breadth and depth within the product lines. Product-line breadth refers to the number of different product lines (i.e., housewares, cosmetics, clothing, or food), and depth refers to the number of items within that line (styles, sizes, and colors). A predetermination of product-line breadth and depth will allow a buyer to plan purchases well within the scope of the store's space requirements as well as within the owner's financial means. Failure to comply with both of these restraints on a retail store's purchasing will often lead to a disorderly system which could lead to considerable inefficiency within the store.

For census purposes, retail stores are classified along product lines—that is, grocery, hardware, or drugstore. But even though a store may be classified as a grocery store, many large grocery supermarkets offer limited assortments of hardware, housewares, children's books and toys, pet supplies, magazines, and other nonfood items. Each of the previously mentioned items belongs to a separate product line, which adds ''breadth'' to the merchandise assortment. When a retailer offers many unrelated product lines, such as the grocery supermarket, it is called ''scrambled merchandising.'' The retail stores' search for nonfood items which offer greater gross margins, and ultimately more profit, has led grocery supermarket operators and other retailers to handle more unrelated items of merchandise. Many retailers in today's market have scrambled merchandise in an attempt to offset sagging profit margins.

As explained above, the depth of a product line refers to the number of items within that line. For example, a specialty store offers considerable product-line depth because a customer is able to purchase almost any size, style, color, or quality of a product from a line of goods. To illustrate more specifically, a specialty store handling pipe tobacco offers the pipe smoker almost any type, variety, brand, and aroma of tobacco that the customer may desire. In fact, almost any type of pipe tobacco manufactured in the world may be available. When compared to a department store, a specialty store offers far greater "depth" or selection in a particular product line.

Even though retail stores appear to be in a stage of product-line proliferation, such as that with scrambled merchandising, we should evaluate the merits of this type of buying. Offering too many lines of merchandise which are unrelated can lead to ineffectiveness in retail merchandising. It is virtually impossible for a buyer to be familiar with all lines of goods; therefore only one buyer should be responsible for a few product lines. Although this will increase the total number of buyers for a store, each buyer will have better knowledge of changes and trends within a product line, and this may save the store money in the long run by making the buyers more efficient.

When a store offers a number of product lines, it may be prudent for a buyer to appraise the sales and profitability of each product line the store handles. It may also be necessary for the buyer to weed out some products in a line or, in some cases, delete a complete line which does not contribute to the profitability of the store. It is difficult to say just how many product lines a retail store should offer because much depends upon the managerial efficiency of the owner-manager. Many retailers in attempting to combat competition are expanding product lines to a point beyond their control. It is sound merchandising and usually a more profitable tactic to offer fewer product lines and to maintain a closer control over these lines. This strategy reduces the amount of funds invested in inventory and affords improved control of stock. Offering fewer product lines with a better selection within each line may be better merchandising strategy than offering a large number of product lines. Basically, it is a retailing myth that a retailer must keep expanding by offering more and more product lines. By expanding too rapidly, it is more likely that the store may lose its effectiveness with the customer. In many instances a retrenchment, or the elimination of a product line, would improve the profits and operations of a retail store. Sound fundamentals of merchandising suggest that a retailer should offer product lines that are most familiar to him or her, and the emphasis should be placed on improving the service, quality, and assortment of these product lines.

DETERMINATION OF PRICE LINES

The determination of price lines, or "price lining," consists of selecting a limited number of prices at which a store will sell its merchandise.

To illustrate price lining, a women's specialty store may sell women's dresses at $29.95, $44, $60, or $110. Or a men's shoe store may sell merchandise priced at $19.95, $24.95, $34.95, or $42. Price lining serves as an aid to the selection of goods by the customer. By offering goods within a short price range, price lining simplifies the buying decision. As customers often know approximately what they wish to pay for a specific item, all they have to do is tell the salesperson what they wish to spend. A customer then can easily shop or be shown the store's offering within that price line.

Price lining also is used extensively as a buying aid for the buyer in that it assists the owner-buyer in planning purchases. A buyer goes into the marketplace looking for goods that can be sold for $29.95, $44, $60, or $110 (or for any certain price range). Each resource or supplier can show a retail buyer what offerings are available within those predetermined retail price lines. Then the merchant can more easily make a selection based on what is available and what can be sold at a profit at those predetermined retail prices.

Price lining may also assist the sales personnel in that it is easier for them to become more familiar with the prices of the merchandise; thus, they might be prone to making fewer mistakes. In turn, improved selling techniques and improved relations with the customers probably will result.

Also, price lining can lead to improved merchandising techniques thereby reducing the number of markdowns and simplifying stock control. Just what advantages occur may depend on how well a retailer has predetermined the price lines. A retailer does not want too few or too many price lines but must maintain a balance. This balance should be distinguishable not only to the customer but should also allow for actual differences in the quality of the items being offered for sale. Care must be taken to guard against having the price lines too close together or too far apart. If the price lines are too close together, the customer has a difficult time distinguishing between the various prices and merchandise quality. If price lines are too far apart, sales may be lost because no choices are offered between the two price levels, and customers will shop elsewhere.

Just how does a retailer go about selecting price lines? For existing retailers, an analysis of past sales will indicate which price lines sold the best. For new retailers, a selection of price lines must be made which are in harmony with the goals and objectives as stated in the retail business plan. It is well for new retailers to select approximately *three* price lines which will represent the target market which the store is attempting to attract. In many instances, new retailers (or even some existing retailers) may select too many price lines, exhibiting the "shotgun" approach to merchandise selection; whereas it is much better merchandising strategy to "zero in" on the target market and offer only lines within the price ranges that these customers are most likely to purchase. Price lining tends to work well for goods that afford price comparison (i.e., brand-name clothing, appliances, tires, or paint); and usually price lining is *not* very effective in the selling of staple or impulse items of low unit value (foodstuffs or snack items).

Although some critics of price lining indicate that it restrains a retailer from offering other lines which may be profitable, in essence, this is a retailing myth. It is virtually impossible for a retailer to offer all price ranges.

The retailer will have little difficulty in changing price lines during periods of rising prices, because as prices rise, the retailer can bring in lower price lines to replace those lines which the customer refuses to buy because of higher prices. The criticism that price lining focuses more attention on the prices than on the merchandise is also a retailing myth. Retailers guilty of this phenomenon are probably derelict in managerial efficiency. In other words, it is the function of a retailer to manage a retail store; and a basic activity of retail merchandising is to provide the right goods, at the right price, at the right time, to the right target consumer group. Any attempt by the retailer to disguise these basic retailing functions is an attempt by the retailer to abandon his or her duties and responsibilities to the customer. When used prudently, price lining is a valuable tool for effective merchandise management control.

DETERMINATION OF MERCHANDISE ASSORTMENT

Closely associated with product lines and price lines is the "assortment" or "mix" of goods and services a retailer will offer to customers. The assortment is the "total" offering of a store and includes both the breadth and depth of the product line. It is the aggregate of goods and services, whether related or unrelated lines of products.

The assortment of merchandise a retailer will offer will ultimately depend on the following: (1) the buyer's experience, (2) the buyer's interpretation and perception of the customers' desires, and (3) the amount of money available for purchases. A merchandise assortment is also influenced by market opportunities, store image, availability of merchandise, and the objectives of management.

A retailer should keep the merchandise assortment under constant assessment because the desires of the customers are in a constant state of change. For example, a buyer should estimate the profitability of each line of merchandise. (This is somewhat difficult to do, but with today's mechanical and computerized facilities, it can be achieved with relative ease.) From this analysis, the retailer may determine that the majority of the store's profitable sales volume stems from a rather narrow assortment of goods and services. Many items may simply take up valuable space in the store and not contribute a fair share to profits. Whether to delete these items or not, of course, is a decision that will have to be made by the owner-manager.

Caution must be exercised, however, in analyzing the profitability of each product in an assortment, since it may be necessary to stock certain nonprofitable goods to support the sale of more profitable items. For example, pen refills may not be profitable, however, they must be stocked if sales are to be made on the more profitable pens. Or a retailer may offer a watch repair service which is not highly profitable in order to attract customers in the hope that they will purchase the more profitable watches.

Model-Stock Plan

A model-stock plan is used as a guide to assist a buyer in a retail store and is an attempt by the retailer to predict forthcoming sales. For existing retailers, a model-stock plan is based on previous sales of items by size, style, color, price lines, and other market factors. The term "model stock" is usually applied to fashion merchandise but is not limited to this type of merchandise. An analysis of past sales or trends becomes an important ingredient in determining a model-stock plan for certain goods. A model-stock plan is designed to achieve the greatest sales volume at a profit to the store. Several such model-stock plans for women's shoes and men's slacks are illustrated in Figure 11-1.

RESOURCE AIDS

Retailers are in the business of purchasing goods and services for ultimate consumers. In order to accomplish this feat, retailers need certain information which will aid them in performing this function.

Width / SIZE	4	4½	5	5½	6	6½	7	7½	8	8½	9	9½	10	10½	11
AAAA							12	12	18	18	10	10	10		
AAA							12	12	18	18	12	10	8		
AA					24	24	36	36	36	24	24	20	18	16	10
A					24	24	36	36	34	20	20	16			
B	10	10	12	12	20	20	24	28	36	30	30	18	12	10	10
C				12	18	20	24	28	36	30	20	20	16		
D				10	12	18	20	24	20	18					
Totals	10	10	10	34	98	106	164	176	198	158	116	94	64	26	20

Colors: Blue and natural   Minimum number required in stock: 1,286
Retail price: $22.95

(a)

LENGTH	WAIST SIZE													
	28	29	30	31	32	33	34	36	38	40	42	44	46	48
28	20	20	20	20	30	30	30	24	20	12	12			
29	20	20	20	20	30	30	30	30	20	20	10	10		
30	12	12	20	20	20	20	24	24	28	30	28	20	16	
31	12	12	20	20	20	20	24	24	28	30	28	20	16	14
32	10	10	10	16	16	16	20	28	28	30	28	20	20	14
33	10	10	10	16	16	20	24	24	24	24	24	20	20	20
34			20	20	24	24	24	24	30	30	30	24	24	20
35							28	30	30	30	30	24	20	18
36							28	30	30	30	30	24	20	18
38									20	20	18	18	18	14
Totals	84	84	120	132	156	160	232	238	258	256	238	180	154	118

Colors: Grey, brown, and blue   Minimum number required in stock: 2,410
Retail price: $19.95

(b)

Figure 11-1 ***(a)*** Model-stock plan for women's shoes and *(b)* model stock plan for men's slacks.

There are many resource aids. Trade associations or trade sources often supply retailers with valuable information on market demand, interpretation of that demand, and changes in retailing activities. Manufacturers and other vendors also disseminate information through their salesmen, catalogs, trade shows, and trade papers.

Manufacturers' sales representatives are essentially specialists. They know the products their firms handle and are a good source of information about the market acceptability of those products. Good sales representatives also know whether the demand for a product is increasing or decreasing. They will readily assist retailers in promoting and selling their goods because a sales representative's future income will depend on the retailers' ability to sell the merchandise at a profit.

Some vendors furnish retailers with catalogs which may be useful for comparative purposes. Product descriptions, prices, sizes, and other product features are shown in a catalog which may be helpful to a retailer in determining merchandise assortment.

Trade shows may also be held periodically during the year by vendors who present their offerings to retailers. These shows allow retailers to inspect new products from many resources. Manufacturers participating in trade shows are usually attempting to test the market demand for their products and discuss technical and marketing problems with retailers.

Trade papers or "flyers" offer the retailer the latest news concerning market demand, market forecasts, and new product acceptability. Some of these trade papers or flyers are issued daily, weekly, or only sporadically. News is funneled into these trade papers by the producers of goods or the manufacturer. Nearly every trade classification has a flyer or trade paper which is available to participating members either on a subscription basis or on a membership-fee basis.

Other resource aids include visiting the actual plant or place of production, visiting or observing competitors, or visiting large metropolitan markets, such as New York, Los Angeles, Dallas, or Chicago. These major market cities have special merchandise marts which display goods from many resources, and a retailer can make a personal inspection by visiting these merchandise marts.

A possible local source of information concerning resource aids may include the Small Business Administration's SCORE. The word SCORE stands for Service Core of Retired Executives. These individuals are often available for advice on various types of retail stores and can aid a person in establishing a retail store or solve a problem for an existing retailer. The Small Business Administration may operate seminars on retailing, and these seminars are often sponsored by the Retail Merchants Associations and Better Business Bureaus. If a retailer needs any information or knowledge to improve the operation of a store, it is available from some source. Sometimes, however, the retailer will have to do a little digging and probing to ferret out this information.

Within an existing retail store, sales records can be analyzed to determine consumer brand preferences, styles, sizes, and colors. It is also extremely important that these data be recorded at the time of sale. Further, an analysis of adjustment records on goods that have been returned for either an adjustment or an exchange, can provide valuable information on whether the merchandise is meeting the expectations of the customer. If for some valid reason the merchandise is not up to customer expectations, it is well to note such characteristics and base future buying decisions on such information. Often it is difficult to determine the "real" reasons for adjustments and returns, so care should be exercised to determine if the goods are actually defective in some way. If the reasons for returning goods are quite specific, such as defects due to a manufacturer's negligence, or material which stretches or otherwise does not hold its shape, then a retailer probably has justification for not reordering such merchandise. Customer satisfaction is the primary goal of every retailer. It is the key to a retailer's success, and every means or avenue must be pursued in order to ensure customer satisfaction.

Another internal source of information, which is easily obtainable because it comes from inside the store, includes stock records. An analysis and evaluation of stock or inventory records will reveal which merchandise has not been sold and which is selling well. If merchandise is not selling well, a determination must be made as to *why* the stock is not moving as expected. It could be due to inadequate display, poor promotion, or simply a lack of consumer demand, and the retailer should remedy this situation.

Some retailers keep a list of customer requests for certain goods. These are referred to as "want slips." A want slip is simply a pad or book in which the salesperson records customer requests for certain merchandise that the store does not currently have in stock. These items should be ordered and obtained for the customer, if possible, because stocking the customer-wanted item will build consumer confidence in the store. A certain amount of goodwill will also be built by the retailer in better serving the consumer. In an era of retailing activity when many items appear to be unobtainable from many retail stores, one would think that retailers should certainly capitalize on the use of want slips. The information is valuable and reliable in interpreting consumer demand since it comes to the retailer "firsthand", directly from the consumer. However, care should be taken so that want slips do not become crutches upon which salespeople rely. For example, sometimes it is easier for a salesperson to fill out a want slip rather than making certain that the item is really not in stock. The item requested may not be on the store's shelf, but it is possible that it is in the stockroom. Frequently goods are found in the stockroom after the customer has been told that the item is not in stock.

Other sources of internal information on what a store should buy may come from the salespersons themselves. Salespeople who remain on the selling floor are in a position to appraise consumer demand. It is well for a retailer to have some provision for eliciting comments from salespeople about what is and is not selling. This can be done through the use of weekly meetings or by using a suggestion box. Involving the selling force will usually stimulate interest, improve morale, and keep lines of communication open between the buyer and supporting personnel. It is extremely important that all supporting personnel

PURCHASING STORES NAME		J. W. ROBINSON CO.	600 West Seventh St. Los Angeles, California 90017	MARKING INSTRUCTIONS
		A Division of Associated Dry Goods Corp. New York Office: 417 5th Avenue, New York 10016		(CHECK ONE)

SHIP ONLY TO ADDRESS MARKED BELOW: (√)

SERVICE CENTER ☐ 15541 East Gale Ave. City of Industry, Ca. 91745	**VALLEY** ☐ 8501 Van Nuys Blvd. Panorama City, Cal. 91402	**NEWPORT BEACH** ☐ #2 Fashion Island Newport Center Newport Beach, Cal. 92660
LOS ANGELES ☐ 600 West 7th St. Los Angeles, Calif. 90017	**ANAHEIM** ☐ 530 N. Euclid Ave. Anaheim, Calif. 92801	**SAN DIEGO** ☐ 399 Fashion Valley San Diego, Calif. 92110
BEVERLY HILLS ☐ 9900 Wilshire Beverly Hills, Calif. 90210	**GLENDALE** ☐ 221 No. Glendale Ave. Glendale, Calif. 91206	**CERRITOS** ☐ 300 Los Cerritos Mall Cerritos, Calif. 90701
PASADENA ☐ 777 E. Colorado Blvd. Pasadena, Calif. 91101	**SANTA BARBARA** ☐ 3805 State St. Santa Barbara, Cal. 93105	**WOODLAND HILLS** ☐ 6100 Topanga Canyon Blvd. Woodland Hills, Calif. 91364

ROUTING

MARKING INSTRUCTIONS (CHECK ONE): NO MARK ☐ STRING ☐ KIMBALL ☐ GUM ☐ PIN ON ☐ ½ SIZE ☐

VENDORS NAME

VENDORS ADDRESS

(A). ROUTING: UNAUTHORIZED DEVIATION WILL BE CHARGED TO YOUR ACCOUNT.

(B). ALL BACK ORDERS MUST BE SHIPPED PREPAID.

(C). MDSE. DESCRIPTIONS ON BILLS OF LADING MUST BE IN ACCORDANCE WITH THE NATIONAL MOTOR OR UNIFORM FREIGHT CLASSIFICATION ACTIVELY IN EFFECT. DEVIATION WILL BE CHARGED TO YOUR ACCOUNT.

SPECIAL INSTRUCTIONS

CITY		STATE		ZIP	

DATE	SHIPPING DATE NOT BEFORE	CANCEL IF NOT SHIPPED BY	THIS ORDER SUBJECT TO CANCELLATION UNLESS SHIPPED IN ACCORDANCE WITH THESE DATES	DEPARTMENT NO.		
				SPECIAL DATING	214715	MFG. NO.
TERMS		**F.O.B.**	**POINT OF ORIGIN**	**FREIGHT ALLOW.**	ORDER NUMBER TRADE DISCOUNT	

MO.								**PACKING SLIPS AND MADE BILLS**		
AMT.										
MO.										
AMT.										
MO.										
AMT.										
MO.										
AMT.										

STYLE	DESCRIPTION	COLOR	COVER							QUANTITY AND UNITS	UNIT COST	TOTAL COST	UNIT RETAIL	TOTAL RETAIL	CLASS

BUYERS OFFICE	BUYER	MDSE. MGR.	TOTAL COST ▷	TOTAL RETAIL ▷	
64S REV. 1/73	THIS ORDER SUBJECT TO TERMS AND CONDITIONS AS PRINTED ON BOTH SIDES				M.U. %

Figure 11-2 Buyer's order form. *(Courtesy of J. W. Robinson Company, Los Angeles)*

understand that the store must operate as "a total system" if it is to be successful and serve the consumer well. When a retail store operates as a total system, any decisions made in one area will directly or indirectly affect the store in other areas. Failure to understand this basic phenomenon will ultimately lead to inefficiency and a loss of profitable sales volume. Thus, every retailer must strive for a total operating system in order to maintain a viable retail business. All the activities and functions of the store must work in unison; that is, there must be a coordination and integration of all the store's functions.

SUMMARY

A retailer must have the right goods, at the right time, at the right price, for the right customer. Failure to comply with any of these fundamentals of retailing management will result in an unsuccessful retail business.

Two broad classes of *resources* or suppliers are available to retailers: producers or manufacturers, and middlemen—who may be wholesalers, brokers, or agents. Usually a retailer will purchase from several sources of supply. Care must be taken so that the number does not become too large, since this could result in a diffusion of orders.

The retail store *buyer* is a key individual in the merchandising activities of a retail store. Purchasing merchandise for resale to final consumers is the primary role of any buyer, whether for a large chain or for the owner of a small store.

The major function of a buyer is to determine what to buy, how to price the merchandise, how to display the goods, and how to promote the merchandise successfully. In addition, a buyer has a responsibility to work with and assist supporting personnel, sustain a profit for the store or department, and maintain a solid working relationship with resources.

Supporting store personnel must coordinate and integrate the store's or department's promotion with other phases of sales promotion, work to create a total system for uniformity of decisions and customer relations, and work with all people and sections of the store for the same basic goals.

When a retailer purchases goods from a *manufacturer or producer,* it is said that the purchase is *direct.* Many large retailers prefer to purchase directly from the producer. Generally, small retailers have to purchase from wholesaling middlemen because they do not possess the buying power necessary to purchase directly from the manufacturer. Generally, purchasing directly from the producer results in fresher merchandise for the retailer. Further, goods bought directly from the manufacturer may cost a retailer less than if he or she were to buy from a wholesaling middleman. If an item must be returned to the manufacturer for any reason, it probably will be returned to the customer more quickly if it does not have to be sent to the producer via the route of the wholesaler. Some resources, such as producers, may provide quicker delivery to the retailer than if goods are purchased from a wholesaling middleman.

Middlemen are used as resources by retailers because certain merchandise may not be available directly from the producer. Some small producers will sell only through a wholesaling middleman. Often, wholesalers represent several producers and offer the retailer a greater assortment of merchandise than can be obtained from any single resource on a direct basis. Also, wholesalers are often better informed about local market conditions than are manufacturers.

The world's largest wholesale market for consumer goods is in New York. *Resident buying offices* are established in cities like New York to facilitate the purchase of soft consumer goods. The independent resident buying office often serves many different, noncompeting retail stores, whereas the store-owned resident buying office may be controlled by either a single large retailing chain or by a group of retail stores.

Resident buying offices provide a retailer with information on new resources, new products, market conditions, and trends in merchandising. In addition to offering a retailer special-order privileges, resident buying offices often settle disputes between a retailer and a resource.

Before a retailer makes any purchase of merchandise, it is wise to determine the number of *product lines* the store will offer for sale. A predetermination of product-line breadth and depth will allow a retail store buyer to plan purchases within the store's space requirements as well as within the store's financial budget.

Price lining consists of selecting a limited number of prices at which a store will sell its merchandise. Price lining is used as a buying aid for the buyer of the store. Price lining can lead to improved selling and merchandising techniques and improved customer relations. In turn, this often leads to a reduction in the number of markdowns and simplifies stock control.

A retailer's *goods and assortment mix* is the total offering of the store. A retailer should keep the merchandise assortment under constant assessment in order to maintain store efficiency. The assessment may determine that a store's profitable sales volume stems from a rather narrow assortment of goods and services.

A *model-stock plan* is used as a guide to assist a buyer in a retail store by providing information on previous sales of items by size, style, color, price lines, and other market factors.

A number of *resource aids* can assist a retailer in purchasing goods. Trade associations, manufacturer's sales representatives, trade shows, catalogs, trade papers, visits to places of production, and visiting one's competitors will provide a retailer with valuable information on what goods and services to purchase for the store. A store's internal records often offer one of the most reliable sources of information concerning what has been sold in the past. At times, the salespeople and the consumer will offer a retailer valuable tips on the type of merchandise to purchase for resale.

REVIEW QUESTIONS

1 Describe the duties and responsibilities of the retail store buyer.
2 Distinguish between the major types of merchandise resources available to a retailer.
3 What are some of the advantages accruing to a buyer who purchases merchandise directly from a manufacturer?

4 What are some of the advantages accruing to a buyer who purchases merchandise from a middleman?

5 Evaluate the buying policy of purchasing merchandise both directly from producers and indirectly from wholesaling middlemen.

6 Explain why it may not be wise to purchase goods from a large number of resources.

7 What is a resident buyer? What are the duties and functions of a resident buyer?

8 Distinguish between the two main types of resident buying offices.

9 What is a product line? Why is it important for a buyer or a retailer to determine in advance the number of product lines, and the breadth and depth of product lines that the store will offer to the consumer?

10 What is the purpose of price lining?

11 Discuss scrambled merchandising and the way or manner in which this retailing concept came into being.

12 What is model stock? A model-stock plan? What is the purpose of a model-stock plan?

13 What are some of the sources from which information can be obtained in making an analysis of the profitableness of handling certain lines of merchandise?

14 Evaluate some of the sources of information available to a retail store buyer in the interpretation of consumer demand. In what ways can this information be useful to a retail store buyer?

CASE PROBLEMS

1 **The Poppyseed** is a 7,500-square-foot specialty store in a Midwestern town of 40,000 population. The store specializes in handling greeting cards, gift wrap, and gift items such as crystal, lead glass, colored glass, ceramics, bathroom soaps, towels, and pewter.

The Poppyseed is located in a downtown area on the main avenue between the First National Bank and Kevin's Bar. Because of the number of people conducting business with the First National Bank, there is considerable foot traffic past the Poppyseed. Kevin's bar caters mostly to the town's state college students and the owners of the Poppyseed are not sure that this group of persons represents a potential market.

The Poppyseed was opened in June 1965 by Minnie and Pearl Offstrand, daughters of "Pappy" Offstrand, a highly successful grain dealer in nearby Osmond, a town of 2,500 people. "Pappy" financed the opening of the Poppyseed complete with inventory. His daughters signed a note for $45,000 which included the financing of inventory only, exclusive of the costs of the building.

Neither Minnie nor Pearl had any previous retailing experience; however, each was a graduate of the University of Minnesota. Minnie received a bachelor of arts degree in sociology and Pearl received a bachelor of arts degree in business administration.

The owners-operators of the Poppyseed never kept any records concerning the store's purchases. Sales data were minimal because the store had an old-fashioned cash register. No sales slip was ever filled out when a customer made a purchase. The Hallmark sales representative came in from time to time to rearrange the Hallmark greeting card section. This person replaced greeting cards that had been sold since the last call on the Poppyseed, and saw to it that the display was properly merchandised. The American Greeting card salesperson called on the Poppyseed four times each year and received orders from both Minnie and Pearl. Minnie and Pearl took turns ordering merchandise, and each ordered when it was deemed necessary to fill the shelves.

The Poppyseed honors Master Charge and BankAmericard, but does not extend any other form of credit to the customer. Because of the small size of the community, the Poppyseed often accepts personal checks from its customers as payment for merchandise.

A new planned shopping center was recently constructed on the western edge of the town where the Poppyseed was located. The center was located on a major highway and provided parking for approximately 2,000 cars. The center has been open about one year, and the merchants are doing a thriving business. It appeared that many of the downtown customers were driving to the shopping center to make many of their purchases.

The shopping center consisted of two anchor stores, Sears, Roebuck and Company, and J.C. Penney's. Forty-two small shops complement the shopping center by offering a wide variety of goods and services. The center even has a greeting card and gift store which has made its presence known to the Poppyseed.

The Poppyseed appears to be having some trouble in maintaining the proper merchandise in stock. Sometimes Minnie would order goods through the catalog distributed to the store by a New York specialty wholesaler. At other times Pearl would order merchandise from a Minneapolis wholesaler, often the *same items* that Minnie had ordered through the catalog from the New York wholesaler. At other times, the store received ceramics on consignment from the college students.

Because of the rapidly rising price of many lines of merchandise, the Poppyseed often paid more for items than the catalog indicated or the wholesaler quoted. This resulted in some bickering between Minnie and Pearl, and each thought something should be done to better coordinate the purchasing function. Each was at a loss as to *what* should be done with respect to buying merchandise and where they could turn for advice.

What is the basic problem with the Poppyseed? Outline your procedures for buying and handling merchandise for the Poppyseed. Can you suggest some policies that should be followed by the store in order that the operation can be more successful?

2   The Readyman Hardware and Building Supply Center occupied a site on a major street approximately two blocks west of the Westgate neighborhood shopping center. The store is located on a piece of property measuring 600 by 750 feet. The building measures approximately 200 by 240 feet, which consists of 48,000 square feet of selling and nonselling space. The sales area has been apportioned 36,000 square feet, and 12,000 square feet are used primarily for the storage of paint, plywood, and building materials.

After completion of the marketing research for site location, this particular location was selected over two other possible sites. It was believed that this location had better market potential than the other two locations. This has proved to be correct since sales and profits have risen steadily from opening day.

Some trade journals have been reporting that the growth areas include floor coverings and plumbing fixtures and supplies. Mr. Lowe, the store's general manager, has given some thought to adding either one or both product lines to the store's present goods and service mix. Either of these product lines would complement the store's present product lines, which include building materials for the do-it-yourself customer, hardware tools, paint and paint supplies, and small household lighting fixtures—in short, many of the items a person might use on weekend projects around the home.

According to the trade journal reports, more homes are being carpeted completely; that is, even the kitchen and bath areas are being covered with a high-density nylon carpet rather than using vinyl tile.

In another trade journal article it was reported that the sales volume of plumbing fixtures and supplies was on the rise due in part to the high cost of hiring a licensed plumber. Mr. Lowe would like to add both product lines to the present goods and service mix, but it was believed by top management that only one line of the proposed products should be added. The store could extend its present facilities by adding 2,500 square feet of space; it was thought feasible to add a wing to the present structure, and this addition would be used for the new product line. The present nonselling area was not to be disturbed since the storage area was well arranged.

The top executives of the store determined after a committee meeting that either of the proposed product lines would be a valuable and profitable addition to Readyman's present product offering. Both lines were expected to attract considerable consumer traffic. Based on previous business experience, either product line would add additional profits to the store. The problem seemed to be one of deciding which product line to add to the store's present lines and what steps should be taken by the store's management.

On the basis of the above data, which product line should Readyman Hardware and Building Supply Center add to its present product and service offering? What other factors would aid in this decision?

Chapter 12

Negotiations with Merchandise Resources

Before any actual purchases of merchandise are made, a retailer will find it necessary to negotiate with the resources or suppliers on a number of factors. One major point, of course, is the purchase price which will vary depending on the quality, quantity, and the various discounts allowed by the vendor. Also, a retailer is concerned with the period of time allowed before payment must be made to the supplier. This time period is often referred to as "dating" and together with the purchase price of the merchandise, is called the "terms of sale." That is to say, purchase price plus dating equals terms of sale. Other factors which are often negotiated between a retailer and a vendor include: (1) guarantees against a price decline, (2) the return of defective or otherwise unsaleable goods, and (3) transportation charges.

It is critical for the retailer and/or buyer to maintain good working relations with the suppliers and to be able to negotiate favorable terms of sale for the desired merchandise. (The term "buyer" will be used throughout the text to denote the individual responsible for purchasing the merchandise for a retail store.) A buyer should not expect to receive unusual price concessions from a resource and still retain the vendor's goodwill. Nor should the vendor place unusual demands on the buyer and still expect to maintain a mutually rewarding business relationship. Improved service and friendly relations are more likely to come from a vendor who believes that the buyer is treating him fairly. In turn, the buyer should obtain and strive to keep the respect of the vendor, thereby creating a solid business connection. Both parties in a purchasing transaction have to be satisfied in order to maintain a long-standing worthwhile business arrangement. Negotiations must be based on the mutual understanding of each other's position.

Perhaps the single most important element in the negotiation for merchandise is the price. From the vendor's viewpoint, the price must cover all the costs plus a profit. From the buyer's point of view, the net price paid for the merchandise must also be low enough so that a retailer can add a markup percentage and remain competitive. In other words, a retailer must be able to buy at a price which will provide a profit. If a retailer is forced to pay a supplier too much for the merchandise, the store will be forced to take less markup in order to remain competitive with other retailers selling the same goods.

Since we are primarily concerned with the buyer's duties, let us focus our attention on the price paid by the retailer. When purchasing merchandise from resources, the amount of the discount received by a retailer depends on the skill of the buyer. A buyer should be firm but not too rigid for fear of losing the goodwill of the vendor. Because it is the buyer's function to obtain the most favorable terms of sale that are possible, a buyer must not be too lenient. As you can see, there is a delicate balance between what a buyer can obtain on "terms of sale" and what can be procured with respect to delivery dates, state or condition of goods on arrival (returns), and continuous information concerning special purchases. Terms become mutual consideration for the buyer and the vendor. Both parties must retain respect in the mutual transactions of buying and selling.

DISCOUNTS AND ALLOWANCES

A discount granted to a buyer is any price reduction by a seller from the suggested or list price of that merchandise. Discounts are grouped as: (1) trade or functional, (2) quantity, (3) seasonal, (4) cash, and (5) promotional. Each of the foregoing is granted to a buyer by a vendor for a specific purpose although a selling-buying transaction may include any or all of the different kinds of discounts. But in order to gain a better understanding of what is involved in the various kinds of discounts, let us examine each of the types of discounts in some detail.

Trade or Functional Discounts

Trade or functional discounts are a reduction from the list price offered to middlemen (both wholesalers and retailers) in payment for performance of certain marketing functions. These marketing functions include: (1) buying, (2) selling, (3) storage, (4) financing, (5) risk bearing or taking title, (6) bulk-breaking units into smaller or single items, (7) transporting, and (8) disseminating market information. The marketing functions listed above are sometimes called marketing activities and are performed by all retailers both large and small. In order to compensate retailers for the performance of these functions or activities, a trade or functional discount is given; that is, a reduction from the retail list price of the merchandise.

For example, a manufacturer of a certain item may quote a suggested or retail list price of $80. The item may offer trade discounts of 40 and 10 percent. Thus, the manufacturer would receive $43.20 for this item. This $43.20 is the amount a wholesaler would pay the manufacturer for this merchandise. When the wholesaler, in turn, sells this same item to a retailer, the retailer will pay the wholesaler $48. The wholesaler keeps the 10 percent ($4.80) to cover the costs of operation and profit. Although the wholesaler is granted both discounts (40 and 10 percent) by the manufacturer, the retailer is granted only the 40 percent discount by the wholesaler. The retailer then offers this particular item to the ultimate consumer for $80, the manufacturer's suggested retail price. As a further explanation, see the following calculations:

Manufacturer's suggested retail price (100 percent)	$80.00
Less a 40 percent trade discount (to retailer)	− 32.00
	$48.00
Less a 10 percent trade discount (to wholesaler)	− 4.80
Price paid to manufacturer by wholesaler	$43.20
Wholesaler's purchase price	$43.20
Plus margin to cover operating costs	4.80
Price paid by the retailer	48.00
Plus margin to cover operating costs	32.00
Retail price to the consumer	$80.00

In order to save time and steps in the calculation of trade or functional discounts, at this point, let us introduce another method of determining the price paid by the retailer. This method is called the "on-factor method" of determining discounts.

In the previous example, we began with 100 percent. From this 100 percent figure, a deduction or discount of 40 percent was made (off factor). This leaves a 60 percent figure which is now called the "on factor." Using the on factor of 60 percent and the manufacturer's suggested retail price of $80 (which also equals 100 percent), a figure of $48 is obtained. See the following calculations:

Manufacturer's suggested retail price (100 percent)	$80.00
Multiplying by the "on factor" of 60 percent	.60
Price paid by the retailer	$48.00

The next step involves taking the second trade discount, 10 percent, from the base of 100 percent (100 percent − 10 percent = 90 percent). In our calculations, 90 percent now becomes the on factor. By using the on factor of 90 percent and the figure of $48, which was the result of the previous calculations, the result is $43.20—or the price paid to the manufacturer by the wholesaler as shown in the following calculations:

Manufacturer's list price* (100 percent)	$80.00
Less 40 percent discount	− 32.00
	$48.00
Multiply by the on factor of 90 percent	.90
Wholesaler's purchase price	$43.20

*The manufacturer's suggested retail price can also be referred to as the "manufacturer's list price"; the words are interchangeable.

Whichever method you prefer to use is a matter of personal choice. However, most business people will use the on-factor approach because of the time and steps saved. Either way, notice that trade or functional discounts are determined or calculated in "chains" (more than one discount). Each discount is computed on the remaining balance after the preceding percentage figure has been deducted. As in the example above, the two discount figures of 40 and 10 percent are *not* added together for a combined 50 percent discount. This is why you must use one of the above calculation methods in order to determine the correct purchase price.

Trade or functional discounts will vary considerably from one type of industry to another. This is due to the differences in the normal markups required by retailers and other middlemen and, in part, because of the differences in trade customs.

"Chain discounts," or a series of discounts, are very common among some types of industries and are used by many manufacturers. Chain discounting is used by manufacturers in order to meet competition and to grant lower prices to buyers depending upon supply and demand. For instance, a manufacturer of rubber products (tires, v belts, overshoes, raincoats, and the like) may offer a buyer a series of discounts as follows: 30, 20, 10, and 2.5 percent. The terms as quoted to the retailer would be: list price less 30 percent, less 20 percent, less 10 percent, less 2.5 percent. This form of chain discounting is common practice for a manufacturer selling tires to a retailer operating a tire store.

In the calculation of chain discounts, a buyer must begin with the manufacturer's suggested retail or list price. Usually the manufacturer supplies a retailer with a printed price list. By taking the manufacturer's suggested retail price, or a total price for the purchase of several items, a deduction is made in the following manner: The suggested or total price, less 30 percent, less 20 percent of that balance, less 10 percent of the next calculated figure, less 2.5 percent of that balance.

For example, let us assume we have a manufacturer's retail price of $900 for a certain number of tires. The buyer, through chain discounting, would pay a total price of $442.26.

Total price of the merchandise (100 percent)	$900.00
Less 30 percent discount	− 270.00
New balance	$630.00
Less second discount of 20 percent........	− 126.00
New balance	$504.00
Less third discount of 10 percent	50.40
New balance	$453.60
Less fourth discount of 2.5 percent	− 11.34
Price paid by the buyer	$442.26

Justification of Trade Discounts   Trade or functional discounts are justified from a retailer's point of view in that a relatively large gross margin is needed to cover operating costs and, hopefully, provide a profit to the retailer. Trade discounts also determine the price a retailer will pay a producer for goods, whether the retailer sells the merchandise at the manufacturer's suggested retail price or sells the goods at some other price.

From the manufacturer's point of view, trade discounts adjust for differences in the cost of the production and sale of the goods. For instance, a producer may sell 10,000 units to a single wholesaler or retailer. Or the manufacturer may sell the 10,000 units to twenty smaller retailers. Thus, there is considerably more selling expense associated with the sale of those 10,000 units to twenty smaller retailers than with selling the 10,000 units to one larger retailer or wholesaler. The sale of 10,000 units to twenty retailers could involve twenty separate calls by a salesperson, twenty separate shipments and billings, and could increase the possibility of greater collection problems. Thus, the differences in trade discounts granted to different buyers and various classes of trade (wholesalers versus retailers) is justified since it is based on the size of the order, the frequency of purchase, and the number of invoices or transactions that must be completed.

Trade or functional discounts also may be justified in that a vendor or seller may wish to maintain more intensive distribution of the products. (Intensive distribution is where a vendor will sell to a number of outlets all offering the same product for sale.) For example, a large retailing chain store may purchase directly from the manufacturer as does the wholesaler. If both the chain store and the wholesaler are granted equal trade discounts, chain stores would be able to undersell smaller retailers on the same items. Therefore, a larger trade discount may be justified to the wholesaler for competitive reasons. It seems only fair that the wholesaler be able to cover all marketing costs associated with selling the same goods to many smaller retailers. Assuming that all other factors are the same, an analysis of a situation of this sort would indicate that the retail price of an item would be the same at both the small retailer's store and the large chain store. At least both retailers—the chain store and the small retailer—have paid the same price for the identical item, except for quantity discounts granted.

Another justification from the manufacturer's point of view is that the principle of intensive distribution of a product (selling a product to many outlets offering the same product) has been accomplished through the use of trade discounts by offering the same goods to the same classification of buyer at the same price. The price differs only for a different type or class of buyer—the wholesaler in this case. By maintaining a policy of intensive distribution through the use of a discount structure, the manufacturer has broadened the market for the product, making it available to a larger number of ultimate consumers. The greater the exposure of a product to the final consumer, the greater the potential for an increased sales volume.

Trade or functional discounts are legal as long as the same discount (reduction) from list price is granted to the same classification of trade. That is, all wholesalers must obtain the same discount, or all retailers must receive the same discount.

Since trade or functional discounts are granted to buyers on the basis of market status classification (such as wholesaler, jobber, or retailer), it may be thought that buyers performing different functions would not be in competition with one another. However, section 2(f) of the Robinson-Patman Act of 1936 does make it unlawful for a buyer "knowingly to induce or receive a discrimination in price which is prohibited by this section."

This provision of the act tends to protect the smaller retailer from the larger buying power of chain stores. Otherwise, large chain stores could demand and receive huge discounts that would not be available to the smaller independent retailers, thus forcing the smaller retailers out of business since they would not be able to compete with the prices of the chains. The Federal Trade Commission and the courts have taken the position that these trade discounts are legal as long as there is no injury to competition. However, the same discount must be granted or made available to all buyers of the same market status (wholesalers or retailers). Any disparity or discrepancy between prices granted to wholesalers or retailers based on trade or functional discounts could give rise to litigation and court actions.

Quantity Discounts

Quantity discounts given to a buyer are reductions from a vendor's list prices for purchasing large amounts of merchandise. Usually, special discount prices are given by the vendor if the buyer purchases a large order. Quantity discounts may be based on either the number of units or the dollar amount of the purchase. The quantity discount also may be stated as a percentage figure or stated in actual monetary units (dollars and cents).

Quantity discounts are granted by a vendor to a buyer because it is more economical for the vendor to sell a product in larger units; the seller's costs associated with billing, shipping, and collecting are reduced when large orders are filled.

The legality of quantity discounts is also subject to the provisions of the Robinson-Patman Act of 1936. For instance, a vendor selling goods in interstate commerce (between states, as opposed to intrastate which is within the state) may not offer greater quantity discounts to one buyer than to another buyer in that classification, if:

1   The goods are of the same grade and quality.
2   The price difference tends to create a monopoly.
3   The price difference substantially lessens competition.
4   The price difference injures, destroys, or prevents competition with a seller or buyer, or customers of either a seller or buyer.
5   The price difference is not making "due allowance for differences in the cost of the manufacture, sale, or delivery resulting from the differing methods or quantities in which such commodities are to such purchases sold or delivered," or offered "in good faith to meet the equally low price of a competitor."

Manufacturers who have been questioned regarding various quantity discounts to buyers in the same trade classification have defended their position on the basis of cost differentials associated with marketing those goods. Or, as stated in (5) above, some vendors have defended their discount structures by stating they are "meeting a competitor's equally low price." This defense is rather weak, and generally the courts have not upheld it as reasonable.

In the final analysis, a retailer should be careful not to become a participant to illegal discounts since under the Robinson-Patman Act of 1936, the retailer is equally guilty. The real offender under the Robinson-Patman Act has been the large buyer, but this charge may be somewhat unwarranted. How is a buyer to know, or how could the buyer even be *expected* to know, whether the price the store is paying is lower, the discount greater, than that of other buyers? To be in violation of the act, a buyer must be reasonably aware of, or have knowledge of, the illegality of the lower price of the goods. In short, both buyer and seller must be aware of any illegality, and this must be proved by the complaining party. However, since the Robinson-Patman Act is explicit on the restraints concerning quantity discounts, a buyer should exercise caution in receiving large discounts based on the quantity purchased.

Cumulative Quantity Discounts   Cumulative quantity discounts are those discounts which are allowed to accumulate over a period of time, usually one year. Whether in units or dollars, cumulative quantity discounts are based on total volume. By using cumulative quantity discounts, a vendor can attract and hold customers over a period of time, say, for the current year. The buyer is rewarded for concentrating purchases with this vendor because the percentage discount is calculated on the year's total business rather than being determined on each individual transaction. In essence, cumulative quantity discounts are viewed as patronage discounts, since the more total business a buyer gives a vendor, the greater the discount.

Cumulative quantity discounts are often used to stimulate the sale of slow-moving items by including with them faster moving goods. The slower moving items are offered at very attractive discounts and sold with the more popular goods as a package deal. A producer is often able to make more effective use of production capabilities by offering retailers cumulative quantity discounts. For instance, assume that a retailing-chain-store system agrees to order a certain amount of merchandise from one manufacturer. A producer can go ahead and produce the goods and, at the same time, allow cumulative quantity discounts on the total order. This is possible even though the individual stores in the chain may purchase smaller orders each month throughout the year. In this illustration, it would appear that cumulative quantity discounts benefit both the producer and the retailer.

There is some question, however, as to the advisability of a manufacturer allowing the use of cumulative quantity discounts. First, even though a producer may be able to regulate production, there are no cost savings in filling and shipping small orders. Any savings in production costs may be offset by increased marketing costs.

Second, buyers may be encouraged to purchase in smaller quantities which will reflect a hand-to-mouth buying policy on the part of retailers. If a vendor allows quantity discounts to accumulate over a period of time for some retailers, all retailers may insist upon this type of buying arrangement.

Noncumulative Quantity Discounts   Noncumulative quantity discounts are based on individual transactions and are given to encourage large orders. There are cost savings to a vendor using noncumulative quantity discounts to encourage large orders. Generally, a vendor's selling expenses, as a percentage of sales, decrease as the volume rises. Therefore, the vendor can afford to give quantity discounts and still make a profit while, at the same time, building goodwill among the customers. For instance, many expenses such as a salesperson's calls, billing, order filling, and shipping to an individual customer are reduced when a vendor can send out one large order instead of many smaller orders.

A buyer may benefit greatly from taking advantage of any quantity discount on merchandise that a vendor may grant. For example, a vendor may offer a quantity discount of 50 cents off each case of tuna providing the buyer purchases 25 cases or more. Or a vendor may allow a 12 percent discount on a single shipment of footwear (canvas or sportswear) if the buyer will purchase a minimum number of 350 pairs. On shipments of mattresses, a producer may allow a discount of 7.5 percent on orders up to and including 24, a discount of 10 percent on orders up to and including 48 units, or a discount of 12.5 percent on all single orders up to and including 72 units. Most buyers will press a vendor for large quantity discounts. In Chapter 11, we learned that a buyer's responsibility was to purchase not only the right merchandise but to purchase that merchandise at the right price. Often, quantity discounts are the only way in which a retailer can pass unit savings or a discount on to the consumer. In other instances, quantity discounts may allow the retailer to obtain a little extra profit from the operation of the store. In today's retailing environment where there is a constant squeeze on a retailer's profits, a wise buyer will have to negotiate for all the discounts that are obtainable from the vendor.

Seasonal Discounts

Seasonal discounts are used by vendors to encourage buyers to place orders early in the season. If a buyer places an order well in advance of the regular selling season, seasonal discounts, amounting to 5, 10, or even 20 percent, are granted by some manufacturers. Seasonal merchandise (such as air conditioners, lawn mowers, snow blowers, or Christmas decorations) are goods that usually carry seasonal discounts. In effect, the vendor is shifting the marketing functions of storage and warehousing to the buyer. Whenever a producer shifts these marketing functions forward to the retailer, there must be some incentive to the retailer. That incentive is usually in the form of a seasonal discount, which is a reduction from the normal price of the merchandise.

Off-season orders for seasonal merchandise allow the vendor or manufacturer an opportunity to level out the production schedule and make better use of production facilities. It is often less expensive for a manufacturer to grant buyers seasonal discounts than it is to close down the production facilities for a period of time, especially if one considers the startup costs and expenses of rehiring personnel.

Manufacturers of toys generally grant seasonal discounts to buyers who are willing to accept delivery of goods well in advance of the holiday season. For example, retailers of toys may take delivery of merchandise in July or early August, which is well in advance of the Christmas season. Also, a manufacturer of snow tires often encourages retailers to purchase and take delivery of shipments by July, which again is well ahead of the snow season.

Retailers may be willing to take delivery of goods in advance of the normal selling season if the discount granted by the vendor is more than what the costs of storage will be. If the cost in time and space expenses to warehouse the merchandise before the selling season is greater than the amount of the discount, the retailer has little incentive to buy early. However, many vendors continue to press retailers to purchase early in the year in order to obtain a better selection of merchandise. Thus, a retailer, in some instances, has little or no choice but to place orders early and accept delivery of the merchandise before the regular selling season. For this reason, warehouse space has become more scarce in some areas. Also, the costs of warehousing merchandise must be added to the retail price of the goods which means the ultimate consumer must pay for these expenses, as they must pay for any other marketing costs incurred by the retailer.

There is a variation of seasonal discounting which is called "forward dating." Forward dating allows the retailer to sell a portion of the merchandise before the invoice becomes due and payable. If a retailer is able to sell a portion of the goods before payment is due the vendor, the retailer—in effect—is able to operate on the vendor's money.

To illustrate how forward-dating terms work, assume that a manufacturer of rubber products offers forward-dating terms to a retail buyer of snow tires. The manufacturer may offer the following terms of sale to the buyer: Take delivery of the merchandise on or before July 15. One-third of the purchase price is due on or before November 10 with a 2 percent cash discount applicable to the amount of the payment; one-third of the purchase price is due on or before December 10 with a 2 percent cash discount applicable to the amount of payment; the final one-third of the invoice is due on or before January 10 of the following year, also with a 2 percent discount on that amount.

In this case, the retail buyer is also entitled to the normal 2/10 cash discount (a deduction of 2 percent for payment within ten days) in addition to dividing into thirds the total payment for the merchandise. A vendor may or may not grant a cash discount to a buyer with forward-dating terms, although this practice is common for the manufacturers of rubber products. Sometimes this incentive of forward-dating terms can also be called a "sweetener" by vendors. Supposedly, forward dating makes the purchasing transaction more attractive to a buyer, and the retailer often will take advantage of forward-dating terms.

In the above illustration, the retailer will have sold much of the merchandise before the final payment is made to the manufacturer. In periods of rising interest rates, buyers may find that it is less expensive to store merchandise for short periods of time than to borrow money from a commercial bank for working capital.

One may ask why a producer would extend forward-dating terms to buyers of merchandise. By granting forward-dating terms to retailers, a manufacturer obtains orders which will allow the firm to commence producing for the next consumer selling season. Thus, the manufacturer does not experience the unprofitable and disagreeable chore of having to close the production facilities for a period of time. This enables the manufacturer to level out production costs and keep the selling price more competitive. Also, storage costs are minimized for the producer, and there is less risk of price changes.

Cash Discounts

A cash discount is a reduction in the total price of an order granted by a vendor to a buyer for prompt payment of the invoice. The cash deduction is from the face amount of the invoice, *after* deducting the trade and quantity discounts from the list price. In other words, the cash discount is computed as a percentage of the amount that remains after all other discounts have been deducted. For example, let us say a vendor offers a retailer a cash discount of 2/10, n/30 terms on an invoice dated January 7. Let us also assume that the retailer owes the producer $800 after the trade and quantity discounts have been granted. The retailer may then deduct a cash discount of 2 percent if the payment is made within ten days after the date of the invoice, or by January 17. If the retailer pays the bill by January 17, a cash discount of $16 may be deducted from the $800 invoice, making a payment of $784 due the vendor. If the buyer does not pay the invoice by January 17, the entire bill (or $800) is due within 30 days (by February 7). Thus, two elements are present in cash discounts: (1) the percentage reduction itself (in our example it was 2 percent) and (2) the time period in which the invoice must be paid (2/10 or n/30).

Many different terms of sale which include cash discounts are offered by various manufacturers. Some vendors offer 2/10, n/30, as in our illustration above. Other manufacturers may grant as much as 6/10 eom (end of month). Such a large cash discount may be offered to buyers of women's ready-to-wear clothing (due to seasonality) or to buyers of carpeting (due to storage). Generally, the practice of the trade will determine the amount of cash discount a vendor will extend to a retailer.

Other terms used by manufacturers include cash discounts of 2/10, 30 extra, which in effect extends the 2 percent cash discount to 40 days (10 days plus the additional 30 days). Terms of 2/10 eom refer to a cash discount period ending the tenth of the month following the month in which the purchase was made. For example, 2/10 eom terms for a purchase made on January 1, indicate that a 2 percent cash discount may be taken by the buyer any time through February 10.

It is extremely important that a retailer take advantage of any and all cash discounts offered by vendors. Even if a retailer must borrow the money from a commercial bank at 12 to 15 percent per annum in order to pay the invoice, it still would pay the retailer to take the cash discount. To illustrate this fact, consider the following: A vendor offers to a buyer terms of 2/10, n/30—one of the most common cash discounts offered to retailers. For the retailer who does not pay the invoice within the ten-day period of the cash discount terms, the effective rate of interest amounts to a staggering 36 percent annual rate. Why is the rate 36 percent? There are approximately eighteen 20-day periods in a year (18 days × 20 days = 360 days). Since the original terms were 2/10, n/30, there are 20 days in which the retailer uses the money of the vendor (30 − 10 = 20 days). So the eighteen 20-day periods times the percentage-rate figure (2 percent in this case) equals the annual percentage rate of interest (2 percent × 18 = 36 percent). If a vendor offers a cash discount of 4/10, n/30, the annual rate of interest would be the equivalent of 72 percent if the buyer did not take advantage of the cash discount. Thus, it becomes readily apparent that a retailer should always take a cash discount if offered. It costs less to borrow money from the bank or another source than it does to "borrow" from the vendor.

Cash discounts, when granted to retailers by vendors on equal terms, as with other forms of vendor discounts encounter little danger of being illegal under the Robinson-Patman Act of 1936. If there is any price differential at the same level of competition (all retailers are considered to be on the same level), price discrimination may be present. This transaction would then be considered to be illegal under the Robinson-Patman Act.

Promotional Discounts and Allowances

Promotional discounts and allowances are price reductions granted by the vendor to the retailer in partial payment for advertising and promotional services performed by the retailer. Promotional discounts and allowances may take the form of a 25-cent-per-case allowance, as for certain food products or a discount or an allowance may be granted in the form of one free case with the purchase of twelve cases of the same product at the regular price. At times, promotional discounts and allowances also may be in the form of point-of-purchase display materials or granted in dollar amounts for special advertising purposes.

Promotional discounts and allowances are used by suppliers so that the merchandise will be advertised and/or displayed by the local retailer. In many instances, the reputation of the retailer is better known to the customer than the reputation of the vendor. Or the opposite may be true. The reputation, reliability, and name of the manufacturer may be more highly esteemed than that of the retailer. In either case, both the vendor and the retailer benefit from the use of promotional discounts and allowances if they are used properly and with discretion.

When accepting promotional discounts, the retailer has a portion of the promotional costs paid by the vendor. At the same time, the vendor is able to take advantage of a lower rate of advertising and promotional cost than would be experienced if the advertising were done on a nationwide basis. If the retailer is local and thus enjoys a local advertising rate, the rate is always lower than national advertising rates. Since the vendor is paying the retailer to advertise for him, it would appear that the vendor is getting more promotion for the money spent.

Manufacturers of well-known brands of merchandise often like to have retailers arrange large displays of their merchandise where they will receive a lot of customer attention. One method that is used to encourage this practice is to provide the retailer with substantial promotional discounts and/or allowances. At times, depending on trade-union regulations, sales representatives of manufacturers will offer the retailer assistance in arranging these displays. Some manufacturers also offer retailers instore demonstrations as a means of encouraging retailers to display, stock, and promote the vendor's brand of merchandise.

Promotional discounts and allowances extended by vendors are considered by some to be pricing strategies rather than promotional incentives. This philosophy probably depends on the intent of the vendor and the reaction of the retailer. In one sense, promotional discounts and allowances can be thought of as a reduction in the cost of the merchandise since the net price paid by the retailer is less than if the merchandise did not have this allowance.

Promotional discounts and allowances to retailers can also be thought of as reductions in promotional expenses. This is logical since the manufacturer is actually paying for a portion of the advertising costs, not the retailer. In whatever manner these promotional discounts and allowances are perceived, it appears that they are extended by a vendor for the mutual benefit of both supplier and retailer and probably will continue as a practice of the trade. Naturally, retailers will continue to seek promotional discounts and allowances because they are a means of assistance in paying for advertising costs associated with promotion of the merchandise.

The Robinson-Patman Act of 1936 does limit the extending of promotional discounts to retailers by vendors. Any promotional discount or allowance extended by a vendor to a retailer must be made on "proportionately equal terms." Although the word "proportionately" is not defined in the Robinson-Patman Act, court decisions have made it clear that neither the vendor nor the buyer should extend or accept promotional allowances unless such funds are reasonable. That is, all retailers must be afforded like discounts and allowances, and these discounts and allowances must be extended for the same or similar services.

In 1968, the United States Supreme Court held that a manufacturer furnishing advertising and promotional allowances to retailers buying directly (large chains) must also offer the same allowances to other retailers who compete with these direct-buying retailers, even though the merchandise may be purchased indirectly from wholesalers.[1] This ruling by the Supreme Court tends to protect the small retailer in that all promotional allowances must be the same. However, large retailers purchase a larger dollar volume which, in effect, yields a larger promotional allowance.

It would appear from this landmark decision that notice has been served to vendors and retailers that promotional allowances must be "proportionately equal to competing firms." If competing retailers cannot take advantage of such promotional allowances, alternatives must then be made available. Vendors must take every precaution to ensure that all retailers receive the same proportion of discount. Further, vendors must also make sure that they receive the advertising services for which the allowance was granted.

SHIPPING TERMS

After a purchase has been made, the cost of transporting the goods from the vendor to the retailer must be determined. Transportation costs may be paid by the retailer or by the vendor or shared by the vendor and the retailer. Shipping merchandise may cause some concern with respect to ownership since the question often arises: "When does the title pass from the vendor to the retailer?" This is an important question because whoever has title to the goods bears the element of risk of owning those goods. Should something happen to the goods in transit, then ownership becomes extremely important and must be determined before a final settlement can be made. Following are several transportation arrangements that can be selected by the retailer and the supplier.

F.O.B. Origin or Factory

When a vendor quotes a price f.o.b. (free on board) factory or point of origin, the buyer pays all transportation charges. Free on board origin or factory is probably the most common means by which merchandise is shipped. Title to the merchan-

---

[1]*Federal Trade Commission v. Fred Meyer, Inc.*, 390 U.S. 341 (1968).

dise passes to the buyer at the point of origin (factory) or the vendor's loading dock.

Assume that a buyer for a large department store in Los Angeles purchased from the Furniture Mart in Chicago a truck load of furniture. The amount of the invoice is $15,000, and the terms of the invoice are 4/10, n/60, f.o.b. Chicago. When the trucking firm (a common carrier) loads the furniture at the dock of the Furniture Mart in Chicago, title to the furniture passes to the department store in Los Angeles. If the trucking firm charges $1,000 for freight from Chicago to Los Angeles, the department store will pay that amount to the trucking firm and then obtain possession of the merchandise. Any loss or damage that occurs to the furniture on its way from Chicago to Los Angeles will be the responsibility of the department store, and they will have to file a claim against the trucking line. The trucking line then will have to settle the claim which is usually done by an outside insurance firm. If the department store pays the invoice within the cash discount period, the store sends the vendor a check for $14,400 ($15,000 less the 4 percent cash discount).

F.O.B. Origin, Freight Prepaid

A vendor may ship merchandise f.o.b. origin, freight prepaid. In this case, the buyer does not pay any freight charges and takes possession of the goods upon arrival. As in the previous example, title to the merchandise passes to the buyer when the goods are loaded on the common carrier.

F.O.B. Origin, Freight Equalized

In a few instances a vendor may share the costs of transportation with a retailer. This allows a supplier to extend the market for the merchandise since the retailer would normally purchase the same or comparable merchandise closer to home. But some manufacturers at distant points when entering a new market area will absorb some of the freight charges. The arrangement to share or equalize the costs of freight vary considerably, and usually the terms are negotiated by the vendor and the buyer before the transaction has been completed.

PRICE GUARANTEES

It is not uncommon for a buyer to seek from the vendor a guarantee against a possible future price decline on merchandise. This practice evolved from early order placement, especially when seasonal goods were involved. It works in this way: In a guarantee against a price decline, the vendor agrees to reimburse the buyer if the price of the goods is lowered after the order has been placed. The amount of the reimbursement to the buyer will be the difference between the price at the time the order was placed and the price at the time the merchandise was shipped. During a time of rapidly rising prices, there is probably only a slight chance that the price will go down on any type of merchandise. However, there is always the possibility that some goods may lose their appeal, and their price would be reduced by the manufacturer. The manufacturer generally uses a price guarantee against a price decline to stimulate early orders from buyers. Or sometimes it may be used to encourage buyers to place large orders on staples (such as flour or sugar) when the price structure is uncertain and unstable. An unstable market condition could emanate from uncertainties in growing conditions or from precarious labor market conditions.

CONSIGNED MERCHANDISE

In some instances merchandise, instead of being sold to the vendor, is "consigned" to a retailer. When merchandise is consigned, it is transferred or delivered into another's custody. No sale of the merchandise by the supplier to the retailer takes place, and the title to the goods remains with the vendor; but the merchandise is left, so to speak, in the custody of the retailer. With consigned merchandise, the retailer is acting as an agent for the vendor.

When the retailer sells some of the consigned merchandise, the store receives a commission which usually is in the form of a percentage of the selling price. The retailer then deducts the commission before the sales price is remitted to the vendor. All the risks of ownership rest with the vendor on consigned merchandise. The consignee (retailer) acts only as an agent, not as a merchant middleman (taking title to the goods). However, the retailer, under a consignment arrangement, is responsible for damaged, lost, or otherwise unsaleable merchandise.

Why do vendors consign merchandise to retailers? There are several advantages. First, by consigning merchandise to a retailer, a vendor has more control over the retail price of that merchandise. The manufacturer or supplier will set a definite price. Since the retailer is being paid a set commission, the retailer has no choice but to charge that set price.

Second, consigning merchandise is often the only way for a vendor to place the merchandise in a retailer's place of business. When viewed from this perspective, the consignment of merchandise places the vendor in a weak position. In reality, however, it may be the only way in which a retailer will display and sell the vendor's merchandise. This is especially true if the vendor is new to the market or is introducing an item which has not proved its marketability and is not supported by a national promotional campaign.

Third, for the financially weak retailer, consigned merchandise may be a real advantage. The retailer is able to operate on the vendor's funds since the retailer need not invest or tie up money in merchandise.

Fourth, manufacturers or producers of certain types of goods, such as carpeting, tires, batteries, and artwork, will consign merchandise to new businessmen to get them started in retailing. Usually, after a certain period of time, the individual retailer will be required to purchase the remaining stock from the manufacturer. But the consignment of merchandise is one method for a manufacturer to establish retail outlets in markets which offer sales potential.

However, consigned goods have one major drawback for the retailer. The retailer cannot share in the profits provided by the sale of the merchandise but must be satisfied with the fixed commission rate.

EXCLUSIVITY OF REPRESENTATION

Exclusivity of representation refers to the right of a retailer to sell certain goods in a protected territory without having to compete directly with another retailer selling the same merchandise. For some retailers, this is a very important consideration. By being made an exclusive agency, a retailer may have to be willing to pay a higher price for certain merchandise. But if a retailer is granted exclusivity to the merchandise, no other retailer within a prescribed area can sell the identical brand of goods. The retailer with an exclusive arrangement on certain goods or name-brand items will enjoy certain market advantages. These advantages include the absence of direct price comparison since this retail store will be the only one in the area selling a particular brand. Also, this retailer will be the recipient of the manufacturer's full cooperation and assistance in promotion and advertising. Under an exclusive arrangement, the retailer may also be able to sell the merchandise at a higher gross margin than can be accomplished with comparable merchandise. This is true because similar goods must compete directly with the same brands offered by other retailers. Under an exclusive representation arrangement, the manufacturer benefits by having one retailer in an area that is thoroughly dedicated to the sale and promotion of the producer's brand of merchandise. Like many of the resource-retailer relationships, exclusive representation by a retailer for a manufacturer is of mutual benefit to both parties.

Some examples of exclusivity of representation include the following: (1) a retailer in an area handling only the Magnavox line of TVs and stereos, (2) a retailer of Ford automobiles protected somewhat by territorial boundaries, or (3) Amana freezers and refrigerators being offered by only one dealer in an area.

SUMMARY

Before any actual purchases of merchandise are made, a retailer will find it necessary to *negotiate with resources*. Negotiations will usually be concerned with the price, quality, quantity, discounts, and with the period of time allowed before payment must be made to the resource. Negotiation terms become mutual consideration for the buyer and the seller.

Discounts are grouped into five areas. These include trade or functional, quantity, seasonal, cash, and promotional. *Trade discounts* are reductions from the list price offered to middlemen in payment for performance of certain marketing functions. *Quantity discounts* given to a buyer are reductions from a vendor's list prices for purchasing large amounts of merchandise. *Seasonal discounts* are used by vendors to encourage buyers to place orders early in the season. A *cash discount* is a reduction in the total price of an order granted by a vendor to a buyer for prompt payment of the invoice. *Promotional discounts* and allowances are price reductions granted by a vendor to a retailer in partial payment for advertising and promotional services performed by the retailer.

After a purchase has been made, the *cost of transporting* the merchandise from the vendor to the retailer must be determined. When a vendor quotes a price f.o.b. factory, the buyer pays all transportation costs; f.o.b. origin, freight prepaid means that a vendor pays all freight charges; f.o.b. origin, freight equalized indicates that the vendor will share the costs of transportation with a retailer.

It is not uncommon for a retail buyer to seek from a resource a *guarantee* against a possible future price decline on merchandise. In a guarantee against a price decline, the vendor agrees to reimburse the buyer if the price of the goods is lowered after the order has been placed.

In some instances merchandise is *consigned* to a retailer. No sale of the goods by the vendor to the retailer takes place, and the title to the merchandise remains with the vendor. The retailer receives a commission from the sale of consigned merchandise.

Some retailers have *exclusivity of representation* of a vendor's goods. This means that a retailer can sell a vendor's merchandise in a protected territory without having to compete directly with another retailer selling the same brand of goods. Exclusive representation by a retailer for a manufacturer is of mutual benefit to both parties.

REVIEW QUESTIONS

1 Why are the negotiations with vendors so critical for a retailer?
2 What is the basic purpose of a resource granting a trade or functional discount to a retailer?
3 What is the justification for a retailer receiving a larger trade discount than a wholesaler?
4 What do we mean by the "on-factor" approach to discount calculations?
5 How can a vendor justify granting quantity discounts to retailers?
6 Distinguish between cumulative and noncumulative quantity discounts.
7 Why do some vendors grant cumulative quantity discounts?
8 Explain why seasonal discounts are used by vendors. Why do retailers take advantage of seasonal discounts?
9 What is a cash discount? What are the three elements of cash discount terms?
10 Explain the basic purpose of promotional discounts and allowances. How does the Robinson-Patman Act of 1936 define the legality of promotional allowances?
11 Indicate who pays the transportation charges and when the title to the goods passes for each of the following terms: f.o.b. origin (factory); f.o.b. origin, freight prepaid; and f.o.b. origin, freight equalized.
12 Explain how a guarantee against a price decline works for a retailer.
13 What is consigned merchandise? Why would a manufacturer use consignment as a means of moving merchandise?

14 What are the benefits to a retailer when a vendor consigns goods to the store? Disadvantages?

15 Explain the benefits to both a vendor and the retailer when an exclusive agency arrangement is used.

PROBLEMS

1 A manufacturer of furniture in Durham, North Carolina offers terms of 4/10, n/30 to a retailer. Modern Furniture in San Diego, California, places an order which amounts to $10,400. The invoice is dated June 27. Modern Furniture pays the invoice on July 6. How much is the cash discount? How much was paid on the invoice? How much would have been saved by Modern Furniture if funds would have to have been borrowed from a local bank at 14 percent for 20 days in order to be able to take the cash discount?

2 A large manufacturer of fine china plates offers the following terms to a specialty store retailer:
    a $450 per 100 plates, 2/10, n/30
    b $475 per 100 plates, 2/10, n/30, less 5 percent
    c $500 per 100 plates, one place setting free, value $44.95
    d $500 per 100 plates, 2/10, n/30, $25 advertising allowance
    Which terms are the most favorable to the retailer?

3 Moss Wallpaper and Paint, a retailer in paint supplies, receives an invoice from the vendor which amounts to $1,750 at the vendor's list prices. The store receives trade discounts of 25, 10, and 5 percent off the vendor's suggested retail list price. The invoice is dated October 19, and offers terms of 2/10, n/30. Moss Wallpaper and Paint paid the invoice on November 1. How much was remitted to the vendor?

4 Smith and Hutchinson, retailers of small garden tools, lawn mowers, and garden tractors, made a purchase of garden tractors from Farmland Industries, Inc., Newport, Rhode Island. Smith and Hutchinson are located in Lincoln, Nebraska. Farmland Industries loaded ten garden tractors onto a truck, Watson Brothers Freight Lines, at the Farmland Industries loading dock. The terms of the invoice were: f.o.b. Factory; 2/10, n/90; the total amount of the invoice was $28,900. Watson Brothers Freight Line charged $457 for freight from Newport, Rhode Island to Lincoln, Nebraska. What did each garden tractor cost Smith and Hutchinson? When did the title to the goods pass to the retailers? Assuming that the invoice was paid within the discount period, what amount would be remitted to Farmland Industries? One tractor was damaged on the route to Lincoln. Who pays for this damage? How does the retailer go about collecting for this freight damage?

5 Mitchel and Sons purchased a carload of appliances from Westinghouse in Philadelphia. The purchase consisted of washers, dryers, refrigerators, and stoves. The amount of the purchase was $13,210. Terms on the invoice were 3/20, n/60, f.o.b. Philadelphia, freight equalized. Westinghouse offered Mitchel and Sons a special promotional allowance of $8.25 per unit, and the carload lot contained 110 units. One of the washers was damaged while unloading and it was believed that the unit suffered $43 damage. The invoice was dated July 5, and was paid on July 23. What is the amount of remittance to Westinghouse? Who pays for the freight? Who is responsible for payment of the damaged washer?

6 Sharon's, a women's ready-to-wear store, received an invoice for a billed amount of

$653.28 from the Cole Company of California. Sharon's is located in Boise, Idaho. Cole's is located in Los Angeles. The date of the invoice is May 3 and the terms are 4/ 10, n/45, f.o.b. Los Angeles. Transportation charges total $8.99. How much money should Sharon's remit to the Cole Company?

7 Jacobson's, a men's specialty store, received an invoice from H. Freeman & Sons, Philadelphia, for the amount of $4,248. The invoice was dated March 13 and bears the terms of 3/15, n/45. If the invoice is paid within the discount period, what amount should Jacobson's remit to H. Freeman & Sons? What is the last date that the discount can be taken?

8 The Dart Shirt Company produces men's shirts and offers terms of 2/10, n/30 to all customers. The Dart Company produces shirts of varying qualities among which one style is sold for $84 per dozen, and each retails for $14. The Dart Company allows cumulative quantity discounts, and last year Larson's, a men's clothing specialty store, purchased 1,200 dozen shirts from Dart. On this amount, Larson's received a 5.5 percent cumulative quantity discount. Larson's always took advantage of the cash discount granted by the Dart Company. What was the net cost to Larson's of a shirt retailing for $14?

CASE PROBLEM

Warehouse Carpets is a retail store offering a full line of fabric floor coverings. The store does not sell tile floor coverings.

Warehouse Carpets opened a new facility on West "O" Street in Linwood, Colorado, a town of 43,000 population. The store has been in operation for the past two years, and sales and profits have been rising faster than management had planned.

The physical structure consists of 12,000 square feet of cinder block construction. Of the 12,000 square feet, approximately 2,500 square feet of space is devoted to a showroom. It is in the showroom where the samples and displays of carpet are placed for the consumer to inspect and compare for color, fabric, and so on.

The storage area contains some 10,000 square feet of heated space in which carpet rolls are warehoused on large rollers. After a customer makes a selection from the samples in the showroom, a roll of carpeting is taken from the rack by an electrical forklift capable of lifting 3,000 pounds. The carpet roll is then spread out on the floor, measured, cut, then rerolled and tied. The customer usually takes the carpet at this time, although sometimes Warehouse Carpets makes the delivery and installation.

Warehouse Carpets recently made a purchase of 10,000 square yards of carpet from a leading carpet mill in Pennsylvania. The mill was making some changeovers and this carpeting was considered to be "mill ends." Mill ends are the last of a particular type of fabric and color which cannot be matched with the production of new carpeting.

The carpet mill ends were purchased for $27,900, f.o.b. factory. Warehouse Carpets had to pay the freight company $3,400 for transportation charges. The terms of the invoice were 6/10, n/60. No special advertising or promotional allowance was involved because this purchase consisted of only mill ends. The invoice was dated February 12. Warehouse Carpets paid the invoice on February 22. What was the amount of the payment to the carpet manufacturer? What would have been the amount of the payment had Warehouse Carpets not taken the cash discount? What was Warehouse Carpet's net cost per square yard of carpet?

Chapter 13

Handling Incoming Merchandise

Once merchandise has been purchased and shipped, a method for receiving, checking, marking, and placing the goods on the selling floor should be established. A shipment of goods should be inspected as it is received from the carrier, and a record should be made. Merchandise also should be checked against the invoice for any discrepancies in price, quantity, or quality of goods. In large stores, these functions are usually delegated to specialized personnel; or at times, a buyer may wish to perform these activities. In a small retail operation, the proprietor or a salesperson may carry out all these functions. But whether a large retail store or a small one is involved, careful planning and organization in handling incoming merchandise will yield important economies and reductions in costs associated with these operations.

Upon the arrival but before the placement of the merchandise on the selling floor, several different kinds of work must be performed. First, when a shipment arrives, it should be received by someone at the store. Receiving refers to taking actual physical possession of the shipment. After taking physical possession of the shipment, it should be inspected and checked. Someone at the store must also sign a document stating that the delivery has been made and acknowledge receipt of the shipment. Next, the cartons should be opened, inspected, and checked against the buyer's purchase order. The buyer's purchase order should be compared to the vendor's invoice and any discrepancies noted. If shortages in shipment occur, a claim for credit should be filed with the vendor. If the shipment compares favorably with the purchase order, the merchandise then will be marked and moved either to the stockroom or, preferably, to the selling floor. Marking merchandise consists of placing the desired information on the goods, including the code and the price of the merchandise, and providing information for better inventory control and guidance for selection by consumers.

Considerable attention should be given to the efficiency of handling incoming merchandise. Efficiency in correctly handling incoming merchandise improves customer service because the goods are placed as soon as possible on the selling floor where the customer can inspect the merchandise. Further, the retailer will enhance profits for the store because merchandise sitting in a stockroom where it cannot be seen cannot be expected to sell; the customer cannot purchase a product that is not visible.

ADVANTAGES OF RECEIVING EFFICIENCY

Since the objectives of the receiving operations are chiefly concerned with reducing operating expenses and improving customer service, let us review the numerous advantages of an efficient receiving operation.

First, by quickly moving the merchandise received to the selling floor, a retailer may enjoy a more rapid rate of inventory turnover (RITO). As mentioned previously, merchandise which cannot be viewed or inspected by the customer has little chance of being sold. The more rapid the rate of stock turn (turnover), the less frequently a store will have to employ markdowns because of merchandise obsolescence.

Second, the more rapidly the merchandise is received, checked, and the invoices sent to the accounting department, the better the chances are that the store will be able to take any cash discounts. If the receiving process is slow, it is possible that the invoices will arrive in the accounting department too late to take advantage of the cash discounts.

Third, any shortage in shipment will be quickly noticed when receiving operations are under careful surveillance. If the amount of goods delivered is less than the amount ordered and billed, suppliers should be asked immediately to credit the store for any discrepancies. Such careful scrutiny on the part of the retail store may also indicate to the vendors the exactness with which the store's receiving department operates. In turn, this might lead to fewer errors in shipping on the supplier's part.

Fourth, if the receiving department is efficient in moving and storing the goods, there probably will be less chance of the merchandise being damaged or otherwise becoming unsaleable.

Fifth, overpayment of invoices may be reduced or eliminated when the receiving department works quickly and efficiently in checking the merchandise.

If done correctly, the store's purchase order can be carefully compared and checked with the amounts appearing on the invoice and receiving records, thereby reducing clerical and shipping errors.

Finally, an alert receiving department will check freight bills for the proper freight classification, rate, and weight. Overcharges may be prevented or reduced when incorrect freight classifications, rates, or weights are noted at the time of delivery. Freight companies tend to make some errors since so many packages and shipments are handled every day. Retailers should check for any errors in the calculation of freight charges since these errors appear to be a major complaint of retailers

THE RECEIVING DEPARTMENT

Receiving is an integral function or extension of buying merchandise. Usually, receiving becomes a buyer's responsibility although this duty is often delegated to someone else. This is especially true if the store is large and has a central receiving department. If the store is small and independently owned, the owner personally may receive, inspect, and mark the goods as they arrive from the freight line.

Inspection of Merchandise

The receiving operation begins with the delivery of goods by the carrier to the store's receiving area or dock. The next process which takes place should be an inspection of the merchandise in the presence of the delivery person.

First, a physical count of cartons is made to ensure that the number corresponds with the purchase order and the packing slip. Thus, any discrepancies can be noted on the carrier's receipt. Cartons and boxes should also be inspected for possible damage or for evidence of having been opened before arrival at the store. These notations should be made on the store's copy of the freight bill, which the driver must sign as confirmation of these losses or damages. A driver's signature is necessary if a store is to file a claim or collect on any goods lost or damaged.

It also is well to inspect the waybill to ascertain the following information: (1) the goods being delivered are the same as those described; (2) the store name is correct; and (3) the number of cartons corresponds to the number of cartons on the waybill. Since common carriers make many stops each day, it is not uncommon for drivers to make mistakes. Discovering the mistake at the time of delivery will eliminate many problems which might arise later when an attempt is made to recover the right goods.

In order to keep the shipment together, the last step in the inspection process requires that the individual in charge mark each carton or box with a receiving number, date, and number of pieces. These data are then entered in the receiving record.

Although receiving records differ from store to store, generally, a record will contain the following:

  1 Date and hour of arrival
  2 Carrier's name
  3 Number of cartons
  4 Receiving number (which comes from the record book at the time of
entry)
  5 Invoice number
  6 Condition of cartons
  7 Delivery charges
  8 Amount of invoice
  9 Department ordering the merchandise
10 Any remarks concerning arrival conditions, damages, or shortages

Checking of Merchandise

After the goods have been delivered and accepted by the receiving department, the next step is to check the merchandise to determine if the contents of the cartons (individual items) are in agreement with the purchase order. The cartons or packages should also be checked for quantity and quality. Several methods of checking incoming goods are discussed below.

    Direct One method of checking incoming goods is known as the "direct check" which is often used in small stores. The direct check is quick and simple. Any discrepancies can be noted immediately and can be followed by a recheck if deemed desirable. A direct check requires a physical count of incoming goods against the vendor's invoice. Sometimes suppliers do not send duplicate invoices in package containers, making necessary postponement of the checking process until the invoice arrives. The result is that the merchandise cannot be moved to the selling floor as quickly, and the retailer incurs storage expenses.

    Blind If an invoice is not sent by the vendor, a store may use what is known as a "blind check." A blind check requires the person who is examining the parcels to prepare a list of the contents in each package. To expedite the blind check, standard forms are provided. However, in some instances a checker's description of the goods does not match the invoice description, which may develop into costly delays and errors.

    Semiblind In order to overcome some of the limitations of both the direct check and the blind check, another method called the "semiblind check" has been developed. A copy of the buyer's order is used to record the quantity of goods in a semiblind check. The buyer's order has all the pertinent information except the quantity delivered which is then provided by the person checking the goods. This system may be slow since the person checking the goods must physically count them. However, an excellent control is provided by the semiblind checking system. Further, invoices are kept by the accounts payable department, and invoice losses are minimized.

Marking of Merchandise

The marking of goods is the physical process of putting the price on an item *after* a price determination for that product has been made. All merchandise should be marked with the selling price unless the goods have been premarked by the vendor. This marking may be done by placing a ticket on the merchandise itself or on a container, shelf, or fixture near the item. In some stores, such as grocery supermarkets, the price is placed on the individual items and also on the shelf. Sometimes gummed lables, a marking machine, or price tags are also used in placing the price on the merchandise.

There are several reasons for marking the merchandise. First, the marking of goods with a price serves as an aid to the customer in purchasing an item. Most customers are interested in the price of a product. If an item is not marked, the first question a customer will ask of a salesperson is "What is the price?" Generally, price and quality are commensurate; that is, the higher the price, the higher the quality; or the lower the price, the lower the quality. If price and quality are not commensurate or if there is no relationship between the two factors, the retailer will suffer from a loss of business when the customers discover the truth.

Second, if a customer is shopping for price only, marking the goods will aid the salesperson in readily assisting the customer. Marking the goods will eliminate the time needed for a salesperson to look for the price in the records. Pricing the merchandise may also increase the customer's confidence in that store since the customer knows the store wishes to serve the consumer better. Also, marking the merchandise has much the same purpose as price lining; that is, the customer and the salesperson can quickly pick out a certain price line.

Third, for self-service and self-selection stores, marking the goods with the selling price is almost mandatory. In these types of retail outlets, the customer must see the goods marked, or there will be a resistance to purchase. It becomes easy for the customer to postpone any purchase for goods that are not marked with the selling price. (There are exceptions to this, of course. In specialty stores, such as those that feature high-fashion goods, the customer may have to inquire about the selling price. This is a deliberate strategy on the part of the retailer so that a salesperson must assist the customer.)

Fourth, merchandise that is marked with the selling price is easily assessed for value for inventory purposes. An assessment may be done several times each year, and the retail selling price may be used for determining the value of inventory.

Marking Fundamentals for Control   Certain fundamentals in marking merchandise can aid management in its control function. First, the price should be legible, easily found, designed so that customers cannot change it, attached in a manner which will not damage the goods upon removal, and yet be permanent. Prompt and efficient marking also facilitates making a sale. Only those persons directly responsible for marking should be allowed to control the price-marking devices and tickets. If marking is too loosely controlled by the management, there will be too many chances for errors.

Pricing information placed on goods varies from store to store and by the type of merchandise. Some retail stores wish to mark goods with cost data in addition to the selling price. If a store decides to do this, the cost of an item will probably be in code with any ten-letter word serving as the code. Each letter in the word will represent a number from one to nine and zero. An example of such coding is as follows:

R E D I N B A U G H
1 2 3 4 5 6 7 8 9 0

Thus, an item costing $3.95 would be coded as DGN. If this item were to sell for $7.95 at retail, the ticket would be coded as follows:

$7.95
‾‾‾‾‾
DGN

Any coined word or name will suffice for coding, although it is well to use a word that is not easily recognized by the public. Foreign words or Latin terms may be good ones to use for coding the cost of goods since many people are unfamiliar with them.

In large retail stores that have access to computerized facilities, price tags often carry additional information. For example, the computerized price tag may have a department number, season, manufacturer's number, style number, class, color, size, and retail price. This information serves as a valuable aid to merchandise control. See Figure 13-1 for a sample price tag with eight items of data.

The price tag that is shown in Figure 13-1 contains all the information a retailer needs for merchandise control. For example, the age of the item can be determined from the ticket, as well as the month in which the item was put in stock. This is indicated in the code. The use of any four letters can be used to indicate the four quarters of each year, or one could use W, X, Y, and Z to represent the four quarters of the current year. Thus, W could represent the first quarter, January, February, and March; X will represent the second quarter, April, May, and June, and so on. If one decides to go into the next year, additional letters of the alphabet may be used. The month of each quarter can then be numbered one through three. Merchandise placed in stock in May would be coded as follows: X2 (X represents the second quarter and 2 designates the month of May). Z3 would indicate that the merchandise was placed in stock during the month of December with Z indicating the last quarter of the season and 3 signifying the month of December, or the last in the series of months.

One may ask, "Of what value is the dated information?" In most stores, merchandise dated or coded early in the season should have been sold by the latter part of the season. If the item has not been sold by the time the third or

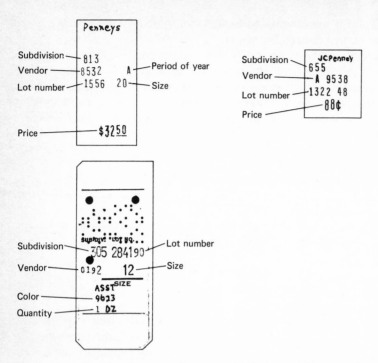

Figure 13-1 Sample price tags. *(Courtesy of J. C. Penney Company, Inc.)*

fourth quarter (season) rolls around, it may become shopworn or obsolete. Thus, dating in code serves a purpose when deciding or determining which items will be marked down.

The information on the price tag which indicates the department and the classification of the merchandise assists the retailer in determining the total sales by department and by classification of good. Most department stores use this information as a guide in deciding what merchandise to buy in the future and as an aid in determining the overall efficiency of the department. Each department is usually required to "carry its own weight"; that is, each department must share in the expenses and contribute to the overall profits of the store.

Some retailers also feel it is valuable to know from what resource the item was originally purchased. Resources are given a number, and this number will then appear on the price tag. The resource number is valuable in determining the movement of merchandise as well as serving as an aid in placing future orders or in reordering the same item. Sometimes merchandise which is defective must be returned to the vendor. This resource number can then be used to identify the vendor correctly and quickly, saving time in returning defective goods.

When marked in code on the price tag, the style, color, class and size aid the buyer and sales personnel in correctly identifying items. Coding this information on the price tag is useful to the retailer when making a determination of what items to reorder. It also serves as a sales indicator of style, trends, colors, and sizes and can be utilized to help facilitate inventory control.

Centralized Receiving

Large retail stores generally have a centralized receiving department. Centralized receiving departments offer many advantages for receiving and handling goods. For instance, there is always the possibility of merchandise losses occurring between the time the goods are unloaded on the store's dock and the time the same goods are placed on the store's shelves. The procedure for receiving merchandise should be routinized in order to reduce errors and minimize the loss of goods and to decrease the costs of handling. Salespeople, generally, are poor choices for handling incoming merchandise in that they often consider such duties a waste of time. Salespersons consider selling to be their prime function, not handling incoming merchandise. Thus, permanent, nonselling personnel should be assigned the duties and responsibilities associated with the receiving department.

A centralized area for receiving should be established with routine standards and procedures for handling incoming merchandise. This standardization will also place the responsibility for execution of receiving duties on certain individuals. By training certain personnel and giving them the responsibility for handling incoming goods, a store will benefit from better control of merchandise. When a store receives proper credit for damaged goods and for shortages in shipments, it probably will be able to reduce its expenses and increase profits. Thus, it is important for the receiving and accounting departments to work together so that these activities are accomplished in the most efficient manner.

Centralized receiving also leads to a more rapid movement of merchandise

Figure 13-2 Centralized receiving operations. *(Photograph Courtesy of FedMart, San Diego)*

to the selling floor. The quicker the merchandise can be moved to the selling floor, the less likely the store will experience stock obsolescence and markdowns. Stockrooms should be used only for merchandise which cannot be adequately displayed on the selling floor. Often, salespeople will not search diligently for goods in the stockroom if the selling area does not have the item on display. The storage of merchandise only results in an expense to the retailer: expenses in moving the goods as well as the loss of the profit from unsaleable items for whatever reason. Although it is necessary to have adequate reserves of merchandise, goods should be moved to the selling areas as quickly as possible.

A centralized receiving area also reduces the expenses associated with receiving goods, checking invoices, auditing, and inspecting the goods as they arrive. Freight charges should be checked at the time of arrival or soon thereafter for the proper classification, rates, and weights. An efficient, centralized receiving department will eliminate and reduce overcharges associated with improper billing by freight carriers. All shipping documents should be inspected and audited for any errors in transportation charges.

SOURCES OF MARKING INFORMATION

Since a great deal of information may be required for coding the price tag, where can all these be obtained? The buyer is usually the person responsible for the information that will be placed on the price tag. In a small store, the information comes from the owner, who probably also serves as the buyer. Of course, a small store may not have such an elaborate price tag as found in Figure 13-1.

The buyer may wish to mark a sample price tag for an item with all the needed information. The invoice, purchase order, or official price list will provide the buyer with the necessary information. After a sample item's tag has been marked and coded, the buyer usually designates someone in the stock room to complete the job of marking the remaining items. Since the buyer is responsible for the complete buying function, it is best that he or she mark the sample item so that it is done correctly. One reason for doing this is that some market changes may have been made since the time the order was first placed with a resource. Consumer demand may have changed, or some items may vary in style, color, or finish. Each shipment and its proper marking requires the careful scrutiny of the buyer in order to provide effective control over the complete buying function.

Since the retailer's net cost of the merchandise is indicated on the invoice, a buyer is able to determine what amount must be added to this cost figure in order to provide a profit to the store. This information is then coded and added to the price tag.

Retailers selling staple items often use an official price list. For grocery stores, the order book may also supply the retail price for the item. Sometimes these official price lists provide the retailer with a suggested retail price range on certain items. A grocery store manager may or may not abide by the official price list because some markets will bear a higher price on the same item than the other markets will support. Usually, an official price list, provided by either a manufacturer or a wholesaler, will give an item's gross margin which has been predetermined by the producer or the middleman.

Some producers wish to control the retail price of an item and when the pricing and marking of merchandise is done by the manufacturer, it is referred to as "premarking." This is usually called a "manufacturer's suggested retail price," "resale price maintenance," or "fair trade"—which strategies will be dealt with in more detail in another chapter. In premarking, much of the work is done by the producer which is an advantage to the retailer. This will reduce the time and expense of the retailer which would be spent in marking assuming that the manufacturer does not charge for performing this function. After the pre-marked merchandise has been received by the retailer, though, it is still necessary to check to see if the price tickets have been attached and carry the correct information.

Some buyers also utilize what is called "preretailing." Preretailing means that the buyer places the price on the purchase order when the merchandise is ordered from the vendor. This practice will cause the buyer, before the good is purchased, to think in terms of the selling price of an item. Some retailers feel preretailing serves as an aid to more careful buying and improved purchasing. One disadvantage of preretailing is that the prices may have changed by the time the goods arrive at the store. If they have changed, the new price must be affixed to the item before it is put on the selling floor.

Equipment and Layout for Handling Merchandise

The arrangement of equipment, the layout of space, and the facilities for handling merchandise must be tailored to each individual retail store. In small stores, no special equipment may be needed. The goods are readily marked and moved to the selling floor or the storage area directly from a receiving area. However, when a retail operation becomes larger, it may be necessary to provide a "system" for receiving operations. Although each store's system for receiving, handling, and moving the goods will vary depending on the space, the amount of goods received, and the time element involved, certain basic fundamentals apply to all retail stores regardless of size.

Since retailing involves the handling of goods with little or no value added other than time, place, and possession utility, it is mandatory that the most efficient means of handling and processing merchandise be utilized. Merchandise should be unloaded, unpacked, checked, and the price marked in a logical and methodical manner. Each step of the handling and processing operation should move the goods one step closer to the selling floor. This process may resemble a production-line facility, which basically it is. Each step builds on the previous phase of the handling process. A minimum of handling, correspondent with each function being performed, will result in a more efficient operation.

The handling of goods can be thought of as similar to a time-and-motion study. The fewer the motions and the less time in each phase of the handling process, the more expedient the flow of goods. A careful study should also be

Figure 13-3 Equipment and layout for handling merchandise.

made of the space available within the retail store for the handling of goods in order to ensure maximum efficiency.

Large retail stores will mechanize handling operations wherever possible. Since retailing is basically a labor-intensive activity, it will pay a retailer dividends to use mechanical devices wherever possible. Wages or commissions constitute the largest single expenditure for most retailers. Thus, a wise retailer will use as many labor-saving aids as possible. Conveyor belts, chutes, tables, moving carts, or portable tables may be and should be used since they are able to carry much more merchandise than a single individual can and can do it more quickly. In turn, this will reduce a retailer's payroll expenses.

Personnel in the receiving department should be trained to perform special handling functions. This will reduce costs associated with breakage and errors in marking. However, adequate supervision in the receiving room is also necessary because this may be one area in a retail store where considerable time is lost because employees engage in "horseplay." In some instances, this often leads to breakage of goods and damage to the equipment used for handling the merchandise.

After the merchandise has been received, unpacked, and the price marked, it should be stored in areas designated for such goods. This will allow quick movement to the sales floor or provide easy access for delivery in the case of appliances. All the merchandise should be arranged according to the floor plan and space available. Nothing is more wasteful to the retailer or more frustrating to the sales personnel than not being able to find an item which is *known* to be in stock. Customers will tend to patronize more frequently those retail institutions where the retailer knows what goods he has and where the items are located in storage. This is one operational area in the retail store in which considerable costs savings can be accomplished if the system is operated properly and efficiently.

Factors Affecting the Location of Receiving

Efficiency in receiving merchandise is dependent on several factors. Among these factors are adequate space and its proper utilization.

What is the value of space in a retail store? Obviously, the most valuable space should be utilized for selling and display. But space, its value, its apportionment, and utilization vary considerably depending on the size of the retail store. For instance, a small retail store may not have space set aside which is used only for the receiving, checking, and marking of merchandise. It is entirely possible that a shipment of goods may be unloaded on a sidewalk and then carried to a back portion of the store. Here the merchandise is checked and marked at the owner's convenience and then put on the selling floor. Some larger retail stores may have a dock at the rear which is used for receiving shipments. The store may have a small but adequate room to which the arriving goods are moved. In this room the containers are checked and the goods are marked. Later, the merchandise is moved to the selling floor and displayed.

A retailer whose store is located in a congested area may find that it is more efficient to receive, check, and mark merchandise at a location other than the physical retail outlet. Often an outlying warehouse is used for such purposes. This is particularly true for a small retailing chain, say, a sporting goods chain of four stores. One store may be located in a downtown area whereas the other three may be located in newer, suburban areas of a city. In this instance, a warehouse facility could be used to receive all shipments for the sporting goods chain. Also, the arriving goods could be checked for shortages, and the items marked at this facility. One advantage of using space outside the retail store is that the entire floor space can be used for display and selling. Many older facilities are small, and the selling floor markedly increases in value. It may be less expensive for the retailer to rent space away from the store for the receiving, checking, and marking of merchandise than it is for the retailer to move the store to a new and larger location.

Another factor which influences the location of receiving facilities is the amount of merchandise that is to be received. A small store does not receive a large volume of goods, and it probably does not need a large amount of space set aside for this purpose. However, the larger retail store which receives shipments daily will need enough space to handle a number of arrivals. As a rule of thumb, enough space should be allocated for receiving so that merchandise is not cramped and damaged because of the lack of space. Inadequate space for receiving usually leads to unnecessary handling of goods which only increases the expenses of the receiving department.

The type of goods received will also help to determine the location of the receiving department. For example, items such as furniture or appliances are quite bulky and need an unusual amount of space. In some instances, retailers of such goods have found it advantageous to locate a receiving department away from the retail store. Again, it may be a warehouse, or a facility constructed next to the store just for receiving purposes. The newer retail warehouse stores, such as Wickes and Levitz, allocate space apart from the showroom and selling areas. Even though the receiving department may be a part of the same building, the areas are clearly designated and separated by walls and special equipment and facilities.

Accessibility for trucks should be considered in selecting space for the receiving department. Many older stores or retailers in downtown city areas may have limited accessibility. It may be difficult for common carriers (truckers) to find the stores because of traffic congestion, one-way streets, no alleys, etc. Usually the most desirable receiving space is at the rear of a store. This location allows the unloading activities to take place out of sight of the customer. It also allows greater freedom on the part of the receiving personnel to move about. Sometimes a store's rear location cannot be utilized because of existing narrow alleys or one-way streets. In these instances, consideration should be devoted to locating the receiving operations away from the store. It may save time and improve relations with the common carriers if the receiving facilities are not readily accessible.

For those retail stores which have adequate space for receiving in the same structure, the department should be located as near the selling area as possible. The less the merchandise is moved, the less likely it is to be damaged; and there is a better chance of reducing labor time and expenses. If receiving facilities are located away from the physical retail outlet, consideration should be devoted to the movement of the goods from the receiving department to the store where they are to be sold. The movement of the merchandise from the receiving department should be kept at a minimum without sacrificing the display and selling areas of the store. Any movement of goods from a receiving area remote from the selling area should be cleared first with the buyer and the merchandise manager.

Receiving Operations

Unnecessary delays in the handling of goods should be avoided. Although the arrangement and space allocation for the receiving department depends on the volume and type of merchandise received, speed and economy are also two very important factors. The flow of goods through the receiving department can be facilitated by having the proper equipment and an efficient arrangement. Basically, there are four methods of handling incoming merchandise.

One of the most common methods of handling incoming goods entails the use of the stationary table. Sometimes this stationary table is called a "check-marking table" because merchandise is unpacked, sorted, and placed on this table. Then after the goods have been checked and marked, they are moved to the stockroom or the selling floor.

Another method for handling incoming merchandise involves the use of portable tables (with wheels). Merchandise is placed on these portable tables where the goods are sorted and checked. The tables are then moved to another area for marking, and from there, are taken to the selling floor.

The "bin method" separates a receiving room into two sections. The first section is used for checking, and the second is used for marking, with a series of bins dividing the two sections. After the goods have been marked, they are then delivered to the selling floor.

Larger retail stores make use of conveyor systems. A mechanical conveyor consists of either a canvas belt or metal rollers, which move continually. Merchandise is placed on the belt or rollers and is rather quickly moved through the checking and marking operations. These conveyor systems are also used to move the goods to the stockroom or to move the goods to the display and selling areas of the store.

Use of a conveyor system speeds the flow of goods through the receiving department. The movement of merchandise should be mechanized if possible since the use of obsolete equipment or hand labor is usually not economical. For the movement of merchandise, modern, powered equipment is preferred over the hand-work methods because of speed and efficiency.

Depending on the type and size of a retailing operation, the use of other modern equipment may be possible. Furniture, appliances, and other heavy items may be easily moved through the use of overhead monorails. Lift trucks (preferably electric because of the noise level and absence of exhaust fumes) may be used in conjunction with pallets (which are wooden skids, frames, or plates upon which goods are placed). The lift truck or forklift, as it is commonly called, inserts two iron prongs into the pallet or skid upon which the goods rest. Then the truck raises the pallet from the floor and moves it where desired. Forklifts will raise 3,000 pounds or more which is usually sufficient for most operations.

Although a rather large initial expense is associated with mechanizing the receiving operations, in the long run this investment will usually result in a savings to the retailer. Mechanized operations have been proven to result in fewer injuries to personnel. Mechanical means will move greater quantities of goods than hand methods, and thus wages may be reduced. The marking of merchandise can also be mechanized. In general, any job in receiving which is repetitive should be mechanized if possible. This mechanization will increase the amount of work that can be performed with less personnel. Since retailing is a labor-intensive activity, it is well to reduce the number of people whenever possible so long as it does not adversely affect the retailing functions.

SUMMARY

Once merchandise has been purchased from the resource and shipped, a *method for receiving, checking, marking, and placing the goods* on the selling floor should be established. Any shipment of merchandise should be inspected as it is received from the common carrier, and the retailer should make a record of the shipment. Merchandise should be checked against the purchase order and invoice for any discrepancies in price, quantity, or quality of goods.

The *objectives of the receiving operations* are primarily concerned with reducing operating expenses and improving customer service. Other advantages which may accrue to a retailer with an efficient receiving operation include the following: (1) a more rapid rate of inventory turnover (RITO) occurs; (2) the retailer is able to take advantage of cash discounts; (3) any shortages in shipment will be quickly noticed; (4) there may be less chance for merchandise to become damaged or otherwise unsaleable; (5) the overpayment of invoices may be reduced or eliminated when the receiving department works quickly and efficiently in checking merchandise; and (6) an alert receiving department will check freight bills for the proper freight classification, rate, and weight.

It is well to inspect the *waybill* to ascertain that: (1) the goods being delivered are the same as those described; (2) the store name is correct; and (3) the number of cartons corresponds to the number of cartons on the waybill.

A *direct check* requires a physical count of incoming goods against the vendor's invoice. A *blind check* requires the person who is examining the parcels to prepare a list of the contents in each package. In a *semiblind check,* a copy of the buyer's order is used to record the quantity of goods in the shipment.

The marking of merchandise is the physical process of placing the price on an item after the price for that product has been established. Marking the merchandise with a price serves as an aid to the customer in purchasing the item. Marking the merchandise will eliminate the time needed for a salesperson to look for the price in the records. For self-service and self-selection stores, merchandise must be price-marked for consumer convenience. Also, marking the goods serves as an aid in assessing the value of merchandise for inventory purposes.

Some retailers have access to *computerized facilities,* which enables them to place certain information on the tags, such as size, color code, class, manufacturer's number, season, or department number. This information serves the retailer in controlling merchandise. It also aids the buyer in purchasing merchandise for future sales events.

Generally, large retail stores have a *centralized receiving* department. Centralized receiving usually offers a standardized routine for handling incoming merchandise which often leads to a more rapid movement of goods to the selling areas. In many instances, centralized receiving reduces the expenses associated with receiving goods, checking invoices, auditing, and inspecting the merchandise as it arrives at the store.

The store buyer usually is responsible for obtaining and placing the information on the merchandise tag. This duty may be delegated to another person by the buyer. *Preretailing* refers to placing the retail price of the items being purchased on the store's copy of the purchase order.

Personnel in the receiving department should be trained to perform *special handling functions.* This will reduce expenses associated with breakage and errors in marking.

The efficiency in receiving merchandise depends to some extent upon the *location of the receiving area.* Care should be taken to apportion and utilize space close to the selling area. This will reduce the amount of time in the movement of the goods from receiving to the selling floor.

To expedite the flow of goods from receiving to the selling floor, retailers should make use of the *latest equipment.* Tables, conveyor belts, and the like will lessen the burden of physically handling the merchandise. For heavy goods, forklifts are needed to move merchandise from one area to another. The initial expense for equipment may be considerable, although it will pay a retailer dividends in the long run. Since retailing is a labor-intensive business, it is well to reduce the number of people handling goods whenever and wherever possible.

REVIEW QUESTIONS

1 There are certain advantages when receiving operations are efficiently performed. What are these advantages?
2 Explain the concept of "centralized receiving."
3 Discuss some of the advantages of centralized receiving.
4 What takes place during the inspection phase of the receiving operations?

5   Discuss the three methods of checking incoming merchandise.
6   Explain the differences in marking merchandise for a full-service store and a self-service store.
7   Explain why some retailers code the merchandise. Devise a code system other than the example provided in the text.
8   Where can a retailer obtain information concerning the marking of merchandise?
9   Explain the basic purpose of preretailing.
10 Visit a receiving department of a local store. Make a report evaluating the layout and design of the department for handling merchandise. Appraise its efficiency.
11 Visit several stores in the area, such as a grocery supermarket, a specialty store, and a large discount retailer. Write a report evaluating the location of the receiving departments and the layout of these facilities for each store.
12 Discuss the current status of the mechanization of the receiving, checking, and marking of merchandise in the stores located in your area. Try to visit a large distribution complex where you can observe a modern mechanized facility.
13 Why should a retailer continue to devote attention to the receiving operations of the store?
14 Explain how a labor-intensive retailing operation can improve efficiency through the use of modern machinery.
15 Discuss the various factors which influence the location of receiving operations.

Chapter 14

Pricing Policies in Retail Merchandising

Before a buyer makes any purchases, a general pricing policy should be established even though the specific retail prices will not be marked on the merchandise until received at the store. The general price levels of goods are determined by many factors, some of which are beyond the control of a retailer, but specific store prices are set by the retailer. Although pricing policies alone will not ensure a successful retail operation, proper pricing of merchandise may maximize profits. In other words, the price of a product or service may determine the demand for that item and may have a psychological effect on the customers. Since customers often rely upon the price of an item as an indicator of the quality of a product, the retailer may temporarily reduce the price of an item in order to attract more customers. This pricing tactic is called "leader pricing." The good or item that is leader-priced may be used as a "loss leader," meaning that the item will be sold at cost or under cost. Presently, there are twenty-nine states which have laws regulating retailers who sell merchandise below cost. Generally these statutes are referred to as "unfair sales acts" or "unfair trade practices." These state laws vary considerably. However, the intent of these laws is to regulate and prohibit larger retailers from selling merchandise below cost in order to eliminate competition. In practice, these statutes are difficult to enforce; hence, one may observe some minor violations of these unfair trade practices with respect to leader pricing.

The retailer's pricing strategy (the overall purpose) has three basic goals:

1 To cover the original cost of the merchandise
2 To cover a retailer's operating expenses
3 To provide a profit to the store

This pricing strategy must have customer appeal. Therefore, a retailer's general pricing policy may follow one of three possible routes: (1) pricing above the competition, (2) pricing below the competition, or (3) meeting competitive prices.

FACTORS AFFECTING RETAIL PRICING POLICIES

Management's prime function is to maximize profits. Merchandise which is high-priced does not necessarily mean that a store's profits will be maximized. Profit maximization is a long-run objective, and a store's management must select pricing strategies which will lead to store profitability. Since many factors affect a retailer's pricing policies, let us look at some of them and how they may interact.

Competition

One major consideration that affects a retailer's pricing policies is the pricing level of competitors. A decision must be made by the retailer to establish prices above the competition, below the competition, or directly at the same competitive level.

If a retailer decides to establish retail prices above the competitive level, the target customer group will probably consist of those persons in the upper income group. Accordingly, the merchandise will have to be of commensurate quality in order for a retailer to be successful in fixing prices above competition. An atmosphere of exclusiveness will have to be reflected in the store's interior. Also, the decor, the sales personnel, and the advertising will have to reflect an image which will justify setting prices above the competition. Many potential customers will patronize a retail store that offers goods priced above competitive levels—if all other elements of the retailing mix are in accord with the higher prices. These customers are willing to pay for certain privileges, but they will expect to receive many services and high-quality goods in return.

For the retailer who is going to price merchandise below competitive levels, there are certain prerequisites. First, in most instances, name brands (manufacturers' brands) will probably have to be offered; although house or private brands may be able to compete on a price basis. Generally, retail pricing below the competitive levels takes on all the aspects of "discount retailing." These retail institutions are commonly referred to as "discount houses." For the most part, the target customer group for a discount house is in the lower income brackets, although you will find customers in higher income brackets patronizing discount houses for certain items. The discount-house customer is seeking a bargain or just does not have the income to shop at a higher-priced retail store. If the retailer is selling lower-priced merchandise, the atmosphere of the store must also reflect an austere image. The simplest fixtures and furnishings will suffice. The physical structure should be unadorned, provide plenty of parking space, and be located in a low-rent district. All promotion and advertising will stress price as the main appeal. Customer services are not expected nor offered. Self-service is preferred over sales assistance, and name brands are consistently offered at prices below those of competitors. Often, leader pricing is used to build a high volume of customer traffic. This type of retail operation is founded on high sales volume rather than on high gross margin per unit. However, there is one danger for the retailer in pricing below competiton. When a retailer competes on price alone, there is nothing else to offer the customers. Prices can only be reduced to a certain level if the store is to be successful. As you will recall, the overall purpose of pricing strategy is to cover the cost of the merchandise, to cover the retailer's operating expenses, and to provide a profit. If this goal cannot be attained, a retail store will not be able to survive.

Pricing directly at the competitive level is used most often when the retailing environment is highly competitive. Certain products are "traditionally" priced at a certain level—soft drinks, cigarettes, candy bars, chewing gum, milk, and bread. Pricing to meet competition "head on" is a pricing strategy that is followed by many retailers. It focuses primarily upon a "me-too" philosophy of retailing. Recalling our earlier discussion of the retail business plan, you may remember the emphasis placed on the determination of goals and potential sales volume. As stated previously, a retailer must be able to "carve a niche" in the market in some way in order to differentiate the store and the merchandise offered from the competitors' stores and merchandise. If these fundamentals have been followed, then pricing strategies also can be differentiated so that customer patronage will be built on store offerings and services rather than on price appeal. Less effort will be expended in attracting customers who are looking for bargains. The retailer will seek either small unit profits on a large sales volume or large unit profits on a small sales volume. The store should be designed to cater to a small segment of the market which will earn a profit for the retailer over the long run. Some individuality and differentiation may become a part of the retailing mix and, thus, the retailer may successfully deviate from the me-too retailing concept.

Income Group

Another major consideration in determining pricing strategy is the income level of the customer group. The target customer group probably has more influence on a store's pricing policies than any other factor. (This is one reason why it is so important in developing a retail business plan to isolate the target market.) Low-income persons are price-conscious while those in higher income brackets are not usually attracted by price-appeal motives. Accordingly, the retailing mix must then reflect whatever will appeal to that specific consumer income group—as to price appeal, goods and service offerings, store image, atmosphere, sales promotion, and location.

Type of Goods and Services

The characteristics of certain goods and services and the various merchandise classifications may determine to a considerable degree the pricing policies of a retail store. For instance, staple goods, which are not affected by styling or seasonality, are sold at lower gross margins than are goods and services which may be seasonal, subject to style obsolescence, or perishable. Other goods and services may require considerable selling effort and are priced accordingly. Items requiring considerable floor space are priced with higher gross margins when compared to more staple items (for example, automobiles and furniture have higher gross margins than staple grocery items).

Retail pricing policies will also usually reflect the degree of risk which is associated with certain items. For example, fashion merchandise is considered to have a relatively high element of risk. Women's high-fashion goods are subject to style obsolescence, as well as seasonality, and they are relatively short-lived. Thus, the markup must be high enough to cover the inevitable markdowns, which are usually associated with high-fashion merchandise. Women's high-fashion retail stores rank near the top in retail business failures due, in part, to the risks associated with this classification of goods, although other factors—such as managerial inefficiency—do contribute to their failure.

Seasonality of goods and services is another factor which influences a retailer's pricing policies. Once a season is over for certain items (e.g., lawn mowers, bathing suits, toys, seasonal greeting cards), the retailer is faced with a decision of either drastically cutting the price or storing the merchandise for another year. Storing the goods until the next season requires a major capital investment with no return until the next season rolls around. Then the leftover merchandise must compete with the new goods. Seasonal goods usually suffer from style obsolescence and are no longer appealing for the consumer. Thus, goods and services of a seasonal nature, like high-fashion goods, must be priced high enough to offset any markdowns that may have to be made at the end of the season.

Goods which are perishable (such as produce, flowers, fruits and vegetables) must also reflect pricing policies which will compensate the retailer for mark-downs, spoilage or other losses which may arise from the retailing of this classification of goods. For example, grocery supermarkets carry a wide range of perishable goods: meats, milk, bread, cheese, and many other dated items. Dated food items must be removed from the shelf after the date on the package. Or the retailer must reduce the price since old merchandise cannot be sold to customers at new merchandise prices. This is why the grocery retailer will use a higher markup to compensate for the risk associated with meat and other perishables. Some dated items, like bread, may be taken off the shelf by the producer and, in turn, offered for sale by the producer in "day-old" stores.

Other goods are priced according to tradition. Diamonds reflect a high gross margin, as does costume jewelry. Men's shoes traditionally carry higher gross margins than women's shoes, due in part to the lower rate of inventory turnover

(RITO) on men's shoes. It may be that men are accustomed to paying higher prices for their shoes than women, or it may be that men do not need as many pair of shoes as women since men's shoes do have a lower turnover rate.

BASIC PRICING POLICIES

Many retailers follow a one-price policy, meaning they charge the same price to all customers. Department stores, grocery supermarkets, specialty stores, are examples of stores that use a one-price policy. Simply stated, there is no haggling over the price.

A variable pricing policy may be used by some retailers selling durable goods or other merchandise such as furniture. Whenever there is an item "traded in" on the sale of another, the pricing policy becomes variable. That is, the same price is not paid by all the customers since the trade-in item will determine the final sales price. The automobile dealer is probably the most classic example of a retailer using a variable pricing policy. Considerable negotiation by the retailer and the consumer over the price of an auto takes place in nearly every sales transaction. There are few exceptions. But this happens only when the demand for a certain style of car exceeds the supply of that model. Variable pricing policies are also used by appliance retailers, some furniture stores, some jewelry stores (those who accept trade-ins of old diamond rings or watches), bicycle shops, gun dealers, and sporting goods stores.

Some retail merchants also make use of odd pricing rather than even pricing, believing that there is some psychological advantage. For example, a retailer will use 79 cents instead of 80 cents or $9.98 rather than $10. But there is little concrete evidence to support the contention that odd pricing serves as a psychological stimulus in encouraging customers to buy. It is more likely that odd pricing is a tradition and a carryover from years ago.

Odd pricing is generally associated with staple goods or other low-unit-priced merchandise. However, automobiles and some appliances violate this rule since their suggested retail prices also end in odd cents. The use of trade-ins, though, usually will overcome the odd-pricing strategies of these retailers.

Multiple-unit pricing by a retailer tends to encourage volume purchases on the part of the customer. Soft drinks, beer, canned goods, hosiery, and men's underwear are examples of items that are usually priced in multiples. However, special events and sales may be promoted with the use of any type of multiple-unit pricing. Multiple-unit pricing has an appeal of economy to the consumer and perhaps even convenience. Usually, multiple-unit pricing is initiated by a manufacturer and then continued by the retailer. Some producers package their items in multiple units, thereby forcing a retailer to price the products as a package.

Price Lining

Price lining is a process whereby the retailer selects a limited number of prices at which the store will sell its merchandise. The price-lining strategy is used quite extensively in selling wearing apparel. For example, a women's ready-to-wear store may offer merchandise at $14.95, $24.95, and $39.95. Or a men's shoe store may offer goods at $19.95, $29.95, and $44. There are some distinct advantages for the retailer in using price lining.

First, price lining aids the buyer in planning purchases. A buyer can go to the market and select the goods which will probably sell at a profit to the store in the predetermined price lines. Thus, price lining is a definite guide to any buyer of merchandise, especially in the apparel goods classification.

Second, price lining also aids the customers in their selection of products. Persons who are price-conscious can readily inspect the items within a certain price line, knowing they are not looking at goods that are priced beyond their means. As we discussed in an earlier chapter, a retailer must initially decide what price lines the store will offer. Critics of price lining say that the use of price lining eases or eliminates the retailer's pricing decisions, thereby giving the retailer much less choice in pricing; but the author feels this point is not valid. Even though he or she uses price lining, a retailer still must decide how many price lines the store will offer. Then goods must be selected to fit the predetermined price lines, and the retailer must maintain the gross margins which were established earlier in the retail business plan. Under price lining, the buyer's basic function is one of buying goods at a certain price so they can be resold within a definite price line. But a buyer for a retail store that does not use price lining will purchase goods in a more random way since no definite price lines must be followed.

Most retailers cannot possibly offer merchandise in all price lines. Thus, a determination must be made by the retailer as to the range of goods a store will offer. This tactic is nothing more than forcing a retailer to zero in on a target customer group. By limiting price lines, a store can offer a wider assortment of merchandise within that price line than could be carried if many price lines were offered. Selection by the customer is also somewhat facilitated, and the planning of purchases by the retail store buyer is made easier.

Leader Pricing

Retailers often will reduce prices of name-brand items in order to attract customers. This is known as leader pricing. Leader pricing can be thought of as both a pricing and a promotional strategy. The purpose of leader pricing is to attract more customer traffic, thus increasing the possibility of increased sales and profits.

Leader pricing is also referred to as "loss-leader" pricing, which is really wrong. Although it may be true that the retailer suffers a loss on the advertised brand-name items, the goods are really intended to be profit leaders. If you stop to think about this idea, it becomes apparent very quickly. If these advertised "loss leaders" were not profitable, why would a retailer use them in pricing and promotional strategies?

Loss-leader pricing works in this way. Merchants may price brand-name items at or below the store's cost, thereby making them loss leaders. However, in most cases, so-called loss leaders are name brands sold at or near cost (not below) which results in no loss to the store, but increases a store's sales and profits (through increased customer traffic). In other words, many so-called loss leaders are not that at all since the retailer is not losing any money.

However, a retailer must be careful because approximately half of the states have statutes which regulate unfair sales acts—or loss-leader pricing. The intent of such laws is to prevent predatory pricing, a tactic used by some chains to drive independent stores from the competitive ranks of retailing. Each state's statutes vary with respect to the use of loss leaders, so it would be wise to check the statute before advertising items below cost.

Any item that is used as a leader to attract customers should be a commonly used household good. The regular price should be well known, otherwise, the advertised item loses its effectiveness as a traffic generator. Each week, grocery supermarkets use loss-leader items to build store traffic. (Take a good look at next week's grocery advertisements in your local newspaper.) Since many of these grocery store operators purchase from the same resources, one retailer's specials may appear to cancel the other retailer's leaders. So considerable thought should go into a retailer's decision of which items are to be used as leaders or traffic builders.

Markup Policy

A retailer's success depends, in part, on how skillfully merchandise is priced. The selling price of a product must cover the cost of the merchandise and all operating expenses as well as give the retailer a profit—if a retailer is to be successful. To the casual observer, this procedure seems to be a relatively simple process. All one must do is purchase some goods, add a certain percentage or dollar amount to these goods, and then sell the merchandise at a profit. But in reality, this is a very complex process.

Consumers are sometimes amazed by retail markups, especially when expressed as 50 to 60 percent, or more, of the selling price. They immediately think that the retailer is experiencing "excessive profits" and that the markups are out of line. But this idea may be due to their lack of understanding of the interwoven relationships of markups, percentage of profits, and the movement of merchandise.

The planning approach to retailing management stresses the concept of the total retail store or system. Carrying this philosophy through the pricing phase of retailing management affords us the opportunity to view products and product lines as part of the total system. In other words, retailers sometimes strive for large profits with overall high markups. But it is suggested that retailers should be more concerned with increasing the total profit of the store (or the total return on investment) rather than being concerned with the size of the markup itself.

It is not difficult for the retailer to add a stipulated percentage to the cost of the store's merchandise, but it may be more difficult to sell this merchandise if the same percentage is used for all product lines. For a specialty store selling one line of merchandise, a markup percentage of 40 percent is easily set. But for a store handling many different product lines, the markup will have to vary because (1) different lines of merchandise have varying rates of movement and (2) competitors may be taking either a higher or a lower markup on similar lines of merchandise.

For example, the success of mass merchandisers can be attributable, in part, to the varying rates of markups on different product lines in order to stimulate the more rapid movement of goods. Part of the secret to the success of mass merchandisers is found in the myth surrounding high markups. To illustrate, a product line which carries a markup of 70 percent and does not sell well is not nearly as profitable as a line of products which carries a 30 percent markup and sells in large quantitites. The key or answer to this example lies in the rate of inventory turnover (RITO). The relationship of markup percentages and RITO must be well understood by a retailer if the store is to be successful. A retailer cannot make much of a profit if the goods do not sell, even if these products carry a "full mark" (i.e., 100 percent markup). Nevertheless, some retailers, and perhaps some consumers, appear to be obsessed with the idea of high markups. However, both may have the wrong impression of the relationship between markup percentages and the movement rates of various products and product lines.

It is this relationship between markup percentages and the RITO that we wish to keep in proper perspective throughout this section on pricing policies in retail merchandising. The blending of these two ingredients is what separates the successful retailers from the unsuccessful ones. Not all retailers are obsessed with high markups; some, instead, are more wisely concerned with the total picture—that is, an ongoing retailing system which incurs costs in the operation of handling goods. These successful retailers understand that a store may be able to offer a lower markup on some goods and still maintain a high dollar profit at the end of the year. Others, who maintain inflexible markups, suffer the resulting consequences of a poor image and reduced profits.

For example, a study by the National Retail Hardware Association (a trade association for hardware retailers) found that many hardware retailers traditionally marked all items in the store with a fixed percentage. When consumers compared some of these items with the same or similar items in discount houses, they found hardware stores were much higher in their retail prices. Because of these higher prices, customers began to patronize discount houses and other retailers for their purchases, buying at the hardware store only items that were unavailable elsewhere.

The National Retail Hardware Association, aware of the cause-effect relationship rate of inventory turnover and profit, sought to convince their members that traditional markups on *all* goods meant relatively low total profits for these hardware retailers. Many of the hardware items carried in stock by these retailers had turnover rates so low that high markups still did not yield any profit for the store. So the association classified product lines according to the rate of movement or what is referred to as "demand sensitivity." The association then suggested to the retailers that they vary the markup percentage according to their rate of sales or movement and the aggressiveness of competition.

Grocery supermarket operators have been quite successful in maintaining flexible markups on items sold in the store. For example, staple items typically carry small markups because they sell very rapidly (sugar, coffee, detergents, flour, and canned goods). Sugar may carry a markup of 4 to 8 percent, coffee may have even a lower markup, since it may be used as a traffic builder (or as they say in the trade, "a football item"—kicked around). Flour and detergents also may be sold at 10 percent markup while items of convenience, such as prepared food mixes, may carry a markup of 40 to 45 percent; prepared cake mixes a 30 percent markup; and fresh produce, 27 percent.

Grocery supermarket expenses average approximately 17 percent of gross sales. Thus, it may appear that selling sugar and flour at a 4 to 10 percent markup (below the average expense rate) will result in a loss to the store. But this is not the case, as this 17 percent is a storewide average. Fast-moving items, such as sugar and flour, may be less expensive to stock and sell, especially since the rate of turnover is much more rapid than for the other items. By taking a small percentage of markup on these staple items and combining it with rapid turnover, the retailer obtains greater total profits for the grocery supermarket.

In conclusion, it can be stated that any markup policy should reflect the volume or number of units that can be sold at a given price. This factor will then determine the markup that will be used on a product line and whether it will have a high or low markup percentage. Generally, a product or product line that is considered to be a staple will reflect a low margin of markup. Those items not considered to be staples—convenience or luxury goods—will carry a higher margin of markup. The reason behind this philosophy is that a customer first buys the staple items, then if discretionary income permits, indulgence in luxury or convenience items may take place. Since most retailers handle both low-margin and high-margin goods, the items which are purchased less frequently must carry a sufficiently higher markup to offset the low-markup lines.

Markup Base

Years ago, retailers would use the *cost* of an item as the base on which to compute the percentage markup and the selling price. Although this is a direct process and one that is still used by some manufacturers, retailers no longer use cost as a base for computing markups. Today, nearly all retailers use the *retail price* as a base when determining the percentage of markup on an item.

The National Retail Merchants Association has had much to do with retailers switching from a *cost base* to the *retail price* as a base for determining markup percentages. A markup based on the selling price facilitates the calculation of estimated profits. This is true because sales information is usually more easily isolated than cost data. The retail inventory method used by most retailers (which will be covered in more detail in a later chapter) is based on the markup at retail or selling price. Thus, this procedure provides a more efficient method for the determination of inventory at cost. By using markup percentages based on selling prices, a retailer is better able to make comparisons between the rate of inventory turnover (RITO), gross profits, and net profits. In other words, many retail selling expenses are based on the selling price of an item (not on the cost). For example, salespersons' commissions are usually based on the retail selling prices. Rents, bonuses, and operating data are also based on total retail sales. Thus, the use of selling price as a base for the determination of markup percentages is entirely compatible with the overall retail store operation. Also, earlier mention was made of consumer criticism of high percentage markups. A percentage markup based on the retail selling price is smaller than a percentage markup based on the cost of an item. To a consumer, a retail store taking smaller markups appears to be less expensive than a store with higher markups. Hence, the store with lower percentage markups may be more appealing to the patrons.

Determination of Markup Markup is computed on the selling price (the base) at each level of distribution—by the manufacturer, wholesaler, and retailer. The manufacturer's price to the wholesaler probably includes a 10 percent markup; the wholesaler's price to the retailer probably includes a 20 percent markup. Finally, the retailer's price to the ultimate consumer may include a 40 percent markup, all percentages based on the selling price. In the case of the retailer, the selling price also becomes the retail price.

Each step in the distribution process, from the producer to the user, includes a markup sufficient to cover the cost of the item, operating expenses, and profit. Figure 14-1 indicates a hypothetical example of how a dress may be priced from the manufacturer to the final consumer.

In Figure 14-1, the production cost of $32.40 represents the manufacturer's expense in producing the dress. To this price of $32.40, the manufacturer must add some residual for profit. As you can see, the markup for the manufacturer is

Production cost (manufacturer's) cost	$32.40
Manufacturer's gross margin (10 percent of selling price)	+ 3.60
Selling price to wholesaler (wholesaler's cost)	36.00
Wholesaler's gross margin (20 percent of selling price)	+ 9.00
Selling price to retailer (retailer's cost)	45.00
Retailer's gross margin (40 percent of selling price)	30.00
Retail price to consumer	$75.00

Figure 14-1 Pricing of dresses from manufacturer to consumer.

$3.60, which is equal to 10 percent of the selling price to the wholesaler (middleman). (Although in many instances, the manufacturer may sell apparel directly to the retailer.) Thus, the manufacturer's selling price of $36 (cost of $32.40 plus $3.60 markup) becomes the wholesaler's cost ($36). If the wholesaler is to sell the dress at a profit, a markup must be added to cover the costs of operation and provide the wholesaler with a profit.

The price of $36 for the dress represents the wholesaler's basic unit cost of the item. In our example in Figure 14-1, the wholesaler has added $9 to the dress as a markup, which then equals a selling price to the retailer of $45 ($36 cost plus $9 markup).

The wholesaler's selling price now becomes the retailer's cost. To this cost figure ($45), the retailer must also have enough markup to cover the costs of operation plus a profit. In this illustration the retailer has added a markup of $30 (the markup being 40 percent of the selling price) to the cost figure of $45, making a retail selling price to the consumer of $75.

This illustration is provided for the purpose of explaining why markups must be provided during each step of the distribution phase—from producer to wholesaler to retailer to consumer. A closer inspection of the markup structure will reveal that each step includes a greater markup in both percentage and actual dollar amount. Can you determine why?

For all practical purposes, as we have just discovered, a markup percentage is based on the selling or retail price of an item. This markup percentage then is used as a guide in pricing at retail so that the projected gross margin (estimated earlier in the retail business plan) can be maintained. It is a common business practice to relate operating expenses and desired profits as a percentage of net sales to the final sales dollar. Prudent retailers continually compare expenses with sales, since management needs to known how much of the average sales dollar is required to cover expenses, yet still allow a given percentage of net profit.

When using the retail or selling price as the base for determining the markup percentage, think of the selling price as being equal to 100 percent. Thus, if the retail price is $75, then $75 equals 100 percent. Then the cost of the merchandise plus the markup is equal to the selling price. This is represented by the following formula:

$$C + MU = SP$$
Cost + markup = selling price

Or if you use the figures from the example in Figure 14-1, you would have:

$$\$45 + \$30 = \$75$$

In this previous example, by knowing any two figures of the equation, it is easy to determine the missing figure. Each side of the equation must equal 100 percent. Using the formula, we can determine the cost:

$C + MU = 100$ percent

Returning to our example, we know the retailer's markup was 40 percent of the retail price. The cost must then be equal to 60 percent of the retail price if the equation is to balance—and remember, the equation must always balance. If the cost to the retailer was $45, and the markup was 40 percent on the retail or selling price to the consumer, then the $45 cost is equal to 60 percent of the retail price. Hence the selling price of $75 is equal to 100 percent. Using our formula, we can determine the cost:

$$C + MU = 100 \text{ percent}$$
$$C + 40 \text{ percent} = 100 \text{ percent}$$
$$C = 100 \text{ percent} - 40 \text{ percent}$$
$$C = 60 \text{ percent}$$

Further, let us assume that the retailer wishes to maintain an average gross margin, or markup, of 40 percent on a line of merchandise. Since the retailer has predetermined that the product line should retail at $75, how much can the retailer afford to pay for merchandise and still maintain a 40 percent markup. Using our formula once again ($C + MU = 100$ percent), we can determine the price the retailer should pay. We know that the retail selling price is $75 and that the retailer wishes to maintain a 40 percent markup, so:

$$\text{Cost} + 40 \text{ percent markup} = \$75 \text{ selling price (100 percent)}$$
$$\text{Cost} = 100 \text{ percent} - 40 \text{ percent}$$
$$\text{Cost} = 60 \text{ percent of selling price}$$
$$60 \text{ percent} \times \$75 = \$45$$

Another formula that is valuable in determining the percentage of markup based on selling price is as follows:

$$MU \text{ percent} = \frac{R - C}{R}$$

where MU percent = markup percentage
R = retail or selling price
C = cost of the item

Using the same figures as in the previous example, we would have the following:

$$MU \text{ percent} = \frac{\$75 - \$45}{\$75}$$

or

$$MU \text{ percent} = \frac{\$30}{\$75} \text{ or 40 percent}$$

Markdowns Even though a retailer has predetermined that the store should have an average markup percentage of 40 percent, at times a retailer will find that it is impossible to maintain the initial markup percentage. It may be necessary for the retailer to mark down the selling price of some goods in order to bring about a sale. Customers have the option to buy goods or not to buy. They care little what a retailer paid for the goods, and they are concerned primarily with the retail price of the merchandise. There is never any certainty that customers will buy the merchandise which has been bought, priced, and marked with the retail store's predetermined markup percentage.

When goods have been in stock for a considerable time, a retailer will usually lower the price of these items in order to sell them. The longer merchandise has been on the shelf, the less likely those goods will sell at their original or initial selling price. Some markdowns are inevitable, regardless of how well the retailer has selected purchases. Market conditions may change, and customer buying habits and tastes may change. Goods are subject to seasonality or may become shopworn, soiled, or otherwise unsaleable. It is also entirely possible that the retailer made errors in pricing the goods. Many times the buyer of the merchandise is accused of making a poor purchase, but in many instances, this is unwarranted. The shifts of the retail market cannot be judged fully by any buyer, especially with seasonal goods. Even the most competent buyers may make occasional errors, which will force the retailer to take some markdowns. There is nothing wrong in taking markdowns; but the markdowns should be kept at acceptable levels.

Markdowns can also be used as a promotional tool. At times retailers may deliberately mark down certain goods in order to stimulate sales by increasing consumer traffic. The usual price of certain items may be temporarily reduced for a special sales promotional event. Thus, this type of markdown is not due to poor buying decisions or to the lack of sales (or turnover) of the advertised items. Rather, it is a retailing tactic employed by the management for a special event. A special event may be, and often is, held near the end of a season. It serves to move the merchandise out of the store into the hands of the consumer and also clears the retailer's shelves for incoming goods.

Control of Markdowns Timing of markdowns is highly critical in that if markdowns are taken too soon, the store suffers from reduced net income. If markdowns are not taken soon enough, the store may also suffer reduced profits. Markdowns should be taken when the first indication arises that the movement of the line may be slowing. This might be a result of the approaching end of the season, or it is possible that a wholesale price is declining, or the producer may be entering the market with a comparable or substitute item. Many producers notify retailers of discontinued lines, thus allowing the retailer to markdown and sell the goods before the introduction of the new items.

In order to facilitate movement of the goods, the retail store should make an honest attempt to take a sufficient markdown the first time so that the item is sold. Generally, the first markdown on an item is the least expensive price reduction for a retail store. If successive markdowns are needed, then there are added expenses and labor associated with these further markdowns. These additional expenses, in turn, tend to further reduce the profits of the retail store. When markdowns are not enough to sell the goods, the items must be carried over to the next season which becomes a costly process for most retailers. Often the price must be reduced again the following season because the style may be obsolete or the items unsaleable. All this tends to reduce the rate of inventory turnover which, in turn, adversely affects the net profits of the store.

Instead of reducing prices yearly or semiannually, some retailers prefer to take monthly markdowns. This is done for two basic reasons. First, a monthly review of the goods is made and all items which have been in stock for a longer period of time, are reduced in price. Second, this practice of reducing prices stimulates customer traffic and sales near the end of each month when sales volume tends to decrease. The marked-down goods can serve as a valuable and reasonably inexpensive means of sales promotion. Monthly markdowns cause bargain hunters to visit the store more often, even if they purchase only the marked-down items, and there is always the chance that these customers will make purchases other than the marked-down goods. The practice of taking monthly markdowns can be a valuable aid in developing a loyal customer following, and it may be less expensive than some other means of promotion.

Markdown Formula For retail accounting purposes, markdowns are usually expressed as a percentage of net sales; but for purposes of internal control and analysis, markdowns may be expressed as a percentage of the lower or reduced selling price (the actual selling price). To illustrate this procedure, let us use our previous example's figures. The $75 dress has to be sold, and the retailer marks it down in order to sell it. Taking $15 off the original retail price of $75, the new reduced selling price will be $60. For accounting purposes, this $15 reduction in price reflects a 25 percent markdown to the retailer. How do we arrive at this percentage? Markdown percentages are computed by the use of the following formula:

$$\text{Percentage markdown} = \frac{\text{dollar markdown}}{\text{actual selling price}} \times 100$$

or

$$\text{Percentage markdown} = \frac{\$15}{\$60} \times 100$$

or

$$\text{Percentage markdown} = 0.25 \times 100 = 25 \text{ percent}$$

This markdown, in the eyes of the customer, however, represents a true reduction of only 20 percent. To illustrate:

$$\text{Original selling price} = \$75$$
$$\text{Actual dollar amount of reduction} = \$15$$

$$\text{True percentage markdown} = \frac{\$15}{\$75} = 0.20 \times 100 = 20 \text{ percent}$$

In advertising markdowns, a retailer must be careful since it would constitute a misrepresentation to indicate to the customer in the above illustration that the markdown was 25 percent rather than the true 20 percent markdown. Actually, markdown percentages should express the relationship of the selling-price reduction to the old retail selling price, since it is the way in which the consumer will look at the price change; whereas the markdown percentage the retailer uses for internal control and analysis expresses the relationship to the new reduced retail price.

Resale Price Maintenance or Fair Trade

Some retailers of well-known, branded goods may be prohibited from taking markdowns or from pricing the merchandise as they think best. This is because some manufacturers establish and maintain the retail prices at which their merchandise can be sold to the ultimate consumer. Items that fall into this category are controlled by "resale-price-maintenance" laws or "fair-trade" laws and are commonly called fair-trade goods.

Ordinarily, a retailer cannot mark down merchandise obtained from manufacturers who adhere to a resale-price-maintenance policy unless given consent to do so.

Resale-price-maintenance laws have had a controversial background, and cases involving fair-trade items have been in and out of the courts for years. But for our purposes in this text, we will cover only certain aspects of the resale-price-maintenance policies.

Beginnings of Fair Trade   Resale-price-maintenance or fair-trade laws came into existence in the early thirties, with California being the first state to pass such a statute in 1931. During the ensuing years, the California law was copied by 46 other states. However, the enforcement of the resale-price-maintenance agreements was applicable only when both the manufacturer and the retailer were located within the same state. Those states which did not pass fair-trade laws were Alaska, Missouri, Texas, and Vermont; and the District of Columbia did not enter into such legislation. These laws contained a "nonsigner's clause" which provided that all suggested retail prices imposed on a retailer by a manufacturer must be strictly adhered to, or a retailer could be taken to court by a complaint signed by the manufacturer.

Then the Congress of the United States passed the Miller-Tydings Act of 1937 which is still on the books and allows manufacturers to establish retail prices for their products in any state that enacts a resale-price-maintenance or fair-trade law. During World War II and the postwar years 1946–1950, fair trade received little attention. But in 1951, a landmark case involving fair-trade items was decided in the U.S. Supreme Court. The Court ruled that the so-called "nonsigner's" clause was illegal under federal law—*Schwegmann Brothers v.*

Calvert Distillers, 341 U.S. 384 (1951). After the Schwegmann case, every manufacturer who wished to specify and maintain retail selling prices had to obtain a signed contract from all the retailers who handled the products. Prior to this case, the manufacturer had to sign a contract with only one retailer under the nonsigner's clause. So the procedure of obtaining contracts from all retailers appeared to be both unfeasible and undesirable, unless a manufacturer had only a few retailers in a small area.

Consequently, the Schwegmann decision was relatively shortlived. The McGuire Amendment to the Federal Trade Commission Act (1952) removed this federal restriction on the nonsigner's clause in interstate commerce. Court cases challenging the validity of the fair-trade laws were very common in the years following the passage of the McGuire Amendment. All fair-trade laws have been repealed in Hawaii, Kansas, Mississippi, Nebraska, Nevada, and Rhode Island. In many other states, fair trade or resale price maintenance is not enforced for reasons which we will discover shortly. At the time of the publication of this book, only a few states retain fair-trade laws, but they include such heavily populated states as California, Illinois, New Jersey, New York, and Ohio. Opponents of fair-trade or resale-price-maintenance laws have said though that the few states which still have fair-trade laws account for more than half of the nation's retail sales.

Effectiveness of Fair Trade   Generally, for fair-trade laws to be enforceable in those states which have these statutes, merchandise must carry a manufacturer's or wholesaler's trademark, brand, or name. In other words, they must be name-brand goods. There are many exceptions, though, even in those states where fair-trade laws are enforced. For example, the following name-brand items or types of sales transactions are exempt from fair-trade laws:

1 Products that are damaged, soiled, or otherwise unsaleable as first-class goods.
2 Going-out-of-business sales.
3 Inventory closeouts on certain items of goods.
4 Sales to charitable and educational institutions.
5 "Seconds" and other goods which have the manufacturer's label removed.
6 Sales involving trade-ins (the value of the item traded in on the new product is increased to compensate for the higher price imposed by the manufacturer through a fair-trade law).
7 Mail-order retailers operating from states which do not have fair-trade laws even though the customer resides in a state where fair-trade laws exist. (This is because mail-order sales are governed by the laws of the state where the transfer of the goods to a common carrier for delivery takes place.)

Low-margin retailers naturally oppose fair-trade laws as their businesses are founded upon the principle of selling name-brand merchandise at a discount. Small independent retailers generally favor fair trade because of their economic disadvantages in competing with either chains or discounters. Fair trade, in this instance, tends to protect the small retailer from the more advantageous pricing of the giant retailers.

Maintaining Fair Trade   A manufacturer may enforce the pricing of fair-trade items on a retailer by employing one of three methods:

First, a manufacturer can refuse to sell a line of products to those retailers who will not uphold the manufacturer's suggested retail price. If brand preference is strong enough on the part of the consumers, the retailer usually will comply with the manufacturer's request. If the retailer is a large discounter, he may simply refuse the arrangement and seek comparable or unbranded goods as replacement merchandise.

Second, in those states where fair trade is enforced, a manufacturer may have a retailer sign a contract which requires the merchant to abide by the producer's suggested retail prices. If the retailer does not comply with the contract, the sale of goods below the established prices becomes an act of unfair competition which then becomes grounds for a civil suit. (A fair-trade contract cannot be enforced in those states which have no fair-trade laws.)

Third, some manufacturers prefer to consign merchandise to a retailer which enables them to dictate or control the retail price. Since there is no transfer of title or sale to the retailer in consignment goods, the retailer merely acts as an agent for the manufacturer. This places the "agency role" on the retailer who must comply with the manufacturer's suggested retail prices. An agency role places the retailer in the position of agent; the manufacturer is the principal, and the agent (retailer) is bound to comply with the principal's instructions.

Arguments for and against Fair Trade   Manufacturers support fair trade because, in many instances, they have spent millions of dollars for promotion in order to build brand image and consumer loyalty. As can be expected, these producers do not want a retailer to use the product as a "loss leader" for building customer traffic. Price reductions could result in a loss of image and prestige, and could damage the reputation of the manufacturer. Also, a manufacturer may wish to help protect small retailers from price competition with large retailers.

Small independent retailers generally favor resale-price-maintenance or fair-trade laws. These retailers may not be able to match the buying power of chains, attain sufficient sales volume to offset any loss from price reductions, or be effective in retail sales promotion because of the expenses incurred. So the small retailer will readily handle fair-trade items.

Large retailers generally favor the repeal of fair-trade laws and feel that the manufacturers should follow a hands-off policy in regard to the pricing of retail merchandise. Most retailers wish to have free reign in pricing their merchandise to meet the market conditions, which may vary from area to area and from time to time. Also, the discount retailers prefer to compete on a price basis and argue that fair-trade laws tend to protect the high-priced, inefficient retailer.

But in actuality, if fair-trade laws have helped small retailers, it is only in a very small way. Evidence suggests that in many cases, small retailers of certain goods have actually suffered from increased competition. For example, grocery supermarkets and discount houses have found drug items and cosmetics to be lucrative. Thus, they stock these items and compete effectively with the more traditional drugstores even though drugstores and pharmaceutical companies generally have supported resale-price-maintenance or fair-trade laws over the years.

From a consumer's point of view, fair-trade-priced items are hard to justify. Generally, fair-trade merchandise is higher in price than other similar merchandise, and consumers feel that the more normal competitive structure should be allowed to operate under free and open market conditions. Most of us like to purchase name-brand items at prices that are lower than normal; that is, most of us like *bargains*. If retailers can effectively compete in the marketplace by offering manufacturer's brands at reduced prices, most consumers will not object. In summary, there is little factual evidence to lend support to the maintenance of manufacturers' suggested retail prices.

NONPRICE COMPETITION

This chapter has focused attention on pricing policies and strategies and how a retailer can profit from pricing know-how. When a retailer focuses all the customers' attention on pricing, or if the store emphasizes price in its promotion, there is little left to attract patronage. After all, there is a limit beyond which a retailer can emphasize price. At the outset of this chapter, it was suggested that a pricing policy have three basic purposes:

1 To cover the original cost of the goods
2 To cover a retailer's operating expenses
3 To provide a profit to the retailer

While keeping these basic purposes of pricing in mind, let us devote some attention to nonprice competition.

In nonprice competition, a retailer maintains a constant price and attempts to improve his or her market position by emphasizing one or more of the following: (1) product offerings, (2) location and convenience of the store, (3) personalized service to the customer, (4) differentiation of retail sales promotion, or (5) improved quality in the service areas (such as liberal returns, credit terms, faster delivery and installation, product warranties, gift wrapping, and convenient hours for shopping). In short, a retailer has many ways in which the store can become differentiated from the competition. Differentiation can come about through design, structure, decorating, and display. Innovation and creativity are the keys to nonprice competition, and many of these factors cost little in terms of money. Expensive sales promotion does not have to be the rule. Creativity in sales promotion is much more effective in obtaining a profitable sales volume. The basic underlying philosophy in nonprice competition is one of striving to make a store different from the competition. There is considerable latitude in being "different." However, it may require considerable effort on the part of the retailer to *accurately* appraise and develop a retailing mix which does segregate a store from those selling the same merchandise. Innovative pricing strategies and tactics which are used by perceptive retail store managers will ultimately reap profits for the store.

SUMMARY

Before a retailer makes any purchases, a *general pricing policy* should be established even though the specific retail prices will not be marked on the merchandise until it is received at the store.

A retailer's basic pricing strategy has three purposes:

1 To cover the original cost of the merchandise
2 To cover a retailer's operating expenses
3 To provide a profit to the store

A retailer's pricing strategies must have consumer appeal if the store is to be successful. A retailer's general pricing policy will follow one of three possible alternatives: (1) pricing above the competition, (2) pricing below the competition, or (3) meeting competition with prices.

If a retailer decides to establish retail prices above the competitive level, the target customer group will probably consist of those persons in the upper income group. If a retailer decides to price merchandise below competitive levels, the target group of consumers will be in the lower income brackets. This pricing tactic is usually referred to as *discount retailing.*

Pricing directly at the competitive level is used most often when the retailing environment is highly competitive.

One major consideration in determining pricing strategy is the *income level* of the customer group. The target customer group probably has more influence on a store's pricing policies and strategies than any other factor.

Retail pricing policies usually reflect the *degree of risk* which is associated with certain types of merchandise. For example, fashion merchandise is considered to have a relatively high element of risk. Thus, the markup must be high enough to cover the risks associated with selling this type of merchandise.

Other factors which bear directly on the pricing of merchandise include *seasonality, perishability, and tradition.* Many types of goods are seasonal. Other merchandise is subject to perishability. By tradition, some goods characteristically are priced at a certain level and offer the merchant a certain markup.

Basic pricing policies may follow: (1) a one-price policy to all customers, (2) a variable price policy where the price of the merchandise is determined by a trade-in or negotiation, (3) an odd-price policy where items are priced in uneven numbers, or (4) multiple-unit pricing where a retailer encourages volume purchases.

Price lining is a process whereby the retailer selects a limited number of prices at which the store will sell its merchandise. Price lining aids the buyer in planning purchases. Price lining also aids the customers in their selection of merchandise. Most retailers cannot possibly offer merchandise in all price lines. Thus, a determination must be made by the retailer as to the range of goods a store will offer.

Retailers often will reduce prices of name-brand items in order to attract customers. This is known as *leader pricing*. Leader pricing can be thought of as both a pricing and a promotional strategy.

A retailer's success depends, in part, on how skillfully merchandise is priced. The selling price of a product must cover the cost of the merchandise, operating expenses, and provide the retailer with a profit.

The planning approach to retailing management stresses the concept of the total retail store or system. The *total store system* affords management the opportunity of viewing products and product lines as part of the total system when determining pricing policy. Retailers should be concerned with increasing the total profit of the store or the total return on investment, rather than being concerned with the size of the markup itself. Thus, different products and product lines will carry varying markup percentages.

The relationship between markup percentages and the rate of inventory turnover (RITO) should be well understood by a retailer if the store is to be successful.

Nearly all retailers use the *retail price* as a base in determining the percentage of markup on an item. A markup based on the selling price facilitates the calculation of estimated profits for the store.

Markup is computed on the selling price (base) at each level of distribution—the manufacturer, wholesaler, and retailer. Each step in the distribution process, from the producer to the user, includes a markup sufficient to cover the cost of the item, operating expenses, and profit.

When using the retail or selling price as the base for determining the *markup percentage,* think of the selling price as being equal to 100 percent. Then the cost of the merchandise plus the markup is equal to the selling price. The following formula represents this procedure:

$$C + MU = SP$$
Cost + markup = selling price

At times a retailer will find that it is impossible to maintain the initial markup percentage. It may be necessary for the retailer to *mark down* the selling price of some goods in order to bring about a *sale.* The longer merchandise has been on the shelf, the less likely those goods will sell at their original or initial selling price. Markdowns should be taken when the first indication arises that the movement of the line may be slowing.

For retail accounting purposes, markdowns are usually expressed as a percentage of net sales. But for purposes of internal control and analysis, markdowns may be expressed as a percentage of the lower or reduced selling price. *Markdown percentages* are computed by the use of the following formula:

$$\text{Percentage markdown} = \frac{\text{dollar markdown}}{\text{actual selling price}} \times 100$$

Some retailers of well-known, branded goods may be prohibited from taking markdowns or from pricing the merchandise as they think best. This is because some producers establish and maintain the retail prices at which their merchandise can be sold to the ultimate consumer. This is known as *resale price maintenance or fair trade*.

Manufacturers support fair trade because, in many instances, they have spent millions of dollars for promotion in order to build brand image and consumer loyalty. Small independent retailers generally favor resale-price-maintenance or fair-trade laws. Large retailers generally favor the repeal of fair-trade laws and feel the manufacturers should follow a hands-off policy in regard to the pricing of retail merchandise. From the consumer's point of view, fair-trade-priced items are had to justify. Generally, fair-trade merchandise is higher in price than other similar goods.

When a retailer focuses all the customers' attention on pricing, or if the store emphasizes price in its promotion, little is left to attract patronage. A retailer should devise some tactics which will differentiate the store from those of competing retailers. This is referred to as *nonprice competition*.

For the most part a retailer emphasizing nonprice competition will maintain a constant price on the merchandise the store offers. The retailer will offer and emphasize product-line assortment, location and convenience, personalized service, improved customer service, and differences in promotional appeals. Innovation and creativity are the keys to nonprice competition.

REVIEW QUESTIONS

1 A retailer's general pricing policy may follow one of three possible alternatives. What are these alternative pricing policies?
2 There are three basic purposes of pricing strategy. Discuss these basic purposes and the relationship to a profitable store operation.
3 Discuss the factors influencing retail pricing policies.
4 Distinguish between a one-price policy and a variable pricing policy.
5 What is the basic purpose of pricing merchandise with odd prices?
6 What is multiple-unit pricing?
7 Discuss price lining and its value to the retailer. What is its value to the customer?
8 Explain how and why retailers use a strategy of leader pricing.
9 What is a markup policy? Why does a markup policy have to vary in a store?
10 What role does the rate of inventory turnover (RITO) play in determining markup percentages?
11 Why do modern retailers use the retail price as a base for determining the percentage of markup rather than using the cost of the item as a base?

12 What is the underlying strategy in taking markdowns on certain goods as soon as possible once it has been determined that the movement has been slowed?

13 Suggest some ways in which a retailer is better able to control merchandise markdowns.

14 Discuss the merits of resale price maintenance or fair trade from both the vendor's and the retailer's perspectives.

15 Under what type of market conditions would you find fair trade working best?

16 Evaluate the effectiveness of fair trade in today's retailing environment.

17 Discuss the merits of nonprice competition. How can a retailer effectively compete with discount retailers by using nonprice competitive tactics?

PROBLEMS

1 Using the selling price as a base, find the indicated items in each of the following:

Given	Find
a Retail price: $40 Cost price: $25	Markup percentage Markup dollars
b Retail price: $69.85 Markup percentage: 33 percent	Cost price
c Cost price: $39 Markup percentage: 60 percent	Retail price
d Markup dollars: $6.50 Markup percentage: 40 percent	Retail price

2 Swanson's, a small department store, desires to offer good values in men's shirts for $16. The wholesale price for men's shirts from one leading producer is $9.50. What percentage of markup is Swanson's getting on the price of men's shirts which sell for $16? Assume that near the end of the season Swanson's must take markdowns on the shirts in order to make room for new stock arrivals. The selling price is reduced to $11. What percentage of markup is Swanson's obtaining on the sale price of men's shirts at $11?

3 A buyer of women's ready-to-wear clothing makes a purchase of knit blouses for $7.95 each. The buyer wishes to maintain a markup percentage of 70 percent. What should these knit blouses sell for at retail in order to return a 70 percent markup?

4 A buyer of home furnishings made a purchase of accessories for the home. These consisted of small items, decorative in nature, ceramic, porcelain, and brass. The buyer is of the opinion that each of the items is unique. The average cost of the items was $14. The buyer wishes to markup the merchandise 250 percent. At what price should each of these items retail?

5 Don's IGA Grocery has just been informed that the producer of sugar is going to raise the price to middlemen. The wholesale price will be $19.92 for twelve 5-pound bags of sugar, and $19.86 for ten 6-pound bags. Don would like to maintain an 18 percent markup on sugar. What should each bag of sugar sell for at retail?

6 The wholesale price of eggs currently is 41.5 cents a dozen. The store manager believes that the store should have a 43 percent markup on fresh eggs. What should the retail price of one dozen eggs be in order to achieve a 43 percent markup?

Part Seven

Retail Sales Promotion

Chapter 15

Promotional Strategies of Retail Merchandising

Sales promotional strategies in retailing may include advertising, personal selling, displaying of merchandise, or any other tactic which will induce a profitable sales volume for the retailer. Essentially, a retailer will combine these strategies —advertising, personal selling, and displaying of goods—to obtain a sales promotional mix which will attract customers into the store and entice them to make purchases.

Generally, there are two major classifications of retail sales promotion. The first one is advertising (via newspapers, radio, television, or direct mail) which is used to attract customers to the store. The second form of sales promotion is the concentration on in store promotion. This includes window displays, floor displays, personal selling, point-of-purchase display materials, and use of various incentives for the store's personnel.

All too often, the retailer will determine the level of a retail store's sales promotional budget through the use of intuition or past sales records. By using these techniques, the retailer is saying that sales promotion is the result of sales, whereas in actuality, sales should be the end result of sales promotion. Thus, a sales promotional budget should be based on the specific goals and objectives that the retailer has established for retail sales promotion. So before a retailer proceeds any further, the store's goals and objectives should be carefully considered.

RETAIL SALES PROMOTION

The basic purpose of retail sales promotion is to increase a store's profitable sales volume at any specified price. In other words, a retailer attempts to broaden the base for a product's use by making it available to more consumers. Retail sales promotion is also used by a retailer to disseminate information as well as to influence and persuade people to become customers of the store. Both of the above objectives have as their ultimate goal a profitable sales volume for the retailer. Thus, as the retailer decides on the sales promotion mix to be used, the store's objectives and goals should be kept firmly in mind.

Retail sales promotion is extremely important today because of the intensification of competition among retailers. As a result, consumers are becoming increasingly more selective in their choices of goods and services. In order to be better able to attract customers to the store and induce them to buy, a retailer must have an effective retail sales promotional program. Through sales promotional efforts, a retailer is able to differentiate his or her store from those of the competition by creating a favorable image of the store in the consumer's mind.

There is yet another reason for an effective retail sales promotion program in today's marketplace. Many manufacturers, through the use of improved physical distribution and logistics, have expanded the geographical limits of consumer goods in retail markets. Thus, it is necessary for a retailer to communicate more effectively with consumers who may be some distance from the retail store. Since people tend to be quite mobile today and will travel a considerable distance in their search for goods and services, the retailer must provide for this in the promotional program. This is an illustration of the consumers' increasing selectivity due to a greater variety and availability of retail goods and services.

Retail sales promotion must be goal-oriented, carefully planned, coordinated with other store efforts, properly timed, and done on a continuing basis. If retail sales promotion is not continuous, it will become relatively ineffective in attracting customers to the store on a regular basis. Through sales promotion, a retailer can carve out a separate target market, cultivate this market for a profitable sales volume, and build an image and reputation worthy of emulation by competitors. Clearly, retail sales promotion is needed by retailers simply because they are selling consumer goods. The communication process between a retailer and the consumers is a significant one. Only through effective communication will a potential customer become aware of a retailer's offering of goods and services.

After a retailer has purchased the merchandise that the customers need or want, these goods must be sold at a profit. In order to effectuate the sale of these products, a retailer must utilize many sales promotional techniques in order to attract customers to the retail store. For our purposes, we will assume that the retailer has established the store in a favorable location and that the market potential exists for these particular goods and services. We will also assume that the store's location and market potential are significant enough to attract some consumers to the store. And here is where the use of retail sales promotional techniques comes into play. Retail sales promotional efforts will assist the retailer in developing sufficient traffic volume. No retailer can afford *not* to use some sales promotional strategies. Retailers must advertise in some manner, whether by newspapers (the single largest medium), word of mouth, identification signs, window displays, or any other means. But consumers must be informed about a retailer's offering of goods and services, or how will they know what the retailer is selling?

Few retailers can afford to depend solely on the people who pass the store. Even those specialty retailers located in the finest shopping centers must advertise in order to support and/or expand their retail businesses. Although shopping centers are usually favorable locations with sufficient market potential, not all the persons who pass the store are prospective customers. For example, many men may pass women's ready-to-wear shops and many women may pass men's shoe stores. But generally speaking, the men are not really prospective customers for the women's shops and the women are not good prospects for the men's stores. However, large amounts of traffic may be more advantageous to certain types of retail outlets. For instance, consumers (both men and women) passing a food store will probably be more likely to purchase food.

Whether in a larger community, a small town, a downtown area, or a shopping center, prospective consumers must be attracted by a well-planned, coordinated, and informational advertising program. This is where retail sales promotion is of value. Retail sales promotional programs integrate and coordinate all promotional efforts toward one common objective—that of getting people into the store to purchase goods and services.

MAJOR FORMS OF RETAIL SALES PROMOTION

Retail sales promotion is a broad term that includes advertising, personal selling, window and interior store displays, location, price appeal, and any other means which will attract customers to the store. Once in the store, customers are then encouraged to browse, compare, and shop for goods and services.

There are two major classifications of retail sales promotion:

1   Advertising through the use of some type of media (radio, newspapers, television, or direct mail advertising) for the purpose of attracting customers to the store, and
2   In store promotion which will stimulate the movement of goods and return a profit to the store (includes window displays, floor displays, personal selling, point-of-purchase display materials, and incentives for the store's personnel).

Budget Determination

All too often a retailer determines a store's retail sales promotional budget based on intuition or past sales. When one of these techniques is used, the retailer is saying that retail sales promotion is a *result* of sales. But in actuality, sales should be the *result* of the retail sales promotional mix. Thus, it is better to adhere to a management policy of developing a retail sales promotional budget based on the goals and objectives of the store.

After a retailer has decided on the specific goals and objectives of the retail sales promotion program, the next step is to determine what amount of money should be budgeted for this purpose. Several methods can be used. The percentage of gross sales, or net sales, method is probably the most widely used because it is simple and easy to calculate or determine. As stated earlier, this method is basically unsound since it uses the theory that retail sales promotion is the *result* of sales rather than the *cause* of sales. For example, when retail sales decline, the sales promotional budget also declines. But in fact, more sales promotion probably should be used to stimulate additional sales volume in order to increase the profits of the store.

A more appropriate method of determining how much money to allocate for retail sales promotion is to define first just what is to be done (set goals) and *then* decide how much money it will take to accomplish those objectives. However, this method is more sophisticated. It requires the management to look at the long-run goals of the store and then to segment the store's objectives and the sales promotional goals into time periods—quarters, months, and perhaps even weeks. By following this procedure, management is better able to view the store as a total system or entity which operates over a long period of time, instead of viewing the enterprise as a day-to-day operation. Also, as the time period is broken into segments, management has a better perspective of the firm and its relationship to the sales promotional goals which have been established. If the goals are unrealistic, then adjustments can be made before the final funds are committed to the sales promotional program. By taking the long-range goals and the time periods and breaking them into segments, management can tailor or design a promotional mix for each period of time. This will allow the retailer to take advantage of the market changes which will inevitably develop. Also, seasonal changes often require some flexibility in the sales promotional mix, as do economic and local business conditions.

It may be well to mention that x number of dollars should be specifically allocated to a store's retail sales promotional program—not just talked about. The money should be there so that a promotional program can be set up and followed carefully. All too often if funds are not actually committed for promotional purposes, the money is used for something else. Then when promotion is sorely needed, no funds will be available.

SALES PROMOTION POLICY AND PLANNING

Naturally, retailers should adopt a sales promotion and planning policy tailored to their individual stores. As with many other facets of retailing, a sales promotion policy suited for one retail store will not work for another store. Regardless of whatever promotional plan is chosen, a retailer should formulate a sales promotional policy or mix that stresses consistency, continuity, intensity, and possesses a central idea or theme. A sales promotion policy could emphasize price appeal, name brands and prestige, bargain departments, service shops, or special events. However, as a result of its retail sales promotion theme, the store will soon become known for a certain type of customer appeal. Thus, it is prudent that the management carefully choose a sales promotion plan since the promotional concepts used will be converted into a store *image*. A store's image is often long lasting and somewhat difficult to change, especially over the short run; so the management should have a definite idea in mind as to the type of image they want. (Store images and how to build them will be covered in more detail later in this chapter.)

Although a sales promotion program focuses attention on the coordination of all promotional efforts toward one common goal and the adjustment of that program to changing conditions, sales promotion plans must be able to adapt to the constantly shifting business environment. Since these business conditions will be either more or less favorable to the retail store, the management must be prepared to adapt quickly to changing conditions. Promotional efforts may have to be increased or decreased as market conditions warrant. New fashions, new merchandise, and seasonal changes should be given special attention. Promotional events may vary in importance, but each should receive special consideration as a part of the overall sales promotion plan.

For example, certain promotional events may last only a day; others may last several days. Some events may necessitate extensive planning and advertising or even require collaboration with other merchants or stores in a shopping center. Sufficient time may be needed to coordinate a store's sales promotional events with employees, merchandise resources, or other scheduled sales. If the outlet is a department store, it will be necessary to coordinate promotional events throughout the store in each department; and each department must be afforded its proper consideration in the overall promotion. Since so much effort goes into a successful sales promotional event, proper planning and coordination is essential.

The Theme Concept

A central theme should be utilized by the retailer for the entire retail sales promotional program in order to provide consistency, continuity, and store impact on the consumer. It will be from this promotional theme that a retail store develops an image which is long-lived. When a retailer makes plans for a sales promotional event, efforts should be focused around this central idea or theme. It should be related to the image of the individual retail store, and the theme deserves careful consideration. Although a theme is usually associated with advertising in the mass media (newspapers, radio, television), it is not limited only to this type of retail sales promotion. Newspapers, radio, and television represent only a portion of a retailer's promotional program. Other sales promotional techniques include window displays, location, interior design and layout, assortment of merchandise, the pricing structure, and, among others, the attitude of sales personnel and office help.

Accordingly, a retailer must select a main idea around which all retail sales promotional efforts will be focused. This theme of retail sales promotion is then designed to implement and provide a base from which all promotional events will evolve. The selection of a central idea or store theme should be as deliberate as possible. A retailer's store theme, as opposed to a campaign theme, will permeate all promotional efforts of the store—whether depicted in advertising, personal selling, window and floor displays, the attitudes of personnel, or the decor of the store. It is important for continuity and consistency that each phase and type of promotional activity carry out this theme as it will form a nucleus for the store's image.

Since every retail store needs a key idea as a nucleus in the store's sales promotional efforts, how does a retailer go about selecting a theme for the store? First, a retailer must consider the store's objectives. A theme is the gist of the retailer's message to customers and potential customers, and it should arouse the consumers' interest and entice them to patronize the store. So the theme selected should relate to and reflect the retailer's objectives. Thus, in accordance with the retailer's goals, a central idea may focus on the customers' desires for (1) economy, (2) dependability, (3) name-brand merchandise, (4) high-fashion goods, (5) ease of store accessibility, (6) prestige, (7) a variety of customer services, or (8) other psychological benefits. The theme should be distinctive and original, and reflect the store's image or personality. A well-chosen theme will attract and hold a certain customer group.

It now becomes even more significant for a retailer when determining a target market to have in mind what image he or she wishes for the store, as well as how the store will encourage this target group to purchase. Correct selection of a store theme will assist the advertising and sales promotional efforts of the store. The use of a theme will help consumers interpret what the store stands for and better understand why they should patronize this store over a competing store. It also may attract prospective customers and hold the interest of the present patrons. A store's central theme binds together each individual advertisement and sales promotional event. It concentrates on or repeats a single concept, which will result in a longer-lasting remembrance by the consumers than otherwise would be possible.

What characteristics are found in a good retail store theme? Since the store's theme serves as a guide for all store promotional events, it should be simple, short, and easily understood by the consumer. In order to be effective, the theme should be tied to the needs and wants of the customers and to the name of the store itself. In addition to being plausible and convincing, the theme should stress consumer benefits and the reasons for patronizing the store. If economy is the main theme, then the retailer must offer merchandise that is lower in price than the same goods found at competing retail stores. If the main theme is customer service, then the consumer has every right to expect a full variety of consumer services from the retailer.

A retailer's main theme should be unique or different or distinctive, but one must realize that seldom can a retailer offer a buyer benefits that also cannot be offered by the competition. However, it is feasible for a retailer to become known for being a leader in a certain retail area—an innovator in merchandising techniques, in distinctive decor, in layout, interior and exterior layout and design, or for having high-caliber sales personnel. All managerial and sales promotional efforts should concentrate on *any* feature which will distinguish a retailer's store from those of the competition.

The selection of a store theme should be attempted only after the target market has been analyzed to determine the attitudes and expectations of the consumer group. A retailer's objectives must also be apparent. One main idea, or several ideas, which can be stressed and turned into consumer benefits can be the central theme. It may be well to stress one central idea rather than emphasize several smaller ideas. Or perhaps, all ideas can be incorporated into a unique store theme. For example, a certain Chevrolet retailer in San Diego, California, utilizes the theme, "What Ever's Right." This indicates to the customer that the firm's efforts will be devoted to customer satisfaction both with the product and the service. A well-known department store chain uses the theme, "We Know What You're Looking For," implying that their merchandise can fulfill your desires and needs. Another national furniture chain uses the central theme of "The World's Largest Seller of Famous Brand Furniture," indicating that regardless of what brand you are looking for, you will find it at their store. Although regional in scope, another retailer of consumer services has coined a distinctive word that is used in its sales promotion. The word, "congeneric," is supposed to indicate to the customer that all the firm's services are client-oriented since the firm is a group of related companies or services working together to serve its clients' needs. One of the leading greeting card manufacturers has used an effective phrase or slogan for years: "When you care enough to send the very best." A retailer offering these cards can also use that slogan in the store's advertising and sales promotion, which is a definite advantage for the retailer since the phrase is so well known.

It is extremely important that a retailer study both prospective customers and present customers for possible themes. Prospects may reveal why they do not patronize the store, and the store's patrons may indicate why they do shop there. Another source of theme ideas may stem from the store itself. Perhaps the location, design, or assortment of goods and services may serve as a nucleus for a store's theme. But whatever theme is selected, it should be based on a central idea and maintained for consistency and consumer acceptability since, together, these concepts will shape the store's image or personality which is long-lived.

The Retail Store Image

As we learned above, a retail store's image or personality develops from the main theme used in all retail sales promotion. It is important when the retailer selects a theme that it be what the retailer wishes it to be, especially since the theme will establish the store's image. And the image, in turn, becomes longer lasting than the theme itself. Themes can and do change over time, but the store image tends to remain the same and be more or less permanent.

It is difficult to separate a retail store's theme from the store's image.

However, upon closer examination, it is evident that the store's main theme develops and often grows into a store image. In other words, a theme is the beginning of the image of a retail store. So it is critically important that a store's image be consistent with the customers' mental view and not with the retailer's perception. How a customer perceives a retail store is more important than how the store's management or owner views the enterprise. Customer concern should always be more important than the retailer's view if the store is to succeed. For these reasons, it is necessary that a retailer get in step with the customers regarding the image of the store.

The image of a retail store is formed in the customers' minds by means of the following: (1) the manner in which the business is conducted, (2) the selection and assortment of merchandise offered, (3) the store's interior design, (4) the layout and display of goods, (5) the lighting and its effects on the merchandise, and (6) the attitude and philosophy of the retail store's personnel. Thus, it becomes readily apparent that the building of a store image is under the retailer's control. For example, Sears, Roebuck and Company has been successful in changing or influencing its image by focusing on a central idea. This retailing chain transformed its image over a period of years by trading up its merchandise lines—this change first becoming evident early in the 1960s. Today, the retailing giant is known as a progressive, modern retailer, rather than a farmer's store for work clothes or a mail-order house. But this change of image is the result of huge sums of money being spent over a long period of time for managerial talent and for sales promotion. Many smaller retailers cannot financially afford to change their stores' images over such an extended period of time. This illustration points out the importance of carefully focusing, selecting, and staying with a concept to build a personality and image for the store, as it is the retail store image which either attracts or repels customers.

THE PROPER RETAIL PROMOTIONAL MIX

In designing a proper advertising and sales promotional mix, a retailer should give considerable thought to the blend of advertising, personal selling, and floor and window displays. The blend a retailer uses will depend on a number of factors. Some of these factors are the nature of goods and services sold, type of retail store, store location, customer grouping, competitive conditions, and funds available. For example, if a retailer is offering convenience goods, the blend will probably be heavily weighted with some form of newspaper advertising. Or if a retailer is selling durable goods, the emphasis will probably be placed on personal selling since durables usually need to be demonstrated. Durables are seldom purchased on impulse, although at times it may appear that this is the case; some shopping and comparing of prices have usually taken place, even if the consumer merely read a manufacturer's advertisement in a magazine.

Advertising   As you probably have already concluded, the most widely used advertising medium for retailers is the newspaper. Retailers use newspaper advertising because they wish to inform as many prospects as quickly as possible. Newspapers can be used to inform customers of special sales events, store hours, credit policies, and services. Newspaper advertising works well for a retailer when consumers wish to purchase certain goods; i.e., a newspaper ad may offer a stimulus to the consumer to purchase the advertised goods. However, it must be remembered that advertising will *not* sell goods or services that consumers do not want.

As we discussed earlier, a retailer will generate more sales volume and have better results if the retail store and its offerings can be differentiated in some way. Naturally, it is easy for a retailer to advertise if the store has something to say to its customers. Thus, retailers of durables (such as appliances, furniture, and automobiles), should advertise in a newspaper because differentiating these items through the use of brand names and specific product features is relatively easy. Retailers who are unable to differentiate their product lines from those of competitors will have to advertise and promote the store's services, image, location, or hours of operation. Other features, such as parking, delivery, and gift wrapping, may also have to be stressed in order to create a degree of difference.

Through the use of advertising, a retailer is capable of developing customer patronage and loyalty. A customer soon learns to rely on the retailer's reputation or be repelled by the store, depending on the consistency of product line quality, the services, and the stocking of certain favorite brands. If a retailer advertises consistently, a consumer's buying motives may be stimulated even though such motives may be dormant. Consumer buying action can also be stimulated by utilizing emotional appeals in advertising. For instance, prestige retail stores have achieved their status largely through the use of advertising which appeals to emotional buying motives.

Personal Selling   Personal selling is used by the retailer in the sales promotional mix to make customers understand that products have hidden features which can be turned into customer benefits. A retailer may also use personal selling to offset preconceived consumer attitudes which focus on low-priced products. Successful salespeople can often convince a customer to buy some higher priced merchandise even though the main attraction was price appeal. This process is commonly known in the retailing world as "trading up."

Window Displays   As a part of the promotional mix, window displays often reflect the image of the retail store. This is found to be true since many customers will judge the character of a place of business from viewing the merchandise in the windows. It is not only the type of merchandise but also the amount of goods in the window which reveals something about the image of that retail store. For example, variety stores or discount houses typically place many items in their windows for display, perhaps even to the extent the windows are crowded. Most of the displayed items are low-priced, and this exhibit reflects the image of a low-priced retail store. Conversely, high-fashion stores often place only one item in a window display which, in turn, mirrors the prestige of that retail store.

The promotional mix (advertising, personal selling, window displays) is used by a retailer to influence and attract customers and to change their attitudes, beliefs, and purchasing habits. When used judiciously, the communication process from the retailer to the consumers via the promotional mix should lead customers to the store and induce them to buy from that store.

Types and Kinds of Promotional Events

Special sales events are often the major highlight of a retail store's sales promotional strategy. The frequency with which special sales events are held vary considerably, although certain sales events are traditional. The list shown in Figure 15-1 provides just a few of the more commonly held retail sales events. Perhaps you can think of other special events that could be added to the list.

The basic purpose of all special sale events is to increase store profits. Other purposes include the moving of seasonal merchandise, clearing and making room for incoming goods, closing out discontinued items, introducing new fashions, attracting new customers, aiding in the establishment of a store's own brand, building good will, and stimulating credit purchases. Thus, any special sale event may have one major goal and several minor objectives. Whatever the major and minor purposes of sale events, the store's personnel should be encouraged to react enthusiastically, which will help make all such events more successful.

The frequency of special sales should be appropriately spaced so that the events do not lose their effectiveness. If sales are held too close together, there is a danger that the store's promotional tactics will fail to attract customers. The timing of special sale events is critical for retailers. For established retailers, the timing of sales can be compared with past sale events to determine their effectiveness. For inexperienced retailers, the timing of special sale events should coincide with favorable weather conditions, good business and economic factors, as well as the pay periods for the majority of the store's customers.

Another factor that a retailer should consider when holding special sale events is the return-goods privilege. Are the goods to be sold "as is"? If so, it is well to inform all the salespeople of this fact and make sure that the customer is also told of the policy of "no returns." This simple act may save the store from some customer complaints.

Cooperative Advertising and Promotion

In many instances, a retailer and a manufacturer (or wholesaler) will enter into an agreement in which the costs of advertising are shared by each party. The manufacturer and the retailer may share anywhere from 25 to 75 percent of the total cost of the advertisement. Generally, they will share the costs equally, i.e., 50 percent for the manufacturer and 50 percent for the retailer. However, any type of arrangement can be made between the manufacturer and the retailer as to how the costs of cooperative advertising will be shared.

Month	Special sales event
January	January clearance sale January tax sale White goods sale
February	Valentine sale
March	Spring arrival sale Pre-Easter sale
April	Easter fashion sale After Easter sale Spring cleanup sale
May	Mother's Day sale Gifts for graduates and brides
June	Father's Day sale Sporting goods week Warehouse clearance sale
July	Fourth of July sale Dog days sale July clearance sale
August	Vacation specials Tire rodeo Kids rodeo Value parade
September	Back-to-school sale Labor Day sale Bargain days
October	Prewinter specials Fall fashions Let's-go-hunting sale
November	Thanksgiving specials Christmas layaway sale After Thanksgiving sale
December	Christmas sale Merry Christmas sale End-of-year clearance

Figure 15-1 Variety of special sales events.

A manufacturer who utilizes selective or exclusive distribution for products will probably list the names of the retailers in the advertising medium and also share the expenses of cooperative advertising. Since local advertising rates are more out of the advertising rates, a manufacturer will spend less money but get more out of the advertising dollar. Second, a manufacturer who shares the cost of advertising with a retailer will tend to foster and build the goodwill needed to sell the products. In some cases, a manufacturer may have to enter into cooperative advertising with a retailer so the retailer will mention the product in the store's advertising. Since some retailers and their reputations are better known to the customers than the manufacturer's name or reputation, a manufacturer may gain from the retailer's prestige and reputation.

Despite these advantages, many manufacturers do not like to enter into cooperative advertising ventures with retailers. The manufacturer's return from this type of investment is difficult to measure, which may account for some of the manufacturer's dissatisfaction with cooperative advertising. Too, some retailers do not care for the assistance they receive from manufacturers in cooperative advertising. Thus, often what should be encouraging goodwill between the resource and the middleman may result in ill will between the manufacturer and the retailer.

Cooperative advertising can assist a retailer in developing advertisements which have considerable pulling power. Generally, cooperative ads are the result of an advertising agency's thoughts and efforts which may develop into a better advertisement than a retailer could develop on his or her own. This does not always hold true, but in many cases, better advertisements are produced by a professional.

A retailer usually does not have to spend money for advertising "mats" because they are furnished by the manufacturer. Mats are plates used in a printing process and usually have the product name, picture, or some other distinctive slogan. Mats are rather expensive, so this can result in a savings to the retailer. When cooperative advertising is used, a retailer benefits from the name, prestige, and pulling power of a manufacturer. A manufacturer's reputation is very important to the consumer, especially with durable goods. If the manufacturer has a proven warranty program, customers will often be attracted to a retailer's store because of the name brand of the product being advertised. Also, the retailer gets considerable coverage from the store's advertising dollars when a manufacturer shares a portion of the expenses.

On balance, a cooperative advertising venture between a manufacturer and a retailer (the most common type of arrangement) should be a mutually beneficial one. The manufacturer cannot sell any more merchandise to the retailer until the retailer sells the goods that are on hand. Conversely, the retailer cannot purchase additional merchandise from the manufacturer until the store has received the money from the sale of the goods. Thus, cooperative advertising plays a pivotal role in the relationship between the resource and the middleman.

Newspaper Advertising

As an advertising medium, newspapers are flexible and timely and are used by a majority of retailers. Newspapers can reach a large number of potential customers. If a retailer places an advertisement in a local newspaper, the retailer can reach practically every home in the trading area.

The advantages of newspaper advertising are numerous. A daily newspaper allows a retailer the opportunity to reach potential customers on any certain day of the week. Through the newspaper, customers can be reached when they are most receptive to the retailer's messages. Also, an advertisement can be cancelled or inserted on short notice and can be quickly adapted to local market conditions. Newspapers also often bring quick responses at relatively low rates per reader. Some of the larger newspapers offer businessmen assistance in developing advertisements, which should help to make the sales promotion efforts more effective. However, one disadvantage of the newspaper is that the advertisement is relatively short-lived.

Direct-Mail Advertising

The most personalized medium of advertising is direct mail since it can be directed to a target market of the retailer's own choosing. Direct-mail advertising can reach a highly selective group. Direct mail can be personal, selective, and the copy extremely flexible. However, direct mail is only as good as the mailing lists that are used which must be current and up to date. Names for use in a direct-mail campaign can be obtained from an existing store's past sales tickets. Or they can be purchased from a mailing house (company which specializes in selling lists of names) if the retailer has not been in business previously. If a mailing list is selective, little waste occurs with direct-mail advertising. Direct mail, when properly used, is not as costly as other mediums of advertising because of the predetermined customer selectivity—that is, only those customers' names should be used who are good prospects for buying from that retail store.

Direct mail often appears to be expensive because of the few pieces which are mailed. However, if carefully constructed and tailored to the prospects, direct-mail advertising can be rewarding in terms of an increased profitable sales volume for the store. The letters or copy used in direct-mail advertising should be original, if at all possible. This will intrigue or interest the consumer who receives it, increasing the likelihood of that consumer taking affirmative action by going to the store and making a purchase. In order to personalize the direct mail copy as much as possible, it is suggested that an automatic typewriter be used to create the impression of originality. Then the letter or copy should be mailed with first-class postage. It makes little sense to mail a piece of advertising by bulk rate if the rest of the message is first-rate.

Magazine Advertising

Magazines tend to be used only by the high-fashion retailers who specialize in reaching a higher income group and by some regional distributors of certain consumer goods. Such retail store as Tiffany's, Neiman-Marcus, Saks Fifth Avenue, Bullock's, Lord & Taylor, Pirie, Scott & Company and Bloomingdale's will advertise in such magazines as *The New Yorker, Harper's, Playboy, Bazaar,* and *Playgirl.* Most magazines are known for high-quality printing and color work, and they reach a national market at a relatively low rate per prospect. However, magazines suffer because they are published infrequently, and because they are rather inflexible as an advertising medium. The initial cost is also quite high which makes magazine advertising rather impractical for the small retailer.

Radio Advertising

Depending on the type of product being advertised, some retailers can use radio advertising quite effectively. In small trading areas, a retailer may have only one station from which to choose; thus, nearly everyone in this area will listen to that station. For those retailers in the more populated areas, selecting a radio station is not so simple. A retailer must first select a station to which most of the store's customers or prospects listen. Then the time spots on the radio station must be selected. If a retailer does not wish to direct the advertising message to those who listen to that station, there will be considerable waste in advertising on the radio. Usually, radio stations are in a position to know each program's audience. Therefore, personnel at the station may be able to assist a retailer in selecting the correct program for the store's target market group.

Television Advertising

Television is one of the fastest growing mediums and is quite versatile for a retailer since it appeals to both sight and sound. Television has an advantage over the radio since the radio appeals only to the ear. Television makes an excellent medium for demonstration of products. However, care must be taken to time the message so that a majority of the potential customers who are viewing the advertisement can be reached. The message should be precise and succinct. One disadvantage of television is that it is quite expensive as a medium. But if carefully and properly used, it can be one of the most powerful and effective sales promotional mediums available to a retailer.

The Importance of Personal Selling

For many retailers, personal selling constitutes a major portion of the sales promotional mix. Personal selling is flexible in that the sales communication can be tailored to each individual customer. A good salesperson should also be a good listener. By listening to the customers, a salesperson is better able to find the products which will fit the customers' needs—thereby benefiting the customer. Personal selling to some degree, like other facets of the sales promotion mix, is based on the emotions and behavioral attributes of the customer. Unlike other mediums of promotion, personal selling allows the customer to ask questions and become a part of the two-way communication process.

Personal selling is quite effective since there is little wasted effort, if the salespeople are properly trained. Training is really the key to effective retail selling. Appropriately trained salespersons are able to react on the spot to customer reactions and overcome customer objections. They can answer any and all questions as they arise which, in turn, lowers the customer's resistance to purchasing.

For the retailer of durable goods, personal selling is almost mandatory. Most durable goods need to be demonstrated to the customer before the purchase takes place, and this can be done only through the use of salespersons.

In any selling process, the salesperson first must attract the attention of the customer. Assuming that the customer came to the store because of an advertisement, part of this attraction phase had already been accomplished when the customer walked into the store. The second part of the process takes place when the prospective customer makes an inquiry. Then it becomes the salesperson's job to answer any and all questions. While the prospective customer is listening to the salesperson's answers and is inspecting the goods, the sales presentation can be made by the salesperson in attendance.

The sales presentation then becomes the medium by which a salesperson holds and further arouses the prospective customer's interest. There is no completely routine pattern or canned sales pitch since each presentation should be tailored to the situation and the prospective customer's inquiry. Since customers buy because of product benefits, it is the function of a salesperson to show the prospective customer just how each product feature will benefit the person. After the salesperson has demonstrated to the potential customer how the product features will benefit him or her, the salesperson should try to finalize or close the sale. If the prospect has further questions, each should be answered carefully. A trial close or suggestion to finalize the purchase will usually elicit any further questions. However, the greatest obstacle for any salesperson is the prospect who does not voice any objections and neither agrees nor disagrees with the salesperson. This situation often indicates that the salesperson has been talking too much. Good salespeople are good listeners, and even the most reticent customers will talk *if* given the opportunity. By allowing the customer to talk, a salesperson is in a better position to ask for the order. If a prospective customer states, "I have to think it over," the salesperson has probably failed to fully answer all questions and overcome all objections. In effect, the customer is thereby saying to the salesperson, "You haven't answered all my questions satisfactorily or given me enough assurance."

Window Displays

Attractive window displays are effective retail sales promotional aids. Many potential customers enjoy "window shopping" and are often attracted to a store because of the merchandise displayed in the windows.

Window displays, like other forms of retail sales promotion, should reflect favorably on the store's promotional policies. When a store has a policy of selling only fashion merchandise, it is well to limit window displays to one item that is shown effectively. This one item then becomes the focal point for that store. Conversely, those retail stores emphasizing price-appeal goods should probably place as many items in a window display as can be wisely merchandised.

Window displays can also be used to add emphasis to the other aspects of retail sales promotion. If the store is having a special promotion, the window displays should also feature the same type of merchandise in order to reinforce the promotion.

Since a window display serves as the silent salesperson, every effort should be made to add items of interest to the scene. A window display serves basically as an open invitation to the prospective customer to enter the store for further inquiry and inspection. A good window display not only arouses interest but also piques curiosity so that a customer will enter the store.

Too, window displays should be coordinated with the merchandise display and assortment inside the store. If a store does not prominently display price tags on the merchandise inside the store, then price tags may be eliminated from window displays. However, if the store openly displays price tags on price-appealing goods inside the store, then this same practice should be followed in the window displays.

Attractive and appealing window displays require considerable time and effort and should be arranged only by persons with some artistic ability. Changes in window displays should be made every few days or periodically in order to maintain customer interest. Merchandise in window displays should never be allowed to become dusty, soiled, or overused since such neglect will repel more customers than it will attract.

TRUTH IN SALES PROMOTION AND ADVERTISING

Retail sales promotion and advertising has its critics. Some feel that advertising is used too extensively which causes unnecessary costs, restricts free competition, and adversely affects the free pricing system. Others complain that sales promotion and advertising serve as poor guides to consumption. Still others criticize the ethics of advertising firms by saying that advertising is misleading. In the retailing field itself, some retailers at times question the effectiveness of advertising in producing a profitable sales volume.

Despite the criticisms of sales promotion and retail advertising, customers have found that they can depend on advertising to learn about the products that are available to them. Advertising also helps the retailer. Through its use, advertising can help the retailer create a certain volume of sales which is necessary in order to offer the customer the best possible assortment of goods and the best personalized service in the fastest time at the lowest cost possible.

For example, when a neighborhood grocery supermarket advertises food bargains in the daily newspaper, its purpose is to induce the customer to shop at that store and to select the advertised items (and hopefully some unadvertised items) from the shelves. The department store that advertises the new season's clothing hopes the customer will come into the store and complete the buying process with the assistance of a salesperson. In either case, if the retailer allows distorted or misleading advertising, the store may well suffer irrevocable damage to its reputation that may never be reclaimed—regardless of the amount of good-will advertising.

Consumers today are better informed and more highly educated than they were thirty or forty years ago. Informed consumers will not base their purchases on store loyalty if that store does not provide what the customers want, at the prices that they can afford, and with qualities which are comparable to competitive products.

Truth in retail sales promotion and advertising is a self-regulatory function of the retailer. Better Business Bureaus and similar consumer groups have had only limited success in controlling advertisements which border on misrepresentation, deceit, or fraud. Taste in advertisements, or an interpretation thereof, is highly subjective and tends to vary from audience to audience. In fact, it may even vary greatly from one time period to another. However, retailers should strive to present advertising that is not questionable as to legality, ethics, or taste and should attempt to present advertisements that are informative and educational. If a retailer's advertising is irritating to potential customers, it will not be effective in attracting customers to the store. Hence, bad advertising will be a waste of time and money and lose potential profits for the retailer.

Every retailer should strive for "fairness" in the store's advertising and sales promotion. Since retailers compete with one another by selling basically the same products, no useful purpose is served in downgrading a competitor's product while stressing the merits of the retailer's own offerings. The downgrading may only serve to draw attention to the competing retailer and cause the customers to go to the competitor's store.

Outright deceptions may be easily recognized by the informed consumer. Bait-and-switch advertising is obviously deceptive. In bait-and-switch advertising, a retailer will advertise a particular item at an especially attractive price. When customers arrive at the store to purchase that item at the low price (bait), the retailer persuades the customer to *switch* to the purchase of a more profitable item, usually at a higher price. This is done by the salesperson pointing out the limitations of the advertised item or by saying that the store does not have the advertised item in stock; or the salesperson may use some other high-pressure sales tactic. This bait-and-switch procedure is, of course, illegal and the retailer should be prosecuted; but it will be necessary for the consumer to file a complaint.

Another tactic which may be used by retailers is known as "puffery" which is nothing more than exaggerating the features of a product or item that is for sale. Retailers resorting to puffery may be asked by regulatory agencies to support their claims. Of course, the degree of exaggeration involved is very important since many consumers have come to expect some fairly "enthusiastic" sales talk on the part of retailers.

It also is illegal to advertise an item that is actually not in stock. Astute retailers will offer customers "rain checks" if leader items are sold out quickly. This tends to build good customer relations, and keeps the retailer from being chastised by consumers or regulatory bodies for not having the item they advertised.

In summary, the basic purposes of retail sales promotion and advertising are communication and persuasion. Failure of the retailer to perform these two basic functions in a tasteful and ethical manner will severely limit a retailer's advertising effectiveness and will cast a cloud of doubt on the store's image.

SUMMARY

Sales promotional strategies in retailing generally include advertising, personal selling, displaying of merchandise, and any other tactic which will induce a profitable sales volume for the retailer. Generally, there are two major classifications of retail sales promotion. One is *advertising* in some form to attract customers to the store. The other form of sales promotion is the concentration on *in store promotion.*

The basic purpose of retail sales promotion is to *increase* a store's profitable sales volume at any specific price. Retail sales promotion is extremely important today because of the intensification of competition among retailers. Retail sales promotion should be goal-oriented, carefully planned, coordinated with other store efforts, properly timed, and done on a continuing basis.

All too often a retailer determines a store's retail sales promotional budget based on intuition or past sales. When one of these techniques is used, it means that retail sales promotion is a result of sales, when actually, *sales* should be the *result* of retail sales promotion. A more appropriate method of determining how much money to allocate for retail sales promotion is to define *first* just what is to be done (set goals) and *then* decide how much money it will take to accomplish those objectives.

Retailers should adopt a sales promotional policy that is tailored to the individual store. Generally, a sales promotional policy suited for one retail store will not work for another store.

A *central theme* should be used by a retailer for the entire retail sales promotional program in order to provide continuity, consistency, and store impact on the consumer. It will be from this promotional theme that a retail store develops an *image* which is long-lived. Accordingly, a retailer must select a main idea around which all retail sales promotional efforts will be focused. This theme of retail sales promotion is then adapted to implement and provide a base from which all promotional events will evolve.

In accordance with a retailer's goals, a *central idea or theme* may focus on the consumers' desires for economy, dependability, national brands of merchandise, high-fashion goods, ease of store accessibility, prestige, customer services, or other psychological benefits.

The most widely used advertising medium for retailers is the newspaper. Retailers use *newspaper advertising* because they wish to inform as many consumers as quickly as possible.

Personal selling is used by a retailer in a sales promotional mix to make consumers aware that certain products have hidden features which often can be turned into customer benefits.

Window displays, as a part of the promotional mix, often reflect the image of the store.

In many instances, a retailer and a manufacturer or wholesaler will enter into an agreement in which the costs of advertising are shared by each party. This arrangement is referred to as *cooperative advertising.* Cooperative advertising allows a retailer to develop advertisements which have considerable pulling power at a reduced cost to the retailer, since the vendor is paying a portion of the cost.

Since *newspapers* are flexible and timely, they are used by most retailers as an advertising medium. *Direct mail* is the most personalized advertising since it can be directed to the consumer. *Magazines* tend to be used only by the high-fashion retailers who specialize in reaching a higher income group and by some regional distributors of certain consumer goods. Some retailers can use *radio* advertising quite effectively. *Television* advertising is one of the fastest growing mediums and is quite versatile for a retailer since it appeals to both sight and sound. *Personal selling* is flexible in that the sales communication can be tailored to each individual customer; personal selling is rather effective since there is little wasted effort, if the salesperson is properly trained.

Retail sales promotion should be *truthful* as well as *informative*. Generally, consumers have found that they can depend on advertising to learn about the store's offerings. Effective retail sales promotion and advertising is both informative and persuasive.

REVIEW QUESTIONS

1 Define retail sales promotion.
2 What is the basic purpose of retail sales promotion?
3 Why should retailers always advertise in some way?
4 Discuss the importance of determining a retail sales promotional budget.
5 What factors determine the sales promotional policy of a retail store?
6 What is a theme? Why is a theme so important to a retailer?
7 How does a retailer go about selecting a theme for a promotion?
8 What role does a promotional theme play in determining the image of a retail store?
9 Define "retail store image."
10 Discuss the importance of a retail promotional mix.
11 Why is the newspaper the most widely used medium for retailers?
12 What type of retail store is most likely to use personal selling as the main ingredient in the promotional mix? Why?
13 Special promotional events are important to most retailers. Why? Can you name some other special promotional events?
14 Explain how cooperative advertising works for a retailer.
15 Discuss the merits of a retailer cooperating with a vendor on a sales promotional event.
16 How can a retailer make the most effective use of direct mail advertising?
17 Discuss the circumstances under which each of the following forms of sales promotion would be used: Window displays; magazines; radio; television; personal selling.
18 Evaluate the truth in today's retail advertising and sales promotion.

CASE PROBLEMS

1 **Al's Grocery** is located in a rural Midwestern town of 15,000. The residents of the town are either employed at Ryan Electronics, are entrepreneurs, or are retired persons.

The store is located on South Street, one of the main roads through the town. There is ample parking for 150 cars, and the structure consists of approximately 16,000 square feet.

Al has taken over the store from his father who has operated the store for twenty-five years in the same location. Al has progressive ideas, which do not coincide with his father's, about how the store should promote sales.

Al's competition comes mainly from two giant grocery supermarkets, both chain organizations. One grocery chain is located within three blocks of Al's store in a new shopping center. The other grocery chain is located on the western edge of the town, along with a national discount chain store.

Al sells all the regular items that today's grocery stores handle. Al is a member of IGA and offers both national and IGA brands of fruits, vegetables, USDA choice beef, grade A chickens, and top quality pork. Al's father was not interested in selling nonfood items, such as children's clothing, garden tools, and pet supplies. Al believed that these items could be stocked by merely rearranging the interior of the store and reducing the number of national brands of canned foods.

Al further reasoned that he could capitalize on the store's location at the junction of the streets where all traffic turned to the shopping center.

Al has been advertising regular grocery items in the *Northfork Daily News* each Wednesday through Saturday. This is what the other grocery stores did, and Al and his father thought it was appropriate.

Last year's sales volume for Al's store reached $457,000—down from the previous year's figures of $587,000. Al was searching for some innovative way to advertise whereby he could attract more customers and increase the store's sales volume. Al believed that his offering was as good as the chain stores; but for some reason, customers appeared to be attracted to the shopping center.

What would you recommend that Al do in terms of sales promotion to attract more business? Outline your procedures.

2   Mini Case Watson Pontiac-Buick was located in a small town of 4,500 population in a Western state. Brad Watson had taken over the business when his father retired. The business had been good to the Watson family in that Mr. T. C. Watson had averaged approximately 175 new car sales each year and about 220 sales of used automobiles. Some used autos were purchased at car auctions in a nearby large metropolitan area. Only clean, low-mileage cars were purchased at wholesale prices and returned to the Watson used-car lot.

The business had been located at the end of Main Street for twenty-eight years. Mr. T. C. Watson had constructed the building shortly after World War II. General Motors encouraged the Watsons to move to a larger facility where more adequate parking would be available and more room for the used-car lot was available. A site was selected on the main highway through town, which was number 200. One square block was purchased, and a new building of 25,000 square feet was built with General Motors' approval. Access to the new building was from four streets, and the building was located in the middle of the block. The showroom floor faced a southerly direction and the repair facility was in the rear.

Since this was a new facility, Brad thought that something special should be promoted for the "opening." His father and the General Motors representative also believed that the time was ripe to develop a new image for the Watson Pontiac-Buick store.

There was another problem with which the Watsons did not know how to cope. The energy crunch of the early 1970s turned many car buyers toward the smaller, compact models. People who previously purchased Grand Villes and Electras—the large models in each product line—were not trading in their cars as they had in the past; previously, these owners traded in their cars about every two to two and one-half years. These models carried a nice gross margin of 25 percent over the dealer's cost. Currently, many smaller models were being sold instead. These models offered Watson a much smaller profit margin—in some instances, only 15 percent.

Design a special promotional program for Watson Pontiac-Buick which will create a new image for the store. Place some emphasis on the more profitable models. Use some innovative techniques to entice owners of older models to trade in their two-year-old cars. Place special emphasis on a theme which can be utilized for some period of time.

Chapter 16

Retail Credit

Buying goods and services on credit has become a way of life for many Americans. Most of us use some form of credit—whether it is for a house, an automobile, furniture, soft goods, or services. We want the opportunity to be able to use goods and services now but not have to pay for them until a later date. We as consumers have come to demand, accept, and extensively use the various forms of credit available. Consumers today show little apprehension or hesitation when they buy merchandise now and pay for their purchases at a future date.

Thus, retail credit has become an integral part of practically all retail stores. Very few retail stores sell on a "cash-only" basis. However, recently, some retailers have attempted to attract price-conscious consumers to the store by offering discounts to cash-only customers. But as we discussed earlier, consumers are pretty well convenience-oriented, and credit is a means of convenience. Since retail credit facilitates the purchase of such goods as automobiles, soft goods, and services, the consumer and the retailer have readily accepted this form of convenience.

Over the years, consumer attitudes on the use of retail credit have changed. This is evidenced by the growth of the total amount of consumer credit sales as shown in Table 16-1. Retailers, too, have come to accept and offer credit sales as a means of expanding sales volume and increasing profits for the store. Since the

Table 16-1   Consumer Credit

End of year	Total*
1960	$56,141,000
1961	57,982,000
1962	63,821,000
1963	71,739,000
1964	80,268,000
1965	90,314,000
1966	97,543,000
1967	102,132,000
1968	113,191,000
1969	122,469,000
1970	126,802,000
1971	
1972	
1973	
1974	177,600,000

*Figures do not include home mortgage loans.

Source: 1974 figures: *Business Week,* May 11, 1974, p. 23; other data came from a publication by the board of governors of the Federal Reserve System.

retailing segment of our economy is based to a large extent on the uses of various types of retail credit, it is important that the student of retailing understand how and when credit should be used by the retailer and the consumer.

RETAIL CREDIT DEFINED

Retail credit may be defined in many ways. However, in its simplest form, retail credit is a medium of exchange of limited acceptance.[1] In other words, no longer does the consumer use a physical item or commodity for trading in exchange for goods and services. Today, when purchasing goods and services, we utilize money (cash) or the various forms of credit as our means of exchange. Credit at the retail level of business activity is a convenient means which allows the exchange process (buying and selling) to take place. With cash money, the retailer collects the full amount of the purchase price immediately at the time of the sale. But with the use of retail credit, before a retailer collects the full amount of the purchase price, a period of time must pass. A credit transaction usually works like this. At the time of the sale, the retailer may or may not collect a down payment from the customer as a partial payment. Then, over a period of time, the retailer receives the remainder of the purchase price (plus a carrying charge) in a series of payments. This part of the retail credit transaction is the "medium of exchange" in our definition.

[1]Robert H. Cole, *Consumer and Commercial Credit Management,* 4th ed., Richard D. Irwin, Homewood, Ill., 1972, p. 5.

However, in this definition of credit, you will note the words "limited acceptance." Credit does have a definite limitation factor, and this limitation is extremely important to both the consumer and the retailer. The credit limitation arises from the fact that each credit customer has a "ceiling" on his or her ability to repay the amount of the credit obligation. This credit limitation or ceiling is determined by the source, type, and amount of income earned by the consumer. In turn, this income is also affected by the consumer's previous and current outstanding obligations. If a consumer's credit rating is to remain unblemished, every credit obligation must be paid. Otherwise, it is possible this consumer should not be extended credit. This is one reason why it is so important for retailers *before* granting credit to determine what current and previous obligations a consumer may have. One's income will extend only so far. Thus, it can be stated that credit has limited acceptance. One of the basic purposes of this chapter is to gain some insight into just what factors regulate this limited acceptance of credit as a medium of exchange.

PURPOSES OF RETAIL CREDIT FOR RETAILERS

Retailers sell merchandise on credit for many reasons. The basic reason, however, is that credit sales tend to increase a store's sales volume and, hopefully, also increase the store's profits. Since retail credit has become an accepted American way of life, many retailers use retail credit as a means of promotion. For instance, if retail credit is properly promoted, some merchandise may be sold that would not normally have been sold if the customer had to pay for it in cash. Generally, there is less consumer resistance to buying on credit. This is especially true if installment transactions are satisfactorily arranged. The consumer is primarily interested in how much each monthly payment will be. Then if the monthly payment can be met without too much difficulty, the consumer will be satisfied and make the purchase. When a customer has to make a large purchase, such as an automobile or an appliance, there may be considerable resistance to parting with the total amount of cash at the time of purchase. For these consumers, retail installment credit is a less painful method of purchasing goods. Also, there may be greater satisfaction on the part of the customer if the product can be used and enjoyed while the monthly payments are being made.

Through the use of retail credit, a retailer may be able to trade up merchandise sales. This is true because it may be less painful and more acceptable to the customer to purchase a higher priced item when payments are spread over a period of time. If the consumer had to pay for the higher priced item all at once, he or she might not be able to purchase it.

Large retailers frequently issue their own credit cards in the hope that consumers will patronize their store more often simply because purchases can be made on credit. Consumers generally do shop where it is more convenient for them. Thus, the store's credit card may facilitate the purchasing decisions for the customers. Mail-order and telephone retailing are also facilitated when credit is used. Credit customers may shop by mail and have merchandise charged to their account. Customers may telephone a store and ask that certain goods be charged to a credit account, with delivery or pickup of the goods at a later time. Again, the convenience for the consumers cannot be overlooked. When customers have to pay cash for goods or services, they may tend to shop around at *many* stores; whereas a store's credit card may virtually tie customers to that particular store. Between pay periods, customers often have little cash; but if they possess a credit card from a large retail store, they may shop and purchase goods anyway.

PURPOSES OF CREDIT FOR CONSUMERS

According to Professor Cole,[2] consumers use credit basically for one of the following reasons: (1) they hope to raise their standard of living and increase their enjoyment, (2) they want to take advantage of the convenience offered by the use of credit, and (3) they are forced to use credit by the pressure of necessity.

Americans generally possess a belief that their standard of living can be improved. They also want to be able to enjoy themselves today and pay later for these luxuries. Today, for the purchase of an automobile, it would be difficult for many Americans to accept the idea that they should pay in cash at the time of purchase. America is a convenience-oriented society. Many of the goods and services provided by retailers are a matter of convenience—whether time-saving or labor-saving. For instance, all prepared foods are convenience-oriented products. Self-defrosting refrigerators, self-cleaning ovens, and garbage disposals can all be grouped into the convenience classification. So it is with retail credit. Through the use of credit, the customer is able to shop without having any cash. Credit makes it easy to purchase goods and services without having to carry money or worry about making a payment immediately.

Some consumers consider retail credit a matter of necessity. It may be necessary for some consumers to purchase on credit because of the large sums needed for certain items (automobiles, furniture, appliances). At other times, credit may temporarily be necessary until a paycheck is received by the household. But regardless of the reasons, consumers will continue to demand and use credit in making their purchases.

In addition to the reasons given above for consumer use of retail credit, there are other factors which every retailer should consider. Some customers find that it is easier to pay for goods or services with one monthly payment rather than paying for each item individually. Some household budgets are planned so that cash for smaller, day-to-day expenditures is available but that the larger payments to various accounts are made only once a month. For those customers who purchase goods by mail or telephone, credit allows them the convenience of not having to make a trip to the store. Once a customer has established credit with a retailer, the customer just has to place a call, tell the store what is needed, and have it charged to the customer's account. Upon the approval of the credit transaction, the merchandise may be mailed or delivered to the customer. The

[2]Ibid., p. 12.

customer is then billed the following month for the purchases. This use of credit is particularly effective for those retailers who advertise in the local newspapers, in "flyers," or by door-to-door circulars.

In some instances, it may be easier for the customer to return goods to a store when the purchase has been made on credit. Most retailers are reluctant to upset their credit customers by refusing to accept returned goods. Since the customer has not yet paid for the merchandise in full, the retailer may be more receptive to accepting the return of the merchandise. When a cash sale is made, the retailer may be reluctant to accept the return of goods. However, the use of cash instead of credit in itself is no reason to refuse the return of goods.

Finally, credit sales may be preferred over cash sales, especially when the customer acts on impulse. Many impulse purchases would not be made if the customers had to pay cash for the items. It is very easy for the customers to add small impulse purchases to their credit accounts or to a credit card account. Many times a customer is short of cash, and a credit card will facilitate the purchase of goods and services. The use of a credit card or a credit account avoids the inconvenience of having to write a check and provides the store with identification and references. The holder of a credit card avoids all the stigmas associated with check writing since a prior investigation of the card holder's ability to pay has been established with the store. Unless the card holder has violated the credit agreement, credit card purchases are nearly as rapid as cash purchases.

TYPES OF RETAIL CREDIT

Retail credit has been classified in many ways. However, in this text, retail store credit will be classified under three general headings.[3]

Revolving Credit (with Option Terms)

Revolving credit, which is used by many retailers, allows a consumer to purchase goods and services and have up to thirty days to pay for these items without any penalty of interest. If the customer does not pay for the goods and/or services within these thirty days, the credit plan then "revolves" each month and minimum payments are made by the consumer on each billing date. Under the revolving credit plan, a customer agrees to pay a fixed amount, usually set up as follows:[4]

    1 If the new balance is under $10, the minimum payment is the amount of the new balance

    2 If the new balance is between $10 and $200, the minimum payment is $10

    3 If the new balance is over $200, the minimum payment is 5 percent of the new balance

[3]Ibid., pp. 19 and 20.

[4]There are other variations of payment schedules imposed by various retail stores. This illustration serves as only one representation of possible monthly payment plans.

Revolving retail credit plans allow a customer to purchase items (usually small in dollar amount) over a period of a month. But the repayment extends over a longer period of time if the customer so desires. For instance, a customer makes a $4.95 purchase in one department of a large department store and an $11.49 purchase in another department of the same store. These sales transactions are then totalled and added to the customer's revolving credit account. For this privilege, the customer must pay an interest charge. The interest charge will be based on the total amount in the revolving credit account and in most states is regulated by statute.[5] For instance, some states allow a retailer to charge up to an 18 percent annual interest rate on the first $1,000 and a 12 percent interest rate on any balance over $1,000. Revolving charge accounts usually do not go over $1,000. Amounts larger than $1,000 generally are paid on an installment credit plan. At the time of this writing, these interest rates (12 and 18 percent) are the maximum allowed by law in approximately thirty states. If you convert these percentage rates into monthly rates, 18 percent per annum becomes 1.5 percent per month; and 12 percent per annum becomes 1 percent per month.

In those states where the law does not permit special interest rates for revolving credit accounts, the courts usually have ruled the following: The maximum allowable interest rate for revolving credit loans will coincide with that state's maximum legal rate of interest for cash loans. In some states, this rate for cash loans may be as low as 8 percent. Any rate of interest in excess of the stated legal rate for cash loans would amount to usury, and the retailer would be subject to fine by the courts.

Retail revolving credit has become extremely popular with both the customer and the retailer because of its two main characteristics: (1) it allows the customer to pay the full amount of the bill within a twenty-five-to-thirty-day grace period without any penalty of interest charges, or (2) it allows the bill to automatically "revolve" into the next month with a charge for interest. The retail revolving credit plan is almost universally accepted in larger department stores and specialty stores. This plan is so flexible that both the customer and the retailer enjoy its many benefits. According to Professor Cole, the most important features of retail revolving credit plans with option terms are as follows:[6]

  1 The customer ordinarily makes a series of purchases. In fact, the retail store would consider its sales promotion program faulty if this were not the case.
  2 There is no down payment.
  3 If the account is not paid within the prescribed time period, a series of recurring payments can be made over a period of time.
  4 There is a finance charge if the account is not paid within the prescribed time period.
  5 In most states, revolving credit transactions are governed by the provisions of a state law.

[5]Ibid., p. 66.
[6]Ibid., p. 78.

6 Under the federal Truth-in-Lending Law, disclosure procedures are spelled out for open-end credit transactions (including revolving credit).

For many retailers, the option-terms revolving credit plan is ideal since it is very flexible in meeting most customers' needs. Since one of the basic purposes of the plan is to increase sales, with the proper promotion, this goal can be accomplished. Also, the revolving credit plan with option terms allows a customer to charge a larger dollar volume than could be charged under a normal thirty-day credit arrangement. Once a customer's credit has been approved by the store for a revolving credit plan, the person is free to buy and charge merchandise at any time without the need for further credit checks. Usually the credit limit is known only to the store. As long as the individual pays each billing on time, he or she need not be aware of the credit limit placed on the account.

Installment Retail Credit

Installment retail credit gets its name from the fact that a customer must make periodic payments which are divided into segments, called "installments." These installment payments are based on: (1) the amount of the transaction, (2) the amount of time needed for repayment, and (3) the customer's ability to repay the loan. The dates for future payments are usually set at a specific time each month, or in some instances, every two weeks. Generally, the customer receives a statement or a payment book, detailing each payment with respect to the interest and the remaining balance.

Installment retail credit differs from revolving retail credit in many ways. First, in installment credit, a written contract is used which is called an installment purchase contract. This contract in every way is a legal and binding agreement for the individual purchaser. Since many of us may use installment credit at some time or another, it is important that both the consumer and the retailing institution understand it completely. A full comprehension of installment credit transactions by both parties will avoid the misunderstandings that often arise from such credit dealings.

Second, installment credit transactions are usually associated with the sale of high-unit-value goods. For instance, retailers of furniture, appliances, automobiles, pianos, furs, and the like, probably will make use of retail installment credit contracts. However, some items of low unit value (such as vacuum cleaners, sewing machines, and inexpensive jewelry) may be sold by a retailer on an installment contract. Thus, what goods will be sold on an installment contract is a relative matter.

Third, when buying any item on an installment contract, a down payment from the purchaser is usually required. In some cases, the down payment may consist of an older item which will be traded in on the newer item; this is probably best illustrated by the trade-in value of used automobiles. How often have you heard the advertisement from an automobile dealer, "Any old car will do." In some instances, retailers of used furniture or appliances take trade-ins when they are used as a down payment for the purchase of a newer item. Some retailers take appliances and furniture as trade-ins only as an attempt to satisfy or serve the customer. Through this service they are attempting to provide a "haul away" service for the consumer. Usually, the retailers who take older items in trade on the purchase of newer merchandise will not retail the goods themselves. Instead they wholesale or sell the goods once each month to a retailer who sells second-hand merchandise. Many retailers who take trade-ins do it only for the goodwill that is gained for the store through the provision of this customer service.

If a customer does not have a trade-in item, the retailer will require from the customer a cash down payment of 10 to 30 percent of the retail value of the item being sold. Even though some retailers may advertise that "no down payment is required," *most* try to get the customer to pay something down before writing the installment contract.

There is a specific purpose in getting the customer to make a down payment toward the purchase of the item. Both the retailer and the customer benefit psychologically from the investment in the merchandise. If the customer does not make a down payment, the customer may feel no sense of ownership. When the customer has a sense of ownership, there is less chance of the individual failing to make the payments on time. The last thing a retailer wishes to do is foreclose or repossess an item from a person who has failed to make a payment on the installment contract. Usually this practice only serves to create ill will. Since the customer is still responsible for any difference between the value of the remaining contract and the sales price of the item sold after repossession, a bad feeling between the store and the customer only makes things more difficult.

Fourth, an installment contract provides for a series of payments. This schedule of payments will cover the total amount of the contract, which includes all the interest charges (which are also referred to as finance charges). It is important for the retailer who uses installment contracts to make sure that the customer is able to make periodic payments to meet the obligations of the contract. Any current outstanding obligations that the purchaser may have must be considered by the retailer in establishing the schedule of payments—or even in deciding whether to grant credit to this purchaser. Although it is highly desirable to maintain an unpaid balance (which is no more than the resale value of the goods), this may not always be possible. In fact, it would be preferable to maintain an unpaid balance that is *less* than the item's resale value. This fact clearly demonstrates the need for a retailer to obtain some sort of down payment from the customer. There must be a proper relationship between the unpaid balance and the resale value of the merchandise—or the retailer may have a problem. In case of repossession of the goods from the customer for failure to make payment, the items are usually sold. But many times the goods may be sold for less than the unpaid balance of the contract. If this is the case, the customer is still liable for the remaining balance of the contract (the difference between the resale price and the unpaid balance of the installment contract).

In order to reduce the probability of the customer's failure to make the payments, it is wise for the retailer to do the following: The retailer should carefully coordinate any installment-contract schedule of payments with the customer's income. For example, if a customer is paid on the first of the month, then a payment schedule should be set so that the person makes the installment payment on or about the first of each month. If this person's paycheck arrives on the tenth of each month, then the schedule of payments should coincide with this pay period. An individual's income and its receipt is easily determined from the credit application which will be discussed later in this chapter.

Fifth, the schedule of installment payments should not be extended into the future beyond the useful life of the item purchased. For example, some automobile dealers are currently writing installment contracts for forty-eight to sixty months (four to five years)—which is beyond the normal life of many cars. In other words, the car may be worn out before the contract has been paid in full which is highly undesirable and risky. If the customer's equity in the item is less than the amount owed on the installment contract, the customer may want to return the item to the retailer and ask to be relieved from the contract. Legally, it is doubtful that this could be done by the customer; however, it is prudent for the retailer to shorten the schedule of payments as much as possible. The shorter the terms of the contract, the better for both the customer and the retailer. The retailer has less worry about the customer failing to fulfill the requirements of the contract; and by having a shorter contract, the customer pays less in finance charges.

Sixth, the finance charges associated with installment contracts are regulated by state and/or federal law. For instance, on July 1, 1969, the federal Truth-in-Lending Act became effective. The act's main purpose is to ensure full disclosure of credit terms (finance charges) in each and every installment contract. Thus, the customer can determine exactly what portion of the payment goes for interest and equity and knows exactly what the unpaid balance is. Supposedly, because of the disclosure regulation, the act enables a customer to shop around and compare finance charges from one retailer to another; however, it is doubtful that the act serves this purpose. Consumers rarely understand the full provisions of an installment contract. Further, many consumers are concerned only with the amount of the monthly payments, not the amount of interest that has to be paid on each installment contract. However, for those persons who wish to be aware of such finance charges, this act forces the retailer to provide this information.

Finally, installment contracts provide to the retailer secured transactions. That is, title to the merchandise remains with the seller until the customer has fulfilled all the obligations of the installment contract (made all the payments). In many states, this contract can also be called a "security agreement" or a "retail installment sales contract." These retail installment contracts are simplified versions of earlier installment contracts, where the customer had to sign a chattel mortgage or a conditional sales contract (actually putting up collateral of some sort). However, security agreements or retail installment sales contracts provide the seller with rights of repossession in case the purchaser fails to make the required payments on schedule. In practice, however, the retailer usually is not interested in repossessing the merchandise. Retailers will even accept delayed payments before taking any action against an individual who is in default of an installment contract.

Finance Charges Associated with Installment Credit   Since most of us will at one time or another make use of installment credit, it is important that we understand how much we are paying for the privilege of delayed payments. These costs go by various names such as service charge, carrying charge, finance charge, or interest charge.[7] But in this text, the amount that it costs us to use installment credit will be referred to as the "finance charge."

Finance charges are those costs over and above what the identical item would cost if the customer paid cash for the item. In other words, if you take the sum total of the installment payments and subtract from that total the cash price of the item, you will then have the amount of the finance charges. Of course, the total amount of an installment contract may include more than just the item's purchase price and the interest paid on the contract. For example, an installment contract may include the following: (1) charges for insurance (usually credit life insurance on the person who is purchasing the item and is signing the contract), (2) the costs of a credit investigation (although this may not be allowed in some states), or (3) any other expenses or costs that may be added to the installment contract. All these charges should be added to the cost of the installment contract. They also should be included in any determination by the customer of the actual finance charges which are for the privilege of using installment credit.

Annual Percentage Rate   Basically, two rates of interest are usually quoted to customers when they apply for credit or wish to sign an installment contract. These two rates of interest are called (1) the nominal rate and (2) the annual percentage rate which is sometimes referred to as the "true annual rate."

The nominal rate of interest is the rate that is usually quoted to the customer by the financial institution involved, such as a bank or sales finance company. With an installment contract, the nominal rate of interest is approximately one-half of the annual percentage rate. Why is this so? The customer never really has the use of the full amount of money over the time period specified in the installment contract. Say a customer is making monthly payments for one year on an installment contract. This, in effect, allows the customer the use of just over one-half of the money for one year, which then virtually doubles the nominal or quoted rate of interest. For example, let us look at the following situation. A customer signs an installment contract for $1,200 for one year, thereby agreeing to make monthly payments. This amount ($1,200) is repayable in twelve equal payments over the next year. This means, in effect, that the customer who signs this installment contract has use of the full amount for only six and one-half months since each month of the repayment period calls for a

[7]Ibid., p. 119.

payment to be made by the customer. The amount of the first payment (which will be $100 plus finance charges and may vary according to the state or credit rating of the customer) must be deducted from the principal amount of the installment contract. Thus, the installment contract calls for a principal amount of $1,200. But to this figure, will be added the finance charges and any other add-on charges. Then this total amount (divided by 12) will determine the monthly payment over the next twelve months. After the first monthly payment of $100 plus the finance charges, the customer really has use of only part of the $1,200. Thus after each monthly payment, the unpaid balance will be reduced, eventually making it, in effect, approximately one-half of the contracted amount of $1,200. According to Professor Cole, there is a formula for determining the amount of time that a consumer really has use of the full amount of the contract.[8] This formula is: $n + 1$ divided by 2. Thus, n equals the number of payments needed to repay the obligation. In the above illustration, 12 months were needed to discharge the debt on the installment contract. Twelve plus one divided by two equals six and one-half months ($12 + 1$ divided by $2 = 6.5$). Thus, the annual percentage rate (the rate used by financial institutions and the accounting profession) will be approximately twice the nominal or quoted rate of interest on installment contracts.

Currently, under the Truth-in-Lending Law, retailers must comply with the law's provision of explaining to the customer and stating in writing the annual percentage rate, as well as all other finance charges which may be a part of the installment contract. Nothing can be hidden from the customer—which is as it should be. All elements of the contractual arrangement must be revealed and explained to the person(s) signing an installment contract. Although most retailers abided by this rule long before the law was passed, there were those who did not comply with these basic requirements. This often led to misunderstandings and, in some instances, illegal abuses of the customer by the retailer. If a customer or a retailer has any question about an annual percentage rate, reference can be made to interest tables which are available for this purpose. Most retailers have these tables, as do banks and other financial institutions.

Retail Open-Charge Credit

A third form of retail credit is the open-charge credit plan. Many small independent retailers allow a customer to charge merchandise over a thirty-, sixty-, or ninety-day basis. This plan allows the customer to pay the account charges some thirty, sixty, or ninety days later without incurring any finance charges. For example, small specialty clothing shops may use the thirty-day open-charge account for preferred customers. Some independent furniture dealers make use of thirty, sixty, or ninety days in which the customer may pay the debt without paying any finance or interest charges. Often this is referred to as "thirty days, the same as cash"; "sixty days, the same as cash"; or "ninety days, the same as cash." This feature or customer service tends to attract customers to the retail

---

[8]Ibid. p. 122.

store and builds customer goodwill. The obvious benefits to the customer include the use of the retailer's money for the period of time stated: thirty, sixty, or ninety days. Naturally, many customers prefer this arrangement to an installment contract since they may be only temporarily short of cash and may be able to pay the obligations within the stated period of time. Too, the retailer may find that, by offering this service, he or she may increase the sales volume of the store, while at the same time, "differentiating" the store from the competition that is not using the open-charge method of selling merchandise.

BANKS AND OTHER CREDIT CARD COMPANIES

The field of bank credit cards is dominated by two large systems—Bank Americard and Interbank (Master Charge). BankAmericard was started during the middle 1950s, but did not become nationally and internationally prominent or profitable for the company until about ten years later. Master Charge started slowly in the field but has been aggressive and likewise successful.

Both credit card companies operate in a similar manner. The sponsoring banks act as collective credit departments for all the retail merchants joining the card system. Some retailers join both systems, as well as offering other credit card systems, such as American Express, Diners Club, and Carte Blanche.

The customer who holds a bank credit card can charge a purchase at any cooperating retail store. The customer is also provided with a convenient credit card which is usable in many stores. After a customer has made a purchase on a bank credit card and has signed the sales slip provided, the retailer sends the sales slip to the bank. The retailer gets credited with the amount on the sales slip, less a deduction of 3 to 5 percent depending on the arrangement between the retailer and the sponsoring bank. The sponsoring bank is then responsible for the collection of the debt, and bills the customer. But meanwhile, the retailer gets his or her money immediately, less the percentage charged by the bank for handling and processing.

One limitation or disadvantage for the retailer is the flexibility the card holder has in being able to use the card for purchases in any cooperating retail store. Thus, the retailer loses the effectiveness of a store-sponsored credit card in tying the customer to the store. On the other hand, many small retailers are not in a position to have their own store credit cards. Thus, the bank card allows them to become more competitive with larger stores. Some large department stores or chains have their own credit cards and will not honor any bank card.

FACTORS INVOLVED IN DECISION TO SELL ON CREDIT

Retailers sell merchandise on credit to stimulate a profitable sales volume for the store. Also, selling on credit may improve the retailer's public relations with customers and increase the number of services offered. A retailer's decision to sell merchandise on credit is one of personal choice, but many retailers feel that they are virtually forced to sell goods and services on credit because their competitors do. This is probably true since a majority of the customers have come to accept credit in some form as the "standard way" of purchasing goods and services. Let us look at some of the factors which may influence a retailer's decision to either offer credit or not offer it and sell strictly for cash.

First, let us assume that the retailer has made a decision to sell the store's merchandise using some form of credit. Now the retailer must make a decision as to the type of credit plan that will be offered to the store's customers. As we have already discussed, the main forms of retail credit include: revolving credit with option terms, retail installment credit, open-charge credit, and bank or company credit cards. A retailer has the option of using any, all, or some combination of these credit plans.

Next, the retailer should make some predetermination regarding the effect of the credit plans on the profit of the store. Hopefully, the store's profits will be increased through the stimulation of additional sales volume. However, it is possible that the costs or expenses associated with the use of credit transactions and uncollectible accounts could drastically reduce the profits of the retail store. Too, some types of merchandise will lend themselves to credit sales. For instance, goods that are sold on credit must carry a high enough gross margin to warrant selling them that way. Generally, food items do not offer the retailer a high enough gross margin to warrant selling on credit. This is just one reason why very few grocery stores sell on credit. Of course, there are some limited exceptions to this basic rule. Some specialty food stores or gourmet shops will sell merchandise on credit because these items generally offer the retailer a higher gross margin than is offered on staple foods in the grocery supermarkets.

Second, a retailer may be forced to sell merchandise on credit because of the competition. If the competing retail stores offer the consumers an opportunity to buy on credit, then the retailer probably will have to offer credit to the customers. Of course, the retailer may have some choice as to the specific type of retail credit which the store will make available to consumers; but most retailers will adopt credit systems similar to those offered by the competition.

Third, the desires of the consumer should always be kept in mind. If the customers demand that credit be offered, then the retailer has little or no choice but to offer a credit plan. The retailer may wish or be able to find out what type of credit arrangements the customers prefer, but in practice this may not enter into the decision to sell on credit. The customers will simply be informed of the store's credit policies and arrangements. However, a few customers may ask about special arrangements for the payment of merchandise purchases. If a customer inquires about a special repayment method, the retailer may have to make some special arrangements for this customer. Or the retailer may have to convince the customer to accept the store's basic provisions of the regular credit plan.

Fourth, as previously mentioned, the type or kind of goods a retail store sells will usually be a significant factor in the decision to sell on credit. If a retailer is dealing in merchandise which carries a relatively high price, credit is almost mandatory for the store. Durable goods, such as furniture, appliances, and automobiles almost always require credit provisions of some sort. These goods are quite high-priced and are not easily paid for in cash by the consumer. Thus, a longer time period is needed in which the customer can pay for the item. Other retailers handling soft goods, such as men's and women's wear, will also allow customers to purchase on credit. This may be due, in part, to the price of the merchandise; but more likely, it is for the convenience of the customers.

Finally, any retailer planning to sell merchandise on credit will have to make some provision in the retail business plan for additional working capital for operating the store. Since there is a time lag between the sale of the item on credit and the receipt of the full payment, the retailer may need additional operating cash. The retailer may have to make arrangements with a bank or other financial institution to borrow additional funds to operate the store. Whether the retailer makes a profit from the extension of credit to consumers obviously depends, in part, on how much the retailer will have to pay for the additional working capital. If the costs of the additional money from a financial source are greater than the profits from the sale of goods on credit, the retailer will lose money. Thus, the retailer must be able to borrow money from a financial institution at a favorable rate of interest. But in addition, the retailer must receive an even greater rate of interest from the consumer if any profits are to be derived from the use of credit sales.

THE CREDIT INVESTIGATION

The retailer, or a credit manager, must have certain credit information on the customers before accepting the customers' credit applications, or rejecting them. Most stores will have a systematic procedure of gathering credit information which must be followed *before* the customer is granted credit. The first step is usually to have the customer fill out a credit application. When the credit application form is completed, the customers themselves will have provided much of the information that is needed. Figure 16-1 shows a typical retail credit application form which would be completed by the customer at the time of the application for credit. Figure 16-2 shows a credit application form in Spanish.

The applicant is asked to complete the credit application, filling in all the blank spaces. Then much of this information can be verified by the retailer or credit manager simply by investigating or questioning the sources given on the application. For instance, one's place of employment, as well as the duration of that employment, can be verified by telephoning the company involved. At times it may be desirable to get this verification in writing, especially if the credit applicant does not have good references. It may be necessary to obtain financial information on a credit applicant from other sources. These sources might include credit bureaus or credit reporting agencies. Usually, a credit applicant is asked for the names of companies or banks where credit has been established in the past. These references can then be checked for authenticity and verified as to the applicant's promptness of payment.

After the credit application form has been completed, someone in the credit

(Please Print)

Ms. / Mr. / Mrs. / Miss _____

Add. _____

City _____

State _____ Zip Code _____

Married ☐   Widowed ☐   No. of
Age _____ Single ☐   Divorced ☐   Dependents _____

Spouse's First Name _____   Phone Res.: _____   Phone Bus.: _____

How Long at Present Address _____ Own ☐ Rent Furnished ☐ Rent Unfurnished ☐ Board ☐ Mo. rent or Mortgage Pymts. $ _____

Former Address (if less than 2 years at present address) _____   How long _____

Name of Employer _____   Street Address _____   City and State _____

Steadily Employed? _____ How long with present employer? _____ Occupation _____   Net Earnings _____ Wkly. ☐ Mo. ☐

Former employer (if less than one year with present employer) _____   How long? _____

Name of Spouse's Employer _____   Address Spouse's Employer _____   Net Earnings _____ Wkly. ☐ Mo. ☐

How long? _____

Explain other income, if any _____

Name of Bank _____   Street Address _____   City and State _____   ☐ Savings ☐ Checking

Relative or Personal References: 1. _____ Street Address _____ City and State _____

2. _____ Street Address _____ City and State _____

Previous Sears account? ☐ Yes ☐ No   At which Sears store _____   Account No. _____   Is account paid in full? ☐ Yes ☐ No

Complete list of all debts now owing. Attach additional sheet if necessary.

Credit References and Addresses (Banks, Stores, Credit Unions, Finance Co's, etc.)	Date Opened	High Credit	Balance or Date Closed	Monthly Payment

Date Opened   SRC   Account Number

Requested Line of Credit

Approved Line of Credit

Authorizer

Date Set

Interviewer   Investigated By   Date

Store Stamp

SAN DIEGO 1078

SRC AUTHORIZED PURCHASER
1.
2.
3.

Social Security Number
Applicant's _____
Spouse's _____

Driver's License Number
Applicant's _____
Spouse's _____

MEMORANDA				
Div	Date	Amt.	Store	Appr. Code

SEARS REVOLVING CHARGE ACCOUNT AND SECURITY AGREEMENT

In consideration of Sears selling merchandise and services for my personal, family, or household use on my Revolving Charge Account, I agree to the following regarding all purchases made by me or on my Sears Revolving Charge Account Identification:

1. I have the privilege of a Charge Account, in which case I will pay the full amount of all purchases within 30 days from the date of each billing statement.
2. If I do not pay the full amount for all purchases within 30 days from the billing date of each statement, the following terms shall be in effect:
   (A) I will pay the deferred payment price for each purchase consisting of:
   (1) The cash price, and
   (2) A **FINANCE CHARGE**, which will be the greater of a minimum charge of 50¢ (applied to previous balance of $1.00 through $33.00) or an amount determined by applying a periodic rate of **1.5%** per month **(ANNUAL PERCENTAGE RATE of 18%)** to the first $1,000.00 of "previous balance" and a periodic rate of **1%** per month **(ANNUAL PERCENTAGE RATE of 12%)** to any part of the "previous balance" in excess of $1,000.00. FINANCE CHARGE is based upon account activity during the billing period preceding the current billing period and is computed upon the "previous balance" ("new balance" outstanding at the end of the preceding billing period) before deducting payments and credits or adding purchases made during the current billing period.
   (B) I will pay for merchandise and services purchased in monthly instalments which will be computed according to the following schedule:

If the New Balance is:	The Minimum Monthly Payment Will Be:	If the New Balance is:	The Minimum Monthly Payment Will Be:
$ .01 to 10.00	Balance	350.01 to 400.00	30.00
10.01 to 200.00	$10.00	400.01 to 450.00	35.00
200.01 to 250.00	15.00	450.01 to 500.00	40.00
250.01 to 300.00	20.00	Over $500.00	1/10 of New Balance
300.01 to 350.00	25.00		

I have the option of paying more than the Minimum Payment each month. If I fail to pay any instalment in full when due, Sears may declare the entire balance due and payable and Sears may also repossess any merchandise for which Sears has not been paid in full.

   (C) Sears shall retain title to merchandise purchased under this agreement until paid in full. Each payment shall be applied to merchandise and services as follows: first to unpaid Finance Charge; then, as to items purchased on different dates, the first purchased shall be deemed first paid; as to items purchased on the same date, the lowest priced shall be deemed first paid. I will not sell, transfer possession of, remove or encumber the merchandise without the written consent of Sears. I have risk of loss or damage to merchandise. Upon my default, Sears may charge me reasonable attorneys' fees and collection costs.
   (D) Sears will send me a statement each month which will show my previous balance (last month's new balance), new balance, minimum payment, Finance Charge, purchases, payments and credits, and the amount of my monthly instalment coming due.
   (E) I have the right to pay my entire balance in full at any time without incurring a subsequent Finance Charge.
3. Sears is authorized to investigate my credit record and report to proper persons and bureaus my performance of this agreement. Upon demand, I shall return my Sears Revolving Charge Account Identification card to Sears.
4. Sears waives the right to retain or to acquire any lien arising solely by operation of law in real property used or expected to be used as my principal residence. This provision is not applicable to judgment liens.
5. The information furnished me or on my application is submitted to Sears for the purpose of obtaining credit, and I understand that Sears will rely upon this information in extending credit to me. I hereby certify that this information is true, correct and complete.

I understand that my Finance Charge and other credit terms will be based on my State of Residence. If I change my State of Residence, I will notify you, and you will provide me with a new agreement containing the Finance Charge and other terms applicable to my new State of Residence.

NOTICE TO BUYER: (1) DO NOT SIGN THIS CONTRACT BEFORE YOU READ IT OR IF IT CONTAINS BLANKS. (2) YOU ARE ENTITLED TO A COPY OF THIS CONTRACT. KEEP IT TO PROTECT YOUR LEGAL RIGHTS. (3) YOU HAVE THE RIGHT TO PAY IN ADVANCE THE FULL AMOUNT DUE.

Signature _____

Sears, Roebuck and Co. ("Sears") by _____ Date _____

MEMORANDA _____

1 0898-057   CALIF. REV. 1/74

Figure 16-1 Sample retail credit application form. *(Courtesy of Sears, Roebuck and Co.)*

SEARS REVOLVING CHARGE SECURITY AGREEMENT
(CUENTA CORRIENTE CON SEARS Y CONVENIO DE GARANTIA)

En retribución de que la tienda Sears me venda mercancía y servicios para mi uso personal, para mi familia, o para mi uso casero en mi Sears Revolving Charge Account, yo estoy de acuerdo en seguir las reglas siguientes respecto a todas las compras hechas por mí o por quien se identifique con mi Sears Revolving Charge Account:

1. Tengo el privilegio de una cuenta de crédito en cuyo caso pagaré la cantidad total de todas las compras en menos de 25 días despues de la fecha de mi estado de cuenta.

2. Si yo no pago en su totalidad en menos de 25 días, a contar de la fecha de mi estado de cuenta, quedarán en efecto los siguientes términos:
   (A) Pagaré el precio del pago diferido de cada compra, consistente de:
      (1) El precio al contado, y,
      (2) Un *CARGO POR FINANCIAMIENTO (FINANCE CHARGE)* que debe ser mayor del cargo mínimo de **50¢** (aplicado al balance anterior entre **$1.00** y **$33.00**) a una cantidad determinada aplicando el porcentaje periódico de **1.5%** por mes *(TASA DE PORCENTAJE ANUAL DE 18%...ANNUAL PERCENTAGE RATE OF 18%)* a los primeros **$1,000.00** del balance anterior y un porcentaje periódico de **1%** mensual *(TASA DE PORCENTAJE ANUAL DE 12%...ANNUAL PERCENTAGE RATE OF 12%)* a la cantidad que sea mas de **$1,000.00** del balance anterior. El *CARGO POR FINANCIAMIENTO (FINANCE CHARGE)* esta basado sobre la actividad de la cuenta durante y entre la fecha de cobro anterior y el cobro corriente que será computado sobre el balance anterior ("balance nuevo") pendiente al final del cobro anterior antes de descontar los pagos y créditos o añadir compras hechas durante el periódo corriente.
   (B) Pagaré por la mercancía y servicios hechos, en abonos mensuales, que serán computados segun el siguiente plan:

Si el Nuevo Balance es:		El pago mensual será:	Si el Nuevo Balance es:		El pago mensual será:
$ .01 a	10.00	El balance:	350.00 a 400.00		$30.00
10.01	200.00	$10.00	400.01	450.00	35.00
200.01	250.00	15.00	450.01	500.00	40.00
250.01	300.00	20.00	Mas de $500.00		1/10 de Balance Nuevo
300.01	350.00	25.00			

Yo pagaré todos mis abonos mensuales segun el plan mencionado arriba tan pronto como reciba mi estado de cuenta. Si yo dejo de pagar un abono cuando corresponde, Sears tendrá derecho de declarar vencido y pagable el balance total, y Sears tambien tendrá derecho de reposeer cualquier mercancía que no haya sido pagada en total.
   (C) Mis pagos mensuales serán aplicados a la mercancía y servicios que no han sido pagados en su totalidad, en una proporción entre el precio de cada compra y el total de todas las compras. La propiedad de la mercancía comprada en ésta cuenta quedará a nombre de Sears hasta que yo haya pagado el precio de la compra en total. No debo vender, transferir propiedad, trasladar o ponerle impedimento a la mercancía sin el consentimiento por escrito de Sears. Tendría peligro de pérdida o perjuicio a la mercancía. En caso de mi incumplimiento, Sears tendrá derecho de cobrarme el costo razonable de honorarios de abogados, como tambien los costos de colección.
   (D) Sears me enviará un estado de cuentas cada mes en el que se mostrará mi balance anterior (el nuevo balance del mes anterior), el nuevo balance, el plan de pagos, Cargo por Financiamiento (Finance Charge), compras, pagos y créditos y la cantidad del mi abono mensual que esta venciendo.
   (E) Tengo derecho de pagar mi balance total en cualquier tiempo sin que se me cobre un Cargo por Financiamiento (Finance Charge) subsiguiente.

3. Sears queda autorizado a investigar y comprobar mi crédito y reportar mi cumplimiento de este contrato a las oficinas autorizadas. A pedido de Sears yo debo devolver mi tarjeta de identificación de mi Sears Revolving Charge Account.

4. Sears renuncia el derecho de retener o adquirir un gravámen sobre la propiedad inmueble que uso o espero usar como mi domicilio principal. Esta estipulación no es aplicable a fallos judiciales.

5. La información descrita en mi aplicación sometida a Sears con el propósito de obtener crédito y entiendo que Sears confía en ésta información al extenderme crédito. Certifico, pues, que esta información es verdadera, correcta y completa.

6. Convengo en que el Carog por Financiamiento (Finance Charge) y demás condiciones de crédito se determinaran de acuerdo con el Estado en que resido. Si cambiase mi Estado de residencia, lo informaré a Sears y Sears me proporcionará un nuevo convenio conteniendo el Cargo por Financiamiento (Finance Charge) y demas términos de crédito aplicables al Estado de mi nueva residencia.

Firma _____

Sears, Roebuck and Co. ("Sears") by _____ Date _____

6728

SEARS, ROEBUCK AND CO.
EASY PAYMENT PLAN — MODERNIZING CREDIT PLAN
RETAIL INSTALMENT CONTRACT AND SECURITY AGREEMENT
(CONTRATO DE VENTA AL POR MENOR A PLAZOS Y CONVENIO DE GARANTIA)

Este convenio provee una serie de ventas de crédito que Sears me ofrece, de mercancías y servicios para mi uso personal, el de mi familia o del hogar.

Estoy de acuerdo con lo siguiente, en relación con todas las compras hechas de acuerdo con mi Retail Instalment Contract and Security Agreement:

1. Recibiré un ticket de venta describiendo cada articulo de mercancía de acuerdo al presente contrato.

   A. Al hacer mi compra inicial, recibiré un testimonio de informes de crédito aplicables a dicha compra. Las siguientes compras efectuadas dentro de éste contrato pueden cambiar el número y cantidad de mis pagos mensuales, el Cargo por Financiamiento (Finance Charge) y la Tasa de Porcentaje Anual (Annual Percentage Rate). Cualquiera de dichos cambios aparecerá en el próximo estado de cuentas mensual.

   B. Sears puede consolidar mis compras siguientes con mi balance pendiente de compras anteriores. En cada una de las compras nuevas, pagaré un *CARGO POR FINANCIAMIENTO (FINANCE CHARGE)* que será mayor que el mínimo Cargo por Financiamiento de acuerdo con los terminos establecidos por Sears en el momento de la compra subsiguiente sin que exceda **$5.00** o: para compras bajo el Easy Payment Plan—una cantidad determinada aplicando la *TASA DE PORCENTAJE ANUAL (ANNUAL PERCENTAGE RATE)* de **18.25%** para los primeros **$1,000.00** de la cantidad financiada (o parte de ella) y **14.75%** de cualquier cantidad financiada en exceso de **$1,000.00**; en el Modernizing Credit Plan—una cantidad determinada aplicando una *TASA DE PORCENTAJE ANUAL (ANNUAL PERCENTAGE RATE)* de **14.75%** a la cantidad financiada.

   C. De acuerdo con los términos establecidos por Sears:
      (1) Todas las compras serán pagadas a plazos.
      (2) El Cargo por Financiamiento (Finance Charge) comenzará a acumularse al cerrarse mi próximo ciclo de cobro.
      (3) El Cargo por Financiamiento (Finance Charge) será calculado solamente en cada nueva compra, y la cantidad financiada y el costo del financiamiento de cada nueva compra será añadido a mi balance pendiente.
      (4) Con anterioridad a la fecha del pago del primer plazo mensual o cada nueva compra, Sears me notificará por escrito el nuevo plan de pagos, el cual incluirá el número y cantidad de mis pagos mensuales y el total de mis pagos.

   D. Al dejar de cumplir una o mas veces los términos de este convenio, Sears está en su derecho de declarar vencido el balance pendiente y exigirá su pago.

   E. Convengo en pagar la cantidad de cada plazo mensual en o antes de la fecha de pago señalada hasta que la cantidad financiada y el Cargo por Financiamiento (Finance Charge) por cada compra esten completamente pagados. Si yo pagara por adelantado el total de mi balance pendiente, cualquier Cargo por Financiamiento (Finance Charge) correspondiente me será devuelto bajo los términos de la Regla de 78.

6727

2. Sears retendrá la propiedad de la mercancía comprada bajo éste convenio hasta que esté pagada en total. Cada pago mensual será aplicado a mercancías y servicios como sigue: en cuanto a artículos comprados en diferentes fechas, el primero que se compró será considerado como pagado primero; en cuanto a los artículos comprados en la misma fecha, el que tenga menor precio será considerado como pagado primero: No vender, transferir la posesion ni destruiré ni gravaré mercancía sin el consentimiento por escrito de Sears. La pérdida o daños que sufra la mercancía serán mi responsabilidad.

3. En caso de mi incumplimiento, Sears puede cobrarme una suma razonable por honorarios de abogado y gastos de colección.

4. Sears renuncia el derecho de retener o adquirir un gravámen sobre mi propiedad inmueble usada en el presente o que espero usar como mi residencia principal. Esta regla no es aplicable a gravámenes originados por sentencias judiciales.

5. Sears queda autorizado para investigar y comprobar mi crédito y a reportar mi cumplimiento de este contrato a cualquier persona u oficina relacionadas con el crédito.

6. Convengo en que el Cargo por Financiamiento (Finance Charge) y demás condiciones de crédito se determinarán de acuerdo con el Estado en que resido. Si cambiase mi Estado de residencia, lo informaré a Sears y Sears me proporcionará un nuevo convenio conteniendo el Cargo por Financiamiento (Finance Charge) y demas términos de crédito aplicables al Estado de mi nueva residencia.

AVISO AL COMPRADOR:

(1) NO FIRME ESTE CONVENIO ANTES DE HABERLO LEIDO O SI EL MISMO PRESENTA ESPACIOS EN BLANCO.

(2) UD. TIENE DERECHO A UNA COPIA COMPLETAMENTE LLENA DE ESTE CONVENIO.

(3) BAJO LA LEY, UD. TIENE EL DERECHO DE PAGAR POR ADELANTADO EL IMPORTE TOTAL DE LA DEUDA Y A OBTENER UN REEMBOLSO PARCIAL DEL COSTO DE FINANCIAMIENTO, SI LO HAY, ACORDADO EN ESTE CONTRATO.

(4) SI UD. DESEA PAGAR POR ADELANTADO EL TOTAL DE LA CANTIDAD DE LA DEUDA, A PETICION SUYA SE LE PROVEERA EL INFORME SOBRE LA CANTIDAD A REEMBOLSARSE QUE LE CORRESPONDE.

ACUSO RECIBO DE UNA COPIA DE ESTE CONVENIO (SECURITY AGREEMENT):

Firma _____

Sears, Roebuck and Co. ("Sears") by _____ Date _____

Figure 16-2 Sample retail credit application form in Spanish. *(Courtesy of Sears, Roebuck and Co.)*

department usually interviews the applicant. This interview should be consistent with the store's policies with respect to the promotion of credit, and the applicant should be informed of these policies and procedures. The applicant should be informed of the following: (1) the arrangement for the repayment of the debt obligation, (2) the store's policies with respect to late payments, and (3) the actual finance charges. Also, the applicant's signature should be obtained. Many business people feel that after an applicant signs a form, he or she has a more positive psychological attitude toward the seriousness of the credit application and the obligations to the store. If the customer's credit application is accepted by the store, the customer will have to sign for any credit extensions. If the applicant is refused an extension of credit, someone in the store's credit department will have to tell the applicant why the credit application was refused. If the applicant has a poor history of repayment, or if most of the "take home" pay is committed for other monthly payments, it may be well to refuse the application. Most people who are refused credit understand why they have been turned down, especially when it is a result of a poor repayment record or the inability to have enough monthly income to pay their outstanding obligations. The refusal to grant credit should be handled with care, however, as the store may wish to retain the applicant's goodwill. It is always possible that, at some time in the future, the applicant may be in a better position to apply for credit with the store.

PROMOTION OF CREDIT SALES

Since the basic purpose of credit sales is to increase a profitable sales volume for the store, it is important that credit be properly promoted by the store. Credit is a promotional tool which will aid the retailer in determining the best promotional mix for the store. As you will remember, the promotional mix consists of various ingredients: various forms of advertising, salesmanship, point-of-purchase display materials, PMs (prize money or push money), spiffs, credit, and various store services. With these thoughts in mind, let us look at several ways in which credit can be promoted for a store.

Customer Sources

Credit sales may be sought from three basic sources: (1) new customers, (2) reactivation of inactive customers, and (3) increased sales to present customers. Any one of these three sources or any combination will hopefully improve a retailer's credit sales. But just how does a retailer go about stimulating credit sales? First, credit should be incorporated into the store's regular promotional themes. Since the credit department is usually a part of the accounting department in most retail stores, we should not look to the credit department for credit sales promotion. Rather, credit should become an integral part of the promotional mix, and the customer should be continuously reminded of the store's credit arrangements. Since credit buying has become a way of life for many people, retailers must promote credit sales.

Second, a retailer that is large enough to have a regular credit department can promote credit sales by stressing "charge accounts" in all the store's promotional programs. These charge accounts may be either existing accounts or new accounts. Large retail stores will also have their own credit cards. When credit sales are promoted in this manner, the customer is more closely tied to that retail store because of the store's own credit card. Since retailers who issue their own credit cards limit that card's use to their store, it cannot be used at any other retail establishment (such as with nationwide bank cards or oil company credit cards). Thus, the promotion of credit sales will also promote a certain customer loyalty to that store.

Third, credit sales can be promoted in a manner which will stimulate the sale of higher priced items. This is referred to as "trading up" the customer. When a customer purchases goods on credit rather than by cash, there may be less resistance to the retail price because payment is not made in a lump sum but is extended over a period of time. Trading up is an important point for the retailer to consider when selling merchandise on credit.

All three of these credit promotional practices may help the store's profits but only if the expenses associated with credit promotion are more than offset by increased profits from increased sales. In other words, certain expenses will be incurred when a store decides to sell goods and services on credit; these expenses would not be incurred if the store sold only for cash. Thus, it is well to keep in mind that operational efficiency must be maintained when credit sales are used as a means of sales promotion, or the store may lose money.

New Credit Customers   How does a retailer go about attracting new credit customers to the store? Perhaps one of the most often overlooked sources of new credit customers lies within the store itself. A store's cash customers are often potential credit customers. If a customer is a regular patron of the store, then the customer must be satisfied with the store. If the customer that is satisfied with the store's services and merchandise keeps returning to the store, then this person should also be receptive to buying merchandise on credit. However, some customers always prefer to purchase on a cash-only basis. But the cash-only customers represent *potential* credit customers—even if it is only on an open-charge account. Because of the convenience of charging purchases, these open-charge account customers may purchase additional merchandise.

A store's present cash customers can be solicited by the store's salespersons to open credit accounts. Salespersons should be familiar with the store's credit policies, and they can be instructed on how to approach cash customers.

Another source of credit customers is the residents who live within the trade area of the store. In today's society, people are rather mobile, and residents constantly move in and out of trade areas. Thus, a retailer may obtain information on residents residing in the store's trade area, and a direct-mail campaign for soliciting new accounts can be used. For instance, the letter shown in Figure 16-3 was used to interest potential customers in becoming credit customers with this particular store. But remember, a letter of this type is only as effective as the

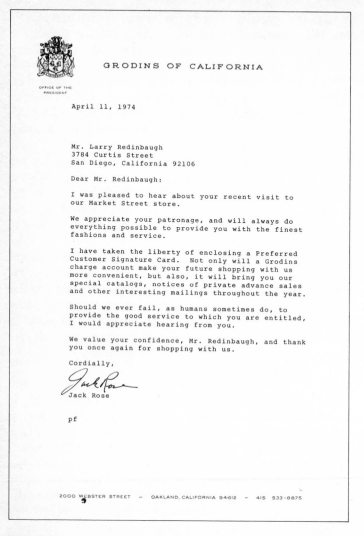

Figure 16-3 Letter to a potential credit customer. *(Courtesy of Grodins of California)*

mailing list of potential customers. The mailing list must be current; that is, the list should be up to date and the letter addressed to a specific person, not to an "occupant." The greater the personalization, the more effective a letter will be in soliciting new credit accounts.

Another means of soliciting credit customers is to include a mention of credit plans in the store's regular advertisements. If a retailer uses newspapers as a means of advertising, he or she should extend an invitation to open an account with the store somewhere in the store's advertisement.

Once the store has a list of credit card customers, it is good sales promotional strategy to acknowledge these customers on special occasions. For instance, some retailers offer their credit card customers advance notice of special sales events and allow them to view the merchandise ahead of the regular non-credit-card customers. Or during special seasons of the year, it might be a good idea for the store to promote directly to credit customers. This helps to retain customer goodwill and to impress upon the credit customers that they are the store's special patrons. From a psychological standpoint, this strategy is quite effective. Most customers enjoy being recognized as someone special in today's environment of depersonalization. Thus, credit customers appreciate recognition and may ultimately become more loyal patrons. This is a rather inexpensive means of sales promotion and should not be overlooked by retailers using credit sales transactions.

COLLECTION POLICIES AND CREDIT INSURANCE

Any retailer selling merchandise on credit will, at some time or another, have to resort to the collection of some accounts which have not been paid in full. Some accounts will be virtually uncollectible, and others may be partially collectible if the right approaches are used. It is inevitable, however, that on occasion the retailer will have the rather distasteful duty of collecting an unpaid bill. The retailer may have to send a collection letter or personally contact the individual who has not met the obligation of the credit account.

General Collection Policies

Retailers selling merchandise on credit must implement some type of collection policy. The nature of this policy will, of course, reflect the attitudes and philosophy of the owner-manager. The collection policy may be strict or lenient, or may be somewhat variable, depending on the nature of the goods, the time elements involved (how long the account is past due), and the type of community in which the retailer is operating.

Some retailers have a policy of sending a "friendly reminder" to the customer after an account is thirty days past due. This reminder may be followed with another the next month (sixty days), or it may be followed more closely with other reminders with the tone of the letter increasing in severity. Other retailers may make some use of the telephone to remind customers that their accounts are past due. In either event, care should be taken to retain the goodwill of the customer. An inquiry may reveal sickness in the family or some other unforeseen tragedy which has kept the customer from making a payment. For many retailers, the last resort is to turn the account over to a collection agency. Collection agencies will attempt to collect the amount due the retailer; but they will, in turn, charge a 50 percent commission for this service. That is, the agency keeps 50 percent of the amount collected for its role in the collection process.

If the account cannot be collected in any other way, the very last measure taken is a court action lawsuit. This measure should be undertaken only when it has been determined that the debtor has sufficient assets against which a judgment can be entered by the court. A judgment alone does not guarantee the creditor that the obligation will be discharged. For if the debtor has no assets, the retailer will collect nothing anyway and will incur additional lawyer and court costs.

Credit Insurance

Nearly all installment credit transactions provide for either "level term insurance" or "decreasing term insurance" on the debtor for the amount of the obligation. Should the debtor (the person owing the money to the store) die before the full amount of the contract has been paid, the life insurance policy's proceeds will be used to pay the obligation. The store is usually named as the beneficiary of the credit insurance policy, and this cost is included in the total finance charges. Generally, premiums for this type of insurance are rather low.

SUMMARY

Retail credit is a medium of exchange of limited acceptance. The limitation factor of retail credit is both important to the retailer and to the consumer.

Retailers sell merchandise on credit in order to increase a store's sales volume and hopefully, a store's *profits*. Credit can be used as one means of retail sales promotion. Credit is used as a matter of customer *convenience*.

Consumers use retail credit to raise their standard of living, as a matter of convenience, and because they may be forced to use credit as a means of necessity.

Retail *revolving credit* allows a consumer to purchase goods and services and have up to thirty days to pay for these items without any penalty of interest. If the customer does not pay for the goods and services within this thirty-day period, the credit plan then revolves each month, and minimum payments are made by the consumer on each billing date.

Installment credit gets its name from the fact that a customer must make periodic payments which are divided into segments, called installments. These installment payments are based on the amount of the transaction, the amount of time needed for repayment, and the customer's ability to repay the loan.

Installment credit makes use of a written contract which is referred to as an *installment purchase contract*. Installment credit is used with the sale of high-unit-value goods. Usually a down payment is required when merchandise is sold on the installment purchase plan. As with all credit plans which extend beyond the thirty-day grace period, installment credit allows the merchant to collect finance charges, called interest.

Finance or interest charges are those costs over and above what the item would cost if the customer paid cash for the merchandise.

The *nominal rate* or interest is the rate that is usually quoted to the customer by the financial institution, bank, sales finance company, or the retailer. The *true annual rate* of interest is the net cost to the consumer over the period of time of the contract.

Retail *open-charge credit* allows the customer to charge goods over a thirty-, sixty-, or ninety-day period, without incurring any finance or interest charges.

The field of *bank credit cards* is dominated by two large systems: Bank-Americard and Interbank (Master Charge). Both credit card companies operate in a similar manner. The sponsoring banks act as collective credit departments for all the retail merchants joining the card system.

When deciding to sell on credit, a retailer should select the plan which best suits the store. It may be that the store can make use of bank credit cards. Or, the store may desire to establish a credit department of its own. In either situation, the retailer may be forced by competition to extend some form of credit to the consumer.

For those retailers operating their own *credit department,* it is important first to have the customer fill out a credit application form. After the credit application form has been completed by the customer, someone in the credit department will interview the applicant. Usually the customer will be informed of acceptance or rejection of the application. If the consumer is accepted, it is important that the customer be informed about the repayment schedule, the store's policies with respect to late payments, and the actual finance or interest costs.

Credit is a *promotional tool* which will aid the retailer in determining the best promotional mix for the store. Credit sales can be sought from new customers, the reactivation of inactive customers, and by increasing sales to present credit customers.

Any retailer selling merchandise on credit will, at some time or another, have to resort to the collection of some accounts which have not been paid in full. Thus, retailers selling goods on credit must develop some type of *collection policy.* The nature of a credit collection policy will reflect the philosophy of the management. It may be a strict or a lenient policy. On balance, a collection policy should be firm but equitable to all consumers.

REVIEW QUESTIONS

1 Why is retail credit considered a "medium of exchange of limited acceptance"?
2 What are the basic purposes of retail credit?
3 Explain how retail revolving credit works for the retailer and for the consumer.
4 How does retail installment credit differ from retail revolving credit?
5 What do we mean when reference is made to "finance charges"?
6 Define the nominal rate of interest and the true annual rate of interest. Why do these rates differ from each other?
7 Explain how retail open-charge credit works for the consumer.
8 Why do some retailers make use of bank credit cards?
9 Discuss some of the factors involved when a retailer decides to sell merchandise on credit terms.
10 What is involved in the credit investigation procedure?
11 What is the best way that the retailer can promote the use of retail credit?

12 Name some of the sources of credit customers.
13 Why should a retailer establish a collection policy for the store?
14 What is credit insurance, and how does it work for the retailer?

PROBLEMS

1   An appliance store sold Mrs. Higgins a washer and dryer for $577. A down payment of 10 percent of the purchase price was required, and the repayment period was to cover two years. An interest charge of $67 was added. What is the true annual rate of interest paid by Mrs. Higgins?

2   Brad Hayman purchased a Datsun 260Z for $6,328. On this purchase he traded in a 1967 red Mustang, for which he was allowed $828. This was the down payment on the purchase of the Datsun 260Z. Brad went to a local bank to finance the balance by signing a note for $6,900. This note was to be repaid in forty-two monthly installments. What is the true annual rate of interest?

Part Eight

Retail Personnel

Chapter 17

Management of Retail Personnel

Retailing can be and often is referred to as a "people" business, meaning that retailers work closely with a relatively large number of people everyday—customers and employees. Thus, the importance of the humanization of all aspects of a retail business cannot be overemphasized. Although the rest of this book is devoted to the planning of a retail business and the attraction and retention of customers, the hiring, training, and retention of employees cannot be overlooked.

Staffing a retail business may be one of the most important managerial functions of retailing. Employees must be organized for the successful operation of the firm, and retailing activities must be performed satisfactorily from the customers' and the retailer's point of view. The management of retail personnel includes: (1) recruitment, (2) selection, (3) training, (4) evaluation, and (5) compensation. These activities may vary considerably with the size of the store. For instance, for a small independent retailer, the number of personnel may be limited to only one or two part-time employees. At the opposite end of the spectrum, a large chain store may have thousands of employees throughout the chain with a formal personnel department which handles all hiring, training, and related employee problems. However, the activities associated with the management of retail personnel must be handled efficiently whether the store is large or

Table 17-1   Retail-Trade Employment 1970–73* (in thousands)

Kind of store	1970	1971	1972	1973*
Department stores	1,511	1,545	1,594	1,658
Variety stores	312	319	330	337
Grocery stores	1,561	1,585	1,651	1,668
Men's & boys' apparel stores	131	131	132	132
Women's apparel & accessory stores	269	276	287	298
Furniture stores	288	289	297	306
Household appliances	88	89	92	95
Restaurants and bars	2,488	2,569	2,684	2,791
Drugstores	453	456	470	479
Total retail trade	11,102	11,333	11,765	12,118*

*Estimated by Bureau of Competitive Assessment and Business Policy.
Source: U.S. Industrial Outlook 1974, U.S. Department of Commerce, p. 153.

small. A retail organization is only as good as its owner, manager, and employees. If retail planning is the key to a viable, profitable business, then the management of retail personnel is a critical factor in the successful operation of any retail store. Thus, the selection and retention of high-caliber personnel will substantially reduce the managerial problems associated with retailing management.

EMPLOYEE REQUIREMENTS

Before the actual recruitment of employees takes place, the retailer must determine two basic factors: (1) the employee needs for the retail store and (2) the nature of the work to be accomplished in the retail store.

The number of employees needed for a retail store will depend on such things as the size of the store, the hours of operation, the nature of the operation (self-service or full-service), and the degree of specialization. The size of the retail business will probably determine how the staffing function is handled. In a large retail organization, staffing is a full-time job which probably will need the attention and direction of a specialist in personnel administration. But in a small retail business, the staffing function will probably not require a full-time specialist because the job is not as complex. It is very likely in a small business that the owner or manager will probably handle this function. The hours of operation will determine, to some degree, the number of employees needed in staffing a retail store. For example, is the store to be open five, six, or seven days a week? Will the store be open for eight, nine, or ten hours a day—or longer? Will the store be open evenings? Any retail store remaining open twenty-four hours a day, seven days a week, will require three basic groups of personnel for each eight-hour shift. If a store is open several evenings a week, some provision must be made to staff the store with part-time people or the regular employees must be paid overtime. Since the number of employees will affect the expenses and hence the profitability of the store, it is an important decision that should be carefully considered.

A full-service retail store will require a larger staff than a self-service store. A store which operates on a self-service basis does not require as many employees because the customers themselves are performing many of the functions that would be otherwise handled by salespeople. On the other hand, a full-service store must provide sufficient personnel to assist customers in their selection of goods and services.

The extent of personnel administration that has to be performed by a certain store will also depend upon the degree of specialization of sales personnel required by that store. For instance, some retail stores will require highly trained sales specialists with technical backgrounds, whereas other stores will need only general sales clerks to perform the store's activities.

A store's management must define and analyze carefully the nature of the work to be accomplished in operating the store in order to determine the type of employees needed. This process of determining the qualitative requirements of a job is called "job analysis."

Job Analysis   Job analysis is a critical part of personnel administration. A thorough understanding of the tasks involved in each specific job is essential because this knowledge is used in several ways. First, job analysis aids in the determination of the personnel requirements for each position. It also sets the minimum standards for the recruitment and selection of applicants who will fill each position. Second, job analysis provides the store's management with the basic facts upon which a division of labor can be organized. It reveals the interrelationship between the various functions within the store such as receiving, marking, storing, and moving the merchandise to the selling floor. Job analysis also indicates what duties should be allocated to each section of work and how each job fits into the total retail store organizational system. Third, job analysis aids in the determination of what type and the amount of training needed in a specific position, and it also helps in the appraisal of an individual job in terms of skill and knowledge. Fourth, job analysis identifies jobs and their relationships and provides information to management which can be used in transfers or promotions of employees. Experience on one job may be necessary for the proper performance of another job, and a job analysis will readily indicate this. Fifth, through its systematic procedures, job analysis reveals the type and amount of work performed in a job, the personal qualifications needed to perform the work satisfactorily, and the responsibilities of each position. These determinants then will provide management with a sound basis for computing the compensation of each employee. Thus, job analysis provides a comparison between the various jobs which helps to create a basis for more equitable payments in accordance with the duties performed. Sixth, job analysis may help to alleviate any misunderstandings between employees that arise on the job. Disagreements about the type and kind of work required by each job often lead to employee grievances. If each job within the store is clearly defined and described, employee discontent will be reduced and morale will be improved.

Finally, job analysis can lead to improved working conditions because of the discovery of an unpleasant working environment due to excessive heat or poor ventilation (which may be characteristic of some receiving room and storage operations).

Job Description

To complete the process of a job analysis, a written report or paper called a "job description" should be prepared. This report or paper should include a description of the work performed, responsibilities, skills needed, the amount of training required, and work conditions under which the job is to be performed. Job descriptions, in turn, lead to job titles and job classifications according to the variation in skills, aptitudes, knowledge, and attitudes required on the part of the employees. A job description utilizes the findings of a job analysis and is a written report which states precisely the personal and technical attributes needed to fill that position. Job descriptions also become a basis for compensation and promotion in the larger retail organizations. Seldom does one find a formalized program of job analysis and job description in the small retail stores. Owners and

Job title:	Department manager
Responsibility:	Department sales, gross profit, operating expenses, merchandising activities associated with the department
Specific duties:	To meet the minimum standards of performance as established by store management to include but not limited to the following: A. To display all merchandise during all hours the store is open B. To have one display featured at all times C. To change each special feature display weekly D. To take markdowns based on merchandise condition not to exceed 50 percent E. To coordinate all sales with other departments F. To schedule work hours for full-time and part-time employees G. To assist in training employees in order that general store policies are followed H. To handle all departmental customer complaints for adjustments and returns I. To maintain normal housekeeping duties J. To keep management and employees informed K. To prepare periodic and regular reports L. To report to the general merchandise manager

Figure 17-1 Sample job description.

managers of small retail establishments feel such formalization of jobs is unnecessary; however, it might be well for the small retailer to take time to analyze and describe work positions in the interest of more efficient retail management.

RECRUITMENT OF RETAILING PERSONNEL

The recruitment of retailing personnel can be divided into two main sources of supply: (1) from within the store or (2) from an outside source.

Employees can be recruited from within the store through promotion from a lower ranking to a higher ranking position, or a person can be transferred from another department or store. Many firms prefer to promote an employee from within the organization because of certain advantages. Promotion tends to result in improved employee morale, utilization of individuals who are already familiar with the firm's policies, and more effective use of employee talents and capabilities. It may also be wise from a financial point of view in that it may reduce expenses associated with the training of a new employee.

In large retail stores or retail chains, some departments may be overstaffed, or some employees may desire to be transferred in the hopes of progressing more rapidly. The transfer of personnel to other departments or to other stores allows a large retailing firm to take advantage of employee training, skill, and work experience which would be lost if the employee were let go. Also, employee morale may be enhanced by utilizing a policy of transfer since all employees are acutely aware of a store's attitude toward promotion and transfer. Also, the expenses associated with employee training are reduced if management transfers an existing employee instead of hiring an inexperienced person from outside the store.

Outside Sources

A number of sources outside the retail business can be sought from which employees can be hired. However, these sources may fluctuate in efficiency depending on the general business and economic conditions (high or low unemployment) in the store's environment. In times of economic uncertainty or high unemployment, unsolicited applications are quite common. Some retailers almost exclusively utilize unsolicited applicants in the belief that it is not only the easiest method of recruitment but is also an indication that these persons are eager to work and will do so if employed. In some cases, there may be some merit to these thoughts. However, one could also argue that these walk-in applicants might have been the first to be relieved from former positions due to a lack of qualifications or for some personal reason. But if a retailer carefully scrutinizes the applicants and their qualifications, these solicitations can be a valuable resource.

Another outside source which can be used in obtaining prospective employees stems from the recommendations of present employees—family and friends of employees. Caution should be exercised in this approach to recruitment, however. An employee may not be very selective in suggesting friends or relatives for possible employment, and this could prove to be embarrassing to an employer. For instance, the recommended friend may be poorly qualified, and the personnel office or the owner of the store may have to refuse to employ the person. Or the person may be hired initially but then may have to be released due to inadequate work performance. This may cause problems with the employee who did the recommending as well as with other employees who know about the situation.

Help-wanted advertisements are often used to attract prospective employees when the supply of personnel is short and the need for additional employees is urgent. Unfortunately, this practice may result in "shot gunning"; i.e., the advertisement is directed to all who read the paper and not just to those who are qualified. Quite often advertising for employees in a newspaper leads to a large number of inquiries from applicants whose qualifications are not suitable for the position(s).

Perhaps a better source from which to obtain future employees for a retail business would be the community college and university campuses. Many colleges and universities have career placement offices which stimulate the flow of applicants because of the number of recruitment interviews held on campus. Some of these student applicants will have retail business experience in addition to their formal education. Others may have little, if any, retail experience; but these students do provide a recruiter with a pool of applicants from which retail trainees may be selected. This method of recruiting employees offers the retailer an opportunity to recruit trainees, for lower sales positions, who can later be promoted to the higher levels of management. As retailing management becomes more sophisticated, the need for college-educated employees will become more pressing. Also, college students provide a valuable source of applicants for part-time employment since many college students need to work in order to supplement their incomes. For many of these employees, only a minimum wage will be paid. (At this writing, the federal minimum wage is $2.10 per hour and after January 1, 1976, will become $2.30 per hour.) However, the student cannot overlook the opportunity to gain valuable work experience, since the more capable and industrious employees will have the opportunity of earning more than the minimum wage while getting valuable work experience. This is especially important to a student who wishes to enter the retailing field after completing his or her education, as most retailers seek employees who have had some retail work experience.

Private and public employment agencies can also be used as a source of employees for a retail business. These agencies usually perform the screening chores for an employer so that the retailer does not have to spend time "qualifying" the applicants. For the performance of these duties, the private employment agency will charge a fee for placing the applicant. The fee may be paid by the applicant, by the retailer, or by a combination thereof. For example, say the applicant is hired and remains with the store for six months. The retailer will then reimburse the employee one-half or the full amount of the fee charged by the private employment agency. As you might expect, almost any type of arrangement can be made. Public employment offices charge no fee as they are supported by tax dollars. Public employment agencies, or offices, perform the same function as does the private agency except that no fee is charged to either the retailer or the applicant. Thus, either the private or public employment agencies can be helpful to a retailer in recruiting and selecting full or part-time employees.

There is yet another source of employees from outside the store—those persons employed by a competitor or similar retail establishment. The practice of enticing these persons to change jobs can be called "pirating" because the retailer "pirates" or takes away another retailer's employee. The practice of pirating is sometimes frowned upon and may have an unstabilizing effect on retailers during a tight labor market. Pirating may be beneficial to employees, however, because prospective employers will offer them additional pay or other benefits if they will move and accept employment with them. A clever or skillful form of pirating often takes place in the upper levels of management. An employee may let it be known that he or she is dissatisfied with the present employer, and the word soon spreads to prospective employers in the same kind of business. The potential employer then makes the individual an offer which, in many instances, the person accepts. This is still pirating in a sense although it may be a bit more subtle. Sophisticated pirating is practiced by many retail firms with many of the management consulting firms acting as an intermediary in the hiring of senior personnel.

SELECTION OF RETAIL PERSONNEL

As we have just noted, recruitment involves the location of promising applicants for employment. After this step is completed, the selection process must take place. The selection of applicants involves a series of appraisals and evaluations from which the more promising applicants are separated from those whose qualifications do not meet the store's requirements. Essentially, the selection process attempts to determine the probable success or failure of an applicant should he or she be employed with that retail organization. Retailers operating small stores often hire on a trial basis. The large stores do not regard the selection process so lightly since they realize that employee turnover is expensive. The costs of training new employees is constantly rising. Thus efficient, effective selection procedures may help to reduce these expenses by obtaining employees who are better suited to their jobs, and, in turn, are more likely to remain with the store.

Application Forms and Preliminary Interviews

The selection process may begin in several ways. Usually, the process will continue with a preliminary interview of the individual applicants who have applied for a position. This preliminary interview is a screening process whereby the interviewer can determine whether the applicant should proceed further by filling out the application forms, taking any tests, or being interviewed more extensively.

The preliminary interview is distinctive in that it usually is quite short, perhaps fifteen minutes or less. During this time period, the interviewer will ask

SEARS, ROEBUCK AND CO.
APPLICATION FOR EMPLOYMENT
PLEASE PRINT INFORMATION REQUESTED.

Date _____

SEARS IS AN EQUAL OPPORTUNITY EMPLOYER and fully subscribes to the principles of Equal Employment Opportunity. Sears has adopted an Affirmative Action Program to ensure that all applicants and employes are considered for hire, promotion and job status, without regard to race, color, religion, national origin, age or sex.

To protect the interests of all concerned, an applicant must pass a physical examination before receiving final acceptance for employment.

NOTE: This application will be considered active for 90 days. If you have not been employed within this period and are still interested in employment at Sears, please contact the office where you applied and request that your application be reactivated.

Name _____
Last   First   Middle

Social Security Number _____
(Please present your Social Security Card for review.)

Address _____
Number   Street   City   State   Zip Code

Previous Address _____
Number   Street   City   State   Zip Code

Current phone or nearest phone _____

Date of Birth _____

Licensed to drive car? ☐ YES ☐ NO
Is license valid in this state? ☐ YES ☐ NO

Have you ever been employed by Sears? _____
If so, when and where last employed? _____   Position _____

Have you a relative in the employ of Sears in the store or unit to which you are applying? _____

A PHYSICAL DISABILITY OR HANDICAP WILL NOT CAUSE REJECTION IF IN SEARS MEDICAL OPINION YOU ARE ABLE TO SATISFACTORILY PERFORM IN THE POSITION FOR WHICH YOU ARE BEING CONSIDERED

What serious accidents, illnesses or operations have you had? _____

Give Details and Date _____

Have your ever had a knee, head or back injury? _____

What physical defects or ailments do you now have such as hernia, heart trouble or high blood pressure, etc.?

List here _____

EDUCATION	School Attended	No. of Years	Name of School	City/State	Year of Leaving	Grad-uate?	Course or College Major	Average Grades
	Grammar							
	Jr. High							
	Sr. High							
	Other							
	College						Degree	

MILITARY SERVICE	BRANCH OF SERVICE	DATE ENTERED SERVICE	DATE OF DISCHARGE	SERVICE RELATED DISABILITY	HIGHEST RANK HELD	SERVICE-RELATED SKILLS AND EXPERIENCE APPLICABLE TO CIVILIAN EMPLOYMENT
				YES ☐ NO ☐		

What experience or training have you had other than your work experience, military service and education? (Community activities, hobbies, etc.)

I am interested in the type of work I have checked:

Sales _____ Office _____ Mechanical _____ Warehouse _____ Other (Specify) _____

Or

The following specific Job: _____

I am seeking ☐ temporary ☐ permanent employment
I am available for ☐ Part time ☐ Full time work
If part time, indicate maximum hours per week _____

Have you been convicted during the past seven years of a serious crime involving a person's life or property?

NO ☐   YES ☐   If yes, explain _____

HOURS AVAILABLE FOR WORK	
Sun.	To
Mon.	To
Tues.	To
Wed.	To
Thurs.	To
Fri.	To
Sat.	To

10534 (F5901) REV. 1/74

(SEE REVERSE SIDE)

Figure 17-2 Application for employment. *(Courtesy of Sears, Roebuck and Co.)*

general questions to determine the applicant's special qualifications, interests, and experiences. This first interview is generally short because the interviewer probably has a few definite questions of concern and will check them off until the applicant is either eliminated or cleared for further consideration. For some applicants, the preliminary interview will be the only step in the entire selection process; that is, the interviewee (applicant) may be turned away because of

REFERENCES

LIST BELOW YOUR FOUR MOST RECENT EMPLOYERS, BEGINNING WITH THE CURRENT OR MOST RECENT ONE. IF YOU HAVE HAD LESS THAN FOUR EMPLOYERS, USE THE REMAINING SPACES FOR PERSONAL REFERENCES. IF YOU WERE EMPLOYED UNDER A MAIDEN OR OTHER NAME, PLEASE ENTER THAT NAME IN THE RIGHT HAND MARGIN. IF APPLICABLE, ENTER SERVICE IN THE ARMED FORCES ON THE REVERSE SIDE.

NAMES AND ADDRESSES OF FORMER EMPLOYERS, BEGINNING WITH THE CURRENT OR MOST RECENT	Nature of Employer's Business	Name of your Supervisor	What kind of work did you do?	Starting Date	Starting Pay	Date of Leaving	Pay at Leaving	Why did you leave? Give details
1 Name				Month		Month		
Address Tel. No.				Year		Year		
City State Zip Code					Per Week		Per Week	
NOTE: State reason for and length of inactivity between present application date and last employer								
2 Name				Month		Month		
Address Tel. No.				Year		Year		
City State Zip Code					Per Week		Per Week	
NOTE: State reason for and length of inactivity between last employer and second last employer								
3 Name				Month		Month		
Address Tel. No.				Year		Year		
City State Zip Code					Per Week		Per Week	
NOTE: State reason for and length of inactivity between second last employer and third last employer								
4 Name				Month		Month		
Address Tel. No.				Year		Year		
City State Zip Code					Per Week		Per Week	
NOTE: State reason for and length of inactivity between third last employer and fourth last employer								

I certify that the information contained in this application is correct to the best of my knowledge and understand that deliberate falsification of this information is grounds for dismissal in accordance with Sears, Roebuck and Co. policy. I authorize the references listed above to give any any and all information concerning my previous employment and any pertinent information they may have, personal or otherwise, and release all parties from all liability for any damage that may result from furnishing same to you. In consideration of my employment, I agree to conform to the rules and regulations of Sears, Roebuck and Co. and my employment and compensation can be terminated, with or without notice, at any time, at the option of either the Company or myself. I understand that no unit manager or representative of Sears, Roebuck and Co., other than the president or vice-president of the Company, has any authority to enter into any agreement for employment for any specified period of time, or to make any agreement contrary to the foregoing. In some states the law requires that Sears have my written permission before obtaining consumer reports on me, and I hereby authorize Sears to obtain such reports.

Applicant's Signature _____

NOT TO BE FILLED OUT BY APPLICANT

INTERVIEWER'S COMMENTS	Date of Emp.		Tested		(Store will enter dates as required.)		Mailed	Completed
	Dept. or Div.	Regular / Part-Time ☐☐	Physical examination scheduled for		REFERENCE REQUESTS			
	Job Title		Physical examination form completed		CONSUMER REPORT			
	Job Title Code				With. Tax (W-4)			
	Compensation Arrangement				State With. Tax			
	Manager Approving		Review Card prepared	Minor's Work Permit	Store/Pers. Rec. Card			
Prospect for	Employee No.		Tickler Card prepared	Proof of Birth	Earnings Rec.			
1.			Timecard prepared	Training Material Given to Employe				
2.								

Job Grade _____   Rack No. _____   Unit Name and Number _____

unsuitable qualifications or some misunderstanding about the nature of the job. Usually, all persons applying for a job will be asked to complete an initial prepared application form or information sheet. These forms are generally multipurpose and ask the usual data such as: name, address, birthplace, birth date, name and address of parents, marital status, age, debts, resources, name of person to notify in case of emergency, and many other similar personal details.

Also, references and work-history data are requested and will be closely scrutinized by the interviewer. References for any applicant being seriously considered for employment should be checked. Similarly, work-history records will reveal a great deal about an applicant and will indicate whether he or she is experienced in a particular type of work or frequently shifts from one employer to another.

It is possible that some retail institutions will use a preliminary interview before asking the applicant to fill out the application forms, but this is normally a personal preference of the interviewer or the personnel director. So it is possible to find some deviation in the way the selection process is handled.

A second interview may be conducted which allows for a broader exchange of information between the interviewer and the applicant. The course of the interview will depend on the philosophy of the interviewer, the nature of the job to be filled, and the type and size of retailing firm. Large retailing firms have a proven definite procedure for interviewing applicants, whereas most small retailers allow a relatively open and free exchange of information to take place. In either instance, the interviewer attempts to appraise the suitability of the applicant by getting the person to talk freely and naturally.

Sound personnel management policy does not allow interviewers to "hassle" applicants in order to test their irritability level. At one time, this was considered to be part of a good interview; but, fortunately, today this practice is frowned upon by most personnel directors. If the stress interview is used, and the applicant is not hired, a bad impression will be created and may damage the store's reputation. If the applicant is hired, the individual may have difficulty forgetting the "stress" of the interview which could lead to lowered morale and a negative attitude.

Since the basic purpose of the second interview is to exchange information, this should be done in an environment of mutual respect. Guidance of this second interview can be facilitated by the interviewer using the application form(s) that the applicant completed. If the interviewer asks about the data on the application form, the applicant feels more at ease since the person will be prepared for that type of questioning. Further, by following the application form, the interviewer may be able to elicit more in-depth information and probe into areas where more details are needed. For instance, omissions or gaps in dates during the school years or term of work experience can be explained by the prospective employee. Why did the person leave the last job? Was it because of personal reasons or poor work performance? In this in-depth interview, any area of missing information may reveal certain personality traits which may not be obvious to the casual observer.

Testing in Selection

In addition to interviews and application forms, many of the large retailing firms will administer an employment test to the applicant. Some retail stores do not administer employment tests because of the expenses associated with testing. Further, some managers cannot see the value of testing applicants, especially for certain types of jobs.

However, the use of employment testing is growing in importance because of the growing recognition that hiring mistakes are expensive. Miscalculations in recruitment, selection, and hiring are expensive because they may cause excessive employee turnover or, worse, may result in less desirable employees remaining with the firm for a long period of time. It is not always easy to dismiss an employee, especially if the employees are members of the Retail Clerks International Union. Although unions may be no more desirous of keeping unfit employees than management, nevertheless, it is more difficult to dismiss a union employee.

Various tests for qualifying applicants for jobs are used by retailers. These tests usually fall into one of the following categories: (1) achievement, (2) aptitude, (3) interest, and (4) personality.

Achievement Tests   Achievement tests measure an applicant's level of capability and what the person can do. Sometimes achievement tests are also called proficiency tests. For example, secretaries must be proficient in the secretarial skills of typing and shorthand. Office personnel may have to be proficient in the operation of calculating and bookkeeping machines or in the use of other office equipment. An achievement test can be set up for any special skill or capability a retailer wishes to measure.

Aptitude Tests   Aptitude tests measure an applicant's ability or talent, which may be developed or latent. Basically, an aptitude test determines whether an individual can learn, has the capacity to learn, or can be trained. Sometimes aptitude tests are called intelligence tests because they seek to measure intelligence—memory, reasoning, vocabulary, and social perceptions.

Aptitude tests are used—perhaps wisely or unwisely—in the screening of job applicants for placement with a retail business. Sometimes people are unwilling to concede that most jobs do not require superior intelligence for success—in fact, attitude may be more important. Actually, above average intelligence in some jobs may lead to frustration on the part of the employee and result in a higher employee turnover.

Of course, for the higher level managerial positions in a retailing firm, the ability to reason and the capacity to learn are essential requirements for success. Considerable mental capacity is needed by the manager in order to be able to cope with and understand the total retailing system and all its interrelated subsystems. But for many jobs, average to above-average intelligence will suffice. Perhaps more important is the possession of a proper attitude toward the job. However, some retail stores require applicants to take an intelligence test and attain a certain minimum score before they can be hired.

Interest Tests   Some tests are designed to determine an individual's special interest areas. Usually areas of interest are arranged on some sort of priority basis, and if an individual has a liking for certain areas of interest, that person may be more successful on the job. For instance, someone handling fashion merchandise should be interested in the latest styles and trends in fashion. A buyer should be interested in all the details which lead to purchasing the right merchandise for the store and its customers. If the applicant for these jobs is not interested in these basic job characteristics, then it is likely that the person will ultimately fail on that job. Through the use of interest tests, it may be possible to eliminate those persons who will fail.

Personality Tests   As was stated earlier in the text, retailing is a people business. In order to be successful in retailing, one has to like working with people since daily contact with all sorts of persons requires a certain type of personality.

In order to make sure that the right people are being hired for these jobs, retailers are increasingly making use of personality tests. These tests appraise and evaluate significant traits in the total personality of a person. An applicant may pass all the other employment tests (achievement, aptitude, and interest) but may not be able to get along with fellow employees or customers.

However, caution is recommended in the use of personality tests. The human personality is so complex that extreme care should be exercised in any attempt to measure significant traits. Some tests attempt to measure an applicant's attitudes and reactions to certain ideas. Sometimes this is accomplished through the use of word association tests; that is, one word is provided and the applicant is to fill in the first word that comes to mind. All personality tests attempt to measure attitudes and feelings and to identify significant traits which influence personality and relate to success on the job.

These tests are useful in the selection of prospective employees if the findings are properly obtained and interpreted. Those who make use of such tests must know what the findings mean since raw scores, in themselves, are not self-explanatory. It is recommended that only professionals be allowed to interpret test scores. Therefore, members of the professional staff who are responsible for testing must also assume responsibility for the accurate interpretation of test scores.

Any test used in the selection of employees must be a valid test; i.e., the test must select the type of employee required in order to be useful to management. Otherwise, the test is unreliable and fails to discriminate among those tested. Care should also be exercised to hold the tests and test scores of the applicants in confidence. But tests which are properly administered and interpreted can be of great value to the employer, and retailers should be encouraged to make greater use of tests in selection procedures in order to improve and increase the range of usefulness of employment testing.

EMPLOYEE TRAINING AND DEVELOPMENT

Once the recruitment and selection process has been completed, many retailers (especially large chain organizations) maintain formal training programs so that individuals may develop and improve their performance on the job. New retail employees must frequently be trained for the specific jobs they are to perform.

Experienced employees may require training in order to prepare them for more responsibilities and positions of higher pay. For instance, retail employees may be given training to improve their performance in the jobs they fill at present. Middle-management persons may be given training because there is a need for greater competence in supervision. Executive training may be provided as a means of improving performance and developing replacements for higher management positions. Employees must have opportunities for self-development if they are to develop and use their highest skills and abilities. Almost all employees look forward to jobs requiring higher skills and greater responsibilities.

Many retailing institutions have come to realize that training responsibilities are necessary. These firms have realized that they cannot secure adequately trained employees; therefore, they must provide a training program. Many times, it is possible for small retailers to hire employees who have been trained by large retailers. Some retail firms operate without formal training programs but will rely on informal training through on-the-job programs supervised by an experienced employee.

Any formalized retail training program must be established with a clear understanding of what is to be accomplished. A basic underlying purpose of all training programs should be that all employees have an opportunity to improve themselves as they work.

Reasons for Employee Training

In addition to the basic purpose of providing all employees with an opportunity to improve themselves in their work positions, there are six other reasons why retail employees should be given training. The reasons are as follows:

1 Training improves productivity and performance on the job.
2 Training reduces employee errors by conformance to store policies.
3 Proper training can reduce total wage costs and improve store profits.
4 Training may reduce employee turnover.
5 Training lessens management's supervision.
6 A properly trained employee performs tasks more efficiently, and this may lead to improved customer service.

Retail employee training improves productivity and performance on the job whether an employee is working in the selling or the nonselling areas of a retail store. The job analyses should indicate what knowledge and skills are required in each position. Then training should be directed to those needs as defined in the job descriptions, with attention focused on the added knowledge and skill essential for increased productivity and eventual promotion. Employee training initially may cost the retailer some money, but it should be considered an investment which pays returns over the long run.

Adequate employee training reduces the number of mistakes made by employees because trained individuals will know and abide by the rules, regulations, and policies of the store. Thus, properly trained employees will be more likely to conform to an established routine which will cut down on errors.

The reduction of wage costs is also one of the goals of employee training. Wage reductions are attained through training whereby employees develop an increased capacity to perform duties. Ultimately, the retailer is able to perform an equivalent amount of work with fewer employees which, in turn, lowers the total wage costs.

Retail employees who have been trained by someone at a certain retail business are more apt to remain with that retailer, thus reducing employee turnover. The proper training of employees instills an attitude of "belonging" to the store. If an employee receives little or no training or attention, he or she may develop an apathetic attitude toward the store and its management, and eventually, the employee may seek work elsewhere.

If retail employees are trained by store personnel, they usually require less supervision because of improved job performance. This improved job efficiency and the need for less supervision allows supervisors and middle management to perform other duties in the store. Less supervision and increased responsibility make the employee feel more important and will probably result in a better job performance.

Finally, a retail employee who has been trained possesses a more positive attitude toward the job and the store which then carries over into improved customer service. Courteous, personalized customer service by a retail employee is one of the best advertisements a retailer can obtain, and the cost is low when compared to other promotional expenditures. To repeat an earlier point, the training of retail employees is an investment which has long-run and long-lasting benefits for the retailer.

Who Receives Retail Training

Since the purpose and need for retail employee training has been established, let us now turn our attention to the problem of *which* employees should be trained. Although one may state simply that *all* retail employees need some type of training, it is not practical to provide the same type and length of training to all employees. It becomes a question of determining which retail employees should receive retail training and how long a training period should be.

Sales Personnel   In many retail stores, salespeople are usually the ones to receive some type of training. Even experienced salespersons must become acquainted with a specific retail store's system: sales transactions, credit policies, deliveries, and returns. The length of time required to train an individual depends on that person's experience and ability to absorb these fundamentals. Generally—but not always—an experienced person requires less training than an inexperienced salesperson.

In some instances, even the most seasoned salesperson will benefit from instruction in the techniques of salesmanship. Retail salesmanship techniques should focus on customer benefits rather than on product knowledge. Even experienced salespeople tend to overlook this important technique. Emphasis on this technique does not imply that product knowledge is not beneficial to a salesperson, but points out that, all too often, product knowledge is stressed to the customer by the salesperson with little regard for the benefits derived from the purchase of that item. This is unfortunate since customers tend to purchase goods and services because of the benefits of prestige, status, security, convenience, or economy and *not* because of an extensive knowledge about the product.

Nonsales Personnel Retail employees not associated with the selling function of a store also need training. But here instruction should be focused on store procedures, practices, and policies. Nonselling retail employees usually consist of office and clerical help, delivery persons, and cashiers. Instruction for nonselling persons can be accomplished mainly through the use of movies, group discussions, and store manuals. The amount of time spent teaching these staff members is determined by the ability of the individuals, the size of the store, and the store's policy on training. For example, in some large department stores, new employees may be trained in groups, and the training period may be for a few hours, a day or two, or perhaps up to one week. In smaller retail stores, training may be quite short. In other words, it may consist of an introduction to the other employees, receiving a copy of the store's rules and policies, filling out a sales slip, being given directions on how to "ring up a sale," and being told when and where to take a break. As you can see, the brevity of this latter type of store training leaves much to be desired. In most instances, a new employee is unsure and insecure as to how to proceed in the ways and methods of the store until some training is given or experience is gained. The new employee—especially if inexperienced—is bound to make some mistakes for which he or she should not be held responsible. If the management believes that the store cannot afford the time and money to train new personnel, then that retailer probably should hire only experienced retail people. Seasoned retailing persons will adapt more quickly to a new routine than inexperienced persons—although experienced persons will command a higher salary. But by hiring experienced people, there may be less expense in training.

Managerial Personnel Many of the large retailing chains have management training programs from which employees are promoted into junior executive and middle management positions. Promoting from within, especially when promotion is tied to a training program, is highly desirable. This policy is desirable because it provides managerial talent that is well trained in retailing management, human relations, and store policies and practices. Also, it usually leads to improved employee morale because of the possibility of advancement for store employees. When a retailing chain is expanding operations, this policy is a relatively inexpensive method of ensuring a source of supply of executive talent.

Training programs for managerial personnel usually are more sophisticated than the other training programs of the store. This training probably focuses on advanced marketing and management techniques, practices, and methods. Formalized executive training may even include study at a college or university or at some special school. Other executive training programs will allow considerable latitude for self-development, with financial or other incentives given in order to encourage continued growth.

Most of the executive development programs sponsored by the large retailing institutions are designed to eliminate some of the manager's shortcomings. Among the most frequently mentioned criticisms of managers are poor judgment, lack of creativity, lack of innovation, lack of leadership, inadequate ability in analyzing problems, and the lack of communicative ability.

Many of the retail executive development programs will include course instruction which is patterned along the lines of the limitations and management deficiencies listed above. The training program will include home study courses, applied training in decision making, report writing, human relations problems, and problem solving. These instructional procedures may take the form of "buzz" sessions, case studies, role playing, and lectures. These techniques, when combined with job rotation, usually provide for a well-rounded junior executive. However, the "polish" or seasoning will come only from years of experience in decision making.

Who Does the Training

In small retail stores, usually the owner, manager, or an experienced salesperson will supervise the employee training. Although some owners, managers, or experienced salespersons make good teachers, experience indicates that many seasoned salespeople do not enjoy training new employees, or they do not wish to share their expert knowledge with less-experienced people. This is particularly true when salespersons work on a commission basis and training duties often take them away from their more lucrative selling functions.

In large retail institutions, a training director and/or the personnel department will carry out the functions of training new employees. The training director probably schedules the programs as well as the subject material, and may call on store executives to assist in instruction even though they are not members of that department. Also, the buyer or a department head is often asked to aid in the training of store personnel.

EMPLOYEE EVALUATION

The effectiveness of employee training and on-the-job work experience is a matter of great importance to retail store managers. In order to determine whether an employee has improved since first coming to the store, some form of employee evaluation is needed. This evaluation information can then be used by the retailer in judging whether an employee can assume greater responsibilities. Also, from these measurements, a manager can determine whether transfers and promotions can be accomplished because of improved employee skills and retailing knowledge. Since employee evaluation is known by many terms (such as efficiency rating, merit rating, employee appraisal, or personnel appraisal), in this text, we will use the words "employee evaluation" to mean any type of measurement of employee skills or techniques.

Employee evaluation is essential to the welfare and self-development of individual store employees. These individual workers, as well as their supervisors, need to know how well they are developing so that greater utilization of labor can be achieved within the retailing system. Thus, employee evaluation can provide a device against which one can measure an employee's accomplishments or which will show the need for further training and development. Good employee evaluation should indicate both what an employee "has" and what an employee "lacks" in the way of skills and/or techniques.

Small independent retailers are usually in close contact with their employees, and thus they may not need a formal system of employee evaluation. However, even workers in a small store need to be evaluated in some way to measure their job performance. The owner-manager should also evaluate employees in order to determine the employee's attitudes and feelings about the retail business and its management. Also, it may be that the owner-manager has the wrong impression of some of the employees, and an evaluation procedure may correct these feelings as well as keep open the lines of communication. As you would expect, a flow of ideas between the management and the employees is important for a successful retail system.

Other advantages accrue from employee evaluations: First, they serve as a major basis for the promotion or dismissal of an employee. Since an employee evaluation rates potential to some degree, it is especially useful in designating personnel for transfer or promotion. Under formalized employee evaluation programs, the discovery of employee potential may come well in advance of any openings. But when a job opening does occur, the retailer has one or several prospective persons from which to choose, thereby saving time and money.

Second, employee evaluation serves as one major index for various types of employee training and development programs. The rating from an employee evaluation will indicate whether the person has shortcomings in some area or whether past training programs have fostered the personal growth of the individual. Using these evaluations as a basis for selecting and developing instructional areas, a retailer may be able to improve the store's training program which, in turn, will help the employee's job performance.

One of the most common uses of employee evaluation is for determining increases in wages and salaries. An employee who performs work effectively should be rewarded since the employee's efforts are contributing to the store's profitability. However, caution should be exercised in using employee evaluations, and they should be done in an objective manner, especially if the evaluations are used as the basis for increasing wages.

There are various ways of evaluating retail salespersons and various bases that can be used, such as total sales, profits from total sales, or efficiency in recording sales transactions. Other evaluation categories might include personal qualities (such as honesty, courtesy, and attitude) or the number of customer complaints against the person. If the latter group of characteristics is used for evaluation, considerable thought should be given to the results because of the "qualitative" nature of the evaluative factors. Employee evaluation when properly used can lead to happier and more satisfied retail personnel. But if employee evaluations are incorrectly handled, or if the employees do not understand how or why the evaluations are being done, employee resentment and decreased productivity may result.

If the evaluation is fair and equitable, it can lead to favorable attitudes and an improved morale among the workers. Employees who believe that there are chances for an increased salary incentive or a promotion will usually perform more efficiently and have better attitudes. Retail employees possessing such attributes often indirectly encourage other employees to act in the same manner. Possessing the proper attitude is a necessary ingredient for retail employees because "retailing is a people business."

COMPENSATION PLANS FOR RETAILERS

Since the expenditure for compensation of employees is usually the largest single expense of a retail store, it is extremely important that a retailer spend money wisely in compensating employees. Also, dissatisfaction with compensation plans is a common complaint among retail employees. Therefore, retailers should be extremely selective in choosing a particular type of pay plan. A variety of compensation plans (or a combination thereof) can be used by retailers. The same retailer may even employ different methods of compensation for different classifications of store employees. For example, sales personnel may be paid by one plan, nonselling people by another pay plan, and executives by some other type of plan. The type of retail business may also determine what basic kind of plan is used.

Compensation of retail employees may be in the form of financial or nonfinancial rewards, or a combination of the two. Nonfinancial compensation includes any and all psychic rewards. These nonfinancial compensations may include recognition, a lateral move on the same level with no pay increase, special awards (such as, "employee of the month") different titles, or coffee breaks. A psychic reward is one that is psychological in nature with no monetary significance.

Financial compensation includes wages, salaries, commissions, or bonuses. As was previously noted, these financial rewards can be based on job classification, duties performed, or on total sales or profits (or some variation thereof). No compensation plan can be perfect and completely satisfy the retailer and the employees. However, certain fundamentals form the basis of all good compensation plans. First, an equitable plan of compensation should have broad, basic goals which are understood by both management and employees. These basic objectives include attracting, retaining, and developing good employees. Further, a sound compensation plan should reward people for their efforts. The management of a store should be interested in a compensation plan that produces the best results in relation to selling costs. Thus, it becomes apparent that each specific retailer must outline a plan of compensation for the business which is equitable and meets the requirements of both the employee and the employer. Further, the ideal compensation plan provides a basic wage plus an incentive and is somewhat flexible, economical to administer, competitive, and controllable by management in order to keep selling costs in line with sales.

Types of Compensation Plans

There are two broad, basic plans for compensating retail employees: (1) the straight-salary plan and (2) the straight-commission plan. These two basic plans can then be varied or combined to form a third plan, one based on a salary plus commission. A fourth plan of compensation, the quota-bonus plan, differs in some respects from the salary-commission plan and is, therefore, treated as a separate entity. Also, some retailers may use a combination of two or three of these plans to meet certain wage requirements for their specific businesses and to motivate their employees. In order to see the differences between these plans as well as the advantages and disadvantages, let us examine them in more detail.

Straight-Salary Compensation Plan Currently, the straight-salary plan is the most common method of compensating retail employees, and it has the major advantage of being easy for an employee to understand. It provides a definite amount of income each pay period and is especially suitable for inexperienced employees. Too, the straight-salary plan allows for relatively easy managerial control over individuals since a flat salary is used. Many small independent retailers choose this straight-salary compensation plan. This plan is also particularly suited for the store's employees who perform duties *not* associated with selling.

Even with all the benefits just mentioned, the straight-salary plan does suffer from some limitations. First, the amount of compensation does not fluctuate in proportion to the retail sales volume. This is a disadvantage to the retail store owner in that a salesperson can work inefficiently for some weeks, yet still receive the same amount of compensation. Second, an employee is not rewarded for increased productivity—at least not immediately although a promotion or transfer may come later. Third, a straight-salary plan also suffers from inflexibility. Determining the proper salary level is often a problem, and once the retailer sets it, the salary remains at that level and is difficult to adjust downward should business conditions so warrant.

Straight-Commission Compensation Plan The straight-commission compensation plan overcomes some of the deficiencies associated with the straight-salary method. Under this plan, the amount of pay varies in proportion to sales. When a salesperson increases the volume of retail sales, the amount of that person's compensation also rises. Thus, when the employee relates direct selling effort with increased income, the employee usually works harder to sell more goods and services.

Retail stores selling merchandise of high unit value, such as durable goods (cars and appliances), furniture, diamonds, or high-fashion apparel, often utilize a straight-commission plan. The percentage of commission (rates may vary anywhere from 2.5 percent to 10 percent of total sales) will vary depending on the nature of the merchandise, the gross margin of the goods, the store manager's personal philosophy, and the season of the year.

In addition to varying in proportion to sales, the straight-commission form of compensation is flexible and provides retailers with some control over wage costs. The straight-commission plan provides an incentive to most salespersons because their pay is tied directly to their level of sales. This plan is also easily understood by salespeople, thereby resulting in less confusion when computing earnings. Because of its flexibility, many salespeople would not work on any other type of compensation plan.

Like all methods of compensation, straight commission also suffers from some limitations. When the sales volume decreases, compensation to salespersons also decreases which may lead to a lowering of employee morale—especially if the decrease in sales is caused by economic factors beyond their control. Unfortunately, the incentive feature also may encourage salespersons to high-pressure customers, thereby antagonizing them. This tactic must then be avoided and discouraged if a retailer is seeking repeat business. For the retailer attempting to build a business on customer service, the straight-commission plan encourages salespersons to avoid those persons who may be "browsing" or "just looking." Too, salespeople will avoid those customers interested only in lower priced merchandise since the rate of commission is lower for that merchandise than for the higher priced goods.

For those stores using the straight-commission plan of compensation, there is some danger in having senior salespersons seeking only those customers who are willing to spend a considerable amount of money for certain goods. The junior salesperson then is left to help all the other customers, many of whom may not purchase a large volume of merchandise. This will then create an employee morale problem for the retailer because the junior salesperson will believe that the senior salesperson should also share in helping some of the less productive customers—and rightly so. In order to overcome some of this resentment among sales employees, a few retailers have used a system of rotation for sales personnel. Under the rotation system, each salesperson takes a turn at greeting and waiting on the customers as they come through the door. Using the law of averages, this system helps to distribute the customers among all the salespersons. Although this system may appear to be practical, experience has shown that it also does not work satisfactorily since senior salespeople usually attempt to wait on previous customers. This tactic then often leads to jealousies between the sales personnel, and morale suffers. But if the rotation system is not used, then junior salespersons with less experience often suffer from a lack of customers and reduced sales. Some retailing firms use this rotation system with an understanding that if the junior salesperson cannot "close the sale," then the customer is to be turned over to the senior salesperson. (In retailing, this is often called a "TO," a takeover or turnover.) Then if the senior salesperson does close the sale, the junior salesperson will share in the commission. This may also be one method by which junior salespersons will learn the techniques of selling, although some instruction should supplement this on-the-job selling experience. If a straight-commission compensation plan is to work effectively in a retail store, it must be closely monitored and supervised by the sales manager.

Salary-plus-Commission Compensation Plan   In an attempt to overcome the limitations associated with both the straight-salary and the straight-commission plans, another compensation plan has been formed utilizing the best features of each. The result is a salary-plus-commission plan. It works in this way. Salespeople are paid a basic salary which is somewhat lower than the basic salary of the straight-salary plan. Then, in addition, they are paid a commission on all *net* sales. The rate of commission is somewhat less in this salary-commission plan than the rate paid under the straight-commission plan.

The salary-plus-commission plan does fulfill two of the basic requirements of all compensation plans: (1) a basic salary so that a salesperson will not have to worry about earning enough each month to cover "ordinary living expenses" and (2) a commission structure or rate which provides a salesperson with an incentive for extra effort. This combination plan also provides the retailer with a compensation plan which permits the salary and wage expenses to vary with sales volume. If sales decline, the cost of compensation to salespeople also declines, perhaps to the level of their straight salary. Yet at the same time, salespersons are provided with some stable income through the basic salary.

Quota-Bonus Compensation Plan   This compensation plan utilizes the salary-plus-commission feature from the previous plan, but differs from that plan in that a commission is paid *only* on sales in excess of a given amount or "quota." Because of its merits, this quota-bonus compensation plan is becoming increasingly more popular with retailers. The quota-bonus plan provides a basic salary which means a steady income for a retail store's salespeople. It also provides an incentive, yet it does not encourage "overselling" or high-pressure tactics on the part of the salesperson. The quota-bonus plan is flexible and can easily be adjusted for seasonal variations in sales volume or for new and inexperienced salespeople.

However, even with all these merits, this method of compensation does have some limitations. First, a retailer must determine the weekly or monthly quota from past sales or adjust it to market or seasonal conditions. As you would expect, fixing the quota can be quite difficult and may determine the success or failure of the plan. Second, setting a basic salary is also difficult and will probably be based on a wage-cost ratio, adjusted to local competitive conditions. Again, if the basic salary is too low, the store may not be able to attract and retain competent people; or if the salary is too high, it may cut the retailer's profit too much. Third, establishing rates of commission on sales in excess of the quota is delicate. If the rate is set too high in relation to the quota, the costs to the retailer become excessive; if set too low, incentive may be lost. To be of the greatest value, the quota should remain within the reach of most salespeople, and the commission rate must be equitable.

In light of the above, the quota-bonus plan suffers from several other limitations. The plan tends to become quite complicated so that many employees fail to understand the merits of the plan. This may result in employee discontent, lowered employee morale, and the loss of incentive. If the commission payment is withheld (because of returned merchandise), an employee may fail to understand the management's reasoning, and this may also lead to employee unrest.

It thus becomes readily apparent that there is no perfect compensation plan for retailers. Each plan has its merits and its limitations. In order to overcome some of the criticisms by employees over methods of payment, some retailers offer their employees other benefits or means of compensation.

Other Benefits or Means of Compensation

One method employed by large retailers (and to some extent by small retailers) for enhancing employees' earnings is "profit sharing." Profit sharing is an arrangement through which employees are able to participate in the profits of their employer; and the sharing usually varies according to the salary level of the employee. Profit-sharing plans are not widespread, although they are becoming more acceptable in retailing, in part, because of union contracts and/or managerial philosophy. The Retail Clerks International Union has had some small success with grocery supermarket chains in establishing profit-sharing plans for employees. Other large retailing chains, such as Sears, Roebuck and Company, J. C. Penney Company, and Montgomery Ward and Company, have adopted general profit-sharing plans for their employees. It should be noted that these retailers instituted profit sharing under their own initiative as each firm lacks union representation.

Prize money or push money (or PMs, as they are commonly called in the retailing field) is another form of extra compensation, paid by retailers to salespersons for selling certain kinds of merchandise. For example, prize money may be given to employees for selling goods which have been in stock for a long period of time, for selling "house brands" (a retailer's own brand or label), or for selling other special merchandise which may carry a high gross margin.

Some retailers may also hold sales contests in which salespeople can win prizes. These prizes may be given in cash, or more frequently are in the form of trips or merchandise.

Another benefit used by retailers is to allow their employees discounts on merchandise purchased in the store. Employee discounts vary considerably, but it is quite common for an employee to receive a discount anywhere from 10 to 25 percent on all purchases made at the store where the person is employed. Usually, this percentage will vary according to the type of merchandise sold at that particular store. For instance, some retailers who operate discount businesses or grocery stores may not be able to allow an employee any more than a 10 percent discount on all personal purchases. But a specialty goods store or jewelry store may allow their employees a 25 percent discount. Care should be exercised by the retailer in granting employee discounts because some employees abuse the privilege by purchasing items for all their friends. But this benefit or feature can help to build employee loyalty toward the store, serve as an aid in retaining personnel, and can be considered a method of promoting the store's merchandise.

Special cash bonuses may be provided by the retailer to the employee for suggestions offered for the improvement of the store's retailing operations. This benefit may encourage workers to take a greater interest in their work and look for ways to improve working conditions. Some retailers may also offer other fringe benefits (such as an extra day off or additional cash) to employees on their birthdays, anniversaries, or on their annual employment date.

Generally, pension plans have not been implemented to any great degree in retailing. A major exception is the employees' pension plan at Sears, Roebuck and Company, which is perhaps one of the best in the retailing industry. Many small retailers find no need for a pension plan for employees or probably cannot afford to maintain one. Beyond Social Security retirement provisions, the retail employee has not been provided for in old age or after retirement by the retailer. The federal government has passed limited legislation in providing for the "vesting" of employee contributions to present retirement plans. (Vesting refers to contributions made to a retirement plan by an employee and an employer becoming the employee's property. If the contributions are vested in an employee after five years, this means the contributions made by the employer become an employee's property regardless of whether the employee quits the job. This is one of the major limitations of many existing pension plans.) Should an employee leave employment prior to the vesting date, all the employer's contributions revert to the employer and do not become the property of the employee. Or in some instances, the employee may lose all rights to the pension plan.

Increasingly, retail firms have encouraged employees to accept group medical and hospitalization insurance. Usually, the retailer pays a portion of the premium for the employee and/or the employee's family. Group rates for medical and hospitalization insurance are always less than employees could obtain on their own, and the premiums are paid through payroll deductions made by the retailer. This is an easy and convenient way for retail employees to receive insurance coverage. With the rising costs of medical care, this fringe benefit may be equal to a considerable amount of money. Generally, all fringe benefits apply to full-time employees only, and part-time help may not share in these employee benefits.

SUMMARY

Staffing a retail store with the right personnel may be one of the most important managerial functions of retailing management. Employees must be organized for the successful operation of the store, and the retailing functions must be performed satisfactorily from the customers' and the retailer's point of view.

Before the actual recruitment of employees takes place, the retailer must determine the employee needs for the store, and the nature of the work to be accomplished in the store.

Job analysis is a critical part of personnel administration. A thorough understanding of the tasks involved in each job is essential in order to determine the personnel requirements for each position. Job analysis also sets the minimum standards for the recruitment and selection of applicants who fill each job. Job analysis also provides a store's management with the basic facts upon which a division of labor can be organized. Job analysis reveals the interrelationships between the various functions within the store.

A *job description* is a written report which describes in detail the work to be performed, responsibilities, skills needed, the amount of training required, and the work conditions under which the job is to be performed. Job descriptions lead to job titles and job classifications according to the variation in skills, aptitudes, knowledge, and attitudes required on the part of the employees.

The recruitment of retailing personnel can be from two main sources: (1) within the store and (2) from outside the store.

The *selection of applicants* involves a series of appraisals and evaluations from which the more promising applicants are separated from those whose qualifications do not meet the store's requirements. Essentially, the selection process attempts to determine the probable success or failure of an applicant should that person be employed by the store.

The selection process usually begins with a *preliminary interview.* For some applicants, the preliminary interview will be the only step in the entire selection process; that is, the person will be rejected as unsuitable for the job.

In addition to interviews and application forms, some retailers make use of *employment tests.* The use of employment testing is growing in importance because of the growing recognition that mistakes in hiring are expensive. These tests may be achievement, aptitude, interest, or personality.

Once the recruitment and selection process has been completed, many retailers maintain *formal training programs* in order that individuals may develop and improve their job performance. Many retailing firms have come to realize that training responsibilities are necessary. These retailers realize that they cannot hire adequately trained employees. Therefore, these retailers must provide a training program.

Training of employees results in a number of *benefits* to the retailer. First, training improves productivity and job performance. Second, training reduces employee errors. Third, training may reduce total wage costs. Fourth, training may reduce employee turnover, lessen management supervision, and allow an employee to perform tasks more efficiently.

Nearly all retail employees need some type of training. Salespersons usually are the employees who need to be trained in the art of salesmanship. Nonsales employees need training in store procedures, practices, and policies. Large retailing organizations often provide executive development programs for middle- and top-management positions. Training programs for managerial personnel usually are more sophisticated than the other training programs of a store.

In small stores, the owner or manager usually provides the training for employees. In large retail firms, a training director may be responsible for training employees.

The effectiveness of employee training and on-the-job work experience is a matter of great importance to retail store managers. *Employee evaluation* is essential to the welfare and self-development of individual store employees. Employees need to know how well they are developing in order that the right training may be provided.

Employee evaluation may serve as a basis for promotion or dismissal of an employee. Employee evaluation also serves an one major index for various types of employee training and development programs. Employee evaluation may be used as a guide in determining wages and salaries.

The expenditure for compensation of employees is usually the largest single expense of a retail store. Employees' wages should be controlled because of the size of the expense.

Two broad, *basic compensation plans* are used by retailers: one is the straight-salary method; the other is the straight-commission method. The salary-plus-commission plan is used by some retailers in an attempt to overcome some of the objections associated with the two basic compensation plans.

Since there is no perfect plan of compensating employees, some retailers make use of other forms of *rewards*. These may include profit sharing, prize money, contests, discounts on merchandise, special cash bonuses, and pension plans. The degree and extent of usage of these employee incentives will depend on the size of the store and the philosophy of management.

REVIEW QUESTIONS

1 Discuss the importance of managing retail personnel.
2 What factors should a retailer consider in determining specific employee requirements for the operation of the store?
3 Compare and contrast job analysis and job description.
4 Relate some of the sources for recruiting retail employees.
5 In the selection of retail personnel, what is the primary purpose of the preliminary interview?
6 What is the purpose of the application-for-employment form?
7 Why should the second employment interview be one of mutuality?
8 Define the following terms: Achievement tests, aptitude tests, interest tests, and personality tests. What is the purpose of each test?
9 Discuss the reasons for employee training.
10 In what manner does the training for sales employees differ from nonselling employees? From the executive development training program?
11 Who should be responsible for training employees?
12 Why should a retailer be interested in employee evaluation?
13 What are some of the main purposes of employee evaluation?
14 Compare and contrast the types of employee-compensation plans used by retailers.
15 Which type of compensation plan is best in your opinion? Why?
16 What are employee fringe benefits? Name some of the most common fringe benefits.

CASE PROBLEM

Cole's is one of the largest department stores in a metropolitan area of 1.5 million people. In selecting employees, the store begins its procedure with a preliminary interview. During the preliminary interview, such definitive factors as age, residence, and work experience bear heavily on whether an applicant receives further consideration. It has been the store's policy to reject anyone over forty-five years of age regardless of experience. This was due to Mr. Cole's insistence that persons over forty-five cost the store too much money for the pension plan.

Applicants were never really informed whether they had passed the preliminary interview. Those rejected were told that they would be contacted later. However, these applicants never were contacted again. For those applicants passing the preliminary interview, the completion of the application blank was required. Cole's had received some criticism of this policy of employment.

During the second interview, the personnel director sought the anwers to personal questions from the applicants. It was the personnel director's opinion that all applicants should be tested for their level of irritability. Since Cole's employees provided full-service to their customers, it was believed by the personnel director that all employees should be very patient and tolerant of customers' criticisms.

If the applicants successfully passed the second interview, they were asked to take a battery of tests. This battery of tests included a twenty-minute achievement test, a twenty-minute aptitude test, and a twenty-minute personality test. The personnel director evaluated all tests and decided whether the applicant successfully passed each test. There were different levels of achievement on each test, and this was known only to the director.

The store has been experiencing a relatively high rate of employee turnover lately. The director of personnel is not quite sure what contributes to this sudden increase in employee resignations. Mr. Cole has talked with the director of personnel, and together they have decided that perhaps some revisions of the present personnel procedures are in order.

Problem Assume that you are the director of personnel. Mr. Cole has asked you to prepare a memorandum outlining the changes you believe necessary to reduce employee turnover. Make any recommendations you deem necessary in altering the selection procedure for Cole's Department Store.

CLASS PROJECT

One class session may be devoted to employment interviewing. An interview panel consisting of two to four members may be assigned with the responsibility for selecting both sales and nonselling employees for a large department store. These employment interviews are to screen applicants for these positions. Each panel member assumes the responsibility for interviewing three to four applicants.

Each class member should be ready to be interviewed for a job with the store. Each class member should prepare a resume describing personal qualifications for a particular type of job with the department store. These resumes will be turned over to the interviewing panel prior to the personal interview.

Every member in the class should be prepared to evaluate the interviews. The interviews should be analyzed from the applicant's point of view, the interviewer's point of view, and as to the general procedural conduct of each interview.

Part Nine

Financial Planning
and Control

Chapter 18

Financial Planning and Control—Sales, Costs, and Profits

It is important in our personal lives that we have an understanding of our financial situation at any given point in time. We should know our exact income, our expenses, and our cash flow. We need to know these things so as to be able to buy food and clothing, pay our rent, and pay our bills, hopefully, without going into debt. Similarly, for either a new or existing retail business, these questions must be answered and dealt with if the business is to succeed financially. And this can be done only through adequate and proper financial planning and control.

Many small independent retailers often begin business without adequate funds or any financial planning. This factor, in turn, has led directly or indirectly to the rising rate of retail business failures. However, adequate financial planning is not limited to small retailers. In some instances large chain stores miscalculate their allocation of income and expenses, thereby causing financial hardships. These errors in judgment may be offset by the overall profits of the chain, however, and may not be readily apparent to the casual observer. But whatever the size of the retail business, adequate financial planning and control is necessary.

To clarify what financial planning and control involves and how it affects the retailer, let us outline briefly its various characteristics. First, the term "financial planning and control'' usually refers to the budgeting or fiscal planning of the operation of a retail business—i.e., budgeting for the *income, expenses,* and the *cash on hand.* In other words, every retailer, large or small, must first have a formal budget which serves as a guide and control over sales or income and expenses for the ensuing year. Sales and expenses must be kept in their proper relationship if the retail business is to be profitable and have enough cash available for the operation of the business. Although many budgets consist largely of estimates (or *guess*-timates), these estimates should be fairly accurate and reasonable for that business in order to be meaningful. If the estimates are not realistic, the budget will tend to lose its significance as a control measure.

Second, financial planning includes the determination and estimation of sales (*x* number of dollars or units) and the control of expenses (*x* number of dollars). As an aspect of financial planning, "financial analysis" is concerned with the controlling of sales, costs, and profits in a ratio that will be beneficial to the retailer. The use of sales analysis, cost analysis, and profit analysis helps the retailer pinpoint any problem areas so that corrective action can be taken. For example, a *sales analysis* (examination of the sales records) may determine that some product lines should be eliminated as they are not profitable. Retail sales transactions are often vital indicators of a store's current performance, and they can be checked against past and anticipated sales for more effective financial planning.

Cost analysis may show the retailer that certain costs or expenses are too high and should be reduced. (Typical retailing costs will include such things as the purchase price of the merchandise, delivery charges, wages, rent, promotional expenditures, equipment costs, and depreciation.) Since in the final determination it is the amount of profit in which the retailer is interested, operating costs must be controlled and kept to a minimum; otherwise a retailer may just break even and end with no profit.

A retailer's *profits* should also be analyzed in several different ways. They should be compared with similar retail operations by product line and compared against the retailer's expected return on investment. If the profit falls below expectations, then the retailer can begin to take corrective action by improving the control and efficiency of the store in order to improve the profit situation.

Again, it cannot be overemphasized that financial planning, control, and analysis must occupy a major position in the total retailing system. Without adequate financial planning, the retailer will not be able to start a business successfully or to function effectively for even a short period of time. In order to aid the retailer in developing effective financial planning and control, we will now devote attention to the various factors which tend to influence the retailer's financial decisions in this area.

THE ROLE OF THE ACCOUNTANT

There may have been a time in which a small retailer could open the doors of a store, pay expenses, and merely hope there was money left in the cash register at the end of the day. But these days are gone forever. Yet some retailers still believe that they can control all aspects of their businesses without any form of record keeping. By closely examining these retailers, however, one is quickly able to discover the absence of any real controls. There seems to be little control over the expenses of the store as well as an obvious absence of any analysis of business results. If there is little analysis of the store's operating results, then a retailer has difficulty making intelligent decisions. An accurate picture of a store's performance can be obtained only from an analysis of the retailing transactions which have been posted to a standardized accounting system. Without an adequate accounting system, a retailer may discover that certain changes in the marketplace have occurred but that it is too late to adjust the store's operations accordingly.

It is to be expected that every retailer should have an adequate understanding of accounting fundamentals in order to be able to maintain the necessary business and legal records. The maintenance of store records is no more difficult than any other phase of the retailing operation, and if properly established, record keeping can become quite routine. In starting a retail business, however, it is advisable for a retailer to employ the services of an accountant who can establish an accounting system tailored to that store's specific needs. For example, a retail store usually will need to keep records on sales, credit transactions, purchases, and expenses. In addition, though, there may be other special requirements for certain types of businesses. Therefore, it is extremely prudent for a retailer to hire an accountant to set up a system that is geared especially to that type of store.

Some retailing organizations have existing, more complex systems of record keeping and control. However, from time to time, these stores may also need to revise and update their accounting systems. Again, this will necessitate the use of an accountant or a public accounting firm unless there is a qualified person on the store's staff. Today, many retailing institutions are making use of data processing or electronic equipment which helps to facilitate and condense the operating results of the store.

However, it is virtually impossible to analyze the operating results of any store—whether by data processing or by manual methods—unless there are complete and accurate records on merchandise bought and sold and on the expenses related to these activities. Whether a new or existing retail business should install data processing equipment or mechanical equipment of any sort is a matter which should be determined by the retailer along with an outside consultant, preferably an accountant.

An accountant can put together for the retail business an accounting system which will provide the data to judge the efficiency of a store's activities and serve as a guide for future decisions.

Another reason for employing the services of an accountant is to establish a proper payroll system. Today's complex federal, state, and local income tax regulations, Social Security laws, and detailed deductions for fringe benefits all need to be considered when setting up a payroll system. Also, it is important for a retailer to comply with standard accounting practices concerning inventory valuations, sales taxes, and business licenses. As you might expect, most retailers do not have the special training or time to devote to this accounting function, making it almost mandatory for the retailer to hire a specialist in this field.

Some retailers probably cannot afford to pay for an accountant on a full-time basis, but instead they may be able to retain an accountant on a part-time or consulting basis. Many small retailers employ a bookkeeper on their regular staff and then have an accountant do their more complicated financial statements as well as their income tax returns. Of course, larger retail stores will employ an accountant (or accountants) on a full-time basis.

If retailers need to borrow money, they will also have to have a satisfactory accounting system which provides the information required by the lender. Bankers or vendors will ask for detailed and up-to-date financial information which will show the financial soundness of the retail firm. An adequate and current accounting system will provide to the lenders some evidence of sound retailing management. Also, lenders of funds tend to look more favorably on those retailers who maintain current and accurate records on their businesses.

SOURCES OF CREDIT BORROWING

All retailers, both large and small, at some point will need financial assistance in order to meet the short- and/or long-term needs of their businesses. The changes that affect retailers, (whether daily, weekly, monthly, seasonal, or cyclical) will require flexibility in their finding sources of financial assistance. What kinds of sources are available and what other avenues are open to the retailer? Although the banking system often provides funds by extending credit to retailers, there are other sources of credit aid—among them are vendors, financial institutions (other than banks), leasing companies, and the federal government.

Bank Financing

Commercial banks are the largest single source for short-term and intermediate-term loans for retailers. No other financial institution is as dominant in the American business system as the commercial bank. Based on the retailer's credit rating, banks will usually provide a retailer with a "line of credit" for everyday business activities. (A line of credit is a predetermined amount of money which a retailer is allowed to borrow.) At certain times, large amounts of money are needed by the retailer, whereas at other times, only small sums are needed to pay business expenses. Since the cash needs of a retailer may vary, a line of credit established with a commercial bank allows a retailer to borrow any amount *up to* the predetermined limit.

For example, a retailer may borrow enough money from the bank to purchase goods for the entire season. The retailer's inventory or the store's accounts receivable may serve as collateral for the loan. By borrowing the money from a commercial bank, a retailer is able to take advantage of the cash discounts allowed by the vendors. When the goods have been sold, the loan is then repaid. Or a retailer may borrow money from a bank in order to take care of a number of business needs, such as meeting a payroll, paying taxes, or using the cash for any other legitimate business purpose.

Commercial bank loans to retailers are usually adjusted to the specific needs of that business. Short-term loans are usually made for a period of less than one year. Intermediate-term loans may be made for periods from one to five years, and long-term loans (normally used for real estate) are made for periods exceeding five years. A line of credit from a commercial bank usually is for a short term and is subject to annual review by the banker and the retailer. During a period of high interest rates, it has been common practice for bankers to limit somewhat the lines of credit which were previously established for retailers. For example, during the summer of 1974, one retailer—with whom the author is acquainted— found his normal line of credit of $200,000 cut in half. The prime rate was 12 percent during the summer of 1974. This retailer used this amount of money (or the line of credit) for stocking the store's shelves for the Christmas season. Obviously, this retailer (and probably many others) had to seek alternate sources of credit because of the high interest rates.

Trade Credit

Another source of funds for the retailer comes from "trade credit", sometimes called mercantile or commercial credit. Trade credit is created when one business (a manufacturer or a wholesaler) accepts the credit of another business (a retailer). It is an unsecured, short-term type of credit which facilitates the movement of goods through the successive stages of production and distribution, ending with the retailer who sells the goods. The retailer is the final link in the chain of trade credit which may extend from the manufacturer to the wholesaler to the retailer. The extension of trade credit is for the inventory of goods that the retailer has in stock for resale. When the retailer makes a sale, this transaction may also be on credit; but this is consumer credit, not trade credit.

Trade credit is used by nearly all retailers. It is used to finance the acquisition of goods from either producers or wholesalers. Usually after a business relationship has been established with a vendor, the transaction is quite informal. No more may be involved than the retailer placing an order with a vendor, either by phone or by talking to a salesperson. The vendor's evidence of the transaction is usually in the form of an account receivable, whereas the retailer's accounting system will reflect an account payable. No factual data are available to support the total amount of trade credit used. However, the majority of retail goods and services is financed in this manner. Trade credit has become the acceptable way—no, the *essential* way—of facilitating the vast distribution process in this country. Also, it is doubtful that commercial banks would be in a position to finance *all* retail business transactions because the value of the goods and services is enormous. As retailers have grown into sizeable stores and/or chains, large-scale transactions must be consummated over long distances, which increases the need for trade credit. By allowing a period of time during which payment can be made for goods and services, producers and wholesalers— through trade credit—finance an important part of the retailing inventory. Without this type of credit, many retailers would have difficulty in finding cash with which to operate.

Accounts Receivable and Factoring

As was noted earlier, in addition to making regular loans to retailers using their inventory as collateral, commercial banks may make a loan using the retailer's accounts receivable as security. However, this procedure involves a degree of risk for the bank because of the possibility that some of the accounts receivable will not be collectible. Thus, banks are somewhat reluctant to use these accounts receivable as security for a loan. More frequently, finance companies may purchase a retailer's accounts receivable, at a discount, for a stated amount of cash. The discount taken by the finance company gives them some "cushion" in case some of the accounts receivable are not collected.

Yet there is still another method by which a retailer can raise the necessary cash with which to operate a business. This procedure is referred to as "factoring." Factoring involves the purchase of accounts receivable from a retailer without recourse for credit losses. The financial institution which does the buying is known as a "factor." This financial organization or factor assumes all credit risks associated with the purchase of a retailer's accounts receivable. A factor assumes the entire credit and collection function for a retailer, and debtors make payments directly to the factoring company. Factoring companies make their money in two ways: (1) by assessing the client (the retailer) a service charge and (2) by collecting an interest charge on the money advanced for the purchase of the accounts receivable. Factoring companies will also give financial advice to their clients in addition to advancing cash for a retailer's accounts receivable.

There may be variations, but in most instances, a formal contract is drawn by the factor and the retailer which stipulates the terms of the relationship. For example, the contract will state what accounts are involved, the amount of the accounts, the amount of money to be advanced to the retailer, the factor's charges for services performed, and any other services the factor may perform.

Factoring is used by retailers to ease the burden of credit and collections and to raise working capital by financing their accounts receivable. Through factoring, a retailer does gain freedom from credit and collection responsibilities, but the expense involved is a drawback. In fact, some students of retailing feel that factoring should be the *last* resort. Although it is true that financially weak retailers may be the first to use a factoring company, some financially strong retailers also utilize a factor—especially in automobile, appliance, and farm equipment retailing. Too, some single-line retailers do not wish to maintain a credit department because costs associated with such a department are high. These retailers would rather concentrate their efforts on the selling functions of retailing and leave the credit and collections to a factoring company.

Each retailer on an individual basis must decide whether the services of a factoring company are too expensive. The rates of factoring companies vary considerably from company to company, depending especially on the type of business involved. Factoring accounts receivable eases the burden for a retailer so that a form of credit insurance is provided, and at the same time, it frees the retailer from having any investment in accounts receivable. When dealing in durables such as automobiles, appliances, or farm equipment, this investment is often sizeable. Factoring increases a retailer's net working capital, which allows the payment of current obligations and may then place the firm in a more favorable position for a good credit rating with a vendor or a bank.

Leasing Arrangements

Another method of gaining working capital is for the retailer to "lease" or rent space within the business to someone else. Leasing space in a retail store is not new. For years, department stores have leased space to specialists in jewelry, furs, or hats. In turn, these specialists have provided the store with managerial expertise in these specific areas. Grocery supermarkets also often lease space in their stores for drugs, liquors, children's clothing, and other nonfood items. Even large variety chains, such as F. W. Woolworth and S. S. Kresge Company, lease space in their respective discount chain stores—i.e., Woolco and K-Mart.

The retailer has the basic advantage in leasing space to a specialist of not having to provide his or her own working capital and staff to operate the department. During times of rapid expansion of the firm, the retailer gains a distinct advantage. Also, leasing affords the retailer an opportunity to experiment with new departments and merchandise without all the risks associated with a new retailing venture. By renting a department to a lessee (the specialist), the lessor (the retailer) benefits from the lessee's specialized managerial skills and buying expertise. The lessee, in turn, benefits from the customer traffic generated by the retailer's store; utilization of the lessor's fixtures, services, and promotion; and the retailer's name and goodwill.

Leasing arrangements vary widely. However, usually a lessor (retailer) provides the space, fixtures, lighting, heat, services, and possibly the record-keeping system. The lessee (the specialist), in turn, assumes full responsibility for the purchasing and handling of the merchandise as well as for the management of the department. A lessee pays the retailer for the space occupied, either on a flat-fee basis or on a percentage of gross or net sales, or on some other basis. In many instances, a lessee will pay the retailer a percentage of gross sales plus a minimum fee. This rent provision allows the retailer to collect a minimum amount for the space occupied by the lessee and, at the same time, provides the retailer with additional income resulting from a lessee's management skills. However, on occasion, the lessee and the store management may decide to terminate the lease; disagreements often arise over the basic policy and philosophy of the store. Often what is a good policy for the store may be unworkable for the lessee. In some cases, a lessee will build a good business, only to have the retailer terminate the lease. The retailer may decide to take over the operation of the department because the net profit potential is greater than the income generated by the lease.

Leasing arrangements are relatively important in the retailing industry and will probably continue to be so in certain segments of large-scale retailing. Even though retailing executives do not agree on the merits of leasing departments within a store, leasing arrangements will continue in many specialty areas such as furs, shoes, and jewelry, as well as in service departments such as travel agencies, optometrists, insurance, and the like.

Unfortunately, one major problem will continue to exist in retailing in regard to leasing arrangements. Many times after a lessor has observed the activities of a lessee and witnessed the profits generated from a leased department, the retailer develops the opinion that the store can operate such a department. In many instances, this may not be true. All too often, a retailer does not possess the experience or expertise needed in that particular area of specialty merchandising; but this may be discovered too late—*after* a retailer has taken over the department and had to absorb some losses. Specialty retailing departments, in most cases, are better left to a lessee.

The Small Business Administration (SBA)

The federal government's Small Business Administration (SBA) is playing an increasingly important role in providing financial assistance to small retailers. The SBA was created by The Small Business Act of 1953, and its existence and authority is derived from this act and its amendments. In addition, the SBA derives authority from The Small Business Investment Act of 1958, as amended; the War Claims Act of 1948, as amended; and Title IV of the Economic Opportunity Act of 1964, as amended. Each of these acts or amendments

---

U.S. Small Business Administration

To apply for a loan—step-by-step procedure:

If, after carefully reading the first part of this pamphlet, you are not sure of your eligibility or about meeting SBA's objectives, credit, or policy criteria, call or write the nearest SBA office for clarification.

If you believe you qualify and wish to apply for an SBA loan, follow this step-by-step procedure (for new businesses):

1. Describe in detail the type of business to be established.
2. Describe experience and management capabilities.
3. Prepare an estimate of how much you or others have to invest in the business and how much you will need to borrow.
4. Prepare a current financial statement (balance sheet), listing all personal assets and all liabilities.
5. Prepare a detailed projection of earnings for the first year the business will operate.
6. List collateral to be offered as security for the loan, indicating your estimate of the present market value of each item.
7. Take this material with you and see your banker. Ask for a direct bank loan and if declined, ask the bank to make the loan under SBA's Loan Guaranty Plan or to participate with SBA in a loan. If the bank is interested in an SBA guaranty or participation loan, ask the banker to contact SBA for discussion of your application. In most cases of guaranty or participation loans, SBA will deal directly with the bank.
8. If a guaranty or a participation loan is not available, write or visit the nearest SBA office. SBA has eighty-five field offices and, in addition, sends loan officers to visit many smaller cities on a regularly scheduled basis or as the need is indicated. To speed matters, make you financial information available when you first write or visit SBA.

Figure 18-1 Loan procedures for new businesses—SBA.

provides the SBA with considerable power and latitude with respect to aiding small businesses, including retailers. (Other small businesses which may receive SBA assistance include manufacturers and wholesalers.)

The SBA's basic purposes are to aid, counsel, assist, and protect the interests of small business concerns, including retailers. Small independent retailers can receive loans from the SBA as well as obtain assistance for the improvement of managerial skills through participation in the SBA's direct action programs. The SBA sponsors these programs, which are designed for developing the management skills of qualified persons seeking to establish small retail businesses.

The SBA is under the management of an administrator who is appointed by the President of the United States and is confirmed by the United States Senate. For those seeking SBA advice, the main office is at 1441 "L" Street, Washington, D.C. There are also eight regional offices, which can be located in the annual directory of SBA field offices.

The Small Business Administration is becoming more important as a supporter of small businesses, including retailers, as evidenced in the following statistics. The San Francisco regional office of the Small Business Administration reported for the twelve-month period ending June 30, 1973, the SBA granted 3,582 small business loans for a total of $196,872,000. For the twelve months

---

U.S. Small Business Administration

To apply for a loan—step-by-step procedure:

If, after carefully reading the first part of this pamphlet, you are not sure of your eligibility or about meeting SBA's objectives, credit, or policy criteria, call or write the nearest SBA office for clarification.

If you believe you qualify and wish to apply for an SBA loan, follow this step-by-step procedure (for established businesses):

1. Prepare a current financial statement (balance sheet), listing all assets and all liabilities of the business—do not include personal items.
2. Have an earnings (profit and loss) statement for the previous full year and for the current period to the date of the balance sheet.
3. Prepare a current personal financial statement of the owner, or each partner or stockholder owning 20 percent or more of the corporate stock in the business.
4. List collateral to be offered as security for the loan, with your estimate of the present market value of each item.
5. State amount of loan requested and explain exact purposes for which it will be used.
6. Take this material with you and see your banker. Ask for a direct bank loan and if declined, ask the bank to make the loan under SBA's Loan Guaranty Plan or to participate with SBA in a loan. If the bank is interested in an SBA guaranty or participation loan, ask the banker to contact SBA for discussion of your application. In most cases of guaranty or participation loans, SBA will deal directly with the bank.
7. If a guaranty or a participation loan is not available, write or visit the nearest SBA office. SBA has eighty-five field offices and, in addition, sends loan officers to visit many smaller cities on a regularly scheduled basis or as the need is indicated. To speed matters, make your financial information available when you first write or visit SBA.

Figure 18-2 Loan procedures for established businesses—SBA.

ending June 30, 1974, the SBA regional office extended 3,153 loans totalling $207,424,000.[1]

Eligibility for financial assistance from the SBA is limited to small, independent businesses. These businesses are defined as retailers or service institutions with annual sales or receipts from $1 to $5 million, depending on the type of business.[2] The type of financial assistance available to small, independent retailers can best be summed up by the following quotation:[3]

> When a small businessman with a financial problem comes to SBA for advice and assistance, Agency loan officers review his problem and suggest possible courses of action. If he needs money and cannot borrow it on reasonable terms, SBA often can help. The Agency will consider either participating with a bank in a loan, or guaranteeing up to 90 percent of the loan. If a bank or other lending institution cannot provide the funds, SBA will consider lending the entire amount as a direct government loan if funds are available. However, most of SBA's loans are made in cooperation with banks.

For many small, independent retailers, the SBA offers the best advice and financial assistance available. In an era of economic bigness, many banks and other financial institutions prefer to lend their money mainly to larger firms. Large firms, in some instances, are better risks than the small, independent retailer—especially in the eyes of some financial institutions. In any case, the chances of obtaining both funds and advice from the SBA are greatly enhanced if the retailer has a carefully detailed retail business plan, complete with accounting records. As was mentioned previously, both a retail business plan and adequate accounting records are evidence of good managerial control and business sense.

SALES ANALYSIS

The value of continuous sales analysis cannot be overstated. Retailers who practice routine sales analysis are able to take advantage of trends in merchandising quickly. Sales analyses also allow a retailer to test customer reactions to certain products, packages, point-of-purchase display materials, advertising mediums, special sales events, retail store layouts, or merchandise assortments. Sales analyses can, and often do, reveal opportunities for new merchandising strategies. A store's sales volume can be analyzed on the basis of individual products, product lines, time periods, customer groups, or order sizes. The sales volume analysis also may be extended to include a survey of: (1) cost of goods sold, (2) gross margins, and (3) expense ratios (these items will be covered later in the text).

A retailer should accomplish sales volume analyses for two reasons: (1) to

---

[1]Reported from a conversation with regional manager of the SBA's San Diego office, October 2, 1974.

[2]*SBA: What It Is . . . What It Does,* Small Business Administration, Washington, 1973, p. 2.

[3]Ibid., p. 3.

determine the trend in sales volume for the retail store over a stated period of time and (2) to determine if the store has captured its share of the market. As you will remember, the store's market share was determined early in the retailing plan by the retailer setting specific goals and objectives. It is possible that a retail store's sales volume may be increasing while at the same time its market share may be decreasing. For instance, if the total retail sales volume is increasing at a greater percentage rate than the individual store's sales volume, the retailer is losing a portion of the market share.

It is relatively easy to determine a store's total sales volume, as these data are readily available from the accounting records. Not so apparent are the sales trends of the store. In order to determine a sales trend, a comparison must be made against some measure—the previous years' sales, industry figures, or some other yardstick.

For a determination of market share, a retailer can use industry figures to determine if the store has achieved its goal. If the industry figures are declining or growing, what is the store's position relative to the industry's figures? When industry figures are used for a comparison, a retailer may find that the store's sales volume has increased by a certain percentage but the store's *share* has decreased as a percentage of the total. It now becomes apparent that further investigation is in order. A retailer needs to determine *why* the store's market position has changed. The causes could be numerous. The store may have weaknesses in pricing or promotion, poor merchandise assortments, a poor location, too many expenses in relation to sales, or poor purchasing judgments. The analysis of a store's weaknesses is what makes a retailer's job most difficult. Any weakness or combination of weaknesses could contribute to a retailer's loss of market position.

Although an analysis of sales volume is time-consuming for a retailer, it is necessary in determining *why* a particular phenomenon happened or did not happen. By using the retailing plan as a standard of performance, a retailer should break sales into components or product lines so that when sales figures become available, a comparison of actual sales with expected dollar volume can be made.

One proven method used for sales analysis is to take the total sales volume for a stated period of time—i.e., quarterly, semiannually, or annually. First, these figures can be easily obtained from the past accounting records for identical periods and then compared for sales trends. Second, a comparison of industry trends can be used to reveal the store's market position. If industry sales are declining, it is not so startling that the store's sales volume on a particular product or product line is also declining. However, if the industry's sales are increasing on a certain product or product line, then a comparison should be made to determine whether the store is also experiencing a comparable rate of growth. If not, corrective action needs to be taken.

Third, a comparison should be made of sales with the objectives set forth in the retailing plan. If the goals state a certain sales volume for a period of time, and if the retailer is on target with this sales volume, then one of the retailing plan's objectives has been accomplished. If the sales volume is not on target with the goals established in the retailing plan, then the retailer must determine the cause. It is possible, though, that the goals set forth in the retailing plan were unrealistically high. This is one reason why the setting of store goals in the retailing plan is so significant. Goals must þe reasonably attainable in order to be useful. Unrealistic goals serve no useful purpose and often result in frustration for the retailer.

RETURN ON INVESTMENT (ROI)

All retailers are in business to serve customers by selling goods or services at a profit. Of course, the amount and percentage of profit varies by the type and kind of retail store, caliber of management, market conditions, and the like. However, most retailers have a definite figure in mind when asked, "What percentage return are you seeking from your investment?"

In setting up the retail business plan, a retailer is asked to state the goals and objectives of the store. Included as a part of these goals and objectives should be a figure which reflects the expected return on investment (ROI). Retailers may figure their ROI in several ways. In establishing a return on investment, some retailers use a percentage of markup on sales. This markup is large enough to cover the purchase price of the merchandise, anticipated costs of operation, and a desired profit for the store. If this method of determining ROI is used, the percentage of profit will remain the same although the dollar profit will vary according to the number of units sold or the volume of sales dollars. If the retailer uses an absolute figure (dollars or cents) to represent ROI, then the percentage markup figure may fluctuate in order to achieve the stated return on investment.

Why do retailers arbitrarily select a particular rate of return (whether dollars and cents or a percentage) on their investment? The philosophy behind it is possibly this: Retailers often state that the rate of return on investment should be fair and reasonable when compared to other investments. They feel that they should receive an ROI which is equal to taking the same amount of money, investing it in another venture, and receiving a like amount of profit. If the return is not equal to other types of business investments, then retailing will not attract enough individuals to operate and own retail stores.

However, should the actual ROI become too high for one type of retail store, many investors will be attracted to this field. This will then lead to a competitive situation where some retailers will fail. For example, the fast-food retailing field has suffered from such an experience. Many of the less efficient, fast-food outlets have gone bankrupt because the "field" attracted too many operators.

In the retailing industry, therefore, an ROI balance is maintained which compensates the retailer for the amount of money invested, the risks associated with that type of store, and the managerial efficiency and efforts put forth by the individual. Fortunately, competition takes care of any imbalance.

Calculation of ROI

The managerial performance of a retailer is measured to some degree by calculating the store's return on investment. In calculating a return on investment, one needs to use the figures found in the balance sheet and operating statements of the business. (This just reemphasizes the need for maintaining proper accounting records.)

The formula for calculating the rate of return on investment (ROI) is as follows:

$$ROI = \frac{\text{net profit}}{\text{investment}}$$

Unfortunately, even by using this formula, there may be some confusion with respect to the calculation of ROI since it makes a difference whether a store has stockholders or is independently owned. For example, stockholders are interested in the return of what *they* have invested in the store's stock (the amount paid for each share of stock × the number of shares of stock). The owner, however, is interested in the return on the *total* investment. Perhaps the following examples will help explain the situation.

Example   A retail store's operating statement indicates annual sales of $2 million and a net profit of $100,000. Year-end balance sheet figures indicate the following:

Assets	$1,200,000	Liabilities	$ 400,000
		Capital stock $600,000	
		Retained earnings 200,000	
			800,000
Total assets ..	$1,200,000	Total liabilities and capital	$1,200,000

The ROI will be different depending on whether we use the $800,000 or the $1,200,000 as the investment figure. Stockholders are more interested in their investment ($800,000) than they are in the store's total investment ($1,200,000). So using the stockholders' equity, the ROI calculation would be as follows:

$$ROI = \frac{\$100,000 \text{ (net profit)}}{\$800,000 \text{ (investment)}}$$

$$ROI = 12.5 \text{ percent}$$

In the above illustration, stockholders are receiving a 12.5 percent return on their investment.

However, the store's management is concerned with the total investment, which in this case is represented by $1,200,000. As one would expect, the ROI calculated with the total investment will result in the following:

$$ROI = \frac{\$100,000 \text{ (net profit)}}{\$1,200,000 \text{ (investment)}}$$

$$ROI = 8.33 \text{ percent}$$

You will notice that management's investment figure of $1,200,000 is much higher than the $800,000 figure used as stockholders' equity. Thus, the $1.2 million investment figure is more realistic and is a better measurement of management's performance, since the additional $400,000 does represent an investment as well, meaning that the *true return* on investment is actually 8.33 percent rather than 12.5 percent.

Retailers may calculate profitability by means of several methods, but a determination of a rate of return on total investment represents a better overall picture of the efficiency of that store. Gross margins expressed as percentages by themselves mean little, as do sales dollars per square foot of space. However, each becomes valuable when used in conjunction with some other yardstick of measurement. Since most retailers have other assets beyond inventory, it makes good sense to determine a rate of return on a business' *total* investment rather than on just a *portion* of that investment. This is particularly true since a retailer can take that same amount of money (total investment) and invest these funds elsewhere and make a profit.

BREAK-EVEN ANALYSIS

When a retailer starts a new business or takes over an existing one, some method should be used to determine the relationship between that store's fixed costs, variable costs, sales volume, and the effect on profits. A break-even analysis will show a retailer at what point a certain volume of sales will meet or cover the firm's total expenses (fixed and variable). Using the break-even method will allow a retailer to determine the relationship between these variables.

A break-even analysis requires a retailer to sit down and determine, as closely as possible, fixed costs, variable costs, and the sales volume needed to break even on these expenses. Fixed costs are those expenses such as rent, taxes, and insurance which must be paid regardless of income, and they *do not* vary with the amount of sales. Variable costs are those expenses which may vary or be changed such as salaries for part-time employees, interest on borrowed funds, advertising, and to some extent, utilities. This break-even analysis allows the management or the owner to visualize a series of sales-volume figures (based on market potential) which the business will need to break even or to provide a profit to the owners.

A break-even analysis includes the developing of charts and graphs. These charts and graphs will then aid management in determining what level of sales will equal costs if you assume certain selling prices and a certain number of units sold. If sales go to a level above the break-even point, a profit to the firm will result. The higher sales go beyond the break-even point, the greater the total profit to the retailer. If sales fall below the level of the break-even point, the retailer will suffer a loss. Stated another way, break-even analysis indicates to management how rapidly profits can be improved if the sales volume can be increased above the break-even level. Also, this analysis reveals the size of the loss at any sales volume below the break-even point.

Break-even analysis is important and useful for considering the relationship between revenue and costs. Figure 18-3 depicts a total-revenue curve and a total-cost curve. Where these two lines or curves intersect is the break-even point (BEP). At this break-even point, total revenue (sales) and total costs (fixed and variable expenses) are equal. Above this point, the retailer is making a profit; below the intersection of the total-revenue and total-cost lines, the firm is suffering a loss.

A critical element in determining a break-even point for a retail store is to determine the fixed and variable costs accurately. All costs, however minor, (including utilities, rent, insurance, salaries, cost of goods sold, fringe benefits, samples, advertising, and interest) should be included in the break-even analysis. If these expenses are not included, the break-even point may be distorted.

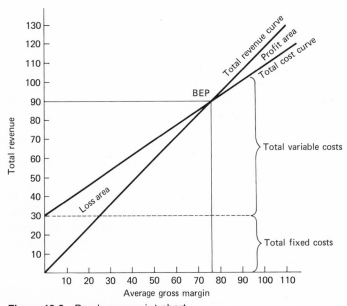

Figure 18-3 Break-even-point chart.

Given all the expenses, a break-even analysis is useful in determining the needed sales volume for a retail store. However, its use is limited by the quality of the imput data. Assuming that the retailer has constructed the retail business plan carefully, a break-even analysis should provide him with a very useful tool for management decisions. It can be helpful in the short run to determine the first year's sales volume which is needed to offset total expenses, and—hopefully— provide a profit to the owner. If the break-even point is considered too high (i.e., the break-even sales volume cannot be attained), the retailer has several alternatives. It may be better to forget the venture, or the variables in the formula may have to be altered (a reduction in expenses). The break-even chart cannot tell the management whether the store can generate a certain sales volume, it can only state how much is needed before any profits accrue to the store.

Let us assume that management has determined that an average gross profit margin of 24 percent (24%) can be maintained on all retail sales. The store's total fixed and variable expenses for the first year equal $109,400. The expenses are classified into the following categories for use in the break-even formula.

$$BEP = \frac{\text{total fixed and variable costs}}{\text{average gross profit margin}}$$

1. Rent	$ 28,500
2. Advertising and sales promotion	36,000
3. Depreciation on store equipment	3,300
4. Utilities (gas and electricity)	3,600
5. Supplies	1,000
6. Telephone	1,500
7. Insurance	1,500
8. Miscellaneous	1,600
9. Interest on $150,000 at 12	
percent	18,000
10. Salaries	14,400
Total fixed and variable costs	$109,400

$$BEP = \frac{\$109,400}{24 \text{ percent}} = \$455,833 \text{ gross sales}$$

In another illustration, a retailer selling electronic organs wishes to know how many organs the store must sell before the owner makes any profit. The average retail price based on previous experience is $2,500 per unit. Each electronic organ cost the retailer $1,850. Salespersons' commissions, handling charges, and financing, have been estimated to cost the store $350 per unit. Fixed costs are $18,000 per year. Using the formula

$$X = \frac{F}{P - V}$$

where X = number of units
   P = retail price
   V = variable costs
   F = fixed costs

$$X = \frac{F}{P-V} = \frac{\$18,000}{\$2,500 - \$2,200} = 60 \text{ electronic organs}$$

where X = ?
   P = \$2,500
   V = \$1,850+ \$350 = \$2,200
   F = \$18,000

If the retailer sells more than sixty electronic organs per year, the store will make a profit. If the store sells less than sixty organs per year, the store will sustain a loss.

Since profit is equal to total revenue minus total costs or $P = TR - TC$, and assuming that the store could sell ninety-five units, the retailer would have a profit of \$10,500. The calculations are as follows:

95 units at \$2,500 selling price		\$237,500
95 units at \$2,200 variable costs	\$209,000	
Add in fixed costs	18,000	
Total costs		227,000
Net profit		\$ 10,500

SUMMARY

Financial planning and control refers to the budgeting or fiscal planning of the operation of a retail business. In retailing, some provision must be made for budgeting income, expenses, and cash on hand. Every retailer needs a *formal budget* which serves as a guide and control over sales and expenses for the ensuing year. Sales and expenses must be kept in their proper relationship if the retail business is to be profitable and have enough cash available for the operation of the business.

Cost analysis determines whether certain expenses are too high or too low or are in the proper relationship to sales. Since the final determination is profit for the store, operating costs must be controlled and kept to a minimum.

Every retailer should have an understanding of *accounting fundamentals* in order to maintain records for the store. If a retailer does not have the proper training, he or she should employ the services of an accountant.

Commercial banks are the largest single source for short-term and intermediate-term *loans* for retailers. Another source of funds for retailers comes from trade credit. *Trade credit* is created when one business accepts the credit of another business. Banks may extend credit to retailers using a retailer's accounts receivable as security. Yet another means of raising funds includes the use of factors. *Factors* purchase accounts receivable from retailers without recourse for credit losses. Thus, a factor assumes all the credit risks associated with the purchase of a retailer's accounts receivable.

Another method of gaining working capital is for the retailer to *lease space* in the store to someone who specializes in selling certain kinds of merchandise. Many department stores lease areas to individuals who sell furs, shoes, or hats.

The *Small Business Administration* plays an important role in providing financial assistance to small retailers. The SBA's basic purposes are to aid, counsel, assist, and protect the interests of small business concerns, including retailers.

The value of *sales analysis* cannot be overstated. Retailers who practice routine sales analysis are able to take advantage of changing trends in merchandising quickly.

All retailers are in business to serve customers by selling goods and services at a profit. Every retailer expects a certain *return on the investment*. The formula for calculating the rate of return on investment (ROI) is as follows:

$$ROI = \frac{\text{net profit}}{\text{investment}}$$

Some method should be used to determine the relationship between a store's fixed costs, variable costs, sales volume, and the effect on profits. A *break-even analysis* will show a retailer at what point a certain volume of sales will meet or cover the firm's total expenses (fixed and variable).

Given all the expenses, a break-even analysis is useful in determining the needed sales volume for a retail store. A break-even chart cannot tell management whether the store can generate a certain sales volume; it can only indicate how much is needed in sales at a stated profit margin before any profits accrue to the store.

REVIEW QUESTIONS

1 What is financial planning and control?
2 Why is sales analysis important for a retailer?
3 What is the importance of cost analysis to a retailer?
4 What is the role of an accountant in retailing management?
5 What financial institution is the largest single source of funds to retailers, and how has this come about?
6 Define trade credit.
7 What is factoring? What is a factor?
8 Why do some large retailers lease departments or areas in a store?
9 What is the purpose of the Small Business Administration?
10 How do you calculate the rate of return on investment (ROI)?
11 What is the purpose of a break-even analysis?

Chapter 19

Retail Merchandise Control Systems

Throughout this book, stress has been placed on the fact that management's primary responsibility is to satisfy the consumer while producing a satisfactory profit for the retail store. In order to fulfill this responsibility, management must utilize certain methods in satisfying the consumer and in producing a profit. Unless certain store activities are well coordinated and store problems readily solved, a satisfactory profit will not be obtained and very likely the customers' needs will not be fulfilled.

Two major problem areas must be closely watched and controlled by a store's management if customer satisfaction is to result and a profit is to be produced; they are: the store's inventory and the store's expenses. Special attention must be given to the control of these two main areas since only by proper control of inventory and expenses can a retail store ever expect to show a profit. Because of their importance, the next two chapters are devoted to merchandise control and expense control. This chapter covers the methods used in controlling the merchandise on hand, and in the next chapter, attention is given to the procedures used in controlling expenses.

BASIC PURPOSES OF RETAIL MERCHANDISE CONTROL

In essence, the basic purpose of any retail merchandise control system is to provide a balanced relationship between investment in inventory (merchandise on hand) and the fulfillment of the customers' wants (sale of merchandise).

Retail merchandise control systems vary in complexity from store to store according to the size of the store, the competitive environment, the type of merchandise handled, and the philosophy of the management. Like all the other elements in the retail business plan, a merchandise control system must be tailored to a specific store. However, all retail merchandise control systems have certain common characteristics that apply to all retail businesses.

Merchandise control systems are designed to aid management in providing precise information on the movement of goods. These data, in turn, aid the buyer in the performance of the purchasing functions and allow the retailer to determine whether certain goods should be moved out quickly (special sales) or should be kept as a part of the regular stock. Merchandise control systems also help to reduce the number of out-of-stock items and keep investments in slow-moving merchandise at a minimum. To summarize again, through the store's merchandise control system, a retailer must strive for a balanced relationship between the inventory and the store's primary function—that of satisfying the customers's needs. If this balanced relationship is not accomplished, the retailer has failed and should take corrective action immediately.

A proprietor of a relatively small retail business may control the store's inventory with little more than a checklist or by visual observation. However, as a retail business becomes larger or the number of items handled increases, it will be impossible to control inventory in this manner. It probably will be necessary to use some step-by-step procedure for determining the amount of the merchandise on hand—either by physically counting the number of units in stock at any given time, or by determining the dollar amount of the units on hand. As you will discover, the determination and the control of the amount of merchandise on hand becomes extremely important in producing a profit for the store, as well as satisfying the customers.

For most retailers, the amount of money invested in merchandise represents the largest single portion of the firm's total capital. On one hand, the goods in stock must be large enough in order to provide prospective customers with a large selection—hopefully resulting in a profitable sales volume. Yet the amount of merchandise, on the other hand, cannot be so large as to be excessive—thereby resulting in losses or excessive expenses for the store. There must be an inventory balance which can be profitably maintained by the retailer.

It is virtually impossible for any retail store to stock enough goods to satisfy the demand of every consumer or potential customer. Any retailer attempting to stock enough merchandise for the satisfaction of all customers would encounter a number of problems. Excessive inventory would result in an unusually large number of markdowns which the management would be forced to take in order to sell the goods profitably. Further, the handling expenses and the carrying charges on a large inventory would be extremely high. Therefore, in order to determine the amount and maintain the proper balance of merchandise in inventory, a retailer must carefully analyze both purchases and sales.

Analysis of Sales and Purchases

Both large and small retailers must analyze purchases and sales which will enable them to implement some form of inventory control. Some retailers may believe that they are able to control the goods on hand and related expenses without a merchandise control system and still maintain a proper balance between purchases and sales. But with the vast assortment of goods available in today's marketplace, this type of merchandise control is virtually impossible. As you have already noted, merchandise in inventory must be matched to the demand of the consumers, and this can be done only by a careful study of the needs and preferences of the store's customers.

Proper merchandise control will also minimize markdowns by closely watching the balance between stock on hand and the sales volume of the store. By analyzing the sales, a retailer is better able to determine the amount of stock that should be on hand to meet future customer demands. Having excessive stock on hand requires markdowns which become costly to a retailer and should be avoided if at all possible. It is inevitable that the store will have some markdowns; but if markdowns are necessary, they should be taken as quickly as possible. Why, you might ask? Financially, it is better for a retailer to take a small markdown at an early date (while the item is still in demand, in style, or unsoiled) than to have to take a larger markdown at a later date (possibly when there is no demand for the item, it is out of style, or it has been soiled by being on the shelf too long). If goods are marked down rather quickly in order to keep the inventory moving, a retailer has a better chance of making some profit on the items or at least may break even (no profit, no loss). If merchandise is kept too long, it ties up the retailer's money and increases the expenses associated with keeping those goods in stock. This, in turn, lessens the retailer's chance of getting his or her money back.

An adequate merchandise control system for a retail business will also help to control stock shortages by indicating areas of shrinkage through stock loss, whether by theft, spoilage, or breakage. Once the shortage problem areas have been determined, a retailer can then take corrective measures to prevent future shrinkages. (Controlling specific types of stock losses will be covered in more detail in the last chapter of this text.)

Inventory Control Methods

Through our discussion above, the need for control procedures has been established. Now we shall take a look at some of the specific control methods available to the retailer.

Merchandise control procedures may be implemented in two ways:

1　By using the dollar-control method (or retail method), which is based on the selling price to the customer of the goods on hand (rather than on the wholesaler's selling price to the retailer)

2　By utilizing the unit method where specific pieces of merchandise on hand are physically counted

Each method can be used independently, or both may be used by the same retailer in an attempt to maintain a balance between sales and consumer demand, thereby more effectively controlling the inventory.

THE RETAIL METHOD (DOLLAR CONTROL)

The retail method of inventory valuation is a system of estimating an ending inventory (for a certain period) and is widely used by chain stores, department stores, and other types of retail businesses.[1] The retail method of inventory valuation is based on the retail (selling) price of the merchandise. It serves as a means of arriving at the value or amount of ending goods on hand and the cost of goods sold *without* taking a physical count of each item in stock. It is much more convenient to take inventory at current retail prices than to: (1) look up the invoices to find the unit cost of each item in stock or (2) to determine the cost of the merchandise from the cost code on the price tag.

When using the retail method, the first step is to determine the value of the inventory at retail prices. Next, the retail price is converted to the cost price by applying the prevailing ratio between cost and retail (selling) price. This converting is done because the underlying basis of the retail method of inventory valuation is the percentage of markup for the merchandise (i.e., the ratio between cost and retail selling prices). If the retail method of inventory evaluation is used, the retailer must maintain the following records: (1) a complete listing of the beginning inventory and (2) a detailed listing of all purchases made during the period in terms of cost to the retailer and selling price to the consumer. Thus, the merchandise available for sale during this period can be stated at both cost and retail prices. This record will then give the retailer a base from which to figure the cost of goods sold as well as the amount of merchandise on hand. Since the retailer now has the total amount of goods that were available for sale, the next step in the retail method is to deduct the sales for the period from that figure. If you deduct the amount of the goods that were sold from the total value of the merchandise available for sale, you will then have the amount of the ending inventory at retail prices. This figure which would represent the ending inventory at retail price is then converted to a cost basis by using the percentage of cost to selling price for this period. The following illustration shows the calculation of inventory estimates by the retail method.

The retail method of inventory valuation is relatively economical in the sense that inventory can be determined when physical inventory counts are not feasible. The retail method, however, does not replace physical counts of goods on hand. Periodically, a physical count of inventory should be taken to check the validity of the retail method.

The retail method is widely used and is sponsored by the National Retail Dry Goods Association and accepted by the Internal Revenue Service.

The retail inventory method allows for more efficient management because operating results can be known for a department or a store without taking a physical inventory. Often it is also desirable to know the gross profit and other information concerning the operations of the store. The use of the retail method of inventory valuation provides a procedure whereby a retailer can reasonably

---

[1]Walter B. Meigs, A. N. Mosich, and Charles E. Johnson, *Accounting: The Basis for Business Decisions,* 3d ed., McGraw-Hill, New York, 1972.

	Cost price	Retail price
Beginning inventory	$40,000	$60,000
Net purchases during the month	23,900	30,000
Merchandise available for sale	63,900	$90,000
Less: Sales for the month	32,000	
Markdowns for the month	5,000	
Stock losses	3,000	
Total deductions		40,000
Ending inventory at retail price		$50,000
Cost ratio ($63,900 divided by $90,000)		71%
Ending inventory at cost (71 percent × $50,000)		$35,500

estimate at any time, the cost value of a closing inventory (i.e., at a given point in time) that is stated at retail value. This then will allow the retailer to determine the store's gross profit.

For instance, if a closing value of inventory at retail is $100,000, it is possible to determine through the retail method the retail book value of the inventory, the cost value of the inventory, the cost of the merchandise sold, and the gross profit. Each of these items can be calculated by using the following procedures shown in the outline below. The retail method of inventory evaluation has four basic steps:

1   The calculation of book value of the closing inventory at retail
2   The calculation of book value of the closing inventory at cost
3   The calculation of the cost of goods sold
4   The calculation of gross profit

The retail method has certain advantages which account for its use. In order to evaluate its usefulness, let us review some of the reasons for the growth of the retail method of accounting.

Advantages of the Retail Method

The overall difference between the two inventory control methods is that with the retail method, operating results can be known for a department or a store without taking physical inventory. As you might expect, this allows management to be more efficient because of the time and effort involved. Some of the advantages of this method are:

1   The operating results of a store or department can be quickly and easily determined.
2   Data are readily obtained which can be used for planning and control of sales, purchases, and inventory.
3   The value of the store's or the department's inventory can be determined.
4   Shortages in stock can be pinpointed.

5   This method can furnish a retailer with a basis for determining the value of any losses for any claims that may have to be made.

To a great extent, then, the retail inventory method of accounting provides a quick way for determining the operating results of a store or department. A store's profits depend upon the gross margin realized which, in turn, depends on the initial markup less any markdowns that have to be taken. Under the retail inventory method, this information is readily available, and it allows management the opportunity to adjust to changing market conditions. Operating statements can easily be prepared from the retail-inventory-method figures which can then be used to observe the profit trend for the store.

As we noted in the retail inventory method, profits are determined by the gross margins on goods sold. By using the retail method, a store's management will be able to spot any downward trend in profits, thereby quickly instituting remedial action (such as reducing expenses in some area).

The retail method also provides information which can be used as the basis for planning and control of sales, stocks, and purchases. When prices are rising or changing rapidly, planning of sales and purchases is highly desirable. Several departments or an entire store may be forced to reflect these changes in prices rather quickly in order to remain competitive. Further, consumer demand can be met more quickly when data are available on sales, stocks, and purchases. Thus, the use of the retail inventory method aids management by giving it the type of information it needs so that it can make satisfactory business decisions.

The retail inventory method also facilitates the comparison of past periods with current results. Future plans for such things as sales promotions, can be directed toward current operating facts. Thus, slower moving merchandise can be pinpointed so that the retailer can reduce the number and amount of markdowns that may be needed to move the goods.

Another advantage of the retail method is that it enables the retailer to determine the total value of the store's inventory. This value can be determined either on the basis of cost or market, whichever is lower. Determining the dollar value in this way prevents the overstatement and inflation of profits for a department or an entire store. When merchandise is valued at the lower of these two figures (cost or market), the cost of goods sold is increased over the amount it would have been if the higher of these two figures had been used. Thus, the greater the cost of goods sold, the lower the gross profit figure, thereby giving the retailer a more accurate inventory value.

The retail inventory method also allows a retailer to determine any shortages in stock more readily. Shortages can be noted by comparing the calculated book inventory with a physical retail inventory. Once the amount of stock shrinkage has been discovered, a retailer can take the necessary precautions or measures to stop or reduce merchandise losses. In a later chapter, special procedures which the retailer can use for the control of stock shortages will be covered in detail.

In the case of unusual losses, such as fire or theft, the retail inventory method furnishes a retailer with a basis for determining the amount of loss and the claim adjustment for insurance coverage. The book value of the goods on hand prior to the loss serves as a valuable aid in determining the amount of the actual loss. The insurance claim can then be adjusted to this value to compensate the retailer for any loss of merchandise.

Disadvantages of the Retail Inventory Method

Although the retail method of accounting is widely used, it does have some limitations. Some retailers consider these disadvantages so overwhelming that they avoid its use entirely.

The retail method of accounting requires an elaborate record-keeping system. Each invoice must be marked with the retail price of each item, and any price changes must be reflected and recorded accurately. Otherwise, the totals and values of the book values, the cost of goods sold, and the gross profit will not be correct. Many retailers find the detailed price records difficult to keep up to date so that they *accurately* reflect the correct inventory values. This point underscores once again the need for a good accounting system.

When using the retail inventory method, the total cost of goods handled and their total retail value are averaged to obtain the cost percentage. As we have noted previously, merchandise of different types and kinds will carry varying markups. Generally, goods which carry a low markup sell more rapidly than goods with a high markup. Thus, by using the retail inventory method, the goods with lower markups tend to be represented to a greater degree than they are in actuality. To a store or a department having wide variations in markups on different kinds of merchandise, this may prove to be a disadvantage. The cost value of inventory may be overstated, although this fact may not be significant to some retailers. If the movement of merchandise is approximately the same for all kinds of goods, then little overstating of value of inventory will occur.

The retail method of accounting may not be suitable for all departments or for all stores, depending upon the type of business and the kind of goods handled. For instance, the retail method cannot be used for retail service stores, such as beauty shops, barber shops, bakeries, prescription departments of drugstores, restaurants, optometry departments, and travel booths. Any retail institution which deals primarily in customer services cannot effectively use the retail inventory accounting method. Also, departments or stores that produce goods (such as draperies or furniture) need to operate on a cost, rather than on a retail basis.

For some departments or stores, the retail method may be costly to operate. There are numerous records to maintain, which can be expensive. The expenses associated with these records should be more than offset by the benefits derived from the system; if they are not, the retailer should seriously consider using another method of inventory control. Even though the retail method requires considerable record keeping and may be expensive to operate, the information gathered and furnished by the system may be worth more to a retailer than the cost of maintaining such a system. This is probably the main reason why many retailers continue to use the retail method of accounting.

COST METHOD OF INVENTORY CONTROL

For those retailers who do not utilize the retail method of accounting, an alternative is the cost method. Under the cost method, goods are marked at the retail price on the price tag and in the accounting records, but the *cost* of each item is also coded and placed on the sales tag and in the accounting records. Thus, the cost code is placed in the accounting records as well as on the price tag. When we talk in terms of cost coding, what do we actually mean? What sort of cost code can be used? Retailers may use many different codes, or combinations thereof, to mark the cost of the merchandise. Usually the retailer using a cost code will devise a code which is known only to the person responsible for price marking the merchandise. The coding system should be kept a secret from the consuming public if it is to be effective.

For example, the use of any word or phrase consisting of ten letters, none of which is repeated, will prove effective in coding the cost of the merchandise. Each letter in the word or phrase represents a number from zero to nine. Below is an example of a word which can be used to code the cost of goods for a retailer.

0 1 2 3 4 5 6 7 8 9
C O S T M A R K E D

By using the above code, any item marked ODDA would have cost $19.95. A retailer can use any ten-letter word or phrase for coding. But, as you can see, no letter may appear more than once or it will invalidate the code. Here is another example:

0 1 2 3 4 5 6 7 8 9
R E G U L A T I O N

By using this code, an item marked RRUA would have cost the retailer 35 cents.

In order to determine the cost of the inventory or the merchandise on hand, a retailer must physically count the goods and make a list of the price-tag information on each tag. The cost is then decoded or determined from the code letters marked on the price tags. As you can imagine, cost decoding can be time consuming, and there is always the possibility of error in the decoding process because each item must be individually counted, listed, and its cost decoded. Then extensions must be made on the ledger and the totals calculated. As you can see, the use of the cost method involves quite a number of steps, whereby using the previously covered retail method, only the total retail selling prices of the goods need to be determined. Thus, it eliminates the physical handling of the goods, as well as the cost coding and decoding.

However, some small retailers generally favor the cost method over the retail method of valuation because they are accustomed to thinking in terms of merchandise-cost figures rather than in terms of retail prices. Confusion can result when a retailer is forced to think in terms of retail prices as under the retail method. The retail method may also lead to mistakes if the store has used the cost method in the past.

UNIT-CONTROL METHOD

Whereas the retail method of accounting is used by many medium- to large-scale retailers and the cost method is used by some smaller retailers, there is yet another system that can be utilized which is called "unit control." The unit-control system is used by various retailers for improving managerial efficiency.

The major difference between unit control and the retail or sales-dollar control is the following: the recording of the merchandise on hand is done in *units* instead of *dollars*. For example, if a retailer is using the unit-control method, instead of stating that the store had sales of $10,000 on a particular item, a retailer would report that 1,000 units were sold (each unit being priced at $10). Thus, the unit-control system—accounting for each unit or item on hand—is particularly valuable as a supplement to the retail method in a number of ways.

By using a unit-control system, for instance, vendor information can be included within the control system where it is easily available to the retailer. Such information as the salability (whether the merchandise sells or does not sell), the number of returns (in terms of units), effective delivery dates by the vendor, and the number of markdowns in terms of units, are readily available from a unit-control system. This information may be placed on the price tag as well as in the regular accounting records (see Figure 19-1). The unit-control method lends itself to computerization since all relevant information can be coded in a data processing system where it is readily available to the retailer. Salespeople can more easily count shelf merchandise in units—rather than dollars—for more accurate inventory reporting. The unit-control system quickly reveals shortages if the number of units do not total the number in the records. Thus, precautions may be taken immediately to curtail any shortages, whether by theft, shrinkage, breakage, or any other cause.

By using unit inventory control rather than the retail method, a retailer is better able to spot which goods are moving more slowly. Thus, markdowns can be taken more quickly, hopefully resulting in greater profits for the store. Other data—such as out-of-stock conditions, reorder points (the level of stock at which reordering takes place), and sales promotions—can also be determined more rapidly when a store operates under a unit-control system. Once a model-stock plan has been determined by the retailer, it is easy to determine at what inventory levels or reorder points staple goods will have to be replaced.

As you can see, dealing with a number of units is more workable in a number of ways than dealing in dollar amounts. For the successful operation of a unit-control system, basically, a card or a page in an accounting book or ledger is required for each item in a store's inventory. This card or page, in turn, should indicate the total number of units on hand, the number of units that have been ordered, and the number of units on hand at the end of each business day.

The unit-control system of inventory accounting is a major tool of efficient

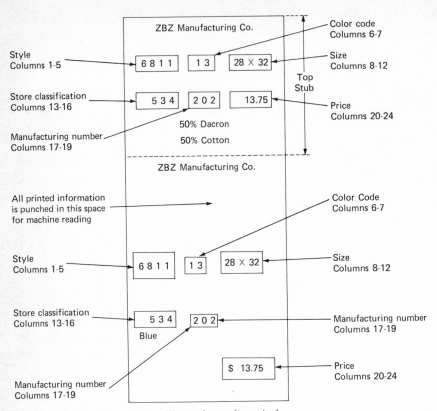

Figure 19-1 Sample price tag illustrating unit control.

retail managers. It provides precise information on the movement of merchandise and eliminates much of the guesswork on the amount of merchandise in stock. By providing current information on the movement of goods, the unit-control system aids the buyer in determining how many items need to be purchased (as well as what kind, style, and color) and when they should be delivered. This assistance to the buyer through the unit-control method helps a store avoid the losses due to out-of-stock items and lessens the likelihood of investing in slower moving goods.

Even with all the advantages noted above, the unit-control system does suffer from some limitations. As a store needs more information on each item (such as sales returns, purchase data, size, and color) or as a store increases the number of goods in stock, the unit-control system requires more cards or pages in a book. This increases the complexity of the control system and, in turn, the cost of operating such a system goes up. In summation, it should probably be noted that it is to the retailer's advantage that *no one system* be used exclusively—whether the retail accounting method, the cost method, or the unit-control method. From the previous discussions, it probably would be best for the retailer to integrate and/or coordinate a dollar method and a unit-control system. By using a combination of both a dollar and a unit-control system, a retailer may improve the efficiency of the store.

EFFECTS OF MERCHANDISE CONTROL ON PROFITS

One of the most important characteristics of any merchandise control system is its ultimate effect on the profits of a retail store. As we have learned, the amount of goods on hand is a basic necessity in the operation of a retail store. Without adequate stock in inventory, a retailer will not be able to compete effectively with other retailers offering a wide variety of merchandise and will not be able to satisfy the customer. Yet too much stock on hand will place a burden on the store's profits. Thus, a retailer must maintain a delicate balance between the two, which takes a certain amount of skill and experience. But an effective inventory control system can do a great deal toward helping the retailer achieve this balance.

Whether based on retail prices, cost data, units, or dollars, an effective merchandise control system should provide a retailer with enough information so that: (1) sales may be controlled, (2) the amount of goods on hand is sufficient, and (3) purchases can be regulated to consumer demand. Also, a merchandise control system should provide the retailer with adequate data so that adjustments within a department or in a store can be made quickly in order to meet changing market conditions. Sales, goods in stock, and purchases must be adjusted to current consumer demand, or the retailer will suffer a loss. A good merchandise control system can be a big help.

An adequate control system will also provide a retailer with enough information on past results from the entire store or from different departments so that a comparison can be made with the current sales. This comparison can then be used in making future decisions regarding purchases and inventory. Further, decisions concerning regular or special sales promotions can be based on current operating information from a merchandise control system. Slow-selling and fast-selling merchandise is quickly spotted through the use of adequate merchandise control systems. Thus, corrective measures can be taken rapidly to adjust the inventory accordingly. As stated above, the merchandise control system plays an important part in a store's profit picture, and it can either enhance that picture or—if not properly administered—detract from it.

RATE OF INVENTORY TURNOVER (RITO)

Another inventory measuring device that should be utilized is called the Rate of Inventory Turnover (RITO). The rate of inventory turnover or RITO is the relationship of retail sales to inventory. RITO indicates how rapidly sales are being made when compared to the inventory on hand. The RITO is usually stated in numerical figures (such as 2, 4, 6, etc.) for a period of one year.

For example, the rate of inventory turnover can be computed by dividing a store's net sales by the retail value of the average inventory (beginning and ending inventory divided by two). However, it also may be computed by dividing the average inventory at cost into the cost of goods sold. Say that a store's net sales for one year are $100,000. The retail value of the average stock is $25,000. Then the rate of inventory turnover (RITO) is 4 ($100,000 divided by $25,000).

As we previously discussed, inventory should be planned and coordinated with sales. Too little inventory on hand will result in a poor sales volume, whereas too much inventory involves the unnecessary investment of capital which might be more profitably invested elsewhere. Also, excessive inventory may result in a retailer having to borrow too much money. Since the money spent for merchandise is the largest single investment for many retailers, considerable attention should be devoted to a balanced amount of stock on hand as well as its turnover. But how does a retailer know how fast the inventory should be turning over? For each general type of retail business, there is available an "average" or median rate of RITO with which a retailer can compare the store's RITO. In theory, these so-called optimum rates would result in maximum profits for that type of store.

Inventory Turnover Rates by Type of Business

The nature or type of retail business will determine to a large degree the frequency of inventory turnover or, as some accountants prefer to call it, the rate of "stockturn." As you will remember from an earlier chapter, the nature or type of retail business is classified according to the kinds of merchandise sold. Thus, it is logical to assume that certain types of merchandise will sell more frequently (turnover) than other types of goods. The greater the frequency of purchase, the

Table 19-1   Percentage of Sales by Department and Number of Stockturns by Department (mass merchandise store)

	Percentage of total sales	Number of stockturns (annual)
Women's apparel	10.60	4.49
Women's accessories	4.82	3.54
Men's wear	8.34	3.53
Children's wear	7.70	3.42
Shoes	4.36	2.09
Household textiles	6.71	2.83
Hardware and housewares	14.33	3.09
Toys	4.69	3.63
Radio, television, appliances	7.95	3.06
Furniture and home furnishings	2.72	2.96
Recreational items	10.17	2.91
Health and beauty aids	7.78	3.77
All other departments	9.80	5.19

Source: "Operating Results of Self-Service Discount Department Stores," Mass Retailing Institute, New York, 1973–74, pp. 71–72.

higher the rate of inventory turnover—other factors being equal. As you can see from Table 19-1, the rate of stockturn of different types of merchandise varies considerably. For instance, women's apparel tends to be purchased more frequently than furniture or shoes—thus resulting in a higher rate of stockturn. Usually, the general level of the RITO will depend on the type of merchandise sold or the type of service(s) offered. This is clearly illustrated by the figures in Table 19-2 which show the rates of inventory turnover for a variety of small retail businesses. A retailer can use these comparative RITO figures in helping to determine the amount of inventory a store should carry and in planning total inventory purchases.

Variations in the rate of inventory turnover (RITO) also occur for other reasons. For example, the location of a retail store may influence the rate of stockturn. Usually, retail stores located in a planned regional shopping center where there is a high rate of customer traffic should have a higher RITO than the same types of stores located in a small, Midwestern rural community.

Table 19-2   Average Rates of Inventory Turnover (RITO) in Selected Retail Stores, 1973 (gross sales volume $50,000 to $100,000)

Kind of retail business	Annual RITO
Combination food stores	10.14
Specialty food stores	10.80
Meat markets	3.77
Confectionery stores	10.80
Retail bakeries	12.94
Men's & women's apparel stores	1.99
Women's specialty shops	2.38
Men's specialty shops	2.21
Children's & infants' shops	4.26
Shoe stores	1.85
Furniture stores	3.36
Appliance stores	2.82
Drugstores	2.79
Liquor stores	4.52
Restaurants	28.09
Cocktail lounges	8.09
Variety stores	3.50
Jewelry stores	1.70
Florists	22.60
Gift and novelty stores	2.30
Photographic supply stores	2.80
Sporting goods stores	3.70
Automotive group stores	3.60
Service stations	16.21
Garages and auto repair shops	6.30

Source: Yearbook, 1973, "Barometer of Small Business," Accounting Corporation of America, San Diego, CA 92101, 1974, pp. 96–102.

Too, the philosophy of the store's management may increase or decrease the RITO in a store in several ways: For instance, if the store's management maintains a selective buying policy, several things will happen. A selective buying policy will eliminate the slower moving items. By carefully selecting certain price lines of merchandise and by excluding those price lines which have little—if any—differentiation, the RITO will be increased. Also, if management can attain a proper balance between styles, sizes, and colors; this will also improve the RITO. The retail store's management can also increase or decrease sales by altering the retail sales promotional program and thus affect the rate of inventory turnover.

What is significant about each of these variables is the fact that all are directly under the control of management. Each of these factors, directly or indirectly, will affect the rate of inventory turnover. Thus, it becomes apparent that through careful retail planning and coordination, a retailer can increase the efficiency of the store. Management's attitude and philosophy cannot be overlooked since these beliefs and ideas will be reflected in all aspects of the business.

Importance of Inventory Turnover

As already stressed, the store's inventory often represents the retailer's largest single expenditure—apart from ownership in land and buildings. Since a retailer's profits come from the sale of that inventory, the retailer's return on investment (ROI) will depend to a large extent on how well inventory investment is managed. Hence, the ROI or return on investment is a good yardstick with which to measure just how well the retailer is doing. Thus, the RITO—or number of times the average inventory turns over during a period (usually a year)—is a measure of managerial efficiency. (It should be noted, though, that some retailers determine their RITO quarterly or semiannually rather than annually.)

As emphasized before, a retailer's prime function is to stock the right goods, at the right price, and at the right time, for the store's customers. Since a retailer's managerial efficiency can be measured by how well these objectives are accomplished, considerable attention should be devoted to the rate of inventory turnover (RITO). A retailer capable of generating a large sales volume on a small investment in inventory probably can be considered to be efficient assuming that sales enhance net profits. Thus, a rapid RITO is highly desirable. However, the student should keep in mind that a rapid RITO is not any more important than any other element in the retailing mix—that is, the merchandise, pricing, promotion, and store location.

Advantages of High RITO

Four distinct advantages result from a rapid rate of inventory turnover: (1) a reduction in the number of markdowns, (2) a reduction in the retailing expenses associated with inventory interest costs, insurance, taxes, and space, (3) an increased sales volume by being able to offer new merchandise more frequently, and (4) an increased return on the owner's investment in merchandise (ROI).

A relationship between the rate of inventory turnover and the percentage of markdowns taken by a store does exist. Overall, large retail stores enjoy fewer markdowns (as a percentage of sales) than do small stores. This may be due, in part, to more efficient purchasing methods on the part of well-trained buyers. However, more likely, these reduced numbers of markdowns are due to improved selection of goods, judicious pricing, and well-planned promotions. An increase in the RITO is usually accompanied by a decrease in markdowns— although a direct, one-to-one relationship may not always exist.

Increased rates of inventory turnover may reduce the expenses associated with inventory interest charges, insurance, taxes, and space. If a retailer is able to reduce the amount of money invested in stock without adversely affecting sales, it logically follows that merchandise interest charges are reduced. The premiums for insurance coverage will also be lowered, inventory taxes will go down, and less storage space will be needed for the goods on hand. If a retailer has to borrow money with which to purchase merchandise (which many retailers do), it is reasonable to assume that the less money borrowed, the lower the interest charges. The same can be concluded for insurance coverage and inventory taxes. As for space requirements, an increased RITO may also reduce the amount of storage space needed for the merchandise. An increased RITO may also lessen the amount of space needed within the store for selling the goods. The released space may then be allocated to the sale of additional goods or put to use in some other way. For the store as a whole, there is no reduction in space charges because the rent for the building continues whether the store is fully occupied or only partially filled with goods. But for a department store, space released in one department may be allocated to another department or leased.

A faster rate of inventory turnover often leads to increased sales because a retailer is balancing the store's inventory to customer demand. In turn, this may lead to a better assortment of goods, styles, colors, and sizes, which then may increase consumer interest and stimulate sales. A higher rate of inventory turnover will also allow the merchant an opportunity to purchase fresh merchandise more frequently, giving the store's customers a greater variety of different goods at more frequent intervals. With more frequent purchases by the customer, a retailer is able to replace sold merchandise with new goods more quickly, which indicates that the RITO tends to be self-perpetuating.

A more rapid rate of inventory turnover will also increase the return on investment (ROI) for the owner(s). It is the goal of every retailer to increase not only the percentage of return on investment, but also to increase total dollar profits. In fact, it is the dollar profits rather than the percentage of return on investment about which a retailer is concerned. For example, a retailer may have a high percentage of ROI if the investment is small, but this also means small dollar profits. Or it is possible for a retailer to have a smaller percentage of return on investment on a large dollar amount invested, but the total dollar amount of profit could be quite large. In order to develop, grow, and remain successful, a retailer must be able to show a satisfactory rate of return on investment. Both the return on investment (stated in percentages) and the actual dollar amount of profits, are important in measuring and analyzing a retail store's efficiency. Since managerial efficiency is measured to some degree by the percentage of the return on investment and the actual dollar profits, shortly we will look at some of the methods by which inventory turnover rates can be increased.

Disadvantages of a High Turnover Rate

Although it is usually advantageous to increase the RITO, always remember that there is a limit as to what can be accomplished. If the RITO is increased beyond a certain point, some retailing activities will suffer because it is uneconomical to perform them. For instance, if the RITO is too high, unusually heavy expenses in receiving, checking, and marking merchandise could result. But if a retail store is suffering from a low rate of inventory turnover and a resulting poor sales volume, some steps must be taken in order to increase the RITO and the sales volume.

Sales may be increased up to a given point since the costs incurred in increasing the sales will be less than the gross profit. Beyond this point, the costs associated with increasing sales will be more than the gross profit derived from the increase in sales. Thus, it would not be wise for a retailer to keep increasing sales indefinitely since the result may be a loss in profit. But in order to increase the RITO, sales must be increased, and inventory must be reduced.

Methods to Increase Turnover Rates

As an indicator of managerial efficiency with respect to the capital invested in merchandise, it is highly desirable for a retailer to increase the rate of inventory turnover (RITO). One way to increase retail sales for a store is to be sure that sales promotion is more properly attuned to the seasonality of the merchandise. Effective use of sales promotion with respect to seasonality reduces the possibility of carryover merchandise. A study and appraisal of current market conditions, customer buying habits and patterns, and competition will ultimately lead a retailer to a more effective utilization of sales promotion.

Another method which can be used for increasing sales is to provide thorough instruction and training for salespeople—whether they have been with the store for a long time or whether they are new employees. Salespersons should be trained or retrained in effective sales techniques, product knowledge, suggestion or "plus" selling, and effective listening. Sometimes a store loses sales because of improper selling techniques and/or poor attitudes on the part of the sales personnel.

Retail store buyers should also be instructed to be more cautious about the appropriate selection and timing of purchases with the selling season. If purchases are timed appropriately through the use of effective sales promotion, these goods will sell readily with few markdowns. Too, if there is any shopworn merchandise left after the sales-promotion event is over, prompt removal of these goods is in order.

However, each of the above merchandising tactics for increasing sales volume should be used with some discretion. For instance, if salespeople oversell the sale merchandise, the regular stock may suffer from lack of sales. This could lead to lower profits for the retailer because, in many instances, sale goods have been marked down and their gross margins are less than those carried on the regular stock.

A retail store's pricing policy should also reflect good judgment on any sale merchandise. Markdowns have to be properly timed, that is, taken only after it has been determined that retention of the goods would be a detriment to the store. Especially depending on the type of store, some customers will wait until sales events are held before committing themselves to purchases. This consumer habit could lead to lower profits for the retailer since in order to optimize store profits, the timing of markdowns is crucial.

Another method of raising the RITO is to decrease the amount of merchandise carried in inventory *without* decreasing sales. As you might imagine, this procedure is very touchy and should be approached with caution. But it is possible to go through the inventory carefully, taking out some items, sizes, or colors, without affecting sales. In fact, a periodic close check of merchandise on hand and a subsequent cleaning out of some items should be done anyway by all retailers. During times of economic turndowns, it also may be wise to reduce a store's inventory. Rather than try to increase sales during poor economic times, it may be more prudent for a retailer to reduce the store's inventory, which cuts down on expenses and which, in turn, may help the profit picture.

Reducing inventory may lead a retailer to "hand-to-mouth" buying practices. Generally, this is not a desirable situation because, in too many instances, the store may be out of stock on items requested by the customers. In today's market, most customers will not tolerate out-of-stock conditions but will simply go to the next retail store where the merchandise is available. Any reduction in inventory should be carefully planned before any action is taken. At times, it is necessary to "prune" certain items from the stock so that the store may offer "fresh" goods. But during times of economic prosperity, it is probably wiser to increase sales rather than to reduce stock in order to increase the rate of inventory turnover.

Summary of RITO

As we have just seen, there is a relationship between the ratio of inventory turnover and profits; and usually, a retailer can enhance profits by increasing the RITO. The rate of inventory turnover, to a point, reflects managerial efficiency. The method, or methods, which a retailer uses to increase the RITO will determine whether or not profits will also increase. Even though sales are held constant, profits may not increase due to a decrease in inventory. This problem occurs because sales become more difficult to make when the inventory is reduced and customers shop elsewhere. Generally, customers will patronize retailers whose stores offer the greatest selection and assortment of merchandise.

Through effective retail management, it is more likely that sales will be increased while the inventory remains stable. The rate of inventory turnover is the *end result* of the efficiency of the retail store's management. Thus, the retailer really seeks increased profits rather than an increase in the rate of stockturn. Often the goal of increased profits leads a retailer to steps which do accelerate the RITO. But rather than being obsessed with the RITO, a retailer should concentrate on such matters as selective buying, wise pricing, well-balanced stock, effective advertising, properly timed sales promotions, and adequately trained salespersons. If this is done, the rate of inventory turnover will take care of itself. Good merchandising management will lead to a satisfactory stock turnover and to increased profits for a retail store.

SUMMARY

The basic purpose of any retail merchandise control system is to provide a *balanced relationship* between investment in inventory and the sale of merchandise. Merchandise control systems are designed to aid management in providing precise information on the movement of merchandise. These data, in turn, aid the buyer in the performance of the buying functions of the store.

For most retailers, the amount of money invested in merchandise represents the largest single portion of the store's total capital. The *merchandise in stock* must be large enough to meet customer demand, yet cannot be so large as to constitute excessive investment.

All retailers should analyze purchases and sales which will enable them to implement some form of *inventory control*. Proper merchandise control will minimize markdowns by maintaining a close watch of the stock on hand and the sales for the store. An adequate merchandise control system for a retail business will aid in controlling merchandise shortages by indicating areas of shrinkage.

The *retail method* of inventory valuation is a system of estimating an ending inventory for a certain period. The retail method of inventory valuation is based on the retail or selling price of the merchandise. This method serves as a means of arriving at the value or amount of ending goods on hand and the cost of goods sold without taking a physical count of each item in stock.

When using the retail method, the first step is to determine the value of the inventory at retail prices. Next, the retail price is converted to the cost price by applying the prevailing ratio between the cost and the retail or selling price. The prevailing ratio between cost and selling price is the percentage of markup.

The retail method of inventory valuation leads a store to the following benefits:

1   The operating results of a store or a department can be quickly and easily determined.
2   Data are readily obtained which can be used for planning and control of sales, purchases, and inventory.
3   The value of a store's or a department's inventory can be determined.
4   Shortages in merchandise can be easily pinpointed.
5   The retail method can furnish a retailer with a basis for determining the value of any losses for any claims that may have to be made from any type of loss.

One major limitation of the retail method lies in the maintenance of an elaborate record-keeping system. Each invoice must be marked with the retail price of each item, and any price changes must be reflected and recorded accurately.

For those retailers who do not use the retail method of accounting, an alternative is the *cost method*. Under the cost method, goods are marked at the retail price on the price tag and in the accounting records, but the cost of each item is coded and placed on the sales tags and in the accounting records. In order to determine the cost of the inventory or the merchandise on hand, a retailer must physically count the goods, and make a list of the price tag information on each tag. Cost decoding can be a time-consuming job, and there is always the possibility of errors from the decoding process.

Whereas some retailers prefer the retail method and others use the cost method, still other retailers make use of the *unit-control system*. When use is made of the unit-control system, the recording of the merchandise on hand is done in units instead of dollars. By using a unit-control system, a retailer can make use of vendor information. This system may aid the retailer in reducing the number of returns, reducing the number of markdowns, and revealing the rate of merchandise movement.

The *rate of inventory turnover (RITO)* is the relationship of retail sales to inventory. The rate of inventory turnover indicates how rapidly sales are being made when compared to the inventory on hand. The RITO is usually stated in numbers for a year.

The nature of the retail business will determine to a large degree the frequency of inventory turnover. Certain types of merchandise sell more frequently than other types of goods.

Since a retailer's profits come from the sale of merchandise, a retailer's *return on investment (ROI)* will depend to a large degree on how well inventory is managed and how many times it turns each year. The ROI is a good yardstick by which the efficiency of management can be measured.

A *high rate of inventory turnover* leads to a reduction in the number of markdowns, a reduction in retailing expenses associated with inventory costs, insurance, taxes, and space, an increase in sales volume, and an increase in the ROI.

The rate of inventory turnover can be increased by coordinating sales events with the proper buying season. The timing of purchases may also lead to an increased RITO. However, the RITO may become an obsession with some retailers, and it may be wiser for a retailer to concentrate on selective buying, judicious pricing, maintaining a well-balanced inventory, making use of effective advertising, and training employees properly. If these duties are performed satisfactorily, the rate of inventory turnover will take care of itself.

REVIEW QUESTIONS

1 What are the basic purposes of any retail merchandise control system?
2 Why must retailers analyze purchases and sales?
3 Name some of the benefits derived from an adequate merchandise control system.
4 What is the basis of the retail method of inventory valuation?
5 What are the benefits of using the retail method of inventory valuation?
6 What are the limitations of using the retail method of inventory valuation?

7   How does the cost method of inventory control work?
8   What are the benefits of using the cost method of inventory control? What are the limitations of this system?
9   Describe the unit-control method of inventory control.
10 Explain the rate of inventory turnover and how it may affect the profits of a store.
11 Discuss the various rates of stockturn for varying types of merchandise.
12 Discuss the importance of emphasizing the rate of stockturn.
13 List several methods by which the rate of inventory turnover may be increased.
14 Why should retailers not be obsessed with the rate of stockturn?

Chapter 20

Expense Control and Analysis

As emphasized in the last chapter, control procedures are extremely important to the retailer. The use of control methods is a necessity if the retailer expects to make a profit and satisfy the customers. Although the control of inventory more directly affects the customer by altering the selection and variety of goods, the control of expenses tends to have a direct effect on the internal operation of the store. Of course, the two are related, but each is different enough to be treated separately.

As a first step in controlling expenses, several things should be done. In order to see what progress has been made toward the objectives set forth in the retail business plan, an analysis of operating expenses incurred must be made by the store's management. By doing this, the retailer will be able to determine not only the dollar amount of expenses but also their classification. The retailer needs to know the dollar amounts for operational purposes, but the classification of expenses is also essential so that the retailer can determine which expenditures should be modified or controlled. Whether expenses should be reduced or increased will depend on the results expected, as outlined in the retail business plan.

As was true with inventory control, expense control and analysis is necessary for reasonable profits. Of course, specific expenses will vary considerably by the type of business (such as self-service or full-service store) and will be affected by other factors (size of store, location of business, or assortment of merchandise). Thus, expense control and analysis should utilize methods by which certain types of expenses can be controlled and/or reduced.

As with most aspects of a retail business, the expenses associated with the operation of a retail store are under the control of management. As with inventory control, a store's managerial ability may, in effect, be measured by how well expenses are controlled. Why is this so? The reduction or the increase of certain expenses will reflect favorably, or unfavorably, on the store's profits as does the store's inventory. For instance, advertising expenses should perhaps be increased in order to enhance the profit of the store. Or it may be more desirable to reduce payroll expenses, since salaries (and/or commissions) is one of the largest single expenses for many retailers.

However, whether expenses should be reduced or increased will depend on what goals have been set by management. Again, management skill and judgment are required to achieve the balance that is needed between the income (sales) and the various retail store expenses. Depending on market conditions, there may be a point where an expense reduction or increase is not justified. Market conditions change, though; and it is the expense controls under these changing market conditions which we wish to pursue.

CLASSIFICATION OF EXPENSES

In order to maintain proper control and allow the retailer to be able to analyze expenses critically, retail store expenses should be classified uniformly. The National Retail Merchants Association suggests the following expense classification, which is referred to as the "Natural Classification."[1]

1 Payroll
2 Fringe benefits
3 Advertising
4 Taxes
5 Supplies
6 Services purchased
7 Unclassified
8 Traveling
9 Communications
10 Pensions
11 Insurance
12 Depreciation
13 Professional services
14 Donations
15 Bad debts

[1]*Retail Accounting Manual,* National Retail Merchants Association, Controllers' Congress, New York, 1962, pp. iii–1.

16   Equipment costs
17   Real property

The above is only one of many ways in which to classify retail store expenses. Therefore, it is desirable for the retailer to tailor the classification scheme to fit the individual store, or the store's accountant may suggest a classification scheme that fits the particular type of business. Of course, by using a similar classification as that above, a retailer may be able to compare the expenses of his or her store with the expenses of a similar store, an industry average, or with a prior period of operation for the same store. In making expense comparisons, however, it is important that *like* or similar expenses be compared; otherwise, you may not get a true picture or comparison of the relationship of the various expenses for the store.

EXPENSE ALLOCATION

After retail store expenses have been classified for each individual store, the next step is to allocate these expenses in terms of dollars and cents. Allocation of expenses means to assign the amount of money that can be used for expenses to areas within a small store, to the selling departments within a larger store, to the branch stores, or to all stores within a chain. This allocation of expenses will then, at a future point in time, allow management to check and analyze the effectiveness of an area, a department, a branch store, or an individual store within a chain organization.

In order to further facilitate the distribution of expenses, the cost items should be placed into one of two broad classifications: direct expenses or indirect expenses. Direct expenses are those that are attributable to a specific function within an area or a department. The salaries of the sales personnel, for example, are considered to be direct expenses of a specific department since they would not exist if the department were closed. Indirect expenses, on the other hand, are all other expenses which are not directly attributable to a specific department or function within that store. In this case, indirect expenses would include such items as rent, office overhead, insurance, and taxes—expenses that continue to be incurred even though the department was removed or closed. These two broad classifications are very important, though, since certain types of direct expenses are more easily controlled than many of the indirect expenses. This one fact becomes even more important, as you will see, since the net profit for a department or a store is determined by taking the total expenses and subtracting this figure from the gross-margin figure. Because of the difference between direct and indirect expenses and their effect on net profit, some controversy has developed among retailers regarding the amount of expenses and the manner in which these expenses should be charged—to a store, a branch, or to a department within a store. As a result of this controversy, three methods of allocating expenses for retail stores have evolved, namely, (1) the net-profit method, (2) the contribution method, and (3) the combination method. Since each method has both strong and weak points, let us devote our attention to each.

Net-Profit Method

The net-profit method of expense allocation requires that all expenses—both direct and indirect—be divided among the various areas of a small store or among the departments of a large store so that net profit can be readily determined for each area or department. Direct expenses are distributed to the selling areas or selling departments which are responsible for them; but indirect expenses are allocated to the areas or departments based on some predetermined formula. Rent, for instance, may be allocated to a department on the basis of the total square footage of selling area. Or other store expenses, such as collection costs, general management salaries, insurance, and taxes, may be apportioned to each area or department on the basis of net sales coming from that department or area. For example, as we stated, the net-profit figure depends on how the expenses for an area or a department are distributed or allocated. Let us assume the following for the television appliance department of a large department store.

Gross margin		$250,000
Direct expenses:		
Salary of the buyer	$25,000	
Sales persons' salaries	45,000	
Travel expenses for buyer	3,000	
Departmental supplies	1,000	
Advertising and sales promotion	12,000	
Total direct expenses	$86,000	
Total indirect expenses allocated to the department	74,000	
Total expenses		160,000
Net profit		$ 90,000

By using the net-profit method illustrated above, note that no particular difficulty is encountered in allocating the direct expenses which are derived from that department. For instance, the buyer's salary and the salaries of salespersons are a direct expense since their full-time duties are directly related to that department.

However, the indirect expenses allocated to the department as in the illustration above, will cause some controversy and friction. Many department heads and buyers heatedly disagree with management's arbitrary allocation of a store's *general* expenses to their department. If possible, some equitable basis for allocating departmental indirect expenses should be established *before* the expenses are allocated. Almost any type of distribution of departmental expenses will meet with some disapproval by someone. However, the store's management should try to choose an equitable plan that will at least attempt to satisfy the largest number of department heads.

Herein lies the major weakness of the net-profit method. When viewed from management's position, the net-profit method of expense allocation does not seem inequitable. Why you may ask? When a store is envisioned as a total operating system, each department is seen as a subsystem. Since each department (or subsystem) contributes a portion toward the total store effort (income), each area must also share in the expenses incurred by the total system (the store). Basically, management is paid to carry out the function of distributing expenses equally and treating each subsystem fairly in the total store system. Thus, the net-profit method is only one way in which to accomplish the store's overall objectives.

In essence, there is a separation of power and authority between the department-level management and the top management; and this is as it should be. Top management is charged with the responsibility of operating the store as a total system and accomplishing the goals as set forth in the retail business plan.

Advantages of the Net-Profit Method   The net-profit method offers several distinct advantages. First, this procedure provides management with a means of determining the net profit for each department. Thus, it becomes a measure of managerial performance for that department

Second, since the net-profit method tells top management what the profit is for that department, the efficiency of each department manager can be analyzed—especially when compared to other managers in other departments.

Third, each department (subsystem) bears a portion of the indirect expenses, which is only fair since each department shares in the benefits of those indirect expenditures.

Fourth, the net-profit method also allows management to detect expense trends by providing a comparison between current expenses and expenses from the past period.

Limitations of the Net-Profit Method   As mentioned earlier, perhaps the greatest weakness of the net-profit method is the possible arbitrary allocation of indirect expenses by management. Regardless of how management determines and distributes indirect expenses, the manner in which it is done is bound to cause controversy. All departments are not identical; some departments will attract more customers than others. But management may tend to view all departments as nearly equal when it is time to distribute the indirect expenses among them. Thus, this one factor can be a major disadvantage unless management takes precautionary steps to combat the complaints.

Second, the bookkeeping associated with the allocation of indirect expenses to each department becomes, in itself, an additional expense. But if the means (the net-profit method) is used to improve the store's efficiency and does so successfully, then this expense can be justified.

Third, indirect-expense allocation is often a complicated accounting procedure and is misunderstood by many of the store's staff. Naturally, there is considerable pressure on department heads and buyers to provide a profit from their store or department. By increasing the expenses allocated to a department or a store, department heads and buyers may become more obsessed with curtailing expenses and lose sight of the primary objective—to supply goods and services to customers. Thus, the distribution of indirect expenses by management becomes a mere roadblock to these people. Should the situation surrounding the allocation of indirect expenses reach this stage of development, remedial action is absolutely necessary. If action is not taken, the store's efficiency will suffer, and nothing will be gained. Department heads and buyers, as well as the store's management, should not lost sight of the perspective of the primary goals and objectives of the total system.

Contribution Method

The limitations and difficulties encountered in using the net-profit method of allocating expenses have led some retailers to adopt another system, namely, the contribution method. Through this expense control procedure, much of the same information can be obtained without having to distribute indirect expenses to various departments or areas.

In using the contribution method, some expenses are distributed to the departments, but other expenses are not. Just how is this determined? The retail store's management makes a determination as to what expenses will be directly allocated to a department, and this total amount is then subtracted from the gross margin of the department. The figure obtained through this calculation is referred to as the department's "contribution margin." For example, if a department's gross margin for a period is $250,000, and the amount of direct expenses charged to the department is $86,000, then the department's contribution margin is $164,000.

The contribution method is simple in that only direct expenses are assigned or allocated to a department. All other so-called "indirect" expenses are classified as general expenses, and no attempt is made to distribute these expenses among the departments. The indirect expenses then become part of the store's general overhead and are used only in determining the total net profit for the entire store.

One issue which has not been satisfactorily resolved when using the contribution method is the determination of the various expenses that should be charged to a department. Some advocates of the contribution method suggest that only expenses incurred in the operation of the department for its benefit should be distributed to that department. For example, a department will have expenses such as salaries, advertising, and supplies. Thus, each department would be charged with expenses which are directly incurred. If the department did not exist, these expenses would not be incurred. Other expenses are placed in a general classification, and no attempt is made to assign or apportion these expenses among the departments.

Other advocates say that only the expenses that would *not* be incurred if the department were not in existence should be charged to that department. Still other proponents of the contribution method think that only those expenses which are under the control of the department head or the buyer should be assigned to that department. So whatever system is used will depend on the philosophy of the owner or manager.

Advantages of the Contribution Method By calculating and using the contribution-margin figure, management can compare one department with another, thereby determining the relative worth of each department. This is a major advantage of the contribution method since the contribution-margin figure obtained is the amount each department contributes toward meeting indirect expenses and providing a net profit for the store. But the major difference between the contribution method and the net-profit method is that a comparison is made between departments or stores before the indirect expenses are allocated which gives management a more realistic comparison.

Second, in order to measure the buyer's or department head's efficiency, a comparison can be made between the past results and the current contribution-margin figures. Again, this is a better comparison because only direct expenses are involved. Under the net-profit method, a buyer or department head might cut the direct expenses, but if indirect expenses were to go up, the profit margin would appear less favorable. Thus, by using only direct expenses under the contribution method, the persons involved become much more directly accountable and proper credit may be given to the buyer who cuts costs.

Third, the contribution method forces employees in selling departments and service areas to be responsible for controlling the expenses incurred in their area. Individuals working in delivery, credit, and accounting are encouraged to control some of the expenses associated with those functions. Failure to do so will be noticeable in the final contribution margin and profit results.

Limitations of the Contribution Method One of the basic weaknesses of the contribution method is that it does not provide a total expense figure for a department. Since all departments or areas within a store enjoy certain services (such as delivery, credit, installation, and record keeping), these departments should also share proportionately in these expenses; otherwise, the profit picture would be somewhat distorted.

Second, some department heads or buyers may demand and use such store services excessively since they are not being directly charged on a proportional basis for these services. Since all departments do not share in these expenses, complete control of the indirect expenses will be difficult for the store's management to attain.

Combination Method

Because of the dissatisfactions or limitations of the two previously mentioned plans of expense allocation, the combination method, or hybrid plan, has evolved. This plan combines the best parts of the distribution of expenses from the net-profit and the contribution plans.

Retailers, seeking more information than could be obtained from either of the previous plans, devised the combination plan for the distribution of departmental expenses. Consequently, this plan shows both a department's net profit as well as its contribution margin. It works in this way: When all direct expenses (in dollars) have been subtracted from the gross margin (in dollars), a contribution-margin figure is obtained. This step is taken from the contribution-margin method. Next, by using an element from the net-profit plan, the contribution margin is reduced by the allocation of indirect expenses for that department. For instance, the steps of the combination plan are as follows:

Net sales	$250,000
Cost of goods sold	− 150,000
Department gross margin	$100,000
Direct expenses of department	− 50,000
Contribution of department	$ 50,000
Indirect expenses distributed to the department	− 25,000
Net profit for department	$ 25,000

Overall, the combination method provides management with more control by providing additional data on the value of the individual selling departments. By having additional facts on each department's expenses, the store's management is in a better position to improve and/or control each department.

When each department's net profit is indicated in the combination method, these data may be used as a guide in determining the selling price of merchandise. Depending on the goals of management, prices may have to be raised or lowered. Also, the department head and/or buyer will be more aware of the indirect expenses and their effect on the department's net profit, thereby making them more responsible to control measures. Usually, you will find among retailers the use of one of the above methods for the allocation of expenses; but depending upon the type of retail business and the philosophy of the management, no one method is predominant.

THE EXPENSE BUDGET

As a management tool, the expense budget is probably without rival and is widely used by many retailers. It is the expense budget that is used to set forth or establish a store's future expenditures for a specified period of time. The budget allows management to examine, analyze, and compare retailing costs; yet it also provides a measure of control over the operations of a retail store.

A store's expense budget is usually set for a period of one year. However, expense budgets may be broken down into monthly figures in order to facilitate control and provide more accurate estimates. Although many of the figures in an expense budget are merely estimates for the coming year, these estimates can be made with reasonable accuracy. See Figure 20-1 for a typical expense budget for a retail store.

Estimation of Budget Expenses

For those retailers who have been in business, expense-budget estimates are based on previous records. These estimates may then be raised or lowered

Typical Expense Budget
Specialty Appliance Store
(one year period)

Salaries (including owner(s))	$ 63,000
Payroll taxes	3,150
Equipment depreciation	3,850
Sales promotion and advertising	38,000
Insurance	3,600
Rent	22,500
Supplies	2,500
Telephone	1,500
Electricity and gas	2,300
Miscellaneous	1,500
Donations	500
Property taxes	2,400
Total expenses	$144,700

Figure 20-1   Typical expense budget.

depending on the objectives of the management as well as the current economic and market conditions.

For the beginning retailer, estimates of retail expenses are somewhat difficult to pinpoint. However, such items as salaries, payroll taxes, depreciation of equipment, advertising allocations, insurance, and rent can be quite accurately determined. Therefore, figures for the items of utilities, supplies, and miscellaneous, are actually the only real estimates in an expense budget. But if the time is taken to plan carefully for a new store, these expense estimates can be reasonably accurate.

Advantages of an Expense Budget

One of the main reasons for setting up an expense budget is to determine the amount of money that will be necessary to support the store for the period of time in question. If this period of time is for one year, a provision for the money which will be needed to pay these expenses should be established—at least on paper. Long before the store becomes profitable, certain expenses will be incurred and must be paid. Some retailers do not realize that it may take three to five years before a store really becomes profitable or profits can be returned to the owner(s). Too many small retailers begin business with inadequate funds, which accounts for the relatively high rate of failure with small stores. This is one reason why an expense-budget estimation is so important.

Second, the expense budget gives a store's management the opportunity to assign the responsibility for expenses and profits to the department heads, the buyers, or other supervisory level personnel. By assigning the responsibility for expenses and profits, the expense budget becomes a management tool. This tool, in turn, allows a "before" and "after" analysis of the store's performance.

Third, the expense budget serves as a management tool for control. However, as with any other method or device which is used in the control of a business (such as accounting, statistics, and marketing research), some provision must be made for flexibility. Flexibility is needed because market conditions change. For instance, sales volume either rises or falls; it usually does not remain static. To ensure an expense budget's effectiveness, some flexibility is needed to cope with any changes such as rising or falling sales volume. Since it may be desirable to increase or decrease advertising and sales promotional expenditures, some allowance has to be made for this change. Caution should be exercised, however, with the element of flexibility. If a budget becomes too flexible, it may lose its effectiveness for control. Or if the store's management is allowed to change budget figures at will without sound fundamental reasons, the basic purpose of the expense budget has been lost.

Fourth, expense budgets force managers to establish goals. By establishing objectives, management must sit down and think about two specific things: at what stage is the business at present and where will the business be in the future? As stressed previously, goal setting is a basic requirement for a retail store's success. If firms are not goal-oriented, they will have no purpose or direction and probably will fail. Stores with no goals will flounder and flit from one retailing strategy to another, which ultimately will lead to an unprofitable retail operation.

Fifth, the expense budget allows an owner to establish the relationship between estimated expenses and projected sales. By using these estimates, the owner is better able to calculate a possible return on investment (ROI). Then if the ROI seems to be too low, a retailer can make some adjustments that will improve the situation. In order to calculate a return on investment (or an actual net-profit amount in dollars), the retailer must plan for expenses and sales carefully and thoroughly. And the planning gives the retailer some idea as to what he or she can expect for the next period of time.

Finally, the expense budget is a sound device against which one can measure performance. At the end of the budget period, a retailer can make a comparison between actual expenses and the budgeted expenses. If actual expenses show any extreme deviation from those that were estimated in the budget, the retailer can carefully analyze the problem to see what happened. Through this analysis, any problem area or weakness in the retailing organization will appear. In some instances, the estimated expenses may prove to be unrealistic in light of unexpected developments in the market. But whatever the cause, the expense budget gives the retailer an opportunity to check the performance of the operational areas in the store.

Importance of Payroll Expenses

Since a store's payroll may be the largest single expense item for most retailers, it is very important that special attention be devoted to the budgeting of this item. In some stores, payroll expenses may exceed one-half of the store's total expenses. For large retailing chains, payroll expenses often run from 6 to 8 percent of gross sales. Since payroll expenses are such a significant part of the retailer's expense budget, it is almost mandatory that careful control be exercised over them. Good control may mean the difference between earning a profit or incurring a loss for the store.

New retailers will have to make an estimate of the amount of work to be done and the number of employees needed to perform the work. If they are not sure how many employees they will need, they should look at similar stores or get outside consulting help to determine the number of employees needed. Hiring an x number of employees on a trial and error system may be costly. If the retailer has too many people, payroll expenses will be unduly high. If a store lacks sufficient help, customer service may suffer, and patrons may go somewhere else to shop. Even existing retailers should review their work force periodically and either add personnel or decrease the staff as needed.

Proper training of employees will ensure higher standards of work performance and may reduce the need for extra help, thereby cutting down the payroll expenses. If special attention has been devoted to store layout and design, the time spent in walking from one area of the store to another will be lessened. Particular attention to such details will aid in reducing the number of salespeople, and more importantly, will increase their effectiveness as salespersons. This, too, can lead to a considerable reduction in payroll expenses.

Increasingly, part-time help is becoming a more important factor for retailers to consider as a means of reducing the payroll expenses. In many large department stores, part-time employees constitute over 50 percent of the total work force. This trend may continue because there are certain advantages in hiring part-time employees: (1) part-time employees are usually paid no more than the minimum federal wage, (2) hiring part-time employees also cuts down on the amount of overtime pay that would have to be paid to regular full-time employees if they had to work additional hours, and (3) fringe benefits, such as insurance or retirement benefits, are frequently not extended to part-time workers. Thus, a retailer's overall payroll expenses will be reduced.

Further, part-time help offers a degree of flexibility for a retailer. Part-time employees, whether sales or clerical, can be used when needed the most—i.e., evenings and weekends when the amount of customer traffic is high. During weekdays when store traffic is minimal, only a skeleton work force may be needed in many cases. In many instances, by utilizing part-time help, a retailer is able to reduce the single largest expense—the payroll.

FUNDAMENTAL STORE RECORDS

Every retailer, large or small, should maintain a permanent set of records which can be used to identify the store's income, expenses, and deductions. The financial record should begin when merchandise is ordered from the vendor(s). Each day, bits and pieces of financial information flow into the store. As sales transactions are made, records should be kept concerning cash, equipment, purchase expenses, payroll, accounts payable, and accounts receivable.

If the retail business is small, usually a simple record-keeping system will suffice. Such a system should consist of a checkbook, a cash receipts journal, a cash disbursements journal, and a petty cash fund.

Checkbook   All the money that passes in and out of a retail store should go through a checking account which is tailored to the store. If the store is small, the proprietor should handle all personal expenses in a separate checking account. When used with other records, a checkbook will aid in proving the amount of cash handled, how much of these funds is considered to be taxable income, and what amount is deductible for income tax reporting.

Cash-Receipts Journal   A cash-receipts journal is used to record cash which the store receives. It is important to keep income that is not derived from sales (advertising allowances and the like), separate from gross sales. Also, sales taxes which a retailer collects for the local and state government must be kept separate as these funds are not business income.

Cash-Disbursements Journal   It is important that every retailer record all funds which a store pays out. These expenditures may be recorded in a cash-disbursements journal, purchases, or expense journal. This may be done at the time the check is written, and each entry should indicate the nature or classification of the disbursement. For instance, the disbursement may be for merchandise, office supplies, rent, wages, or utilities. These disbursements should be totaled each month in order to maintain proper record-keeping control.

Petty Cash   Most retailers keep a petty cash fund with voucher slips to document each expenditure. In this manner, the retailer is able to prove each cash expenditure, especially those small cash payments for which a check is not written. If the amount is too small, usually a check is not written, and the amount is often paid from the petty cash fund. Many of these expenditures are income-tax deductible. The petty cash fund also eliminates the necessity of the proprietor to pay for miscellaneous small expenditures from his or her personal account.

Importance of Cash Flow   Experience has shown that all too often the small retailer fails to establish a sound record-keeping system containing the facts and figures which make up a clear picture of the business. One of the most important assets of any retail business is sufficient operating capital. If a retailer does not put aside working capital (cash), current bills cannot be paid, and the store soon falls into a "cash crisis." There is no adequate substitute for a liquid or cash position. A lack of cash may alarm vendors or employees and may lead to bankruptcy even though the store may appear to be profitable.

Cash Budget   In order to avoid a cash crisis, a retailer should determine the cash needs for the normal operation of the store. The amount of cash needed by a retailer will depend upon the nature and the size of the store.

Generally, as a rule of thumb, 10 percent of a store's working capital should be in cash.

A cash budget serves as an effective managerial tool for planning cash requirements for the store. The cash budget tells at a glance the amount of cash a store expects to receive and the disbursements which must be met. The basic objective of a cash budget is to be able to maintain a liquid (cash) position for any emergency which may arise.

Using a cash budget is beneficial to the retailer because it helps him to:

1 Maximize the efficient use of cash by timing cash disbursements with cash receipts. (This practice will minimize the need to borrow additional working capital.)

2 Pinpoint periods when cash deficiencies arise and the need for additional working capital is needed.

3 Make a determination of periods for the repayment of loans.

4 Determine when cash and trade discounts should be taken.

5 Reveal periods of surplus cash which may be used for investment in inventory.

6 Determine the adequacy of, or the need for, additional permanent operating capital in the business.

It is important that the retailer make the cash budget as realistic as possible. A retailer should not *over*estimate sales or *under*estimate expenses. A sales forecast (determined from the market potential) should be as accurate as possible, because it serves as the basis for the estimation of cash and expenses. An accountant can offer valuable advice on the amount of money needed to operate the business for the next period—month, quarter, or year.

PROFIT-AND-LOSS STATEMENT

A retailer utilizes a set of records to facilitate managerial decisions. These records contain facts and figures which reveal the viability of the store. These facts and figures must be sorted and arranged in order for us to have a clear view of the business and to determine the extent of success or failure. This determination may be done by studying the profit-and-loss statement. The profit-and-loss statement (P & L) reveals what profit or loss the store had during a certain time period. Figure 20-2 illustrates a sample P & L statement for a small retail service business.

Figure 20-2 reveals considerable information concerning this small-service retailer. For instance, the net profit appears to be rather small as a percentage of sales (actually 5.14 per cent); this may be due to the apparently large payroll figure. If this figure includes the owner's salary, the net profit is not too bad; but, if the owner's salary is not included in this payroll figure, then there appears to be too much waste in the payroll portion of the business. Thus, it would appear that payroll may be out of proportion for this retail business. Another item to analyze in the P & L statement is the rent. For example, it is possible that this retailer is

Profit and Loss Statement
for
XYZ Appliance Service
For Year Ending December 31, 1975

Gross sales		$70,000
Cost of sales:		
Opening inventory	$13,000	
Purchases	25,000	
Total	$38,000	
Ending inventory	− 14,000	
Total cost of sales		24,000
Gross profit		$46,000
Operating expenses:		
Payroll	$26,000	
Rent	3,000	
Payroll taxes	1,500	
Interest	600	
Depreciation	1,400	
Delivery expense	4,100	
Telephone	3,400	
Insurance	1,400	
Miscellaneous	1,000	
Total		$42,000
Net profit		$ 3,600

Figure 20-2   Profit and loss statement for XYZ Appliance
Service for year ending December 31, 1975.

paying more rent than is necessary for the size and type of retail business. Also, the average inventory for the year is $13,500 (opening inventory $13,000 and ending inventory $14,000). Since the cost of sales is $24,000, this service firm's average inventory was used less than twice a year, which requires some management attention. These areas of the P & L statement reveal that certain weak areas are evident in this small retail business and that the owner should make attempts to rectify these areas of weakness. In summation, the P & L statement determines the pulse of the business, whether it is healthy or sick.

BENEFITS OF EXPENSE CONTROL AND ANALYSIS

It is wise for a retailer to make an analysis of the operating expenses incurred by the store. However, this analysis should lead to corrective measures if it is to be used properly as a managerial tool; otherwise, there would be little point in making it. The main advantage of expense control and analysis is that it permits management to take immediate remedial action should some expenses be out of line with sales. Monthly reports will reflect the nature of these expenses and will allow for their comparison. In turn, this analysis allows the store's management the opportunity to keep closely in touch with the store's day-to-day activities and to pay closer attention to actual expenditures. However, any deviation may require the attention of the controller, the accountant, or the owner. Budgets are made for a purpose, but if expenditures go beyond the budget's limits, remedial action must be taken or the store may suffer a loss.

Management can improve its efficiency through the use of expense and control analysis. The analysis of such expenses is not a control measure within itself; but instead it is the corrective action that is taken which becomes the control. Like other tools that managers use—accounting, research, and statistics—expense control and analysis need to be conducted properly if the store is going to be successful. Expense control and analysis can help to improve the decision making of the store's executives.

SUMMARY

The use of *control methods* is a necessity if the retailer expects to make a profit and satisfy the customers. Control of expenses tends to affect the internal operation of the store directly.

In order to determine what progress has been made toward the objectives set forth in the retail business plan, an *analysis of operating expenses* incurred must be made by the store's management.

In order to maintain proper control and allow the retailer to be able to analyze expenses critically, retail store expenses should be *classified* uniformly. It is desirable for the retailer to tailor the classification of retail store expenses to fit the individual store.

After retail store expenses have been classified for the particular store, the next step is to allocate these expenses in terms of dollars and cents. The *allocation of expenses* requires the assignment of expenses to areas within a small store, to the selling departments within a large store, to branch stores, or to all stores within a chain.

There are two broad *classifications of expenses:* direct and indirect. *Direct expenses* are those that are attributable to a specific function within an area or a department. *Indirect expenses* are those expenses which are not directly attributable to a specific department or function within a store.

The *net-profit method* of expense allocation requires that all expenses, both direct and indirect, be divided among the various areas of a small store or among the departments of a large store. The net-profit method is used in order that net profit can be readily determined for each area or department.

The net-profit method of expense allocation enables the retailer to determine the net profit for each department, to measure the efficiency of each department, to divide the expense burden among the departments, and to detect expense trends by being able to compare the current expenses with the expenses from a past period.

One of the major limitations of the net-profit method is the assignment of indirect expenses to areas or departments within a store. Some managers are of the opinion that this may not be done on an equitable basis by management.

The *contribution method* of expense allocation is simple in that only direct expenses are assigned or allocated to an area or department within a store. All indirect expenses are classified as general expenses. One of the basic limitations of this method of expense allocation is that it does not provide a total expense figure for an area or a department within the store.

The *combination method* of expense allocation is an attempt to overcome some of the objections of the two previously mentioned plans. This plan combines the best portions of the distribution of expenses from the net profit and the contribution plans.

It is the *expense budget* that is used to set forth or establish a store's future expenditures for a specified period of time. The expense budget allows management to examine, analyze, and compare retailing costs. The expense budget also provides a measure of control over the operations of a retail store.

For those retailers who have been in business, expense budget estimates are based on previous records. For the beginning retailer, estimates of retail expenses are somewhat difficult to pinpoint.

One of the main reasons for setting up an expense budget is to determine the amount of money that will be necessary to support the store for the period of time in question. The expense budget also provides the store's management an opportunity to assign the responsibility for expenses and profits to the department heads, buyers, or other supervisory-level personnel. And finally, an expense budget serves as a management tool for the control of the store.

Since a store's payroll may be the largest single expense, special attention must be devoted to the budgeting of this item. In some retail stores, payroll expenses may exceed one-half of the store's total expenses.

One of the main advantages of expense control and analysis is that it permits management to take immediate remedial action should some expenses be out of line with sales. Monthly reports will reflect the nature of these expenses and will allow for their comparison. Management can improve its efficiency through the use of expense control and analysis.

REVIEW QUESTIONS

1 Why should every retailer make an expense classification for the store?
2 What is the next step after retail store expenses have been classified?
3 What do we mean when we speak of direct expenses? Indirect expenses?
4 Explain the net-profit method of expense allocation.
5 What are the advantages and disadvantages of the net-profit method of expense allocation?
6 Explain the contribution method of expense allocation.
7 What are the advantages and disadvantages of the contribution method of expense allocation?
8 Explain the combination method of expense allocation.
9 What is the basic purpose of the expense budget?
10 What are some of the advantages of the expense budget?
11 Why are payroll expenses so important to the retailer?
12 What are the benefits of expense and control analysis?

Chapter 21

Control and Analysis
of Stock Losses

Stock losses, regardless of source, are of primary concern to every retailer because: (1) these losses must be passed on to the ultimate consumer in the form of higher retail prices and (2) additional sales dollars must be generated in order to offset the loss of any merchandise.

Stock losses will vary according to the type of retail store and the efficiency of the store's management. In a well-managed department store, stock losses may range from about 0.5 to 1 percent of sales. Stock losses in a store which is not so well controlled may range as high as 3.5 to 6 percent of sales. Although these figures are estimates, it is believed that they accurately reflect the increasing problem of stock losses.

Basically, two major classifications of stock losses account for the major portion of shortages within a retail store—employee theft and shoplifting. Of course, there are other reasons for merchandise shortages, such as breakage, cash register mistakes, burglary and robbery, mysterious disappearance, and the failure to weigh or measure certain types of goods correctly. But the main percentage of stock losses result from employee theft and shoplifting. Although a retailer cannot completely eliminate stock losses, positive steps can be taken to keep these losses at a minimum. As with other control measures for such items as inventory and expenses, the key to preventing stock losses is proper managerial control.

PREVENTING EMPLOYEE THEFT

Employee theft, or pilferage, is more serious than some retailers might think and, unfortunately, it is on the increase. In some retail stores, dishonest employees may account for two-thirds of the store's stock losses. As you might imagine, merchandise-theft-loss estimates vary by the type of retail store and the efficiency of management. As previously mentioned, merchandise losses may range from about 0.5 to 1 percent of sales for a well-managed store. For a loosely controlled retail store, this stock loss figure may range from 3.5 to 6 percent of sales. Of these amounts, employee pilferage may account for about two-thirds of the store's total stock losses with the remainder being due to shoplifting and other reasons.

Stock losses and the prevention of theft are under the control of the store's manager. It is encouraging to note that, although the management will not be able to eliminate stealing entirely, positive steps can be taken to keep stock pilferage at a minimum. Therefore, the key to proper stock loss minimization is to maintain proper control.

Perhaps one of the best precautions a retailer can take is to hire employees whose honesty is beyond question. But too many retailers take integrity for granted and, in many cases, a person's honesty cannot be correctly determined until they have been hired. Thus, the need remains for management to install effective theft deterrents and to take measures to uncover dishonesty.

Experience has revealed that often the "most trusted" employee is the one who pilfers the largest amount of merchandise. One possible explanation for this occurrence is that the most trusted employee, who has had many years of experience, knows the store procedures well. Because this employee is so trusted and knowledgeable, he or she is in a better position to pilfer goods than anyone else. Once an employee begins to steal merchandise, whether for personal use or for a friend, the temptation for taking more goods is irresistible.

Many owner-managers of small retail stores feel close to their employees, and they trust their employees with keys, safe combinations, cash, and records. Thus, these employees have the tools and accessibility for easily committing a crime. There are few businesses in which dishonest employees are not found. Usually these employees are protected by management's indifference since they take only a few items. Then the "few items" may eventually lead to a considerable amount in dollars and cents.

Specific Measures for Preventing Employee Theft

Just what type of measures can a retailer use in order to protect the business from employee theft? First, one fact becomes obvious. The retail store with the greatest proportion of honest employees suffers the least from theft loss. Every retailer should take precautions to ensure that the people who are hired are honest. An applicant's background should be checked since it may reveal some insight into an individual's character. The reasons for a person's discharge from previous employment should be thoroughly investigated before an applicant is hired. Although this procedure may take a little more time, effort, and money on the part of the retailer, it will probably result in the employment of more reliable and trustworthy employees. To reiterate, improving the caliber of retail personnel is largely a matter of careful screening, checking, selection, and hiring (which we discussed in an earlier chapter). Reference checks can and should be made on all applicants. In addition to character references, many retailers will also undertake a check on an applicant's credit rating. Usually, a credit check can be obtained on an individual through a local credit bureau for a nominal fee, say $5 to $7. This investigation may reveal how well the applicant handles personal financial matters, which may have an effect on his or her attitude toward temptation.

Second, in many cases, a security bond is also a wise investment for a retailer. A security bond is provided by a bonding company and is an insurance policy against theft by the store's employees. The retailer pays a fee for the security bond, but all the investigative work on the employees is done by the bonding company. In a case of theft by a bonded employee, the bonding company reimburses the retailer for any loss. For a retailer handling large sums of cash, or for certain businesses such as jewelry stores and the like, it is especially wise for a retailer to bond all employees.

Third, a retailer should take precautions to ensure that the store reflects an atmosphere of honesty and integrity. This, in turn, will encourage employees to stay honest. By creating this type of store environment, a retailer will discourage employee pilferage. A store which operates on this basis will tend to bolster employee morale by encouraging honesty throughout the store. How can this be done? To begin with, a retailer creates an atmosphere of honesty by maintaining high standards. The standards established and followed by senior employees will be passed on to new employees who will also follow them. A retailer should not settle for a "small write-off" or loss but should strive to keep all shortages to a minimum. Merchandise loss figures should be kept from employees. If the retailer's attitude is that of accepting small losses as inevitable, store employees will also come to accept this philosophy. Thus, the retailer should adopt the storewide policy of "no losses" and use checks and balances for ensuring this.

Fourth, the retailer through his or her actions sets the tone for the store. For example, if all overshipments and overpayments are returned promptly, employees are able to witness management's honesty. Hopefully, this policy may be contagious. The owner should make it known that the rules of the store should apply to everyone—the manager, employees, and the owner.

Fifth, it is essential that a retailer establish an environment of trust and respect and take an interest in the store's employees. A retailer who is interested in and who respects and trusts employees preserves their dignity and individuality. These sound personnel practices can be expected to elicit greater cooperation from a store's employees as well as reduce merchandise losses.

Sixth, if a retailer provides employees with the proper incentives, it may reduce the temptation to take goods from the store. An employee should not be placed in a position or job where lying or cheating is required in order to meet a performance standard. In providing proper incentives to employees, a retailer needs to assign duties and responsibilities with clear lines of authority. If these duties and responsibilities are put in writing for an employee to study, the result will be less error and waste and, in turn, less employee indifference to the store.

Seventh, employees should be given the necessary resources needed to perform their functions well. Otherwise, circumstances beyond their control may lead individuals to cheat and steal just to get even with management and the store. It is much wiser for management to remove all opportunities which encourage employees to be dishonest.

Eighth, there is no substitute for well-implemented measures and controls which help to eliminate or prevent stock losses. The use of continuous training of employees may lead to improved methods of stock control since the employees will more thoroughly understand the procedures being used. This training may also (1) suggest new and better ways in which employees can reduce or eliminate stock shortages and shrinkages, (2) lead to improved employee attitudes toward the problem, and (3) give them added incentive for helping to eliminate all shortages.

Finally, a retailer probably does not need to worry too much about new employees if he or she has been relatively careful in the selection process. Usually, a lack of knowledge about a store's routine restricts a new employee's chance of taking merchandise or money. Merchandise cash-control procedures and/or a close watch of daily receipts and personal observation will usually detect any shortages for which a new employee may be responsible.

MEASURES TO REDUCE SHOPLIFTING

Shoplifting accounts for approximately one-third of all stock losses in retail stores and, unfortunately, it is also on the increase. All ages and types of people shoplift goods from retail stores. One can easily be fooled by the outward appearance of shoplifters. Shoplifters include the rich, the poor, the professional thief, the teenager, the kleptomaniac, the drug addict, and the housewife—in short, no one type of person can be identified as a shoplifter.

The largest amount of shoplifting takes place in the self-service and self-selection retail stores. The reasons for this may be the smaller number of sales-people at hand in the display areas and the fact that the merchandise is openly placed on gondolas and shelves for the customers' inspection. Obviously, it is not difficult under these circumstances for shoplifters to steal a large amount of goods since there are few deterrents in these types of stores.

Retail stores located in metropolitan areas have a higher rate of shoplifting than do stores located in rural areas. This could be the result of more customer traffic in metropolitan areas; or it may be due to sociological factors. For example, most customers are better known in the smaller, rural communities; hence shoplifting is much more difficult. Regardless of location, however, no retailer can afford to ignore the problems of shoplifting and not try to do something about it.

Specific Measures to Prevent Shoplifting

Methods employed by shoplifters vary widely from the amateur's sneakiness to the professional's boldness. In fact, the most conspicuous shoplifters may go unnoticed by retail personnel. On the other hand, any customer who walks into a store with a shopping bag, a large purse, or a coat over his or her arm is a possible shoplifter.

Professional shoplifters will probably use accessories of some sort; one of the most common is known as a "booster." The booster is a large box tied with a heavy cord which looks like an authentic package. The outside appearance of a booster gives one the impression that the package has been purchased and tied simply for easy carrying. One end of the box, however, is hinged so it can be quickly opened and merchandise stuffed into it. A large booster may hold as many as five men's suits or six or seven women's dresses.

Another trick used by shoplifters is to wear a coat which has a pillow case, or cases, pinned to the inner lining. This pillow case then serves as a container for the storage of merchandise that is picked up. Usually, the coat is large and loose fitting so that the goods placed inside the pillow case do not show from the outside. Women shoplifters may also wear large bloomers which can be stuffed with large quantities of goods.

As you can see, shoplifters use such a variety of methods so that combating the problem is a major task for any retailer. But what can a retailer do to reduce shoplifting? Several inexpensive methods can curtail the amount of shoplifting. First, a retailer should keep a close control on washrooms and fitting rooms. Customers attempting to shoplift merchandise often use fitting rooms or washrooms when concealing goods beneath outer garments. A retailer can also schedule employee work hours so that enough personnel are available for covering aisles during the peak periods of customer traffic. Doors which are not used frequently, including rear doors, should be locked at all times.

Second, the prominent display of mirrors and antishoplifting signs may have a psychological effect of shoplifters and may stop the amateur. However, it probably will have little effect on the professional shoplifter.

Third, some of the large retail stores use plain-clothes personnel, or floorwalkers, to patrol the store. These people are paid to walk continuously; they shop and monitor the aisles, looking for any person who arouses suspicion. Many shoplifters are caught this way, or if a shoplifter becomes aware that he or she is being watched, they usually will move on to another store.   ·

Fourth, there is an alternative for the smaller retailer who feels that his or her store cannot afford floorwalkers. By having salespeople or someone from the store's staff greet all customers at the door, shoplifting will be discouraged. When a person is spoken to upon entering a store, that individual knows that the store personnel are alert, and this may tend to discourage individuals who are thinking of stealing goods. Shoplifters do not like to feel that they are being watched or even that they have been noticed entering a store. Thus, if this impression can be given to the customers, it usually will discourage even professional shoplifters.

Fifth, small items and expensive goods should be kept behind the counter or in locked cabinets. The larger, more expensive items such as suits, furs, gowns, jewelry, and the like should be kept on locked racks, or salespersons should be on duty at all times to provide customer assistance. Diamonds, watches, and other small expensive items should be placed in showcases and be inspected by customers only with the assistance of a salesperson. Using the above procedures tends to discourage most shoplifters.

Finally, some large self-service stores make use of in store closed-circuit television with monitors. This is an expensive means of preventing shoplifting, but it is most effective. And, if the store is unusually large, the system probably will pay for itself. This in store television system works in this way: Usually, each aisle in the store is covered by a television camera, which is connected to a monitor in a small room near the rear of the store or to one side of the building. One or more full-time employees (or security guards) monitor these television sets watching for any unusual customer activity or potential shoplifting. This is a good theft prevention system since people can be watched without their realizing it; but this system is probably too expensive for the small retailer.

Legal Aspects of Shoplifting

Although laws governing shoplifting differ from state to state as well as from community to community, a few basic legal rules must be observed. Retail employees should be thoroughly instructed about what they should do if they observe a customer in the process of stealing goods. First, the retail employee should approach the suspicious customer quietly and inconspicuously. If the customer is still in the store, the employee should inform the customer that he or she has merchandise which has not been paid for and should ask the customer to pay for the goods. If the potential shoplifter has walked out of the store, the employee should still try to inform the customer that the merchandise has not been paid for and ask the customer to return to the store. The merchandise should be taken from the suspect at this time. If the suspect customer refuses, only a small amount of force may be used to take the person into custody. Retail employees should use extreme caution when a woman is involved, and if possible, only female employees should stop a female suspect.

Second, the police should be called to the scene. If the potential shoplifter has been apprehended, the store employee and the police will probably question the suspect. This procedure has two basic purposes: (1) to get the suspect to admit his or her guilt and (2) to have the suspect turn over any other merchandise which may have been taken. If the shoplifter has not been caught or taken into custody, complete details and a description of the individual involved should be given to the police.

Third, any merchandise taken from the suspect should be marked and identified as evidence. When the case goes to court, the items taken from the suspect must be positively identified by store personnel. The store employees involved in the apprehension of a shoplifting suspect should make notes with respect to time, date, and conversations as those detailed notes can become a valuable reference in refreshing one's memory when testifying in court.

Court Procedures   Although court procedures may vary in different areas of the country, basically three elements are needed to prosecute shoplifters: (1) a witness to the theft who can positively identify the stolen goods and the individual who stole the merchandise, (2) a store employee who can identify the merchandise as belonging to the store and attest to its value, and (3) documents indicating that the store is a corporation, partnership, or sole ownership business in good standing. If a retailer does not have all of this information for use in the court, it is likely that the shoplifting case will be dismissed.

Although the individual philosophy of many retailers differs concerning what to do about shoplifters, failure to prosecute is in itself an offense against society. Someone must pay for the goods stolen from retailers. If restitution is not made by the shoplifter or the goods recovered, the result is usually higher prices on the store's merchandise. The retailer, in effect, must pass on these expenses to the store's customers in the form of higher retail prices.

Although most people are honest, it still is wise for a retailer to remove all temptations to shoplift merchandise. A retailer can obtain advice from several sources concerning shoplifting and its prevention. For instance, the Merchants' Protective Association, The Retail Credit Bureau, The Better Business Bureau, the local police department, and the local district attorney's office will provide advice, assistance, and information to a retailer about shoplifting and theft prevention measures.

PREVENTING BURGLARY AND ROBBERY LOSSES

Because of the known concentration of merchandise or cash, small retail stores are prime targets for burglars and holdup people. Burglars usually operate at night, seeking dark and easy-to-enter stores. In contrast, attracted by careless displays of cash, holdup people often strike at opening or closing time or when customer traffic is light.

Burglary is defined as any unlawful entry to commit a felony or a theft, even though no force was used to gain entrance. Since burglaries are costly for the retailer, and are on the rise, every retailer should take definite preventive measures to discourage such thefts.

Preventive measures must begin with the retailer. Merchants must be sure to use the right kind of locks on the store's doors. Strong locks not only offer an obstacle to entry but also serve as insurance protectives. Under many standard burglary insurance policies, evidence of forced entry is necessary in order to collect on burglary insurance.

Burglary experts agree that pin-tumbler cylinder locks using three to seven pins provide the best security against unlawful entry. Professional burglars can pick a pin-tumbler lock with less than five pins, but this type of lock is more difficult to force open. Another measure that should be taken by retailers is to make use of dead bolts wherever possible, especially on rear doors. Dead bolts are devices which serve to secure an entrance with a rod which slides into a hole drilled in the door. There is no way for a burglar to pick a dead bolt to gain entrance.

Another relatively simple theft prevention measure is adequate lighting. All entrances, rear doors, and dark corners of a store should be well lighted, because most burglars are somewhat hesitant about being seen working where there is proper lighting.

It was stated earlier that a retailer should hire only honest employees. But, along with this, another measure for protecting a store from unlawful entry is for the retailer to issue as few keys as possible. This practice prevents keys from getting into the hands of unauthorized store personnel. A retailer should keep a record of every key that is issued to the store's employees. Store employees who have been issued keys should be cautioned not to leave store keys with parking lot attendants, in top coats at restaurants, or lying about in the stockroom or coffee room. Should an employee lose a store key or fail to turn in any key upon leaving the store's employ, the lock on that door should be changed immediately. It is sound business practice for the retailer to code each key so that it does not have to be visibly tagged. In this way, only store employees authorized to use keys will be aware of which lock a specific key fits.

Security Systems

A silent, central-station, burglary alarm system provides a retailer with the best protection against unlawful entry. If triggered, a burglar will not hear this alarm as he or she would if it were a local, bell-ringing alarm system. A silent alarm system alerts only those persons who know how to handle burglars—the police or security officers of private companies.

These silent security systems can be leased or purchased from private firms in large cities. In smaller rural communities, these silent systems may be wired directly to the police station. The use of a silent security system also often leads to a reduction in the insurance premiums paid by a retailer for burglary and theft protection.

Lighting

It was stated earlier that all entrances and dark corners should be well lighted as this tends to discourage would-be burglars. Outdoor lighting is an inexpensive method of protecting a retail store from burglary as nearly all break-ins occur during the night-time hours. Darkness conceals a burglar and allows this person to work without interruption. Mercury and metallic vapor lights work best because they cover large areas and also can withstand many of the weather elements. These lights may be controlled by photoelectric "eyes" or time clocks. A photoelectric eye turns on the lights at dusk and turns them off at dawn, both automatically. Thus, there is no need to rely on individuals to perform these functions.

Indoor lighting is equally important for a retailer to consider as a means of discouraging theft. When a store is well lighted inside, shoppers tend to be cautious about pilfering goods. During the night hours, a well-lighted store interior allows security officers to notice any disorder or any person who might be inside. If a store is left dark, a burglar can see police officers approaching, but the officers are unable to see the burglar. In order to facilitate the vision of the security officers into the store's interior, it is well to arrange the store's display windows so that one's vision is not obstructed from the outside.

Preventive Measures for Cash

Every retail merchant should have a strong safe in which money and other valuables can be placed during the hours the store is closed. A safe should not be placed in the rear of a store where it cannot be seen from the outside. To do so is an invitation to theft. Safes should be visible from the sidewalk and should be located in a lighted area. If possible, a retailer should also deposit on a daily basis all excess cash. Even the best safes are not burglar-resistent when torches or explosives are used.

Cash registers should be emptied of cash and left open each night as a forced entry will ruin a cash register. If a retailer has to leave cash in large amounts in a safe over a weekend, it would be wise to record the serial numbers of the large bills.

Every retailer should take special precautions to discourage would-be robbers. Large amounts of cash on hand are an open invitation to a holdup person. A retailer should make daily bank deposits if at all possible, or make use of an armored car if the service is available. If armored car service is not available, a retailer should vary the trip to a bank each day. Most robbers survey a retailer before staging a holdup. They look for patterns of behavior, e.g., the retailer going to a bank at the same time each day with the cash receipts.

High-Risk Store Locations

Some stores are located in high-risk locations which have a reputation for high crime rates. Retailers located in these areas of high risk should not leave merchandise in window displays overnight. Some jewelry stores or other specialty stores make use of a heavy piece of glass hanging on chains behind the regular store window. Since this glass is suspended from the ceiling by chains, it is difficult to break. As the glass moves freely, a blow with a heavy instrument does not affect this hanging glass even though the outer window may have been broken. Other retailers also make use of window bars, window screens, burglar-resistant glass, watchdogs, and private police patrols.

Burglar-resistent glass aids in the protection of a store's contents in that it does not break easily. It will withstand a continuous beating, and its high tensile strength makes it a favorite for retailers located in riot areas.

Watchdogs have become one of the most effective means of protecting a store from burglary. Once the word gets out that a store has watchdogs, burglars usually cross that store off their list of possible targets. The sight and sound of an angry watchdog makes most burglars very wary of entering a store.

Training Employees to Handle Robbery Attempts

The training of retail employees should also include instructions on what to do in case of a robbery. Emphasis should be placed on the protection of lives, and retailers should warn their employees not to become heroes. Heroic action by a retail employee often ends in tragedy. Thus, a retailer should instruct the store's employees to cooperate with holdup persons in every way. While the store's employee is cooperating with the holdup person, mental notes should be made on the person's physical structure, hair color, complexion, voice, apparel, and anything else which would make it possible to identify that person. Although it may seem impossible, employees should try to remain calm during a holdup or robbery. Amateur holdup persons become nervous when confronted by an employee who is also nervous or one who wishes to become a hero. If the holdup person has a gun, shots may be fired, and a tragedy may result.

Opening and Closing the Store

Generally, opening and closing a store is a two-person job. When a store is being opened for the day's business, one person should be stationed outside where observation of the other's actions can be seen. One person should enter the store, check the burglar alarm if one is used, then investigate for any unusual signs of uninvited callers in the store. This amount of time should be predetermined and agreed upon by both parties, and if the person entering the store does not appear within the stated time, the person outside the store should call the police.

Night closing should be done in a similar manner. Last-minute checks should be made in washrooms, storage areas, and other hiding places where persons could hide and raid the store after it has been closed.

Much of this chapter on the control and analysis of stock losses appears to be common-sense advice, especially for experienced persons. However, from time to time, one may become complacent about such retailing functions and duties. Robberies usually occur because someone was forgetful. Stock losses also occur because of negligence on the part of the retailer. Thus, retailers cannot afford to relax their guard when dealing with the public. Even though most of the public is honest, it takes only one individual to ruin a retailer's life whether by staging a holdup, stealing a large amount of goods, or otherwise being responsible for stock losses.

OTHER TYPES OF STORE LOSSES

Other types of retail store losses include the passing of bad checks and the use of stolen credit cards. The passing of bad checks has increased because merchants readily accept customers' personalized checks in their eagerness for more business. But there are times when it *does not* pay to do business with certain customers.

In dollar amounts the passing of bad checks in the United States exceeds all other crimes. The Small Business Administration estimates that bad checks in the amount of $1,500 per minute are passed every day in retail establishments. Yet, less than 1 percent of the checks written are by customers who would be considered bad risks. The passing of bad checks is the most popular crime because it is easily done and often the bad-check artist goes unprosecuted. Typically, the bad-check artist, as opposed to the less sophisticated regular customer, talks to confuse the clerks or divert their attention while the check is being accepted. By training the sales personnel, a store can make them aware of some of the factors which denote good checks. For example, checks which are good contain the following elements:

1 The company name must be printed, not typed or written on the check.
2 The check must be issued on a locally existing company.
3 The customer must be employed at the above company.
4 The check must be negotiable and drawn on an existing bank.
5 The check must not be predated.
6 The check must bear the location and code of the bank.
7 The amount written in words must agree with the numbers.
8 The signature must be clear and legible.
9 Payroll checks usually will end in odd cents.
10 Watch for printed restrictions either stamped or typed on the check.
11 Have the payee (customer) endorse in ink the name exactly as it appears on the face of the check. If already endorsed, ask the payee to endorse the check once again so that the signature can be witnessed.
12 Obtain all pertinent identification data, and record it on the reverse side of the check.

Some counties have a regular reporting service on bad checks which is usually available to retailers. It is estimated, however, that only 10 percent of bad checks are reported due to the low dollar amounts of many of the checks. A retailer should retain all forged checks and identification and stolen credit cards, because these can be used to prosecute those individuals responsible for using and passing these financial instruments.

SUMMARY

Merchandise losses are of concern to every retailer because these losses must be passed on to the consumer in the form of higher prices, and additional sales dollars must be generated in order to offset the loss of goods.

Stock losses will vary by kind of retail store and the efficiency of that store's management. Although stock-loss figures usually are only estimates, it is believed that they range from 0.5 to 6 percent of sales.

Basically, stock losses occur from two major sources—*employee theft* and *shoplifting*. Dishonest employees may account for nearly two-thirds of a store's merchandise shrinkage.

Stock losses are under the direct control of the manager or store owner. One of the best safeguards a retailer can have is to hire employees whose honesty is beyond question. Many retailers provide security bonds for their employees as an insurance policy against theft by the employee. Every retailer should strive to maintain an environment of honesty and integrity. A retailer sets the tone for employees by conducting business in an atmosphere of honesty. This will lead to employee integrity and honesty. Continuous training may reduce the amount of merchandise shrinkage due to employee errors.

Shoplifting takes place in all retail stores; however, self-service and self-selection stores suffer the greatest losses. A retailer should maintain control over fitting rooms and rest-rooms. Customers attempting to steal merchandise will make use of these facilities when concealing goods. Mirrors may be used to discourage the amateur shoplifter, however, mirrors are relatively ineffective against the professional shoplifter. The use of *floorwalkers* or plain-clothes personnel will aid in reducing shoplifting. Certain types of merchandise should be kept on closed racks or in cases provided with locks.

Since the legal aspects of shoplifting vary from state to state, it is well for a retailer to become familiar with the local laws governing this crime.

Although *court procedures* may vary, usually three elements are needed to prosecute shoplifters. These include a witness to the theft who can positively identify the stolen goods and the person who allegedly stole the merchandise, a store employee who can identify the goods as belonging to the store and attest to its value, and documents indicating that the store is an existing firm.

Because of the known concentration of merchandise or cash, small retailers are prime targets for burglars and holdup persons. *Preventive measures* must be taken by the retailer. Secure locks, adequate lighting, irregular schedules to the bank to make deposits, and the guarding of keys will prevent losses due to burglars or holdup people.

Proper and adequate *training of employees* also serves as a deterrent to stock losses for a retailer.

REVIEW QUESTIONS

1 Why are stock losses of primary concern to every retailer?
2 How can a retailer reduce the amount of employee theft?
3 What measures can a retailer take to reduce the loss of goods from shoplifting?
4 Discuss the legal aspects of shoplifting and the retailer's appearance in court at the prosecution of the alleged party.
5 What are some of the preventative measures a retailer may take to reduce the chances of burglary and the possibility of a holdup?
6 What aspects of training should a retailer emphasize in order that the store's employees know what to do in case of a robbery?
7 Discuss the valid elements found in a check that would be honored by a bank.

Index